The Believing Heart

To Dr. Callahan
with Best Wishes

Choonsug Song

The Believing Heart

An Invitation to Story Theology

C. S. SONG

FORTRESS PRESS   MINNEAPOLIS

Library of Congress Cataloging-in-Publication Data

Song, Choan-Seng, 1929-
    The believing heart : an invitation to story theology / C. S. Song.
      p. cm.
    Chapters 3 and 7 were delivered at the Shuang Lian Lectures,
Taipei, Taiwan, Mar. 23–26, 1998.
    Includes bibliographical references and index.
    ISBN 0-8006-3142-0 (alk. paper)
    1. Narrative theology. 2. Storytelling – Religious aspects –
Christianity. 3. Theology, Doctrinal – Asia. 4. Christianity –
Asia. I. Title.
BT83.78.S66 1998
230 – dc21   98-32213

Manufactured in the U.S.A.   AF 1–3142

03   02   01   00   99   1   2   3   4   5   6   7   8   9   10

To the memory of my parents,
who first told me the stories
of Jesus' life, hope, faith, and love.

Contents

Preface xi

Part One
INVITATION
1

1. **We Piped for You and You Would Not Dance** 9

    A Marketplace Called "the Circle"   9

    Jesus at the Marketplace   11

    The Handmaid of the Church   13

    Theology as the Practice of Amen   16

    Entering the City with Bliss-Bestowing Hands   18

    What Is God-Talk?   23

    Theology as Human-Talk   27

2. **Birds of the Air and Lilies of the Field** 31

    Freedom from Anxiety: Jesus' Theology of Life   31

    Who Is My Neighbor? Jesus' Theology of Human Community   37

    What Is the Reign of God Like? Jesus' Theology of God's Reign   41

    Remove This Cup from Me: Jesus' Theology of God's Will   44

3. **Come and See** 50

    Come and See in Five Stages   52

    Stage One: God's Other Plans   52

    Stage Two: Breaking a Theological Bottleneck   57

    Stage Three: Not Christ-Centered but Jesus-Oriented   60

    Stage Four: Into the World of Stories   65

    Stage Five: A Story from Taiwan—A Theological Exploration   70

Part Two
L I F E
77

4. Death Is Not the Wages of Sin 79

A Doctor's Testimony 80

A Life-and-Death Matter 82

God as Source of the "Serious Command" 84

Death Is Not the Wages of Sin 90

The Phenomenal and the Ephemeral 92

The Glory of God 97

5. In the World There Is Suffering 104

Nikita's Story 105

A Disease Called Poverty 106

Thorns and Thistles 109

My Name Is Legion 122

Part Three
H O P E
131

6. Elusive Hope 133

Shattered Dreams 135

Scarce Work, Low Wages 136

Fly Now and Pay Later 141

Let My People Go? 142

7. Ethics of Hope 162

Incense Sticks Named "Hope" 163

Ethics of Hope 182

Part Four
FAITH
189

8. Faith in the World of Divided Loyalties 191

    Three Loyalties   192

    Testifying to the Spirit of God   212

9. Our Faith and God's Grace 215

    Before . . . but Now . . .   215

    Faith in God's Grace   235

10. The Heart That Believes 241

    The Parable of the Raft   241

    The Believing Heart   254

Part Five
LOVE
265

11. The World-Soul of Love 267

    A Song of Enlightenment   267

    Justice and Virtue Must Prevail?   269

    A Human Shield   274

    A Temple Bell   281

    Essence of Nonviolence Is Love   287

12. The Saving Work of Love 292

    Love That Saves Others   293

    Suffering unto Love   299

    Life-Force Called Love   308

Notes 317

Index 333

Preface

Christian theology has at last awakened to the pluralistic reality of our world. The awakening has ushered in a new theological era in which increasing numbers of Christians and theologians endeavor to think through complex relationships between the Christian faith and the world in which it finds itself. The result is the releasing of theological energy embedded in all parts of the world, creating exciting theological developments and fresh theological insights. With the onset of the twenty-first century, Christian theology has entered a reconstruction stage with a promise of more disclosure of how God has been dealing with nations and peoples.

The book that is now in your hands is a modest contribution to this theological movement, focusing on four major themes that concern human beings, Christian or not: Life, Hope, Faith, and Love. In writing this book I tried to listen with one ear trained on the Christian Bible and the other to voices and sounds coming from different quarters of our world. As I listened attentively, trying not to miss hidden notes, I found myself engaged in intense conversation with the stories of, on the one hand, human beings in search of God and, on the other hand, God in the company of human beings.

Central to these stories is the believing heart, the heart that believes in spite of hardships and despairs, the heart that struggles to make sense of what seems senseless in life and history. It is this believing heart that gives content and form to theological thoughts and formulations. That is why the book bears the title *The Believing Heart*, with a subtitle, *An Invitation to Story Theology*. This book shows the believing heart in practice.

Is it possible to do story theology without first developing theories of story theology? Well, why not? Men and women of all times from all places—particularly those of us from Asia—have been practicing story theology. Are there reasons why the practice cannot continue in this scientific and technological world? Precisely because our world, East and West, South and North, has been affected by developments in science and technology, there are urgent reasons to recover the art of story theology and to refine it when necessary. Theories can come later. Theories should not stand in the way of story theology as an art, an art practiced by people from different walks of life in different life situations.

As this volume goes to the press I would like to thank Dr. Chen Chia-Shi, president of Taiwan Theological Seminary; Dr. Chen Yang-Un, the dean, and their colleagues. They invited me to deliver, from March 23 to 26, 1998, the Shuang Lian Lectures, a prestigious lectureship established with funds provided by the Shuang Lian Presbyterian Church in Taipei, Taiwan. Two chapters, "Come and See" (chapter 3) and "Ethics of Hope" (chapter 7), formed part of the lecture series.

The lectureship represents an effort on the part of the seminary and the church to relate theology to church and church to theology. The effort is not new, but is urgent particularly in countries such as Taiwan where Christians and churches need to reexamine their theological past and to explore alternative theological approaches within different religious cultures. I felt privileged to have been a part of such effort.

Words of sincere thanks to Michael West, senior editor of Fortress Press, and to the Fortress Press editorial staff are in order. For these past several years I have been very much indebted to Mr. West for his unfailing support and encouragement. He is the kind of editor who inspires you to want to continue putting your thoughts and reflections in writing. To Ms. Audrey Englert, too, I express my appreciation. She ably and graciously prepared the manuscript for this project.

To my wife and our two daughters go my heartfelt gratitude. As they continue their music making, I go on with my theology making, and the twain, even though not always in harmony, are not dissonant. From them I have learned to sing theology as much as to tell theology, though not always with success. But theology, after, all, is an experiment of life, and as with all other experiments in theology there are failures and accomplishments, though perhaps more failures. This is what theology ought to be—an unending journey toward the City of God.

Part One

INVITATION

This is an invitation to all of us *thinking* Christians to reflect on what we believe, to explore what Christian faith means in our life, and to think through how it is related to the world in which we live.

Why such an invitation? The reason is simple: it is not easy to be a Christian today. It used to be quite different, at least in the West. Until the recent past, say until the end of World War II, to be a member of the Christian church in Europe and in North America was the most natural thing in the world. Your status in the community would be in question if your name was not found in the church register; a baptismal certificate was once accepted in lieu of a birth certificate for official purposes. In the old days you were suspect if you were not a regular churchgoer. To stay away from the church was to stay away from God. Lost to the church, you were lost to God. You were born into the church, baptized in the church, married in the church, and died in the bosom of the church. Church was your life and your destiny.

Such a relationship between Christians and the church was best expressed by Cyprian, bishop of Carthage on the northern shores of Africa in the third century: "One cannot have God for one's Father who has not the Church for one's Mother."[1] He also proclaimed in a more famous dictum: "There is no salvation outside the Church" (*salus extra ecclesiam non est*).[2] The dictum, once proclaimed, has remained, and not only in the Latin church—also known as the Roman Catholic Church—that Cyprian served as a bishop but also in the Protestant churches. Even today many Christians, perhaps more Protestant Christians than Roman Catholic Christians, still hold the dictum as central to the profession of their faith.

So to be a Christian was an inseparable part of your life. You did not have to choose to be a Christian. In fact you had no choice. As you grew up, you would come to know the society in which you lived as a "Christian" society. You were taught to distinguish your world, the "Christian" world, from the world beyond or outside it, the "non-Christian" or "pagan" world. In short, you were brought up as a Christian and taught "Christian" moral values. Christianity stood for all that was good and true. Those who did not hold the Christian faith represented the false and bad. This is the extent to which the Christian church dominated not only the external life of people in Europe and North America, but their internal life—their minds, their souls, and their psyche. These were the good old days.

1

Then something happened. A change came with what Nazi Germany did to millions of Jews deep in the heart of the "Christian" Europe during the Second World War. How were those men and women who had "the Church as their Mother" capable of committing such atrocities? How could a society so deeply rooted in the Christian faith, recognized no salvation outside the church, foster such a heinous crime against humanity? That demonic forces of destruction were hidden in the depths of the religious culture shaped by Christian spirituality is hard to comprehend.

There were also the atom bombs that in a flash of a second devastated Hiroshima and Nagasaki and claimed the lives of hundreds of thousands of people, mostly civilians. Was there no other way to end the war waged by Japan? Was there no other means to bring the military government of the nation of the Rising Sun to its knees, which itself had caused such horrendous devastation in Southeast Asia, leaving countless homes in ruins and family members without number dead or scattered (*chia pho jen wang* in Chinese)? One cannot help asking. It was the United States of America that first manufactured the atom bomb and used it, the nation that has the coin bearing the inscription "In God We Trust."

After the Holocaust and the atom bombs, being a Christian should not be easy. But strangely, the practice of Christian faith and theological reflection on that faith in the West during the past half-century have gone on largely unchanged. Most Christians and churches have not thought it necessary to revise their textbook answers to the questions of faith and life in the very different world of today. The world, once dominated by the West, has become globally oriented, politically and economically. The economy of power has shifted and diversified. History has come full circle. The Pacific or Asian century has already begun. Asia, as in the early centuries, is going to play a decisive role in the life and history of the world community in the twenty-first century.

Cultures and religions shall not remain unaffected by the political and economic reality of the post–World War II era. If the West no longer dictates the world politically and economically, it cannot dominate it culturally and religiously. Some Christians and theologians have at last come to reckon with this fact. "There are now," a prominent European theologian noted in 1986, "4.8 billion people living on this earth. Of these 1.4 billion are nominally Christian— almost one-third of the world's population. That compares with 724 million Muslims, 583 million Hindus, and 278 million Buddhists. We can already see from these figures, calculated over many years of painstaking research by the staff of the *World Christian Encyclopedia* (Oxford, 1982), just how much is at stake here."[3] This is an acknowledgment that the religious situation of the human community is very different from what many Christians think it to be. Implied in this statement is also a warning, perhaps even an alarm.

At first the statistics—admittedly outdated—seem to present Christians a heartening picture. Even if not in the absolute majority, we number more than the members of any of the other religions surveyed. We can still speak and act from the position of strength. We have nothing to worry about or to fear. On top of this, consider that the number of Christians in Africa has increased by leaps and bounds. In the twenty-first century, it is said, there are going to be more Christians in that continent than in Europe and North America put together. Elsewhere, at least a quarter of South Korea's population is now Christian. Christianity is a power to reckon with in that country not only religiously, but socially and politically. Why, then, should there be so much at stake for Christianity?

There is something in Hans Küng's statement above that makes us feel less confident about the status of Christianity in the world today. The number of Buddhists in the survey, for instance, seems too low. Are there only 278 million Buddhists in the world?[4] In Asia, the majority of the population in countries such as China, Japan, Taiwan, Thailand, and Sri Lanka practice Buddhism in one form or another. Their number must far exceed 278 million. Moreover, Buddhism and other religions cited are not on the wane; they are increasing their numbers not only in their traditional habitats but in the West, to which adherents have emigrated in great numbers. For Christians concerned about living in a "Christian world," there must be much that is at stake in the picture these statistics present.

Some Christians may also find a note of alarm in Küng's statement. Of 4.8 billion people in the world, "1.4 billion are *nominally* [emphasis added] Christian," we are told. The word *nominally* makes one sit up and ponder. "Nominal Christians," by definition, are Christians in name only. They were baptized and christened in church as infants but are not practicing Christian faith. How many of the 1.4 billion Christians are nominally Christian? No one knows. At least one can say that the number may be considerable. Does not this lead to the conclusion that the number of practicing Christians today is not anywhere near 1.4 billion?

If nominal religious practice occurs in Christianity, it must be the case with other religions also. There must be nominal Buddhists, Hindus, Muslims, or Confucianists. The actual number of those who practice their faith must not be as large as the official statistics. But the point is that when people of these other religions are taken together, they are far more in number than Christian believers. If those who practice primal religions and ancestor worship are counted, and they must be counted to gain a more complete picture, people of other religions far outnumber the Christian population.

Even after all these centuries of Christianity's expansion from the West to other parts of the world, the expansion accompanied by the domination of the Third World by Western colonialism, the world has not been made Christian. And all signs today tell us that the world will not be made Christian in the future. With the radical shifting of political, economic, and cultural dynamics, the religious dynamics have also shifted. The world of religious pluralism is here to stay. Christians cannot simply wish it away. The stakes for Christianity are indeed high if the Christian church ignores what religious and cultural pluralism means for human community, if it carries on business as it has always done, if it refuses to reenvision how God is at work in the world and in the whole universe.

Christians today, especially those of us who do not come from the traditional Christian West, need to develop a self-understanding different from that of our forebears, whose life and faith were shaped by the view of life and world prevailing in their times. We have to learn to perceive in the hearts and souls of women, men, and children outside the church both sorrows and joys, hopes as well as despairs, and not only godforsakenness but the presence of God's redeeming love. We must realize that we have often misrepresented God, erred in the claims we make for God, and pronounced wrong verdicts on others in the name of God. Is this not what we read over and over in the Hebrew Scriptures? Is this not what the scrutiny of church history discloses to us? We tend to forget that those of us inside the Christian church perhaps have tried God's patience much more than those outside it. We ourselves are in need of repentance as much as those we have made targets of conversion to Christianity.

There must be change in what we believe and do as Christians. What you will read in these pages is an invitation to change—change in our attitude toward those who do not believe and practice their faith as we do, change in our assertions about God and how God is at work in the life of peoples and in the history of nations, change in the way we have treated Jesus as an object of worship, an article of faith, and a system of doctrine and not as the living presence of God, as one who brings hope to the hopeless, courage to those in distress, and love to the human community racked by hate, conflict, and division. Should we not for once let Jesus tell us about God, and how we Christians together with women, men, and children around us fare in God's sight?

What follows in these pages is also an invitation to adherents of other religions. This book is addressed to them as well. But what do reflections on Christian faith have to do with us who do not share that faith? they demand. We are excluded from the Christian community of faith unless we are converted to it, they say. We are regarded as lost to your God until we become members of your church. We are told that there is no salvation for us unless we give up what we believe and accept Jesus as our savior. We are reminded that our conversion is the sole purpose of Jesus' life and work, that this is the reason he died on the cross.

The problem, they say, is that in Asia there are so many of us—Buddhists, Hindus, Muslims, Confucianists, Shintoists, and those who observe ancestor rites. We make up a large part of the world's population, almost two-thirds of it, in fact. Does this mean that so many of us are lost to God? Do you believe that your God wants to see us lost? What kind of God is this, then? Some of your preachers and evangelists never tire of telling us that we are not really capable of doing good. The good we do is done with wrong motivation and amounts to little in the sight of your God. Did Jesus share this view? Did he also think that, no matter what we do, we are going to perish forever if we do not become Christians?

This is not the only problem, say adherents of other faiths. They remind Christians that in the West the religious situation has changed visibly. In Europe many cathedrals—centers of Christian piety for centuries—are deserted by Christians and flocked to by tourists. When the ski season begins in winter, ski slopes will be crowded with people on Sunday and churches will be half-empty. Come summer, there will be more sun worshipers on the Mediterranean beaches than God worshipers in the house of prayer. Once the bastion of Christian spirituality, Europe has become secularized. Christianity in its traditional form ceases to appeal to an increasing number of women and men. Most in Asia are more "religious" than European Christians are, at least outwardly.

In North America the religious situation is not quite the same as in Europe. That the mainline churches have suffered a steady loss of membership in recent years is well documented. Between 1965 and 1989, reports an April 1993 issue of *Time* magazine, each of these mainline churches has lost one to two million members, some less and some more.[5] Does this mean that religion is on the decline in the United States? Not at all. It is noted that "when West Europeans drop out of church, as large majorities do, they typically lose interest in belief too, but America remains unpromising ground for atheism and agnosticism."[6] On the whole Americans are religious people.

But how is the religious life of men and women in the United States shaped today? The *Time* report goes on to tell us that "churches on either side of the spiritual spectrum are growing fast: the conservative evangelical Protestantism on one hand and an assortment of Eastern, New Age and unconventional religions on the other."[7] We are outsiders to Christianity, admit our friends and neighbors of other religions. The growth of conservative evangelical Protestantism neither interests us nor excites us. As a matter of fact we know little about it except that its strong advocates want to make Christian converts of us. But the growth of "Eastern, New Age and unconventional religions," particularly Eastern religions, intrigues us. We had not thought that our faith, deeply rooted in the lives, histories, and cultures of people in Asia, would be attractive to the women and men of this country shaped by Christian culture.

At any rate, we are puzzled because most Christians in Asia told us that what they believe is fundamentally different from what we believe, that there is little in common between their faith and our faith. They also make a point of saying that they as Christians are essentially different from us as Buddhists, Hindus, or ancestor venerators, although in everyday life at home, at the market, at the workplace, we often cannot tell that they are Christians from the way they do things and conduct business. The truth of the matter is that most of the women and men who did their utmost for our nations, and who even gave their lives for our people, were not Christian.

Why, then, do our Christian friends and neighbors insist that what they believe is true and what we believe is not, that their faith leads to salvation and ours does not, that they are better than we are in every way? Of course the answer depends on what one means by salvation, and we would like to know more about it. As to what we say and what we do, how do they know what motivates us deep in our hearts? Our hunch is that what they insist on as true reflects much of what they have been taught by Western Christian missionaries. Most of them and most Western missionaries know little about what we believe and how we live. As human beings we are vulnerable, but are they less vulnerable because they are Christians?

We also wonder whether what they say to us is what Jesus would have said to us. Do they regard us as Jesus would have regarded us? On the basis of the few things we know about Jesus, our question is not entirely unfounded. Our own religious experience prompts us to raise the question with our Christian friends. We know, for example, that what the Buddha is reported to have taught is not what most Buddhists practice in their daily life. The Buddha taught his followers to cultivate "the heart of boundless kindness and mercy" toward all creatures. But we are pained and saddened by the bloodshed that continues between the Buddhist Singhalese and the Hindu Tamils in Sri Lanka. We also feel shame at rampant child prostitution in Buddhist Thailand. We cannot of course extend our own failures to Christianity, but our suspicion is that there could be discrepancy between what Jesus actually taught and did in his day and what most Christians teach and do today.

What I can say at this point is that these questions are not entirely groundless, and the suspicion is not totally without reason. It may be that we Christians and you adherents of other religions have been at odds with one another for wrong reasons, suspicious of one another because of false claims we all make, and harsh to each other based on doctrines that misrepresent what the pioneers and founders of our faiths have taught. This is unfortunate, to say the least. It does not mean that we basically agree on matters of faith and morals. This is not the case. There are bound to be fundamental differences in what people of different religious traditions believe and do. But there is one problem we must avoid as much as possible, and that is coming to odds because of mutual misrepresentation and intentional or unintentional distortion of what each tradition believes and does.

What you will read is also an invitation to you, adherents of other religions, to reflect with me on Christian faith as I see and experience it. In contrast to the ways in which that reflection has often been done in the history of Christianity, I am not going to lay out the doctrines that have shaped the life and faith of Christians and dictated their approach to the life and faith of people outside the Christian church. Some of these doctrines, developed in the West and conditioned by Western views of life and world, often hinder understanding and appreciation between Christians and their fellow human beings outside the West. You may be interested to know that these doctrines have also caused division among us Christians. It has become increasingly evident that doctrines are not an auspicious place, among Christians of different hues and colors, to start a discourse on life and faith. Nor are they always conducive to the task we all have in common—striving for peace, justice, and love in the world today.

Having said all this, I must hasten to stress that my purpose is to make neither one more effort toward unity among Christians nor one more attempt at mutual understanding between Christians and people of other faiths. Rather, it is my view that Christian faith is relevant to the life we live and the hope we cherish as human beings. I am also convinced that it is to this life and to this hope that Jesus addressed himself in his life and ministry. This is to say, reflection on what Jesus said and did, and on the faith developed from his sayings and deeds, should be closely related to the problems and issues we Christians face as human beings, and to how we relate to the people and the world around us. As we Christians look at ourselves in the depths of our own finite humanity, we may be able to encounter the world of meaning of Jesus that the church has not shown us. We may also find deeper resonance with the creative Spirit of God at work in the human community at large and in creation.

What is presented in this book, in other words, is a Christian theology focused on life, and the meaning or meaninglessness we human beings experience in our life. At the heart of this theology is Jesus, who lived and died for the meaning of life as he saw it, who, according to John, author of the Fourth Gospel, came so that all people "may have life, and may have it in all its fullness" (John 10:10 [REB]). Through his vision of life Jesus tells us who we are and what our problems are. In his life of hardship and suffering he discloses what life in all its fullness really means. In his struggle with the powers of this world, both political and religious, he reveals who God is and what God wills. As he stares death in the face, he envisions the life eternal in God's love.

It is Jesus himself who invites both Christians and those who are not to look deeply once again into what he said and did. After all, what the Christian church has insisted about Jesus is not important, only what Jesus himself must have meant by declaring himself "the way, the truth, and the life" (John 14:6). Should not this latter statement inspire us to say what Jesus means for us today?

Chapter 1

We Piped for You
and You Would Not Dance

We as Christians living close to the turn of the century have reasons to be worried and at the same time excited: worried because the religious map of the world we have inherited is outdated, excited because the new map contains surprises and new opportunities. We are under pressures, both internal and external, to seek a new understanding of ourselves and to be prepared for change. New understanding is necessary because much of what we have held to be true as members of the Christian church has become disconnected from much of reality. Change will come because we can no longer superimpose our Christian ideas and practices on others not dominated by Christianity and the culture shaped by it. Many of us Christians, faced with a situation not under our control, continue to fortify ourselves with traditional values and ways, rejecting new insights that seem to contradict our basic convictions. There are also others of us who, liberated from ignorance and arrogance, perceive new horizons of life and faith that both broaden and deepen our search for what it means to live, believe, and hope.

We should be excited, rather than worried, about the new situation that has unfolded. We are called to engage in new understanding and creative change so that we may play a constructive role. We must liberate ourselves, on the one hand, from our ignorance of how others live and what they believe, and, on the other hand, from the arrogance that has strained and distorted our relations with them. What lies ahead is a challenging task. To prepare ourselves, we need to have plans, to develop guidelines, and to set directions. In short, we need to learn to tell stories very different from the stories we have inherited. This calls for change in our Christian psyche, reorientation in our theological mind-set. How should we go about it? Where should we start? We will begin at the most mundane place of all—the marketplace.

A Marketplace Called "The Circle"

There used to be a busy open-air market called "The Circle" on East Gate Road in Tainan, the old capital city in the southern region of Taiwan. "The Circle" disappeared many years ago, a casualty of irresponsible city planning, and has been replaced by motorways hazardous to pedestrians. It used to be a popular marketplace about thirty meters in diameter, cluttered with small stalls selling all sorts of food and drink, both cold and hot. There were also shops that sold inexpensive clothes and household wares.

It was a noisy place—shopkeepers soliciting customers at the top of their voice, customers bargaining over the price of a broom or a piece of cloth, friends and neighbors greeting one another, engaging in loud conversation. Dogs and cats barked and mewed when fighting over crumbs of discarded food. Smells of all sorts came from food cooking on the stove and served on the table, from spices, used liberally, that enhanced the aroma. Noise and smell combined to fill the atmosphere, and to create a human community assembled to fulfill the need for food to delight the palate and to nourish the body. "The Circle" was open day and night, seven days a week, all the year round. It was a great place at night. People looked forward to it after the day's work was over. There they would enjoy delicacies not available at home and meet friends and neighbors to chat and exchange gossip.

Cities in Asia abound in marketplaces such as "The Circle." These are "people's markets" in every sense of the word. Men, women, and children from all walks of life, young and old, rich and poor, are to be found there. Nothing could stop them from returning day after day, night after night—not even the perpetual tropical heat in such places as the island nation of Singapore. Singapore, in fact, has one of the most fabulous night markets in Asia, where people can eat and shop to their hearts' content, despite the temperature and humidity. Of course Hong Kong is full of markets. These markets not only serve the needs of the local inhabitants, but also travelers from abroad. Once the traveler's business is accomplished and shopping done, he or she can look forward to a visit to the people's marketplace to taste the local food, to glimpse indigenous customs, and to smell the smell of native humanity. It is to these marketplaces that hosts will be glad to take their foreign guests for an evening of exposure to the "exotic" culture.

Very few Christians, even pious ones among us, will have qualms about taking their visitors to such marketplaces for a brief immersion in the native culture. They know that these places where people sell and buy and enjoy themselves have little in common with the world they find in the church and among Christians. It may be that their "Christian" sensitivity makes them frown upon some of the carryings-on. But which world is more real, the world of the Christian church or the world of the people's marketplace? If the world of the marketplace is as real, if not more real than the world of the church, is it not in the marketplace that we as Christians are challenged to rethink our faith, to redream our dreams, and to reenvision our vision? As the result of such rethinking, redreaming, and reenvisioning, do we not have to do our Christian theology all over again?

Jesus at the Marketplace

It seems that Jesus did a lot of theology at marketplaces. In the parable of children in the marketplace, Jesus tells his critics:

> To what then will I compare the people of this generation, and what are they like? They are like children sitting in the marketplace and calling to one another, "We played the flute for you, and you did not dance; we wailed, and you did not weep." (Luke 7:31-32; also Matt. 11:16-17)

The parable depicts a scene in the marketplace in which children are playing games in two groups—"the one group plays airs for a wedding on the flute, and the other will not dance; the second group chants a dirge, and the other will not play up to this lead by acting as mourners (beating breast)."[1]

Few passersby would take notice of a group of children playing wedding and funeral games at the marketplace. Fewer still would ponder what these games might mean for them. Perhaps no one would see the parabolic significance of these games for their life and faith. Unlike other passersby, Jesus did notice the children. Also unlike them he pondered what these games could mean. Jesus might have thought to himself: Life and death, the mystery of it all! The hope and despair of it all! Neither Luke nor Matthew pauses to tell us whether such thoughts went through Jesus' mind. They do, however, tell us how Jesus saw a parabolic meaning for the religious leaders of his time in the games children were playing: *We piped for you, but you would not dance.*

Jesus must have frequented marketplaces. Where else would he have associated with people from all walks of life? Where else would he have become "a friend of tax collectors and sinners"? Where else would he have heard those stories that he transformed into parables of the reign of God—the story of a woman who turned her house inside out in search of the coin she had lost (Luke 15:8-10); the story of a servant, forgiven by his master for the enormous debt he had incurred, who threw into prison his fellow servant who owed him a pittance (Matt. 18:23-35); the story of the rich fool who built himself large barns and who sat back to relax for the rest of his life, not knowing that death would be visiting him that very night (Luke 12:16-21); or the story of the landowner who hired laborers for his vineyard at different times of the day but who paid them the same wages in the evening (Matt. 20:1-16)?

Jesus must have learned more about human beings, about the world, about his own religious tradition, and about God outside the synagogue than inside. With what he had learned in the company of the people he did two things: he developed a message that made God's reign relevant to the people he met, and he directed sharp criticism against prevailing trends within his own religious tradition. This was his theological approach, an approach that differs from the methods developed in traditional Christian theology. These traditional methods have been shaped by the internal concerns of the church and designed to defend what the church teaches and to explicate concepts and ideas inherited from the past.

But these were not Jesus' methods. Places such as the market were his theological arena. For him the market was a little universe within the universe, a small creation within creation. It was a place where the most spontaneous selves of women, men, and children are found, where these selves expose who they are and what they think. A market is not just a place where people engage in the routines of everyday living and commercial activities. It is where dramas of life are played, the moral strength of the society is tried, and the ethical sensibility of one's faith is put to the test. In other words, it is a world in which human beings face the rigor of living in not always friendly company. In the market they encounter day-to-day issues of life and death, issues not solved by a stereotyped formula taught in a religious catechism. It is also there that a believer is confronted with naked forms of questions about God and humanity, which are not packaged in the familiar language of faith and adorned with liturgical trappings, layer after layer.

Jesus did a lot of theology in markets outside the synagogue, the house of prayer and worship. He developed his message of God's forgiving love in the complex reality of the world. He felt the strong presence of God in the midst of the people whom he had come to know well. In the midst of the crowds he talked about God and God's compassion for women as well as men, children as well as grown-ups, the outcasts, and the disinherited. It was from those the religious authorities had given up for lost that he came to know how the official religion had failed them, and thus God. Armed with his "marketplace theology," he confronted the religious leaders with questions of what it means to believe in the God of mercy, justice, and love.

Women, men, and children in everyday life make theology possible. What they face in daily life makes theology necessary. Unless we Christians and theologians find ourselves in their midst, how can we hear what they are saying? Keeping ourselves aloof, how can we understand what they are asking? As we listen to these people of the marketplace attentively, we begin to perceive that we are in fact listening to the recesses of our hearts. What the people are saying is in fact what we want to say but dare not say in the church. What they are asking is what we have always wanted to ask but are afraid to ask in the company of other Christians. It begins to dawn on us that what concerns us all, Christian or not, is the meaning of the life we live, the world in which we happen to be, and the God who may have something to do with our life and world.

Returning to "The Circle," let us consider a young mother, for example, with a suckling baby on her back and a toddler with unsteady steps in tow—what is occupying her mind, salvation in heaven or her daily cares and burdens? A man showing wears and tears of old age—what is going through his mind as he casts glances here and there, trying in vain to recapture in the young beaming faces and jovial voices his youth long gone—hope for the unknown future or fear of it? What about an old woman, her face full of wrinkles and her back stooped, knowing that her days of toil and hardships are almost over—what is utmost in her heart, gratitude for relief from the burden of life or a feeling of helplessness that her life is slipping away? There are students who resort to "The Circle" after school. They seem carefree, spontaneous, and happy, "fearing neither heaven nor earth" (*t'ien pu pha ti pu pha*), to use a Chinese saying, meaning "fearing nothing and no one." Do they really fear neither heaven nor earth? Are they actually afraid of nothing and no one? What of the wage earners, blue-collar and white-collar, who cannot earn enough to support a growing family?

Obviously "The Circle" to which I refer is symbolic in meaning. It symbolizes what we do and how we live. It reflects what is going on in our minds and souls, often unknown to ourselves. It is a world in which we try to make ends meet, to outdo one another at school and at the workplace, in business and in research, in private disputes and at the law court. It is a world novelists write about—a world of hate and love, despair and hope, conflict and reconciliation. It is a world artists reproduce in painting, sculpture, and music—a world of beauty and ugliness, nobility and depravity, piety and bigotry. It is a world in which we, unwittingly or not, expose our baseness and vulnerability as human beings for immediate gains, be they fame, power, or money. At the same time it is a world that shows us how it is also possible to rise above personal gains and interests to reveal a noble and divine quality buried deep within us.

"The Circle," in other words, represents not only the reality of everyday life, but what the world could become. It serves not only as the external sphere of our existence, but the internal space in which most of our ideas, fears, and ambitions are conceived and nurtured. If this is the case, where else can we go to have what we believe as Christians tested, challenged, and reshaped? The faith most of us Christians hold today is not tested in the real world in which we live. As a matter of fact, we are withdrawn from the world, having retreated to the safe haven called church where we can talk about God, Jesus, or mission among like-minded believers. How people outside the church live and believe is either the target of our criticism or of no immediate concern. It is also within the Christian community that we practice love and show charity for one another. But we try not to ask ourselves how we may put our Christian love and charity into practice in the world of conflicts of power and interest, though we are often part of those conflicts.

The Handmaid of the Church

Do we not, then, have to question the traditional assumption that theology is the handmaid of the church? As handmaid, theology must know its place in the church. It cannot be above the church. It is the church that dictates what theology must be and what it should do. Theology must serve the church, which is its master. Theology takes orders from the church. It explicates what the church

believes to be right. It defends the church from heretics. It fortifies the church
with intellectual resources to combat infidels. It is the guard posted by the church
to keep out intruders, to look out for those who disseminate beliefs and teachings that contradict what the church believes and teaches. This is how theology
must function. It derives its raison d'être from serving the church. It has no
independent status apart from the church.

But theology is *not* the handmaid of the church. Yes, theology must serve
the church, but it renders its service to the church with freedom and in freedom.
Theology does not have to claim authority for itself like the church, but it has
to claim freedom from external coercion, even from coercion of the church.
Authority has to be a by-product of freedom. Where there is no freedom, there
is no authority. The authority that suppresses freedom is no authority at all,
because it commands no credibility and possesses no authenticity. The authority
that is not credible and authentic is nothing but a violent power. It violates truth.
It violates humanity. And it violates God. History tells us how much violence
authorities have committed against truth, humanity, and God, not only in the
realm of politics but also in the world of religion!

What is true of the church is also true of the academic community. The
search for truth, be it scientific or humanistic, is carried out within an academic
institution. The latter provides the resources and environment for the former.
But the search for truth is compromised when the institution in which the search
takes place interferes with it, invades it, even manipulates it for whatever reason.
When this happens, the truth revealed and made public is untruth. It is a lie.
The lie masked as truth not only discredits the search itself but the institution as a whole. It destroys the very foundation of an academic community. An
academic community gains authority only when it respects freedom, cultivates
it, and encourages it. Freedom creates space within an academic community. It
gives the community the moral power to be part of the human search for what
is true, good, and beautiful.

Let us return to the relationship between theology and the church. If theology should not be above the church, it should not, it was maintained, take place
outside the church either. Such an assertion used to make sense in the part of the
world that embraced Christianity, notably Europe. Until the Enlightenment in
the eighteenth century the world of Europe was the world of Christianity. The
church was the world and the world was the church—hence the word *Christendom,* meaning "those parts of the world where most of the inhabitants profess
the Christian faith."[2] The church had the final say about practically everything
from the cradle to the grave, and of course beyond the grave. It made little difference where one practiced and reflected on the Christian faith. The church
was the final arbiter not only in matters of faith and morals, but in social mores,
views of life and the world, even one's private thoughts.

The idea that the Christian church stands for the world persisted long after
the Enlightenment, although it eroded gradually in Europe, the very heart of

"Christendom," as human reason began to disclose a world different from the world represented by the church. The world has since grown apart from the church. The relation between the world and the church has been reversed. As the world gained in influence, the church lost influence. While the world expanded activities that did not relate to the church, the church was compelled to withdraw into itself. The once respected word *Christendom* has disappeared from common usage. Most Christians in the West today spend a few hours in church on Sunday; the rest of the week they spend at home, at the workplace, in the business world. They live a so-called secular life that has little to do with what they think and how they behave in church. They are not very different from others who spend their Sunday on the golf course, on the ski slope, in department stores, or in front of the television.

These observations are in no way meant as an indictment of the "secular" world or as a call to return to the type of church that once dominated the world. They simply describe prevailing trends in the relationship between church and world. The trends tell us one important thing: the Christian church has erred in its desire and effort to put the world under its control. This desire not only has distorted the relationship between church and world, but, lamentably, it has corrupted the church. The reason is simple. To control others one has to have power. Without power, one cannot control others. It is as simple as that. This certainly is the case in politics, whether domestic or foreign, national or global. The same situation extends to almost all spheres of life, from family to clubs to associations. How the world today is dominated by economic power! In this post–Cold War era, economy is the decisive power that creates "the wealth of a nation" and enables it to gain political clout over other nations. Money talks— the power of money. According to a Chinese saying, "Money can make the devil work for you" (*ch'ien kho shu kwei*). Is this not how power gets corrupted in politics, in the business world, and in human relationships?

When religion is wedded to power, it gets corrupted, too. The corruption in this case is at once sad and repulsive. Again a Chinese saying tells us that "money can move the gods" (*ch'ien kho thong shen*). Power, and particularly power of money, is a crisis for a religion. Much intrigue and crime related to the desire for power have been hatched in the inner sanctum of religious hierarchies and institutions, all in the name of God and in the promise of salvation in heaven. This makes reading the religious history of humankind a heavy reading, and the history of Christianity is no exception.

The miracle is that men and women of genuine piety toward God and deep compassion for the suffering humanity are, from time to time, raised from the debris of corrupt religion to bear witness to God's redeeming love. But such miracles do not justify a religion corrupted by power and greed. Of course not. John the Baptizer was entirely right when he said to the religious leaders that had come for baptism: "Bear fruit worthy of repentance. Do not presume to say to yourselves, 'We have Abraham as our ancestor'; for I tell you, God is able from these stones to raise up children to Abraham" (Matt. 3:8-9). Religious reformers, be they Christian, Buddhist, or Hindu, are the stones raised to restore and revitalize the spirit of the pioneers of their faith. Could have this been in Jesus' mind when he remarked, quoting Psalm 118, "The stone that the builders rejected has become the cornerstone" (Matt. 21:42)? The same statement could apply to many a religious reformer who graced the pages of the religious history of humankind.

We usually understand religious reforms as directed to the religious establishment, to what it teaches and how it conducts itself. This is true. A reform movement is a renewal movement. It gives a religion a new lease on life. It also gives birth to a new religious tradition when it is rejected by the religion in power. A religious reform is generally concerned with the status quo of the religion in question. But one aspect seldom gets highlighted: a religious reform also compels a religious community to turn itself to the human community outside. The movement causes a religious establishment to turn inside out, to reform itself in light of the realities it has to encounter in a larger human community and to refashion its self-image and ministry. The establishment has to take into account how women, men, and children struggle to make sense of life in society.

Theology as the Practice of Amen

In the sense of turning a religious establishment inside out, Jesus was the reformer of reformers. What he said in the Sermon on the Mount at once comes to mind. "You are the salt of the earth" (Matt. 5:13). He continued: "You are the light of the world" (Matt. 5:14). Jesus was speaking to an odd assortment of listeners: his disciples, wage earners, housewives, children, even religious leaders. They were different in background, in education, and in what they did to make a living. But one thing they had in common: they all belonged to the same religious tradition. True, though many of them were not accepted as members in good standing because of their profession and social status, they still longed to be part of the religious community that assured its members security, not only in this life but in the life hereafter. But Jesus did not tell them to be good members of the synagogue, faithful observers of the law, or strong advocates of the interests of the religious community to which they belonged. Instead, he told them to be the *salt of the earth* and the *light of the world*.

In saying what he did, Jesus tried to draw their attention to what was going on around them in society, to how people "out there" fared, to how God regarded them and cared for them. In Luke, Jesus summed it up in the parable of the Good Samaritan (10:25-37). "Who is my neighbor?" This was the question. To that man robbed and injured on the road from Jerusalem to Jericho, no matter what the priest's and the Levite's reason for not extending a helping hand, they were not his neighbor. There should be no doubt that the priest and Levite preached and taught about neighborly love, but that love did not extend beyond their own religious circles. No doubt they stressed the practice of that love, but the practice was kept within the bounds of their religious tradition.

For Jesus such love is not love, at least not the love of God he experienced. God's love is boundless, having no boundary, social or political, cultural or religious. That love is limitless, and is not restricted to a certain kind of people for whatever reason, particularly for the reasons of race, gender, class, or creed. That love is not conditional, and is not predicated on fulfillment of certain conditions, be they ideological or confessional. Jesus had the Samaritan in the parable manifest that love of God—the love that is not sectarian, not doctrinal, not calculating, the love that has to prevail for the world to be a livable place, for the earth to be a creative part of God's creation. To know God's will, one must be the salt of the earth. To experience God's love, one must be the light of the world. This was the heart of Jesus' message of God's reign. This message was the core of his ministry. There is an irony here: a religion tends to alienate people from God, but the pain and suffering one sees and experiences in the world draws one to God.

Is this not the way the prophets of ancient Israel went about their ministry toward those in power? They brought political and religious leaders to their senses and reminded them of their divine duty toward the men, women, and children they ruled. Are we not familiar, for example, with these words from Isaiah, a prophet of Israel in the eighth century B.C.E.—words he was sure represented what God wanted to say?

> Your new moons and your appointed festivals
> 　　my soul hates;
> they have become a burden to me,
> 　　I am weary of bearing them.
> When you stretch out your hands,
> 　　I will hide my eyes from you;
> even though you make many prayers,
> 　　I will not listen;
> 　　your hands are full of blood.
> Wash yourselves; make yourselves clean;
> 　　remove the evil of your doings
> 　　from before my eyes;
> cease to do evil,
> 　　learn to do good;
> seek justice,
> 　　rescue the oppressed,
> defend the orphan,
> 　　plead for the widow. (Isa. 1:14-17)

Jesus would have said Amen to these words. Faith is a practice of this Amen. Theology is reflection on that practice. A religious community responds to the Amen in hymns, in words, and in actions.

Isaiah was right. Jesus, of course, was right. Many a religious reformer has been right. Religion cannot resist being an end in itself. Its own survival, the expansion of its interest in the name of God, obscures the Amen and suppresses it. This kind of religion is a mockery of God, a religion that "sells dog meat while hanging a sheep's head outside the shop as advertisement" (*koa yang-thou mai kou jou*), to use a Chinese expression. It is a piety that benefits from believers' innocence and fear. What Isaiah indicts are the religious practices that use God as a means to selfish gains and personal well-being at the expense of the poor and the disinherited in society. A true religion, a genuine piety, and the religious practices that please God and edify people, Isaiah says, should be oriented not to what is right and good for the religious community itself but to what is right and good for the world. This is also Jesus' contention with the religious establishment of his day. Other religions, too, have no lack of persons with foresight and enlightenment who have striven to restore genuine piety and the true spirit of love and compassion to religion.

Entering the City with Bliss-Bestowing Hands

A story from China may further point to the importance of a theological reorientation. In the twelfth century, during the Sung dynasty (960–1279 C.E.), there lived a Zen monk by the name of Kuo An. He likened the Buddha's nature in a human being to a cow, a familiar domestic animal, and created ten pictures to illustrate stages of spiritual progress by depicting how a cowherd went about looking for the lost cow in the fields and on the hills. Each picture is explained by a short introduction in prose and a commentary in verse. This series is known as "The Ten Cow-Herding Pictures," which has been a popular introduction to Zen Buddhism. These ten pictures tell the story of how the lost cow (the Buddha's nature) is found, tamed, and brought home. At the end of the story, however, the cow disappears. There appears, in the place of the cow, a monk with all smiles "entering the city with bliss-bestowing hands."

These pictures are parables. The simple strokes of the Zen monk's brush that give form to the ten pictures develop into a compelling parable—a parable of the simplicity that contrasts with the world of complexity that human beings have created. That simplicity is a symbolism that has the power to evoke in the human mind a response to the primordial oneness of life. Altogether "The Ten Cow-Herding Pictures" conveys a profound message addressed to the life one lives in the world. The ten pictures show the aspiring Zen monk how the search for the lost cow begins in deserted places and ends in a busy marketplace. They also tell Christian seekers of truth how and where we should engage ourselves in the practice of our faith and theology.

What intrigues us is that the cow, after a Herculean effort to find it, disappears. At the last stage of the spiritual progress a smiling monk extends his blessings to his fellow human beings. This is what Kuo An, the author, says in his introduction to this tenth and last picture:

Entering the City with Bliss-Bestowing Hands. His humble cottage door is closed, and the wisest know him not. No glimpses of his inner life are to be caught; for he goes on his own way without following the steps of the ancient sages. Carrying a gourd he goes out into the market; leaning against a stick he comes home. He is found in company with wine-bibbers and butchers; he and they are all converted into Buddhas.

This prose introduction is then followed by a poetic commentary, also from Kuo An:

> Barechested and barefooted, he comes out into the marketplace;
> Daubed with mud and ashes, how broadly he smiles!
> There is no need for the miraculous power of the gods,
> For he touches, and lo! the dead trees come into full bloom.[3]

These lines are beautifully crafted. They are words with sounds and images, and they show us that the extraordinary is to be found in the ordinary, the otherworldly in the this-worldly, the heavenly in the earthly, the eternal in the temporal.

The enlightened monk "is found in company with wine-bibbers and butchers." This sounds quite familiar even to our Christian ears. Does this not conjure up the image of Jesus his opponents ridiculed as "a glutton and a drunkard, a friend of tax collectors and sinners" (Matt. 11:19; also Luke 7:34)? Whether wine-bibbers and butchers in the ancient Orient or tax collectors and sinners in ancient Israel, they are not "prominent officials and eminent personages" (*ta kuan hsien yau*), to use a Chinese idiom, to be found at the royal court or in the religious hierarchy.

On the contrary, they are common folks who eke out their living in the streets and in the marketplaces. They are wage earners, small-shop owners, tenant farmers, housemaids—what are called "small-town people." They are men and women who would rather avoid setting foot in a government office to have their grievances settled. They can also be those religious devotees without means and status, marginalized and slighted. A Buddhist monk enjoying a company of people such as these? An enlightened sage mingling with living beings preoccupied with their mundane life? What a contrast a monk "entering the city with bliss-bestowing hands" poses to our notion of Buddhism as a world-denying religion!

It is true that in Buddhism a monk or a nun is called *chhu chia jen,* one who leaves home, or *chhu she jen,* one who goes out of the world to devote oneself to-

tally to the Buddha. Buddhism itself has developed the teaching of detachment
from the world, the practice of asceticism, and the tradition of monasticism.
But according to Kuo An's "Ten Cow-Herding Pictures," which illustrate the
stages of spiritual progress, a *chhu-chia-jen* has only moved halfway toward becoming a monk or nun and is still not liberated from ignorance (*avidya*), having
not realized that world-denying asceticism itself is futile for religious enlightenment. Does this not sound similar to the experience of Martin Luther, the
young Augustinian monk turned reformer, in his effort to win salvation by asceticism? This understanding, as a matter of fact, is what the Buddha himself
is reported to have realized after practicing extreme austerities in the forests for
six years. Compassion for all living creatures in the world cannot be practiced in
separation from the world. This world-affirming aspect of Buddhism has tended
to be suppressed by Buddhism itself and to be ignored by Christians.

In some quarters in Asia today Buddhism has been making a renewed impact on society as Buddhist monks and nuns who have left home and the world
reenter the world to practice Buddhist faith and to carry out acts of mercy. She
Cheng Yen, a Buddhist nun in Taiwan who developed The Mercy and Kindness
Association (*ch'u chi kong te huei*) and gained as many as three million members in a few years, writes: "When you are engaged in the study of Buddhist
teachings, you must not think that leaving the world of mortals (*jen chien*) to
follow the ways of heaven would enable you to attain the law of the Buddha
(*Buddhadharma*). As a matter of fact, once you leave the world, there is no law
of the Buddha to be attained. All Boddhisattvas have achieved their way in the
world."[4] Kuo An, the Chinese Zen monk of the twelfth century, was right in
his "Cow-Herding Pictures": spiritual progress is not completed until you find
yourself "entering the city with bliss-bestowing hands."

Kuo An also says something that should startle us thinking Christians in
Asia. Those who seek enlightenment, he tells us, "go on their way without
following the steps of the ancient sages." This sounds like antitraditionalism,
elevating rejection of the past to a virtue. At first this statement seems to contradict the Zen tradition of seeking enlightenment by repairing to the master's
abode. The training is rigorous, sometimes almost cruel. The will and spirit as
well as the bodies of the students are subjected to terrible hardships and rigorous
discipline. Only the few who have stood the test are granted admission to the
company of the enlightened ones.

Many stories, some undoubtedly of legendary nature, are told about those
who attained the lofty summit or the profound depth of enlightenment. One
such story is related about Hui-k'o (487–593), the second patriarch of Chinese
Zen Buddhism. As the story goes, the monk traveled to Shau-lin monastery (in
the present Honan province) to seek instruction from Bodhidharma, the first
Zen patriarch. He tried to gain an audience with the master, but the latter,
always sitting silently facing the wall, paid no attention to him. "On the ninth
day of December of the same year," the story continues,

he stood in the fast-falling snow and did not move until the morning when the snow had reached the knees. Bodhidharma then took pity on him and said, "You have been standing in the snow for some time, and what is your wish?"

Replied Hui-k'o, "I am come to receive your invaluable instruction; pray open the gate of mercy and extend your hand of salvation to this poor suffering mortal."

Bodhidharma then said: "The incomparable teaching of the Buddha can be comprehended only after a long and hard discipline and by enduring what is most difficult to endure and by practicing what is most difficult to practice. Men of inferior virtue and wisdom who are light-hearted and full of self-conceit are not able even to set their eyes on the truth of Buddhism. All the labor of such men is sure to come to naught."

Hui-k'o was deeply moved, and in order to show his sincerity in the desire to be instructed in the teachings of all the Buddhas, he cut off his left arm with the sword he carried and presented it before the quietly meditating Bodhidharma.[5]

This is the famous story of "cutting off one's arm in the search of truth (*dharma*)." True or not, the story moves its readers and makes them think deeply. For seekers of truth in ancient China the road to enlightenment was hazardous, unpredictable, and full of hardships. Does not a story such as this remind us of similar stories in the history of Christian monasticism?

The search for truth may take years. Aspiring monks find themselves completely under the authority of their master. Deviation from the strict discipline of the Zen community brings punishment, and serious offense against its rules results in excommunication. Why, then, does Kuo An, himself a Zen master, describe the monk, at the end of his search for truth in the "Cow-Herding Pictures," to be "on his own way without following the steps of the ancient sages"? What brings about this departure from the past? It is the enlightenment. As long as a monk is enslaved by the tradition of the past and the teachings of his master, he is still unenlightened. His mind is still clouded. He is still not free to receive the truth he seeks. But when the moment of enlightenment arrives, all that has gone before, including what his master has taught, is superseded. He is ready to strike out on a new path, leaving the secluded mountain to enter the rough-and-tumble of the world, and to share the life of all living creatures.

It is this freedom from the past traditions, enabling the service of the divine truth continually disclosing itself in "the world of mortals" (*jen chien*), that is very much absent among Christians in Asia. We have inherited the Christian traditions from the West and discarded our indigenous traditions. True, we are indebted to Western Christianity for what we are as Christians, but are we less indebted to our native traditions for what we are as Taiwanese,

Thais, Malaysians, or Japanese? We have to recover our indebtedness to our own traditions and reaffirm ourselves in them even though we are Christians. This is the discipline we have long neglected, to the detriment of our own self-understanding as Asian Christians. But we have to know that the recovery of that indebtedness will not result in a happy marriage to the Christian traditions from the West. There are, in fact, more tensions and conflicts than peace and harmony, both in the practice of Christian faith and in theological reflections on it.

By all means we need to deepen our experience and understanding of both Christian traditions and Asian traditions. But, as long as we pursue them both as if our grasp of the final truth depends on them, we are not going to get anywhere near the truth. At most we shall become competent in parroting what others have said about these traditions. It is at this point that what Kuo An, the Zen master, advises seekers of truth may enable us to extricate ourselves from the double binding of Western Christian traditions and indigenous Asian traditions in which we find ourselves. He advises that one should "go on one's way without following the steps of the ancient sages." For those monks who had come to him for enlightenment, did this not mean that they were to go on their own way, without following the steps they had learned from him? Yes, it did. This is why one of the fundamental tenets of Zen is *pu li wen tze, chiau wai pieh ch'uan,* that is to say, not to establish teachings in writing but to develop traditions beyond traditions.

The history of Zen Buddhism makes fascinating reading because it is full of stories of enlightened monks striking out on new paths in their grasping for the truth. There is a celebrated story of how Hui-neng (638–713), the sixth patriarch of Chinese Zen Buddhism, arrived at the moment of truth. "One day," the story tells us, "the fifth patriarch [Hung-jen], wishing to decide on his successor, wished to see how much of his teaching was understood by his followers." The poem composed by Shen-hsiu, the most scholarly of his five hundred disciples, ran as follows:

> This body is the Bodhi-tree,
> The soul is like a mirror bright;
> Take heed to keep it always clean,
> And let no dust collect upon it.

Hui-neng was not satisfied with it and composed another, which was inscribed beside the learned Shen-hsiu's:

> The Bodhi is not like the tree,
> The mirror bright is nowhere shining;
> As there is nothing from the beginning,
> Where can the dust collect on it?[6]

The contrast between the scholarly Shen-hsiu and the intuitively creative Hui-neng cannot be more striking, representing the contrast between faithful adherence to the tradition accumulated from the past and the bold break from it.

Most of us Christians and theologians in Asia are more like Shen-hsiu than Hui-neng. But in seeking to extricate ourselves from the double binding of Western Christian traditions and our Asian traditions, Hui-neng cuts a far much more exciting and challenging figure than his learned counterpart. "With Hui-neng, Zen begins to shoot out its own native roots, that is to say, what used to be Indian now turns to be genuinely Chinese. Zen has become acclimatized by Hui-neng and firmly rooted in Chinese soil."[7] Could what happened to Buddhism in China also happen to Christianity? Or is it too difficult, if not impossible, at this stage of Asian history for Christianity to become "acclimatized and firmly rooted" in the soil of Asian communities in which it has come to stay? I would like to believe that the task is not impossible, although it will be difficult. The awareness of this difficulty should excite and challenge us.

What Is God-Talk?

The questions raised above prompt the quest of what our main preoccupation in theology should be. We should, of course, be preoccupied with God. This is what theology, derived from two Greek words, *theos* (God) and *logos* (discourse), means. It is commonly assumed that theology is a discourse on God, study on the nature of God, exploration into the mystery of God, reflection on God's activities in the world. As to questions such as how the world began and what its destiny is going to be, who Jesus is and what he means for us, how individual souls are to be saved and gain eternal life—all such questions are to find answers from who God is and what God does. No wonder theology is said to be "God-talk." Is this not self-evident? Does this not sound simple and clear? All things—things in heaven and things on earth, things related to life and death, things that have to do with time and eternity, things concerning human beings—all such things logically follow from what God in God's own self is and how God relates Godself to us.

But is theology as simple and clear as what God-talk is supposed to be? Are answers to questions such as who God is in God's own self and what God's purpose is for humanity and for individual persons so obvious and evident as some Christians, preachers, and theologians want to have us believe? Why, then, did Jesus have to wrestle, from time to time, with what his mission must be, as the story of his temptation in the Gospels of Matthew and Luke seems to tell us? Why did he have to struggle for the last time in the Garden of Gethsemane, before his arrest by the Temple police, to comprehend what God had in store for him? How is it that many saints in the history of the Christian church tell us, in many different ways, how they have to pass through terribly dark nights of the soul to attain a vision of God, and even then how the vision may not be as transparent as they like it to be? Why have there been many seekers of the way and the truth who underwent much physical torture and spiritual agony to attain the experience of enlightenment? And why did Kuo An, the Chinese Zen monk, find himself turning to the world and entering the marketplace to make friends with common men and women, to share their life of joy and suffering, hope and anxiety?

It may not be simple and clear, this business of God-talk. Theology may be God-talk, but it is still necessary to know who does the talking: God, of course! A response to one's inquiry comes back loud and clear. Is this not what the expression "God-talk" means? *God* talks. Is this not what the story of creation in the Hebrew Scriptures tells us? "God *said*," we are told, "'Let there be light'; and there was light" (Gen. 1:3). That seer on the island of Patmos in the last book of the New Testament tells us how he, in his vision, heard the one sitting on the throne declare, "See, I am making all things new" (Rev. 21:5).

Discourse in most parts of the Bible is discourse in the name of God. Prophets in ancient Israel used to declare, "Thus saith the Lord," before they launched into indictments of social and religious evils of their day. Most of the hard things they said against the people, however, came from astute observation based on their keen religious and moral sensibilities. What they said carried moral authority because it was motivated by their deep love for the people and inspired by their profound sense of what was holy and divine. In vivid and strong language they said what they considered to be God's will and purpose for their nation and people. It was language of faith and discourse in faith. They could not have meant that the language was God's word for word and that the discourse was uttered directly by God.

The situation becomes more ambiguous and confused when considering the discourse of the church. At Sunday worship the Scripture reading begins with these words: "Hear the word of God." This phrase echoes "Thus saith the Lord," the resounding pronouncement of the prophets in Hebrew Scripture. Whether or not the passages read from Genesis, Jeremiah, or Psalms in Hebrew Scripture, or from John's Gospel, the Book of Acts, or the First Epistle of Peter in the New Testament, are literally words uttered by God is a theological question that often brings out the worst in otherwise devout Christians. When it comes to the divine elocution in the Book of Leviticus, prescribing religious and social codes for the community of ancient Israel, the Song of Songs with its exquisite and often explicit love between a man and a woman, or the Book of Revelation, which contains many violent scenes, the debate on Scripture as "the Word of God" has to be conducted judiciously. Whether or not what preachers proclaim in their sermons reflects the word of God is another question.

This leads me to say that the term "God-talk" has a twofold meaning. It means *God* talks, and it can also mean *talks about* God.[8] The verbal phrase "God talks" and the phrase "talks about God" are two entirely different things. In the former it is God who does the talking, whereas in the latter it is we human beings. Confusion of one phrase with the other or identification of one with the other has caused conflict within the church and tension between Christians and non-Christians. What we, Christians and theologians, have often done, sometimes knowingly and sometimes scarcely knowing, is to correlate our talks about God for the talk God is supposed to be doing. We speak for God, although often it is doubtful whether God is willing to identify Godself with what we say in God's behalf. We speak in God's name, not thinking whether we are just using the name of God to give credence to what we are saying.

This is the problem. It is a serious problem not only for Christianity but for all religions. It is often the case that the authenticity of the person speaking in the name of God is very much in question. The credibility of the religious establishment that communicates God's will and purpose for believers, and even for humanity, more often than not does not stand up to scrutiny. History tells us that many crimes have been committed in the name of God. Many religious pretenders have misled innocent women, men, and children and brought tragedies to them, to their families, and to their community while quoting God and God's purpose. We are familiar with one tragic story after another in the chronicles of every religion. How many people have had to suffer and even perish on account of "God's truth" invoked by the religious authorities? Trials of the so-called heretics and infidels make sordid chapters in the history of almost all religions.

The assertion that our God-talk, that is, our talks about God, is equivalent to the talk that God is doing is the root cause of religious fanaticism. The practice prompts some believers to make hasty judgments about what others believe and how they practice their faith. Once our talks about God are taken for the talk done by God, they take on the air of sanctity. Talk about God cannot be contradicted without grave consequences. It cannot be defied without incurring the wrath of the religious establishment, who argue that doubt is the work of the devil to poison the minds of the faithful and to undermine the peace and harmony of the religious community. Faith is not faith unless it is irrational. What contradicts nature and common sense is held to be divinely inspired. God, accordingly, is not God unless God behaves whimsically with the world God has created. Consequently, the absurdity of some religious claims and the irrational nature of some religious practices are not exposed until tragedy strikes the people involved. That this process is repeated shows how dangerous religious authoritarianism and fanaticism can become.

Christianity has been one of the religions that has made God-talk its main concern. Some Christians claim that they take part in God-talk, that is, that God talks directly to them. They call Christianity a revealed religion, a religion that deals directly with God. What it says is what God says. What it teaches is what God teaches. It affirms what God affirms. It commands what God commands. It is this self-understanding of what Christianity is that has shaped the nature and mission of this church and determined the function of their Chris-

tian theology. The church is the community of those women and men elected
to be saved. Some Christian theologians have even mobilized their theological
power and talent to develop the rational basis for why God has chosen Christianity to be the sole instrument of God's saving purposes for humankind. Of
course they have had to contrive theologically why other religions and their communities are not instrumental to God's grand redemptive design for the world.
Even though the human community has always been religiously and culturally
pluralistic—the reality to which we Christians were rudely awakened by the
demise of Western colonialism and by the end of the Western domination of
the world—for many Christians views of life, history, and the world that center
on Christianity are still deeply rooted in their religious consciousness.

Since Christianity is a revealed religion, the argument goes, it is fundamentally different from other religions. Christianity, in the last analysis, is not a
religion. Never mind the religious rites and ceremonies that resemble those of
other religions. Never mind the mundane nature of its organization and structure. And never mind that it seems to share with other religious communities
some common ground in what it teaches and practices and in what it anticipates
for the life hereafter. Christianity is, it is asserted, founded on a revelation of
God not shared by other religions. No, Christianity is not a religion. It is revelation. Its origins lie in the "revealed truth" from above, which is not found
anywhere on this earth. If it is a religion, it is a divinely inspired religion and
unlike other religions that developed out of human needs and fears.

The question as to whether Christianity is a religion or not does not have
to detain us. It is a rhetorical question. Christianity *is* a religion, even though
it claims to have its root in God's revelation. We need to know, however, that
some other religions too make the claim that divine revelation has led them to
what they believe and to how they practice it. If this is the case, the critical
question both for Christians and for others concerns the ways in which we have
come to know what is revealed to us. How do we know what we take to be
revealed comes from the good God and not from sinister forces in the universe
and in the human community, or even from our subconsciousness? What is the
basis of our claim to the divine truth? By what means and through what chan-
nels have we come to be inspired by it? And how is it related to our everyday
experience?

These are not idle questions. They force us to *think about* what we believe, to
reflect on the truth we take for granted, and to *test* how we practice our faith in
relation to the people and the world around us. If you say that you know what
you believe is from God, and therefore that it is true, then that's that. There
can be no further discussion, no more argument. You ask others to take what
you say at face value, or just to ignore it. But if you want others to take you
seriously, you have to show them *how you have come to believe what you believe.*
This is what is called "testimony." One must testify to faith to friends, strangers,
skeptics, unbelievers, and even to those who oppose it.

Theology as Human-Talk

How do you testify to your faith? To testify to something, in this case to faith, is part of the most common and necessary activity of our daily life—communication. All living beings, and not just human beings, are engaged in communication, from plants to birds to insects. Modes of communication differ from species to species. Communication may be a sound, a movement of the body, an odor, a touch, or a combination of these. For human beings, communication takes place mainly through language, following rules of grammar, syntax, and semantics. Even body language and sign language share the basic elements of the spoken and written language. But language is not limited to words and sentences, whether spoken, written, or in signs and gestures. The language of painters is color; the language of musicians is sound; the language of dancers is body movement. Still, these languages have grammar, syntax, and semantics unique to the art form and at the same time basic to the appreciation and comprehension of others.

Language is, then, both a personal possession and communal property. The language or languages I use is the history of my life. It is me. It discloses my past and my present. It anticipates my future. It can also hide and suppress my life and my history. This last statement does not mean that if language is taken away from me I am rendered "languageless." On the contrary. I have to go underground to devise another kind of language, to communicate what cannot be communicated publicly in the language taken away from me. This is what happens in a totalitarian society.

It is because language is so personal that it is also so communal. A community is built around a language. More correctly, different languages and different nuances and variations of a particular language, representing different experiences, take form in different communities. Language is the bridge between the personal and the communal. It is the medium by which we share with one another our physical needs and spiritual aspirations at various levels and in different dimensions of community life. Next to kinship, language—and for that matter, dialects—ensures the identity of individuals in the community and maintains the coherence of that community.

Language creates affinity, sympathy, and community. But it can also do just the opposite: it can also give rise to misunderstanding, discord, and hostility. We all know from our experience and from history how wars of words can develop into disruptions of personal relationships, social disturbances, civil wars and world wars. In a situation of tension and conflict what is said is not taken for what it is supposed to mean, but for what it is not supposed to mean. Language thus becomes a weapon, and a potent weapon at that, for achieving one's own interest at the expense of others. Is it not because of language as a potential cause of tension and conflict that ancient sages admonish us to be wise in our use of it? "Never be rash with your mouth," says the seasoned sage and teacher of the ways of life in ancient Israel, "nor let your heart be quick to utter a word before God, for God is in heaven, and you upon earth; therefore let your words be few" (Eccl. 5:2). Jesus also knows better than all of us Christians. This is what he is reported to have said to his disciples about praying to God. "When you are praying, do not heap up empty phrases as the Gentiles do; for they think that they will be heard because of their many words" (Matt. 6:7). How much of the Gentile lurks in us Christians when we think of the prayers offered at Sunday worship or in prayer meetings? We pray as if "we think that we will be heard because of our many words."

Lao Tzu, an ancient sage of China and contemporary of Confucius (551–479 B.C.E.), was right: "One who knows does not speak; one who speaks does not know."[9] Do we not have to take to heart the wise remark of this Chinese philosopher of life? Those religious teachers and preachers who speak so much about God's judgment and the imminent end of the world—do they really know of what they speak? And if they know, how do they know? Those evangelists and Christians who talk so much about God, God in God's own self, about the chosen people of God, and about the destiny of those who are not Christian—how are they sure that what they assert comes totally from God's own self and not, at least partially, from their experiences formed and conditioned by their personal, historical, and cultural circumstances?

The language we use to testify to religious truth is no exception to the basic truth that language is culturally determined. To put it simply, language is culture and culture is language—language in the broad sense mentioned above, including all sorts of artistic expression as well as spoken and written language. It is difficult to say which comes first, language or culture. But this does not have to be an egg-and-chicken proposition. The fact is that culture is a language in diverse forms and that language embodies a culture.

Religious language, insofar as it is also a language, is in this way experience-based and culturally conditioned. Some may argue that religious experience is a particular kind of experience; that is, it is a *religious* experience. Here is the crux of the matter. Is not religious experience an *experience?* Is it not a part of *human* experience? If it cannot be reduced entirely to human experience, it still cannot be intelligible when totally separated from it. It may be a sublimated form of human experience—human experience inspired, moved, and transformed by a divine power, a power outside us, a power from above. It may be an experience caused by a creative power not under our control and not at our disposal. But we are not God, nor are we angels. A "divinely caused experience" must be related to "human" experience to be perceived as such. It is we as humans, not as God or angels, who perceive that particular kind of experience as divine experience. It is by means of culturally formed and conditioned language that we seek to express it.

This fact is so obvious that it hardly needs further explication. But it may not be obvious in some religious circles, Christian and non-Christian. That it may not be obvious is why Paul the Apostle had to deal with the issue of speaking in tongues at the Church of Corinth. He did not deny the gift of speaking in tongues, but said that "those who speak in a tongue do not speak to other people but to God" (1 Cor. 14:2a). That one is speaking to God can neither be objectively proved nor disproved. It is a question of whether one is sincere in one's claim. But there is another issue, that is, intelligibility. What use is speaking in a tongue to God if it is not intelligible to other believers? This is what Paul contended. "If in a tongue," he argued, "you utter speech that is not intelligible, how will anyone know what is being said? For you will be speaking into the air" (1 Cor 14:9). Precisely! How much of what is said in church gatherings, to quote Paul, is "speaking into the air," not to mention what is practiced as "speaking in tongues"?

At this point reference to the Chinese character for "faith" or "to believe" (*hsin*) can be instructive. It consists of two parts, with *word,* or *speech,* and *human being* as its radical. This combination indicates that even faith in something mystical is not divorced from the human speech that stands for certain human experiences. The same Chinese character is also used to mean "truthfulness" (*hsin*). A sincere person is "a person of words," a person who does not go back on his or her words, a person who keeps words. Confucius considered "truthfulness" as one of the most basic and important human qualities. "I do not know," he once said to his disciples, "how a person without truthfulness (*hsin*) is to get on. How can a large carriage be made to go without the cross-bar for yoking the oxen to, or a small carriage without the arrangement for yoking the horses?"[10]

When this twofold meaning of *hsin* is applied to a religious situation, faith (*hsin*) in God and truthfulness (*hsin*) in human relationships have to go hand in hand. Further, truthfulness (*hsin*) in human relationships is a test, a potent test, of faith (*hsin*) in God. Ethics has to be very much a part of religion, faith, and theology. This is the heart of Chinese religious thought and practice. Christianity has taken this aspect lightly and dismissed Chinese religion as nothing but ethics. How wrong we Christians have been! "Faith without works," says James, "is dead" (James 2:26). Should not ethics be reinstated in Christian theology, particularly in the theology of the churches of the Reformed tradition that stresses the principle of *sola fide,* by faith alone?

That human experience should relate to faith is evident, is it not? Take one of our central Christian assertions that "God is love," for example. If love is not part of human experience, if it is not part of what it means to be human, how can we experience God to be love? How can we know God is love? And how can we tell others that God is love unless they also experience love as an essential part of their humanity? Considering the interrelatedness of faith (*hsin*) and truthfulness (*hsin*), how are we to convince ourselves and others that God is love unless we can refer to acts of love in human relationships? Love is from God, so assert Christians. John, the author of the letter that bears his name, is emphatic on this point. In his circular letter to Christians he writes: "Beloved, let us love one another, *because love is from God*" (1 John 4:7; emphasis added).

God is love and love is from God. But John does not stop there. "Those who say, 'I love God,' and hate their brothers or sisters, are liars," he continues, "for those who do not love a brother or a sister whom they have seen, cannot love God whom they have not seen" (4:20). Is this not to say that truthfulness (*hsin*) in human relationships can reveal whether one's beliefs are credible or true? What you believe is confirmed or discredited by what you do. I am not saying that our experience of love and our practice of it amount to God's love and to what God does for humanity. Our love is imperfect. It is deformed. It is motivated by self-interest. There is no way we can identify human love with God's love. But the fact is that if we are not capable of love, if we refuse to practice it, there is no way we can talk about God's love, not to mention testifying that God is love or that God deals with us in love.

Christian theology is, then, human action and human talk. It is how we Christians respond in deed and thought to what we believe to be true, good, and beautiful—to all that we believe to manifest God. It is this kind of theology in which Jesus was engaged. That is why he told stories and parables—stories and parables derived from his own experiences and from those of the people to whom he addressed himself. Inspired by the children playing the wedding and funeral games at the marketplace, he likened himself to a piper who piped "God-talk." But the religious leaders and theologians of his day were not impressed. They refused to dance to the tune he was piping and did everything in their power to stop the piper. But they were not able to stop him, not even on the cross on which they crucified him.

There have always been Christians and theologians who try to dance to the tunes Jesus the piper played. They are in the minority. They are often censored by those who have the power to decide what theology must be and what tune it has to play. But in our day the number of thinking Christians responding to Jesus' piping and dancing to the tunes he played has increased dramatically. For an increasing number of Christians and theologians in the world today Christian theology has been transposed from heaven to earth, from the life hereafter to the life here and now. Is it any wonder that theology has once again become serious business, a business conducted not only in the secluded community of Christians but in the wide world, where people struggle to live with meaning and hope?

Chapter 2

Birds of the Air
and Lilies of the Field

Freedom from Anxiety:
Jesus' Theology of Life

Human beings have been preoccupied with God since the dawn of civilization. The word *theology* sums up this human preoccupation with God: *theo*-logy practiced as experience of God, study on God, reflection on God, talk on God. But here is the problem: the God who has been the subject of our experience, concern, devotion, and study is not the object of our human sense perception. God is beyond our immediate grasp. That is why philosophers and theologians use their brain power to gain access to God, and mystics tell us how they find themselves in the presence of the mystery surrounding God. As for some evangelists and preachers, they reduce God to the sum total of our emotional upheavals and personal desires.

Jesus was no less preoccupied with God than his contemporaries and human beings before and after him. But he was no metaphysician who speculates about the nature of God. He was no philosopher of religion who tries to prove the existence of God. Nor was he a theologian who speaks about a God unrelated to the everyday life of people. Nor was he, like fast-talking and emotion-rousing preachers and evangelists, at pains to represent God as a projection of our longings and desires. He was not only totally devoted to God, but his was the business of doing God's will, making sacrifices every step of the way. As we all know, his life culminated in his death on the cross, and not in a Hall of Fame or in a home of riches and comfort.

Jesus was acquainted with the beliefs and teachings on God handed down by the religious traditions of his nation. He was no stranger to the ways in which the God of the religious authorities held ordinary men and women in fear and awe. He could have pursued the career of a religious teacher, defending and refining the faith and theology of the religious establishment. That would have been for him an easy path that could have led to a "successful" religious career. But this was not the path he took. Why?

The answer to this question must be found in his daily association with

31

people, not people high and mighty, whether political or religious, but people of little means—women, men, and children outside the high circles of power, wealth, and prestige. What concerned these people, Jesus must have realized early in his career, was life, above all the anxiety that makes life uncertain and precarious. He was engaged in a "theology of life."

Anxiety comes in all forms and shapes. It varies in sizes and quantity. Anxiety unsettles us; it must have also unsettled Jesus. Anxiety gives us sleepless nights; it must have also from time to time given Jesus nights without sleep. Anxiety deprives us of zest for life; it must have, every now and again, overshadowed the life of Jesus. Anxiety assails the very core of our being and makes us unsure what is in store for us; it must have often rendered Jesus uncertain about what he had to do, when opposition to his mission became vicious and threats to his life mounted. There is anxiety that our trust in the God of love and justice seems to have no basis in reality, that it seems a mere comforting thought, that even if there is a God of love and justice, it does not seem to make a difference in a world of injustice and violence. Jesus himself was not entirely free from such anxiety, as his advocacy for the poor and the oppressed was only making his opponents all the more determined to obstruct his cause.

In short, Jesus knew and experienced anxiety of all kinds firsthand and not secondhand, in person and not in theory, as a matter of everyday experience and not as an occasional project designed to "immerse" its participants for a day or a week in a slum to see for themselves how people live in dire conditions, or in a poorly ventilated factory to experience how young women workers work ten hours a day for subsistence wages. There is, for example, the story of a young scribe who expressed his interest in joining the company of Jesus. "Teacher," he said to Jesus, "I will follow you wherever you go." Even though he was a scribe, someone who belonged to the religious elite, there is no reason to doubt his sincerity. He could have been impressed more by what Jesus taught than by how he went about his ministry. He must have seen in Jesus a rabbi destined for prominence in the company of great rabbis. That could be why he addressed Jesus as "teacher" (rabbi).

If Jesus had been politically astute and calculating, if his purpose was to re-place by political means the old traditions, oppressive hierarchies, and corrupt religious leadership of his day with what he understood to be "the kingdom of God," he would have encouraged that scribe to join him. This would surely have been a gain for him politically. It would have raised the morale of his followers and perhaps enhanced his cause. Here was someone defecting from the religiously powerful group to join the rank of the fledgling religious move-ment. Jesus could have embraced him with open arms. This would at least have been a propaganda coup. It would certainly have increased the credibility of his movement in people's eyes.

This, however, is what Jesus said to the scribe: "Foxes have holes, and birds of the air have nests; but the Son of Man has nowhere to lay his head" (Matt.

8:20; also Luke 9:58). In this response Jesus was saying how he lived, not just occasionally but daily, not only once in a while but constantly, not when his whims prompted him but as his lifestyle. As a wandering teacher Jesus had no security of a home and did not enjoy the warmth and comfort of a hearth. Jesus did not talk about the anxiety of other people from a position of luxury. Anxiety was his daily experience. It accompanied him everywhere he went. It taxed his resourcefulness and sapped his energy to do what he took upon himself.

If anxiety is what Jesus and the people associated with him had to face, it is also what we have to face every day. But how is anxiety dealt with in the Christian church and its theology? How are people in the pew at Sunday worship told not to be anxious? How do our pastors and theologians "theologize" about anxiety, or do they only theologize it away? Here is how anxiety is made into a "theological" subject:

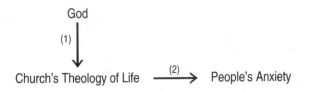

In this theological process God is at the top, in direct relationship with the church and its theology, while people come at the end. In this process people have no relationship with God.

This is the way the church has done its theology for centuries. It always begins with what it understands God to be and with its understanding of what God does in matters big and small. In the name of this God the Christian church in the Middle Ages mobilized kings and princes in Europe to send expedition forces to Palestine to fight the Muslims, known as the Crusades. At the beginning of the modern era the churches in the West expanded to what is now called the Third World to conquer the pagan lands and to convert "pagans" to Christianity. This was the so-called great missionary expansion of Christianity. Of course many pagans were converted to the Christian faith, and Christianity became a "universal" religion. But along the way the people converted to Christianity lost their own culture, in many cases even their ancestral names. They came to be linked with a God who did not recognize their names and who did not appreciate their cultures.

If this disappearance could happen to cultures and names, such neglect also can happen to the problems and challenges people have to face in their daily lives, especially people without means, power, and privilege. Until the end of 1997, when economic turmoil erupted and swept through Asian countries such as Thailand, Indonesia, Korea, and even Japan, many Christian churches in Asia had been affluent. They rode on the bandwagon of the so-called economic miracles. They became rich and powerful. In many cases they replaced still respectable church buildings with big, imposing, and shining buildings to display their wealth and power. Church building became a status symbol. It proudly "testified" how successful Christians could become, how worthwhile it was to be an earnest Christian. It also became the measure of how God blessed Christians.

Many church buildings in Asia today epitomize a theology of how God and mammon can cohabit in peace and with pride. There is of course no room for anxiety in this kind of theology. To be preoccupied with anxiety is a sign of weakness on the part of Christians. To harbor anxiety in their hearts amounts to distrust in God. Anxiety, whether of a material or spiritual nature, has no place in a church glittering under a gilded cross and flashing a brilliant sign saying, "Jesus is the Savior of the World." Anxiety has been banished from the church and from the hearts of the Christians who dutifully present themselves at worship on Sunday.

But the fact is that anxiety has not been banished either from the world in which we live or from the hearts of many a Christian woman and man. True, our world has at last seen the end of the Cold War era, but it has yet to see the end of the threat by nuclear destruction. In science and technology the world can sing the glory of human ingenuity and power, but its rivers and seas are polluted, its resources depleted; increasing numbers of plants of the earth, birds of the air, and fish of the waters become extinct each year. Our streets and homes are not safe. They have been invaded by violence, crime, and murder.

Christians may put aside their anxiety in a make-believe world, created by the economic success of the church, and feel safe within the splendid church buildings. But are we really anxiety-free? Once outside the church compound, we, like anybody else in society, are imprisoned in anxiety—anxiety resulting from the rise and fall of the stock market, from economic turmoil, and from all sorts of abuses, from drug abuse to alcohol abuse to spouse abuse to child abuse. Deep-seated anxiety has also grown out of dislocation from one's homeland in search of freedom from starvation, political freedom, economic prosperity, and educational opportunity in alien lands. Such geographical dislocation creates disruption of human relationships, separation of families, and uprootedness from one's culture and loss of identity.

Anxiety has eroded confidence in our own selves and in our human destiny. This is a serious theological problem. As the church practices a theology of a God high and mighty in rhetoric and irrelevant in reality, its theological responsibility has been yielded to psychiatrists and counselors, who have become high priests in charge of our souls. The mainline churches have also relegated the care of the souls of many of its members to the preachers and evangelists who prescribe instant "evangelical sedatives" to calm their restlessness and to put their frightened spirits to sleep.

But this is not the way Jesus dealt with the anxiety of the women and men around him. Nor is this how he coped with his own anxiety. He saw the worried look of his audience; in that look he must have seen his own worry. He heard their hearts beating in anxiety over what to eat tomorrow and how to clothe their children; in these hearts Jesus must have heard his own heart beating also in anxiety—foxes have holes and birds have nests, but tonight I have nowhere to lay my head. He could perceive the question of questions, though unspoken and unarticulated, that these men and women carried—the question of the meaning of a life laden with difficulties and uncertainties. That must have been his own question as he felt the visible and invisible forces closing in on him to plot his downfall.

The anxiety of the people around him, as well as his own anxiety, was apparent in his talk with them about God, about the world, and about their life and destiny. Then an exchange at this down-to-earth level took an unexpected turn. He told them: "Look at the birds of the air; they neither sow nor reap nor gather into barns, and yet your heavenly Father feeds them" (Matt. 6:26; also Luke 12:24). As he said this, his listeners must have raised their eyes to follow his fingers pointing to a flock of birds in the sky.

While they were still lost in thought about what Jesus said, watching the birds finally disappear from sight, they heard Jesus saying: "Consider the lilies of the field, how they grow; they neither toil nor spin, yet I tell you, even Solomon in all his glory was not clothed like one of these" (Matt. 6:28-29; also Luke 12:27). Was it springtime when Jesus had this discourse with the people? They must have been in an open field covered with spring flowers, including lilies in full bloom. Many in the audience must have noticed those flowers for the first time, and realized how beautiful and charming they were.

As their eyes were still fixed on the flowers, they heard these words: "If God so clothes the grass of the field, which is alive today and tomorrow is thrown into the oven, will God not much more clothe you?"[1] Before they were able to decide whether to agree with him, Jesus lost no time in adding this pithy phrase: "You of little faith" (Matt. 6:30; also Luke 12:28). Grass of the field and their faith. Are they not two entirely unrelated things? And how does God come into all this? They must have been puzzled. This is not the way they had been taught to think about themselves and God.

But this is the way Jesus engages himself and others in trying to make sense of life in relation to God. It can be illustrated as follows:

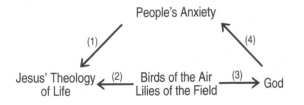

Note in this illustration that people's anxiety has a direct impact on Jesus' theology of life. That theology is further illuminated by "the birds of the air and lilies of the field." Hence the arrow is directed from the birds of the air and lilies of the field to Jesus' theology of life. Only after such illumination are insights gained as to how God deals with people in need and anxiety.

This is quite a departure from the way people of Jesus' day were accustomed to understanding their faith. It is also a striking contrast to what many Christians today regard theology to be—"God-talk," the talk God does, the words God says to us, the discourse God directly addresses to us. How could theology be "bird-talk," or "lily-talk"? Is this not what is branded as *natural theology,* a great enemy of what is known as *revealed theology?* In some modern theological traditions the term *natural theology* has come to be associated with theology that is bad and illicit, theology done behind the back of God, or theology that enters from the back door. But if this is how Jesus did his theology, so be it. Let us all be theologians of "natural theology" like him!

But the so-called natural theology does not have to be bad or illicit. If it is, then the Bible contains much of what is bad and illicit. Psalms in the Hebrew Scriptures, for example, are full of "natural theology." "The heavens are telling the glory of God," intones the poet in Psalm 19, "and the firmament proclaims God's handiwork" (v. 1). In Psalm 148 all created things are called upon to praise God:

> Praise God, sun and moon;
>   praise God, all you shining stars!
> Praise God, you highest heavens,
>   and you waters above the heavens!
>
> Mountains and all hills,
>   fruit trees and all cedars!
> Wild animals and all cattle,
>   creeping things and flying birds!
>   (vv. 3-4, 9-10)

The psalm echoes the stories of creation in Genesis 1–2. It is a poetic version of the creation stories.

Since all things are created by God, it is only right that they praise God. All this poetry is symbolic language, but the images are not just symbols without substance, metaphors that refer to something beyond themselves but that in themselves have no meaning. In other words, these images are not merely signs that can be erased or discarded after they have served a certain purpose. Mountains, trees, rivers, animals, and birds do embody the power, love, beauty, and majesty characteristic of God and God's creating power. They are integral parts of God's creation. They are created for definite purposes, not just as means to a purpose. Without them how are we to know that God is the Creator? If they owe their existence to God, God also needs them to be witnesses to God, who has brought them into being.

It might be that such thoughts crossed Jesus' mind when he saw the worried looks of the people he was addressing. Creation must be the key to the solution of human anxiety, including the anxiety of Jesus. It must be the answer for human beings, himself not excepted, to gain freedom from worry. The birds of the air that catch Jesus' attention remind him of the vastness of creation. The lilies of the field that delight his eyes tell him how rich that creation is.

Anxiety deprives us of the space in which we live and makes us blind to the richness of which we are a part. It separates us from the outside world and imprisons us in our own selves. In our anxiety time stops its flow and space loses its dimensions. What to eat and what to drink become almost our total concern. What to wear and how to add to "our span of life" absorbs our entire energy. This is the heart of our problem, Jesus is saying. Look at the birds and lilies. Do they not make us realize that we human beings are not the center of the universe? Is it not true that when we learn to remove ourselves from the center of everything, we begin to see ourselves in relation to other things and creatures? Does this realization not give us a space that enables us to cope with our daily anxiety?

Birds of the air and lilies of the field provide this inner space. We hold creation in us and creation holds us in itself. It is this inner space, Jesus seems to be saying, it is this spiritual capacity within us that gives us the strength to deal with our everyday problems and the courage to meet the challenges of life. This theology of life is at once spacious and deep. It is spacious because it is related to creation. It is deep because it enables us to fathom the depth of God's caring love in us. This must be what Jesus wanted to say to his listeners. He was not offering an instant solution to their problems. What he was doing was empowering them to relate themselves to God and God's creation. Once space was created in their minds and room developed in their spirits, they could then go about their daily toil and labor with trust in God and hope for the future in their hearts. The theology of Jesus is, thus, a theology that takes creation seriously, a theology that calls upon human beings to derive strength and grace from God's creation to live in faith, hope, and love.

Who Is My Neighbor?
Jesus' Theology of Human Community

As the space in our minds and souls shrinks and as the room in our hearts and spirits becomes crowded with our beliefs and claims, the community we create around us also shrinks. This is one of the problems Jesus tried to drive home to the people of his time. He had a vision—a vision of a community that has plenty of room for all people, a community that can expand its space to accommodate men, women, and children from different walks of life and from diverse religious and cultural traditions. What he strove for was a theology of human community that embodies the richness of God's creation and that is shaped by its marvelous plurality.

Jesus came up against the concept of a religious community reduced in size and impoverished in content. Both in theory and in practice this is how that theology of community was developed:

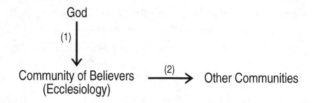

In this theological formula there is no doubt as to who plays the central role. The community of Christian faith that claims God's special favor is the principal player. The Bible, both the Hebrew Scriptures and the New Testament, provides the source of the claim. That claim is the heart of what Christians affirm church to be (ecclesiology).

Such a community of faith is developed as a self-contained community based on what it stands for and, on the other hand, in separation from others and what they stand for. For the community to which Jesus belonged that exclusiveness was rooted in history and validated in tradition. The Exodus from Egypt, the event remembered as liberation from the land of bondage, became the historical memory that created the faith and bonded the people as a community. History was transformed into faith and then into a community organized around that faith. This was a long process, and along the way that faith, derived from history, gave rise to the self-contained community and developed into separation from other communities. God was believed to be preferential, through thick and thin, toward that particular community.

Jesus had to wrestle with this community of his own. The tradition that had grown out of it and that in turn fortified it is long, strong, and invincible. What could be more dangerous than calling the tradition into question, not to mention changing it? But he went ahead anyway, anticipating the consequences. How did he go about it? What did he do to challenge his own self-contained community and its separation from other communities? He did it by associating himself with those excluded from the community. And he did it by telling stories and parables. One of the celebrated story-parables is that of the Samaritan who went out of his way to lend a helping hand to a man robbed and injured on the road to Jericho (Luke 10:25-37).

We are all familiar with the story. It casts in a bad light the priest and the Levite who pass by the injured person, "undisturbed by what they have seen" (*she ruo wu do* in Chinese, meaning "seeing as if not seeing"). They deserve to be cast in a bad light. In contrast, the Samaritan, prompted by "natural compassion and innate mercy" (*ce wen zhi un chi hsin*), to use a Chinese expression, took care of the injured man and made sure that he was nursed back to health.

Most homilies usually stop here to draw moral lessons from the story—the lesson of not leaving people in suffering in the lurch, of helping strangers in trouble even if it means it would affect your plans and delay your appointments. All this is right, of course. When a conclusion is drawn, however, to the effect that Christians are capable of such a deed of care and charity because of their special relationship with God, something is not quite right. It makes one wonder whether this is what Jesus wanted to stress to his listeners. The theological process by which Christians usually draw their conclusion from the story seems to go like this:

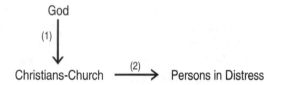

The way Christians understand themselves in relation to God and to the human community, demonstrated above, is typical. It is premised on their particular and, by implication, privileged relation with God. It is this relation that makes what they do different, even though others are also capable of doing the same thing.

This kind of theological reasoning is highly problematic, which becomes evident when we deal with Jesus' parable more carefully. First of all, the priest and the Levite shun the injured man perhaps because they do not want to become ritually contaminated in contact with the wounds or with a corpse. That they are doing something right according to their religion does not mean that they are in the right with God. The theology that does not allow them to turn aside and look after the injured man is wrong and perverted. Jesus did not hesitate to make this clear in what he taught and did. Is this not one of the points Jesus tried to make in the parable we are considering?

There is another important point in the story. Jesus has a Samaritan do what the priest and the Levite failed to do. The Samaritan is not afraid to come into contact with the injured man, to give him first aid, and to take him to an inn for rest and further medical care. Jesus seems to be saying that the person motivated to act solely by compassion has to be a Samaritan, someone from outside the religious community to which the priest and the Levite belonged, someone who is not incapacitated by its faith, theology, ritual, and law. A self-contained community that exists for itself and that protects its own interest has to give way to a community that is open, a community that consists of people from different backgrounds and traditions, a community prompted by service to others and dedicated to the well-being of the human community.

This interpretation is quite different from the theology that undergirds the traditional self-understanding of a religious community, be it the Jewish community of Jesus' time or the Christian community in the past and of today. Jesus must have developed his "theology of the community of believers" in this way:

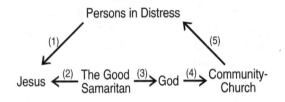

What kind of community would that be, a community in which a Samaritan—a Gentile, a stranger—plays an essential role? What kind of "church" would that be?

A church that could be envisioned on the basis of Jesus' parable of the Good Samaritan is not something given but something that happens. It happens when those women and men carrying heavy burdens are given rest (Matt. 11:28), when release is proclaimed to the captives, sight restored to the blind, freedom won for the oppressed (Luke 4:18-19). It happens when one of the least of brothers and sisters is given drink, food, clothing, or shelter in a dire situation and is visited in prison (Matt. 25:31-46). The church that comes into being in this way is a movement and not an institution, a community of persons and not a hierarchy of clergy, the bearer of the good news and not a structure erected on power and privilege.

In contrast, a religious establishment that does not come about in this way, even though adorned with pomp and glory, boasting of long and illustrious traditions, and celebrating religious festivals with meticulous observance of the church calendar, is not church. A religious community that does not perceive what God is doing in the Samaritan, in the persons of other cultures and religions, is not a part of the "church" that happens. A community that erects for itself an expensive and luxurious sanctuary for worship on Sunday, displaying piety decked with wealth, is anything but holy. In essence it is a place for religious gatherings, as "secular" as those structures constructed for business purposes. To be sure, even a religious community that "happens" as church has to become organized. But organization is a means to an end and not an end in itself. Since it is not an end in itself, there is nothing sacrosanct about its structure, its constitution, its laws and by-laws. Those organizational, structural, or constitutional matters can change and have to change, dictated by the church that happens.

That injured man on the road to Jericho and that good Samaritan, good not because he was a moral man in an immoral society, but because he was capable of being moved by compassion to help a stranger in need—it is they who define for Jesus what a community must be. That man injured on the road and that Samaritan who stopped to give him a helping hand "called into being" a community of men and women "called into being" to serve God by serving one another. This seems to be how Jesus gained his experience of what a religious community should be. This is also why he directed severe criticism at the religious community of his time. Would he not also have some very strong criticisms of most churches today?

What Is the Reign of God Like?
Jesus' Theology of God's Reign

What inspired Jesus to engage in his ministry with people is what he understood to be the reign of God.[2] How did he come to grasp its meaning? How did it become the heart of his life and work? What made him identify himself with it to the extent that he was to die for it? Questions can also be raised in a different way. Why did the religious leaders of Jesus' day find his message of God's reign objectionable? Why did they consider it a threat to their power and authority? What was so dangerous about the message that they went to the length of having Jesus convicted by the Roman colonizers?

There is no simple answer to questions such as these in a situation as politically and religiously complicated as that of Jesus' time. But one thing seems certain. This certainly is the way in which Jesus and the religious authorities of his day came to understand and believe what the reign of God should be. More specifically, it is possible to trace the theological process by which the two parties arrived at what they meant by the reign of God. Let us first consider "the theology of the kingdom of God" held by the religious authorities.

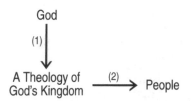

In this scheme it is clear that the phrase "the kingdom of God" is taken literally, that is, as the dominion that "belongs to God," the empire ruled "by God."

The kingdom of God is "God's." This is what the religious authorities taught and what people believed. Do not most Christians, including most theologians, also teach and believe this about "the kingdom of God"? This theology of God's kingdom has become the very core of the Christian worldview. First of all, the phrase *basileia tou theou* in Greek is taken to mean territory, domain, and par-

ticularly kingdom, terms strongly reminiscent of territorial conflict and political
power struggle between one princedom and another princedom, between one
nation and another nation. It is also militaristic, implying conquest and war.
Has this interpretation not led to a militant faith and theology on the part of
Christianity? Has not this, then, been translated into an aggressive theology of
mission practiced in Africa, Asia, the Pacific, and Latin America?

"Much of the 'divine right of kings' and the theory of 'holy war,'" it is noted,
"rested on the presupposition that Jesus Christ was king, and so did much of the
eventual rejection both of all war and the divine right of kings."[3] Such theology
contributed to, among other things, legitimation of papacy. "Christ was king,
the church was a monarchy, the pope was a monarch, and it was by his authority
that earthly monarchs exercised their authority."[4]

The territorial expansion of the church had its basis in a theology that emphasized God, and by inference, Christ, as king. Almost everything that has
been taught by the Christian church to condition the Christians' worldview, and
to shape their practice of faith, can be traced to the idea of God as a supreme
and powerful ruler. The image of God sitting on a high and mighty throne has
come to dominate the Christian experience of God. This God is remote from
ordinary people, inaccessible to women, men, and children outside the community of the chosen. Ordinary people have no part in the kingdom of this God,
the kingdom that, if it does not bedazzle them, intimidates them.

Over against this theology of God's kingdom, Jesus articulated his own experience of *basileia tou theou, basileia* not in terms of kingdom, but in terms of
"reign," that is, in terms of love, justice, and freedom among men, women, and
children. This is how Jesus did his theology of God's reign:

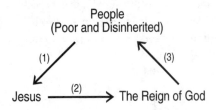

Jesus made people who are poor, hungry, oppressed, and persecuted (Luke 6:20,
21; Matt. 5:3, 10) the subject of the heart of his message about the reign of
God. Can we paraphrase what Jesus said about the sabbath and apply it? The
reign of God, Jesus could have said, is made for people, and not people for the
reign of God.

The reign of God consists, then, of human dramas. The reign of God happens in the life and history of people as individuals and as a community. It has a
strong moral overtone, and relates strongly to the ethical sensibility of a human
community. It is ethical first and then theological. In other words, the theological meaning of God's reign is predicated on its ethical demand. Is this not what

Jesus wanted to drive home to people when he told disciples the parable of the unmerciful servant (Matt. 18:23-35)?

What a human drama Jesus develops in this parable! "The kingdom of heaven," Jesus begins, "may be compared to a king who wished to settle accounts with his slaves." This is the prologue to the story. Contrary to the view commonly held, the focus in the prologue is not the king but the reign of God. This becomes evident as the story unfolds. Who then are the main actors? The king or the two servants? Again, unlike what has been assumed, the answer is not the king but the two servants, particularly the first servant. The first servant did not practice justice and mercy, thus failing to manifest the reign of God. By failing his fellow servant, he failed the reign of God.

One of the servants owed the king "ten thousand talents." This was an enormous sum, beyond redemption. Since "a talent was worth more than fifteen years' wages of a laborer,"[5] ten thousand talents were worth at least 150,000 years' wages in Jesus' day. The servant owed the king 150,000 years' wages! How many lifetimes would it take to repay the sum? It did not require much wit for the servant to realize that he was in serious trouble. His debt was a life-and-death matter. Jesus does not tell us how the servant incurred such an incredible debt. But did he have to elaborate? Did not the amount of the debt itself tell his audience what kind of a fellow the servant was—a ruthless fellow, using his position of power to presume upon the king's goodwill and to defraud him?

There was only one thing the servant could do. He fell on his knees at once and begged the king to spare him, his wife, and children, saying he would repay the debt. Of course he was not able to repay it; he was just trying to gain time. But the king was moved with pity and forgave him the debt. What is highlighted is that God's mercy is as enormous, infinitely more so, as the servant's debt.

Is this what Jesus wanted to say in the parable? Was he telling people how God forgave the servant unconditionally? Was he trying to draw a picture of the reign of God, with God playing the decisive role? This is not what I understand Jesus to say. If this is what Jesus meant by the reign of God, he could have ended the story at this point. But he did not. He continues, and tells us what happened after the servant, who was forgiven without condition, left the king. By continuing the story, Jesus brings it to a new height of suspense.

What follows is the heart of the drama that Jesus scripted for his audience. The forgiven servant, having left the king's presence, runs into a fellow servant who owed him "a hundred denarii," one denarius being "the usual day's wage for a laborer."[6] Thus he was owed one hundred days' wages while he himself had owed the king 150,000 years' wages. The contrast is absurdly colossal.

The contrast Jesus highlighted must have drawn a spontaneous response from his audience: Of course the servant will forgo the debt his fellow servant owes him. He must. He should let it go. He is obliged to forget it. Having been forgiven an incredible debt, there is every reason for him not to take account of a comparatively tiny debt. In contrast to his own debt, it is nothing. But since he does not forgive him, the first servant fails to make the reign of God happen. By taking his fellow servant to task for owing him a pittance, he becomes everything the reign of God is not—ungrateful, unscrupulous, unjust, and lacking compassion.

The reign of God is down-to-earth. It is not something in the sky. Nor is it to come only at the end of time, at a time no one knows. It is not a concept to be handled in abstraction.

If this is the way Jesus did his "theology" in relation to the central concern of his ministry, how are we to do our own theology? The answer is that it has to begin with human beings and not with God. Our theology must relate to earth and not to heaven. It is something that we act out in life and history, not predetermined and ready-made by God for members of the Christian church. If what Jesus has said and done is to guide us Christians, then faith must be our response to what we perceive to be God's will for the destiny of humanity and for the well-being of the world in which we live.

Remove This Cup from Me: Jesus' Theology of God's Will

Many Christians, particularly some evangelists and preachers, profess to know what God wills. They make no secret of the fact that they are in God's confidence. They can read God's will like they read the palm of their hands. They know what God has in store for those who do not confess Jesus as their Lord and Savior. Some are even bold enough to declare when God is going to end the world. And when the awful time of divine judgment comes and goes without incident, they are quick to assert that God has changed the plan just in time for the world to be spared the cosmic battle of Armageddon (Rev. 16:16). But this does not mean, they insist, that God's enemies will not someday be defeated decisively.

How do they know all this? This is not a facetious question. How can one be facetious about things of such importance? Nor am I making fun of the matter. How can one make fun of human destiny and the destiny of the universe? The question of how one knows the answers is not only directed to evangelists and preachers, but to some theologians. Theologians have provided the theoretical basis of what the church teaches and what Christians must believe, from what God is like to how the world came into being, from what one should do to gain eternal life to why the Christian church is the sole vehicle of God's salvation. Again one cannot help asking, and men and women outside Christianity in particular are increasingly asking, how theologians can be sure about their answers.

Evangelists and theologians may differ in the way they communicate what they presume to know. Evangelists tend to exploit emotion more than reason, while theologians seek the ground of their assertions more in reason than emotion. For both evangelists and theologians, however, the final court of appeal is the same: revelation, that is, God disclosing to them what God is like and what God plans and wills. That one has this knowledge is a big claim to make, but it has been assumed that faith is not faith and theology is not theology without such a claim.

This must be why Anselm, a theologian of the eleventh century, prefaces his theology with a prayer:

> Lord, I am not trying to
> make my way to your height,
> for my understanding is in no way equal to that,
> but I do desire to understand a little of your truth
> which my heart already believes and loves.

The sincerity of the heart in quest of God's truth in this prayer moves us. The humility of the spirit longing for God's mystery makes us humble. Then comes the famous dictum that has impressed many theologians:

> I do not seek to understand so that I may believe,
> but I believe so that I may understand;
> and what is more,
> I believe that unless I do believe I shall not understand.[7]

Theology must be faith seeking understanding, an exploration of the faith already given.

Our quest for God's truth cannot begin with nothing. It has to begin with something. This something is faith. Faith precedes theology. It is prior to all our reasoning about God and God's truth. But how does faith come about? Where does it come from? The answer is self-evident: faith comes from God. What takes place can be represented as follows:

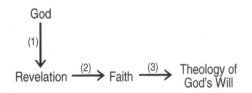

From God, through revelation, to faith in God, to a theology of God's will—this is how Christians are expected to understand their relationship with God. This is supposed to be how we come to know God's will.

From beginning to end it is God who plays the active role, even the sole role. There is only a passive role for human beings to play. The story of how God appeared to Samuel and spoke to him about the terrible fate of the house of Eli, Samuel's mentor (1 Sam 3:1-18), seems a good illustration. In response to God, who addressed him, Samuel replied: "Speak, for your servant is listening." This story seems to confirm that direct communication between God and certain people is not only possible but real, if we are attentive enough. This is what most evangelists and preachers tell us. This is also how many theologians develop their theological systems on "the word of God." Theology, in other words, begins with God and ends with God. In faith and theology God dominates.

But the story of Samuel does invite us to explore another dimension of faith and theology. When Samuel first heard his name called, he thought it was Eli his teacher who called him. He ran to Eli and said: "Here I am, for you called me." As it turned out, Eli had not called him, and Eli sent him away. Samuel was puzzled. This happened three times, and the third time Eli realized something unusual was happening. He then instructed Samuel: "Go, lie down; and if the Lord calls you, you shall say, 'Speak, Lord, for your servant is listening.'" Only then does the story tell us how God revealed to Samuel that Eli and his house were going to be punished for the sins and iniquities Eli's two sons had been committing. After he had to hear this from Samuel, Eli said: "It is the Lord; let the Lord do what seems good to the Lord."

The story seems to suggest that Samuel, "a boy" (1 Sam. 3:1), innocent and inexperienced, was merely a shadow of Eli. There is nothing new in what is "revealed" to Samuel. As a matter of fact, in the preceding chapter there was a vivid description of how Eli's sons had abused their power and taken advantage of people who had come to worship God and offer sacrifice at the temple of Shiloh. There is also an account of how "a man of God" warned Eli about his impending downfall. All this news must have been public knowledge. The entire story from the birth of Samuel to the prediction about Eli and his house, disclosed to Samuel in the first three chapters, is to pave the way for the transition of priesthood from Eli to Samuel. In other words the story is about the religious culture of ancient Israel.

This story is just one example from the Bible of how God communicated with men and women. But does not the story of Eli and Samuel caution us not to take these stories as they are, paying no attention to what these stories try to say about human conflicts and struggles in certain social-political and religious-cultural situations? Is it not too hasty and thus misleading to construct our theology of God's will without exploring these very human situations? Does not the history of religions, including Christianity, tell us believers are prone to make God responsible for their likes and dislikes, their successes and failures, their views and prejudices, and even their violence and acts of aggression?

We must also ask whether the God of our faith and theology is God in God's own self or whether that God of ours has anything to do with God in God's own self. This is not a hair-splitting question. On the contrary, it is a serious question. Is not the God we have come to know in the church an austere God, a revengeful God, a judging God, a God who most of the time seems to take the side of the religious authorities against "sinful" women and men in the pew? In the name of this God those who have sinned are forbidden to come to the Lord's Table, those who question the teaching authority of the church are excommunicated, and those who remain outside Christianity are destined to perish eternally. But perhaps this God of our faith and theology is not the God Jesus addressed as Abba, Father-Mother; and perhaps what is pronounced as God's will is not God's will as much as the will of ourselves and of the religious authorities.

If there are grounds for the questions just raised, much of Christian theology on God and God's will perhaps does not have God as its beginning and end. One may begin to wonder whether God in God's own self speaks through many Christian evangelists, preachers, and theologians. I emphasize the little word *perhaps,* for who besides these individuals can prove or disprove that God in God's own self speaks through them? Still, it is dangerous to be in the audience of those who speak in the name of God. God in God's own self may not be the one who controls and shapes such discourses on faith and theology. Who then is most likely to control and shape the way we Christians must believe in God and God's will? Let us look below:

Church

(1) ↓

God —(2)→ God's Will
for the World

If this is how God's will should be known, then a lot of what goes by the name of theology is not *theo*-logy after all. It is *ecclesio*-logy, discourse *of the church* on faith. Theology with its varied subjects is in fact a part of ecclesio-logy.

In his confrontation with the religious authorities of his time, Jesus came to realize that ecclesiology determined how they did their theology and exercised their power on behalf of God. When he took the authorities to task, he was taking their theology to task at the same time. When he questioned their theology, he was also questioning the God in whose name they exercised their power and authority. He was saying that theology should not be derived from ecclesiology. Theology, according to the original meaning of *theo*-logy, has to engage people in different situations. It is people in distress and suffering who tell us who God must be and what God wants to do. Jesus challenged the theology monopolized by the church and engaged suffering women, men, and children in new experiences of God. The diagram on the following page shows how Jesus did his theology:

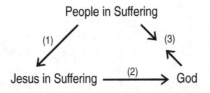

Docs this mean that in Jesus' theology people have replaced God? Absolutely not. For him, people in suffering are his own suffering. In the suffering that he and people share, they encounter not an almighty God in the Holy of Holies, but a suffering God in their midst—in the streets, in their homes, in the world of pain, despair, and death.

This is a crucial theological reorientation. Luke shows deep insight into this reorientation when he has Jesus read Isaiah 61:1-2 in the synagogue at Nazareth:

> The Spirit of the Lord is upon me,
> because he has anointed me
>   to bring good news to the poor.
> He has sent me to proclaim release to the captives
>   and recovery of sight to the blind,
>   to let the oppressed go free,
> to proclaim the year of the Lord's favor.
>   (Luke 4:18-19)

This statement was not just a manifesto of Jesus' ministry. It was at the same time a pronouncement of how he was going to engage people in redirecting their practice of faith and their reflection on it.

People referred to in the passage are specific kinds—*the poor, the captives, the blind, the oppressed.* The good news—the gospel—mentioned is also very specific: *good news* to the poor, *release* to the captives, *recovery of sight* to the blind, *freedom* of the oppressed. When any of these events happen, then that time is the year of the Lord's favor. The year of the Lord's favor takes place in human community. It is not a concept. Nor is it a doctrine.

Can one also say that God is a happening? God is an event when any of these events takes place. God is not an idea. Nor is God a dogma. God happens!

Jesus, in his life and ministry, had to strive for that God that "happens," and to wrestle with the will of that God almost until the last moments of his life in the Garden of Gethsemane, where he said to some of his disciples: "I am deeply grieved, even to death" (Mark 14:34; also Matt. 26:38). "Abba," he called to God from the depth of agony and turmoil, "for you all things are possible; remove this cup from me; yet, not what I want, but what you want" (Mark 14:36; also Matt. 26:39; Luke 22:42). God's will for him was not ready-made, something that came in the cool of the night or in a blissful state of mind. He had to wrestle with it in the midst of the forces, political and religious, working against him.

These incidents describe how Jesus engaged himself, his disciples, the crowds, and even the religious leaders and theologians of his day in practicing faith and doing theology. If Jesus were here today, this is the way he would engage us in doing Christian faith and theology. He would question the way Christians assume ourselves to be favored by God and regard others as outside the pale of God's saving grace. He would encourage us to develop different ways to relate to women, men, and children shaped by cultures, religions, and histories different from Christianity. He would urge us to test what we believe and do in the church, whether Sunday worship or the celebration of the Lord's Supper, against the life, faith, and history of people outside the church.

Would not this approach enable us to come to deeper insights into what God wills for us, Christian or non-Christian, in Asia, in the world, and for the well-being of the entire creation?

Chapter 3

Come and See

According to the author of the Fourth Gospel, it was John the Baptizer among Jesus' contemporaries who first discerned something unusual in Jesus from Nazareth. Was it the way Jesus carried himself? Was his mien so distinct that he could not fail to draw attention from a person such as John the Baptizer? Did his voice have a tone capable of rising above the din and noise around him? Or did an energy or power of spirit emanate from the depths of his person and touch the hearts of those spiritually awakened and alert? It might have been any of these reasons, or more likely, the combination of all of these reasons with others that prompted John the Baptizer to exclaim: "Here is the Lamb of God!" (John 1:36; also 1:29).

John's exclamation must have aroused curiosity in some of his disciples. To them, he was master and teacher. His was the voice crying in the wilderness of a religious tradition corrupted by power and greed, a religious institution compromised by political opportunism and that sought its own survival. His words were sharp and to the point, striking at the roots of social malaise and religious complacency. How could their master, then, fail to draw attention to a man he referred to as "the Lamb of God"? Skillfully, the author of the Fourth Gospel has shifted the focus of his story from John the Baptizer, a stern preacher of God's judgment, to Jesus as "the Lamb of God" who lays his life down for his friends (15:13).

What follows John the Baptizer's exclamation opens the first chapter in the life and ministry of Jesus—the initiation of the first two disciples into the rank and file of his followers. Was Jesus surprised when he realized that two of John the Baptizer's disciples were following him? Was he suspicious of why they were following him? Or did he feel awkward, because they had left the person who had baptized him and made him a part of the growing community disillusioned with the social and religious status quo? Such questions may intrigue some readers and tempt them to pry into the mind of Jesus to find answers. Less than a master storyteller may have allowed the focus of the story to divert to answering these questions.

Instead, the author of the Fourth Gospel, as a master storyteller as well as a theologian of deep insight, develops a question-and-answer exchange between

Jesus and the two disciples of John the Baptizer as cryptic and fascinating as Zen *mondo* (question-and-answer).

> Jesus: "What are you looking for?"
> Disciples: "Teacher, where are you staying?"
> Jesus: "Come and see." (1:38-39)

What is one to make of this exchange between Jesus and John the Baptizer's disciples? What can possibly be implied in this Zen-like question-and-answer session? And what does it say about doing Christian theology in a way that is different from what we are familiar with?

What *mondo* in Zen seeks to achieve between the master and disciples may shed light on these questions. Through *mondo*, Zen "aims at the opening of satori [enlightenment], and a new point of view as regards life and the universe."[1] Leaving the question of enlightenment aside, we are attracted to the idea of Zen aiming at "acquiring a new point of view as regards life and the universe." Is this not the heart of the matter in the *mondo* between Jesus and the two disciples of John the Baptizer?

"What are you looking for?" Jesus asked the two men following him. If Jesus had not known who they were, this would have been a simple question directed to strangers. Of course Jesus did not know them—their names, where they lived, their family background, even how they earned their living. But he must have known that they belonged to the circle of disciples formed around John the Baptizer; thus, his question would have had special meaning. In other words, he must have sensed that they were following him with something specific on their minds.

Their response to Jesus' question, however, strikes us as odd. "Teacher," they asked Jesus, "where are you staying?" Is this simply a question about his lodging? Did they just want to know where Jesus made his home? But the strange thing is that they did not answer Jesus' question. Judging from the circumstances that prompted them to seek out Jesus, their question must have indicated more than just curiosity about where Jesus was staying at present or where he was living permanently. The question seems to indicate that they are curious about Jesus himself, that they want to know something about him, that they cannot help being attracted to him. If this is the case, did Jesus suspect their interest? Did he perceive what was in their minds? Did he have an idea of what they wanted from him? From what Jesus said in reply to the disciples' question, one can be quite certain he did.

"Come and see," Jesus said to them. This is an invitation. But what did he invite them to come and see? Surely he did not invite them to come and see where he was staying. He had neither a permanent residence nor a permanent address. Is he not once reported to have said: "Foxes have holes, and birds of the air have nests; but the Son of Man has nowhere to lay his head" (Matt. 8:20; also Luke 9:58)? Jesus was inviting them to see *what* he was doing and *how* he was doing it. There is authority in the way he speaks and there is power in his voice—authority and power that render his invitation irresistible. Even at this initial stage of his career he seems to indicate that life is going to be different with him—different from the religious tradition the disciples have grown up with, even different from the way their master John the Baptizer carries out his religious tasks. But they have to come and see for themselves.[2]

Come and See in Five Stages

People did respond to Jesus' invitation to come and see, among them his immediate disciples. And the number who responded increased quickly. But did they understand what they saw? There are indications that they did not. Even the disciples who stayed with him, and who sat at his feet day and night for three years, did not seem to grasp most of the time who he was or his true mission. Did they see what Jesus wanted them to see? Again, they did not. They only saw what they wanted to see. That is why they had to wait until Easter morning to be told again how Jesus strove to bring about "God's will on earth as in heaven." What took place, then, between becoming his disciples and their experience of the risen Jesus?

The same question can be directed to Christians in each historical period. The distance between many of those who profess Christian faith and Jesus as he really was has grown with the passage of time. Since Christianity came to Asia and Africa, for instance, that distance has continued to grow. It is that distance, not Jesus himself or his message, that has alienated Christians and their churches from the world of cultures and religions in which they live. How to recover Jesus and his message, how to shorten the distance between Jesus and their experience of him, and how to give witness to his life and ministry—these become important questions for the Christian church today. To these questions we now turn. Let us "come and see" in five stages in an effort to engage our faith in Jesus more deeply and to explore theological implications of that faith for Christianity in Asia and elsewhere.

Stage One: God's Other Plans

Let us come and see what we have been told is God's plan for the Christian church. What we have been taught to see is a movement worked out in advance, a progression based on a deductive method. The movement follows a blueprint every step of the way. There have to be revisions from time to time, but they are insignificant. What is important is the main theme running from creation, to Israel, to Jesus, to the Christian church. The theme is beyond doubt and dispute. Is not the Bible itself structured in this way? Does not the story of God creating the heavens and the earth in the beginning (Gen. 1:1) develop into the story of God's promise to make Abraham "a great nation" (Gen. 12:2)?

Of course the story is by no means uneventful. The story of the "chosen" people of Israel is full of dramas, often traumatic, including the bitter experience of long enslavement in Egypt, a nation that worships gods and idols. But God does keep the promise made to Abraham. The Israelites eventually make their escape from the land of bondage, an "exodus" that is dramatic and full of excitement. The Exodus leads to the conquest of the land God promised to them and to the establishment of the kingdom of David. Just as God's promise to Israel is about to come true, the kingdom becomes divided, followed by the tragic end to the national sovereignty of Israel and Judah, thus beginning a long captivity in the lands of their conquerors. History repeats itself and reaches its rhetorical height in the vision of return from the exile to Jerusalem.

The New Testament picks up the pieces the debacle of Israel has left behind. Onto the stage of God's plan of salvation comes Jesus to replace Israel as the principal actor. The old hope has died and a new hope is born. But Jesus, the new hope, is to meet his death on the cross. This is another debacle, but is it as seemingly irreversible as the loss of Israel and Judah in ancient times? No. For his disciples and the community around them Jesus rises from the grave to become a new Moses, a new David, a new Messiah, to lead the new chosen people of God to victory, replacing the powers and principalities of this world with the kingdom of God in which Christ reigns and Christians reign with him.

This is to make a long story short, but with such faith and theology the Christian church has shaped and conditioned the way Christians deal with the people unrelated to their story and with the part of the world that is indifferent to it. Theirs is the story of God's saving purpose for humanity. It plays the central role in the divine scheme of salvation. According to this story, even Jews fare no better than other non-Christian peoples. By rejecting Jesus, Jews have disqualified themselves as the chosen people of God. The mantle of God's election now falls on the Christian church. Christians have emerged as the "new Israel" to carry out God's plan of salvation.

A neat and straightforward story, is it not? But is it not too neat to be true, too straightforward to be convincing? It gives rise to more questions than answers. Is the God that the story portrays still the God who created the heavens and the earth? Does a God who has invested such favor in a particular people and in a particular community of believers have time for other peoples and other communities of believers? How can we Christians be so sure that in our story alone, and nowhere else, God's plan for human destiny is made completely transparent? How then do we account for the life and history of the peoples and nations that remain outside God's saving activity? Are they of no significance? Do they exist solely as targets of God's displeasure and judgment?

This divine scheme of salvation, when tested in Asia or Africa, becomes questionable. It makes one wonder whether God has intended to deal with people outside the Christian church with displeasure. According to the scheme neatly developed by the Christian church, the great majority of people of the world have no place. They have no part in God's salvation reserved for Christians. But is this not precisely the urgency of the Christian mission? Do not Christians have to make all efforts to evangelize them? Is it not our responsibility to bring them the gospel of salvation? Is it not our task as Christians and churches to make the name of Jesus known to them? Is not our "great commission" to christianize the world? But as we know, Christianity has failed to christianize the world. There is no evidence that it can do so in the foreseeable future.

China is one example. Since its doors were forced open by the military, political, and economic forces of the West in the nineteenth century, China has never ceased to fascinate Western nations. Through their missionary enterprise the churches in the West have played an enormous role in keeping Western fascination with China alive. Of course that fascination has often turned into puzzlement, illusion, and then into despair. But no matter. How could a nation that prides itself as the "Middle Kingdom" cease to be a challenge for missionary enterprise as well as for political and economic exploits? This same history of Western fascination is being repeated today. After a self-imposed isolation finally ended in 1976 and China opened its doors, the world returned to China with a vengeance. China is destined again to play the role of the "Middle Kingdom" with undisguised pride, mingled with glee. It has brought world political leaders to its court. It has attracted entrepreneurs to share in its cities' frantic efforts toward modernization. China is setting out to be the center of the world in the twenty-first century.

The Christian churches in the West are not to be left behind in the competition of nations to outdo one another in this vast market. The churches' fascination with China has been rekindled as places of worship are reopened and are crowded with worshipers on Sunday. Testimony of Christianity's resurgence in China gives the impression that China is going to be "christianized" sooner than expected. This confidence translates into the liberal funds Western churches make available to the churches in China, and into missionary personnel posted as teachers and fraternal workers. These efforts come despite the Three-Self Movement of the National Christian Council of China, which stresses self-government, self-support, and self-propagation. The euphoria of Western churches is joined by many overseas Chinese Christians who, because of their faith and ethnic origin, claim their ancestral land for Christ and for themselves. Christian missionary enterprise is not solely a Western concern anymore. This makes mission to China somewhat different from what it was in previous days. But the faith and theology that undergirded the missionary movement of the past remain largely the same.

As it turns out, more sober and less euphoric stories have been told in recent years by some thinking Chinese Christians. Christianity in China, it is said, "is small and backward. Although the church has been growing rapidly in the last two decades, it still remains a tiny minority of less than one percent of the total population. Most of the increase of believers are in the rural areas and among the less educated and poor strata. A large number of them are attracted to Christianity hastily by preaching of 'cheap grace' and lack of proper Christian education and pastoral care."[3] Does this not sound familiar? Does it not remind one of "rice Christians," a derogatory term used to describe some Christians in the old China?

To make the matter worse, the old "orthodoxy" exported from the West continues to be alive and well. "The narrow exclusivist view of salvation," laments the paper just quoted, "rooted in fundamentalist orthodox theology to shut out all 'non-believers' from the gospel will eventually lead to [the] self-isolation and alienation of the Christian church from the broad masses of the people, to keep the church in a sort of cultural enclave."[4] Does this not sound familiar also? China has changed and is changing the world. But Christianity in China seems to remain the same yesterday, today, and forever—locked in the pseudo-orthodoxy developed during the heyday of Western colonial hegemony in the Third World. Would the Christian church again miss the boat were another revolution—this time, a democratic revolution—to overtake China?

Most Christians in China, and in Asia for that matter, who remain faithful to what I call "pseudo-orthodoxy," have not faced the fact that the "christianized" West has become irreversibly "secularized." That secularization includes the Christian churches, right, left, or center. To make things more complicated, more churches in Asia, as in the rest of the Third World—churches that are "fruits" of Western missionary endeavor—have themselves become "secularized." They allow themselves to be preoccupied with self-interests, power, and greed, thanks to what is known as the "economic miracle." Often they become countersigns and counterwitnesses to Jesus rather than signs and witnesses to Jesus in his ministry of God's reign. What we are seeing today is a moral crisis of the Christian churches in Asia, including churches in China. Here the logic of salvation the Christian church has used to deal with Israel applies: If God rejected Israel as the chosen instrument of God's purpose in the ancient world, are there reasons why God would not reject the Christian church as God's chosen instrument for the renewal of human spirits and the reconstruction of human community in the century to come?

Such a question is serious enough to make Christians think deeply. It implies that God may have other plans for the world, plans that embrace women and men not converted to Christianity. The question also suggests that the Christian church may have excluded the people God has included in God's saving activity in the human community. God's other plans? How could God have dealings with other people behind the back of the Christian church? The truth is that God does not have to work behind the backs of Christians. It is we Christians and the church that have tried to outsmart God, to make ourselves the center of God's relation with humanity, and to marginalize billions of people who, though unrelated to us, are related to God.

The Christian church has marginalized not only the great majority of Asians, for example, but also Jews, sisters and brothers whom we Christians owe beyond measure for our faith. We call Hebrew Scripture the *Old* Testament and our own Scripture the *New* Testament. The words *old* and *new,* in the way we use them, are loaded with value and judgment. What is old is not as valuable as what is new. The old is to be superseded by the new and replaced. Is this not how many of us Christians view "the Old Testament" in relation to the New Testament? Contained in "the Old Testament" is the old covenant, no longer valid and effective. God is no longer bound by it. In contrast, one finds in the New Testament the new covenant God has made with the Christian church. It replaces the old covenant as the sign of the salvation God has bestowed on the church and its members.

For the Jewish people, however, their Scripture is anything but old. Hebrew Scripture has been their scripture since the day their ancestors received the Torah from God through Moses on Mount Sinai. It will never grow old; it is going to be their scripture for generations to come. God's covenant with them, too, will remain valid and true forever. They may have committed sins against God and disobeyed God from time to time in the course of their history. They have been punished severely for it. But God has not abandoned them. God is still their God, and they are still the people of God. It is this tenacity of faith that enabled them to survive horrendous tragedies such as the Holocaust in which several million perished in Nazi Germany.

The Christian church carries its logic of the old and the new even further. What is given in "the Old Testament" is the promise of God. But that promise is fulfilled only in the New Testament. This theological scheme of promise and fulfillment has dominated Christian faith and theology throughout its history. Such a scheme deprives the ancient people of Israel of direct contact with God's salvation. In fact, most Christians think that God broke a direct relationship with Jews. That relationship is now ours. It is a Christian privilege and not a privilege of Jews. For Jews to regain that privilege, they must be converted to the Christian faith. Hence Christian mission to the Jews!

The Christian church applies essentially the same logic to other people outside the church. Most Christians in Asia today in their practice of faith and theology are still shaped and conditioned by that same old logic. God may have made covenant with all humanity through creation, but that covenant does not lead those outside the Christian church to salvation. They have some knowledge of God and God's salvation, but that knowledge is useless because it has nothing to do with Jesus. In making such an assertion, most of us do not stop to ask how Jesus would respond. We refuse even to consider the possibility that God also may be working outside the church. That God may have plans other than the plan we believe God has entrusted to the Christian church is an impious thought. Is it any wonder that we have nothing but disdain for the quest for truth undertaken by people of other faiths?

But it is not impious to surmise that God has always had other plans for different situations, both social-political and religious-cultural. It is a real possibility. Christians and theologians in Asia have to face the possibility and respond. That God has other plans is our theological agenda, although it may not be the theological agenda for our counterparts in the West. It must be our response to God's plans that shapes our practice of Christian faith and theology. Theology in Asia can no longer be a repetition of what we have inherited. To explore the ways of God that are not comprehended by traditional Christianity, we need to read the Bible with new eyes and fresh perspectives. We must equip ourselves to tell Asian stories as stories of God with Asians involved. We have to learn to see our history in Asia as Jesus would have us see. We have to assume theological responsibility for ourselves, believing that God has always had other plans for Asia and means to implement these plans that go beyond the experience and knowledge of Western Christians and churches.

Stage Two: Breaking a Theological Bottleneck

We have taken a bold step. We have addressed ourselves to the heart of our faith. We have raised a critical question about our theology of God's relation with the world. And we have wondered whether God has plans for the world other than the world with which we are familiar. The stage is now set for our exploration into the great mystery surrounding God and into what God has been doing in relation to Asia. But there is much in what we believe that holds us back from further exploration. One of these restraints relates to Apostles Peter and Paul, especially Paul. It is a long story—a story that began almost as soon as the life and ministry of Jesus on earth abruptly ended and that has continued ever since. But I have to make this long story short. I will only point out some events that contributed to what I consider to be one of the theological bottlenecks in Asia and in the rest of what is called the Third World.

The story begins, as mentioned, with the apostles, including Peter and Paul, but with Paul in particular. The experience of the risen Jesus was the watershed in the apostles' life and career. It roused them from their slumber of faith and dispelled their fear of the religious authorities. They came out from hiding to bear witness in public to Jesus crucified and risen. Peter, as the story goes in the Acts of the Apostles, was arrested by the religious authorities for healing a lame man in the name of Jesus. In a scene reminiscent of Jesus' trial before the Jewish council he found himself standing before the religious rulers and leaders that had condemned Jesus. This is what he testified: "Let it be known to all of you, and to all the people of Israel, that this man [the lame man who had been healed (Acts 3:1-10)] is standing before you in good health by the name of Jesus Christ of Nazareth, whom you crucified, whom God raised from the dead" (4:10). This was an open challenge to the religious authorities. This was, at the same time, an appeal to the Jewish public to acknowledge Jesus as the Messiah for whom they had been fervently waiting for centuries.

As for Paul, the encounter with the risen Jesus on the road to Damascus proved traumatic. It turned Saul the persecutor of the new faith in Jesus into Paul the pioneer missionary of that faith. It was this extraordinary experience that gave rise to his faith in Jesus as the Christ, the Messiah, the Savior. Later he wrote to the Christians at Corinth: "Last of all, as to one untimely born, he [Jesus] appeared also to me. For I am the least of the apostles, unfit to be called an apostle, because I persecuted the church of God" (1 Cor. 15:8-9). This is a revealing confession, particularly his mention of having persecuted the church. It seems evident that what he had done before his conversion continued to trouble his conscience. It must have affected him profoundly. It may be that he was not quite able to get over his deeds, even as he was doing his utmost to bear witness to Jesus. Could one suspect that his drive for the cause of Jesus came partly from the sense of guilt for what he had done to the church? It is not entirely groundless to believe that what Paul said about sin as disobedience to God—and he said a lot about it—had a great deal to do with his persecution of the church. Does this not mean that salvation for him was essentially forgiveness for what he had done to the church, and doing away with the associated guilt?

The same can also be said for Peter. He denied Jesus three times when Jesus was brought to the Jewish high court for trial. That all three authors of the Gospels told the story in some detail indicates that the incident must have weighed heavily not only on Peter's heart but on the heart of the community of Jesus' followers. After all, did not all of the disciples desert Jesus and flee (Mark 14:50; also Matt. 26:56)? As for Peter, he "remembered that Jesus had said to him, 'Before the cock crows twice, you will deny me three times.' And he broke down and wept" (Mark 14:72; also Matt. 26:75; Luke 22:61-62). Peter was conscience-stricken. One can be certain that his betrayal of Jesus never ceased to trouble his conscience. His message of repentance could have been deeply affected by it. When asked by his listeners what to do on the day of Pentecost, he said: "Repent, and be baptized every one of you in the name of Jesus Christ so that your sins may be forgiven" (Acts 2:38). Repentance and forgiveness of sins were the core of Peter's message, and have been the message of the Christian church ever since. For his listeners on Pentecost the sin to be forgiven was the sin of disobedience to God; for Peter it was the sin of having denied Jesus.

In the speech at Pentecost (Acts 2:14-36) and in his later defense before the Jewish council (4:8-12), Peter urged people to repent and accept Jesus as the Messiah their nation had long expected. There was no mention of the gospel, the good news of God's reign, for which Jesus toiled, labored, and died. Or at least Luke, the author of Acts, did not tell us what else Peter might have testified on other occasions.

Paul, however, did refer to the gospel many times in his letters—nearly eighty times! He considered himself "set apart for the gospel" (Rom. 1:1) and was "not ashamed of" it (Rom. 1:16). To the church in Corinth beset by division, he made it clear that "Christ did not send me to baptize," thus becoming a party to the divided church, "but to proclaim the gospel" (1 Cor. 1:17). He even went so far as to declare: "Woe to me if I do not proclaim the gospel!" (1 Cor. 9:16). He exhorted the Christians in Philippi to "live your life in a manner worthy of the gospel of Christ" (Phil. 1:27).

One is, however, prompted to ask: What did Paul mean by the gospel when he referred to it? Put another way: Is the gospel invoked frequently by Paul in his letters what Jesus meant by it? Of course it is the same gospel! one may answer with an exclamation mark. But is it? As we all know, Jesus identified the gospel with "the kingdom of God."[5] "The time is fulfilled," he said, "and the kingdom of God has come near; repent, and believe in the good news" (Mark 1:15). "The kingdom of God" is the heart of "the good news" (the gospel) to which Jesus dedicated his entire life. What is so good about the news that the kingdom of God has come? The gospel is good news because it belongs to the poor, because it means the hungry will be fed, because those who weep will laugh (see Luke 6:20-22; also Matt. 5:3-12).

Jesus did call upon people to repent. But he left no shadow of a doubt that it was the rich and the powerful that he was urging to repent. They must repent and turn from the ways in which they abuse their riches and power, exploit the poor and powerless, and make religion a matter of privilege that only they deserve. Repentance for disobedience to God was not his particular emphasis. But this is not how Peter and Paul used the words *sin* and *repentance*. For Jesus sin is sin because it is an act against one's fellow human beings; then, and only then, is it sin against God. This concept of sin is the reason he did not refrain from taking issue with the leaders of his own religion. It is this sin committed against dispossessed and marginalized women, men, and children for which they had to repent.

But Peter and Paul seem to have understood sin in a different sense. They reverted to the traditionally held notion that sin is what one has done to offend God. For the majority of believers in those days this meant an offense against the law. For Peter it also meant his denial of Jesus, and for Paul his persecution of the church.

Is it by accident, then, that Paul refers to "the kingdom of God," the heart of Jesus' message and ministry, only fourteen times in his letters? It does appear that "the kingdom of God" was not the heart of the gospel he mentioned much more often. In instances in which he referred to the kingdom of God, one has the impression that he was talking about something other than what Jesus meant. For him the kingdom of God "is not food and drink but righteousness and peace and joy in the Holy Spirit" (Rom. 14:17). At one point in his letter to the Corinthian Christians he stressed that sexual offenders would not inherit the kingdom of God (1 Cor. 6:10). In short, according to Paul, "flesh and blood cannot inherit the kingdom of God" (1 Cor. 15:50; cf. Gal. 5:21). What Paul

did was, on the one hand, to moralize the notion of God's kingdom and, on
the other hand, to make it the goal of conversion to Christ. Thus with Paul
began the tradition of identifying the kingdom of God with salvation for eternal life, which is prepared for those who believe in Jesus Christ as their Lord
and Savior.

Sin, repentance, salvation—Paul and the early Christian community seem to
have understood the gospel of Jesus in terms of these religious experiences. One
hears the strong echo of John the Baptizer, who preached the repentance of sin
in the wilderness of Jordan. The reign of God that occupied the central place
in Jesus' message and mission is, if not entirely absent, at least muted in the
message of the apostles and in the community they brought into existence. The
Jesus who insisted that the reign of God belonged to the poor, the oppressed,
and the marginalized was bypassed. Salvation replaced what Jesus had meant by
"the reign of God" as the principal concern of the early church.

It is this concern for salvation that the Christian church in the following
centuries assumed; the church developed it out of proportion to other concerns
of faith and life. The self-understanding of Christians as a new people of God
chosen for salvation has not only distorted our perception of Jews as people
of God, but has shaped negative attitudes toward people of other faiths and
religions. Being saved or not being saved has become the paramount theme of
Christian preaching and mission. As for the reign of God that preoccupied Jesus'
life and ministry, it is either spiritualized or made the prize of striving toward
salvation. It is not the reign of God as understood and lived by Jesus that defines
salvation, but salvation as a special privilege granted to Christians both on earth
and in heaven that defines their understanding of the kingdom of God. In this
way the Christian church has also bypassed Jesus.

We now know better, do we not? God is more than Christianity. Jesus is
more than the Christian church. This God invites us to come and see how God
engages human beings, Christian or not, in the colossal enterprise of renewing
God's creation. This Jesus also invites us to come and see how he is present in
the world of human suffering, and how he identifies himself with those women
and men, again whether Christian or not, who struggle to be free from demonic
forces, be they social, political, economic, or religious, that enslave their bodies and spirits. With this God and with this Jesus we must now move to the
third stage in our effort to redirect our theological orientation and to rechart our
theological course.

Stage Three: Not Christ-Centered but Jesus-Oriented

As pointed out above, salvation of Christian souls has become almost the sole
business of the church. It is also widely believed that the church holds the key to

that salvation. The power that the church thus has come to possess is enormous, but over time this power has become a problem. The history of Christianity provides ample testimony of how the church becomes corrupted when the power it holds gets out of hand. That it has often gotten out of hand is one of the costs of church-centered faith and theology. It is a heavy price to pay, because overstepping the bounds of power undermines the integrity of the church and the witness of Christians.

In spite of all these problems, is it not still a matter of course for Christians to hold the church at the center of what we believe and do? Should not what the church preaches and teaches guide us as we deal with people who do not share our faith? Are we not as Christians expected to be church-centered in our relationships with the community? Is not this the only way to show that we are different from others? Did not Paul in fact admonish us not to "be conformed to this world" (Rom. 12:2)? Did he not tell us that "God chose what is weak in the world to shame the strong" (1 Cor. 1:27)?

The Christian community in Paul's time was, indeed, a fledgling church, small, fragile, and weak. During the first three centuries it was harassed, persecuted, and driven underground. These words of Paul have to be read in light of the church's precarious existence in that period. But things changed after Christianity became the religion of the Roman Empire. The Christian community set out to become strong, and at times even led the world in knowledge, power, wealth, and privilege. It was no longer the church with which Paul had to deal—a church struggling to live in an inhospitable, even hostile, environment.

In more recent times, when the church was no longer in command, it entered into alliance with political powers intent on territorial expansion and acquisition of wealth in what is now called the Third World. In this dramatic history the church has often confused its own dubious ambition with the divine purpose of salvation. The church has often erred miserably. Reading the history of the Christian church, and, for that matter, the history of other religions, makes one appreciate the miracle that God has outdone human attempts to be more than God.

But it is not the flaws of the church that make me question whether Christian theology should be church-centered. The church as a human institution will always be flawed. The church as an earthen vessel cannot but succumb to wear and tear. What prompts me to question the central place the church has occupied in our faith and theology is, in fact, not the church, but Jesus, on account of whom the church has come into being. If Jesus is the heart of what we believe and testify, is it not right that our theology should be Christ-centered, and not focused on the church?

I have said that the church has erred and continues to err. There are many reasons for such errors, but the most fundamental reason is that the church has made itself the center of all things. It has replaced Jesus as the center. Church-centered faith and theology is wrong faith and bad theology. When the church makes itself the center, it preaches and teaches the church itself, its own survival and ambitions—not Jesus.

Having admitted the mistake of making the church the center of what we believe and do, we are therefore willing to replace church-centered faith and theology with Christ-centered faith and theology. Christ must be restored to his place of honor and must command our undivided attention. He must be allowed to tell us what we believe, what the church should be, and how the church should do theology. But these resolutions do not solve all problems related to church-centered faith and theology.

This sounds rather strange. Is not Christ already present in the worship of the church? Is not Christ constantly on the lips of Christians who profess themselves to be "spiritual"? In addition, does not what is known as Christology, study on who Christ is, take up much of the space in learned theological treatises?

But is this Christ in fact Jesus himself or the Jesus projected by the Christian churches of different confessions and denominations? Does this Christ reflect Jesus himself or the interests and needs of individual Christians? Is this Christ actually the Jesus who lived, toiled, suffered, and died on the cross, or the Christ of Jesus-cult, which sees Jesus as a cultic object or icon that inspires our piety but not our discipleship? Does the church worship the Jesus who walked the earth and endured all sorts of pain, even the pain of dying on the cross, or the Christ that is treated as an object of endless theological debates?

Christ-centered faith and theology often is church-centered faith and theology in disguise. Hence, instead of solving the problem generated by church-centered faith and theology, we come back to it. A Jesus disarmed by the church, stripped of his message by the Christian community, and repackaged by sectarian Christians does not help at all. That Jesus does more harm than good. This becomes most evident today when people from different cultural and religious traditions must learn to live in peaceful coexistence. But, sadly, ours remains a conflict-ridden world, and religions, Christianity included, continue to be one of the main causes of social and political tensions.

I can therefore understand those theologians who propose that being theocentric is more important than being christocentric, and who even go so far as to replace christocentrism with theocentrism. They correctly point out that Christ for many Christians divides instead of unites; that Christ excludes men and women of other faiths from God's salvation. That Christ does not do justice to God who is the Creator of heavens and the earth and all things in between. This partisan Christ does disservice to a human community badly in need of healing and wholeness. This Christ causes racial conflict. This Christ is the reason for discrimination against women. This Christ has no sympathy for people outside the Christian church.

The list of grievances against Christocentrism could continue. I agree with most of them. But the problem is that by getting rid of Christocentrism, one may at the same time be getting rid of Jesus. The simple fact for me as a Christian is that I do not know God apart from Jesus and Jesus apart from God. I cannot replace God with Jesus, nor can I replace Jesus with God. To be theocentric rather than christocentric is to me a false alternative. As a Christian I cannot set Jesus against God, nor can I set God against Jesus. What then is the heart of the problem? It seems to be that Jesus, for "christocentric" Christians and theologians, is "Jesus apart from God," while for "theocentric" theologians God can be apprehended as "God apart from Jesus." Theocentric theologians also committed an oversight in taking the Jesus of Christocentrism for Jesus of Nazareth—Jesus who lived, labored, and died for "the reign of God," the Jesus who, in the power of the Spirit, broke the barriers of race, gender, and class, and who expanded religious frontiers.[6]

Over against these two opposing views, it has to be said that Christian faith is faith in "Jesus-God" and in "God-Jesus." Note the hyphen in both expressions. The hyphen is not an equal sign. While the hyphen does not identify Jesus with God, it does not separate Jesus from God either. It neither equates God with Jesus nor alienates God from Jesus. It is in what Jesus said and did that a Christian comes to know God, leading to an important point: the God that comes to be known through Jesus is the God who is active not only inside the church but outside it, not only among Christians but among people not related to Christianity. If God cannot be confined to the Christian church and its members, how can Jesus, who shares an experience of this God, be restricted to the Christian community?

At this point the hyphen that related Jesus to God and God to Jesus develops into the preposition *in*. What we encounter, then, is "Jesus *in* God" and "God *in* Jesus." Jesus was able to say what he said and to do what he did because he was "in" God and God was "in" him. Perhaps it would be more accurate to say that Jesus was in God *through the power of the Spirit* and that God was in Jesus, also *through the power of the Spirit*. As we know, what makes the Spirit Spirit is freedom. The Spirit cannot be controlled, not even by Christians. The Spirit is not subjected to any other power, even the power of the Christian church. If our theology is oriented in this "Jesus in God" and in this "God in Jesus" in the power of the Spirit, we no longer have to choose between being christocentric and theocentric. As a matter of fact, the Jesus advocated by christocentric Christians and rejected by theocentric theologians is the Jesus *of the Christian church*, with an exclusive claim to God's salvation. The Jesus who gives witness to God outside and inside the church has eluded both theocentric and christocentric theologians.

If our faith and theology cannot be centered in the church without doing injustice to who Jesus really was and what he did, neither will faith and theology centered in Christ help the church. My proposal is, then, that our faith and theology must be *Jesus-oriented*. Is there any difference, one may ask, between being "Christ-centered" and "Jesus-oriented"? A world of difference. First of all,

Jesus, who lived, engaged in the ministry of God's reign, and who was executed on account of it, may not be the same as the Christ that Christians from early times to the present have come to know and worship. Even though there is one Jesus of Nazareth, are there not many "Christs" in the history of Christianity?[7] Should not Jesus of Nazareth be the focus of our theological attention and not a variety of Christs that have come and gone?

Saying that our theological effort is going to be Jesus-oriented, and not Jesus-centered, is not merely a play on words. The problem has to do with the word *center,* from which the adjective *centered* is derived. *Center* is "the point around which anything revolves," or "a place from which ideas, influences, etc., emanate."[8] In Christian usage the word *center,* be it Christ or Jesus, excludes other centers. It does not tolerate them. The Christian center claims to be the sole center, around which everything revolves and from which everything emanates. The word develops into *centrism,* a worldview that takes itself to include all truth. That is why "Christocentrism" has given Christians a sense of superiority to women and men of other religions, and endowed them with militant urgency in mission.

The word *oriented* implies different meanings. *Orientation,* the noun form of *oriented,* refers to a "position with relation to the other points."[9] The key idea in this definition is relation. Orientation is shaped by relations. Each component in the relation is related to other components, and its importance does not negate the importance of the others. Rather each component enhances the importance of the others, and is enhanced in return. Orientation is not restrictive. An entity interested in orientation is not bent on consolidating itself at the expense of others. Rather it establishes relations with others and, together with them, develops and expands the sphere of activity and the sphere of meanings. In this way *orientation* refers to actions that are reciprocal rather than single-minded, expansive instead of constrictive, open instead of closed. The term relates to concepts and realities that are imaginative rather than stereotyped, creative rather than static.

Faith and theology oriented in Jesus do not have to be replaced by theocentric faith and theology. Jesus was and is the living presence that embraces other presences. He did and does break out of social and religious restrictions and creates new space in the human community and in the human heart. He ventured, and still does, into the unfamiliar world to explore what it means to live and believe outside the well-defined social and religious conventions. In so doing, he discovers the world of stories—the world he shares and to which he also belongs. That world of stories expands and stretches. It also deepens and enriches. It is the world of human beings, and not of religious precepts. The world of stories is a community of women and men who struggle to live with human dignity. It is a realm of human spirits seeking the meaning of life in God and in one another. And it is a communion of hearts and minds reaching out to the world beyond the present world. It is this Jesus who leads us to the next stage, in which we leave the realm of concepts and enter the world of stories—stories of women, men, and children, stories of Jesus and stories of God.

Stage Four: Into the World of Stories

In the beginning, to paraphrase the prologue of John's Gospel, were stories. Did not that "Word" that was with God, that "Word" that was God (John 1:1), unfold itself in the story of creation in Hebrew Scripture (Gen. 1:1—2:4a)? And did not this story of God come to be told in the stories of "the heavens and the earth ... and all their multitude" (Gen. 2:1)?

God, according to this creation story, called the light Day, the darkness Night, the dome above Sky, the dry land below Earth, and the waters gathered together Seas. This God also made the sun, moon, and stars in the sky. If this is God's story, is it not also the story of human beings from the beginning to the end of time? Do not our stories concern the sun, the moon, and the stars, the day and night come and gone, the cycles of seasons? Do we not, in this way, live the creation story of God and experience it as individuals and as community? Is not, then, the story of creation the story of how we human beings live both in time and in eternity?

God's work of creation continues, so the story tells us. The story has become the story of the earth putting forth vegetation and the waters and dry land bringing forth swarms of living creatures, including birds flying over the land. All this is God's story. But is it not our story as well? Is not the story of creation told about human beings, who live in total dependence upon the earth, the sky, and the seas?

It has been a colossal enterprise—God engaged in bringing "the multitude" into existence. The job is not yet finished, and it never will be finished. As if to make a special point, the story of creation goes on to say how God created human beings to take care of what God had already made.

> So God created humankind in God's image,
> in the image of God God created them;
> male and female God created them. (Gen. 1:27)

What does being created in God's image mean? It does not, and should not, mean that we human beings are superior to the sun, moon, and stars, that we are to subject the earth and all things to our whims and desires.

Far from it! "In God's image" means that God has endowed human beings with the imagination of the soul and the facility of words to tell over and over God's story of creation as part of our stories and to integrate our stories into God's story. God's image in human beings is thus the power to tell stories—the power of imagination and the power of words. To be human is to be aware of this power. It is the power of our body, mind, and spirit to resonate with the sun, the moon, the stars, mountains, rivers, and trees in response to God's work of creation. It is the power of speech to tell our stories in the service of God's story.

In the world of stories we are born. Into the world of stories we enter. Is this not what John means when he tells us, "The Word became flesh and lived among us" (John 1:14)? This is difficult language and an abstruse thought. To understand it, we have to translate it into our language and express it in our own words. We render it as follows: the story of God became the story of Jesus that lives in our stories. Is this not the miracle of miracles, the miracle of God's story unfolding in human stories by means of the greatest story ever told, the story called Jesus? Does this statement not represent the possibility in human beings doing *theo*-logy, that is, the possibility of encountering God in our human stories in light of that story called Jesus?

This is the excitement of doing theology in the world of stories. Because of this world of stories in which the story of God unfolds for Christians in and through Jesus' stories, there is nothing in us and around us that does not become relevant to the theological venture. Into the world of stories, then, we must go. After all, the Bible itself—the greater portion of it—is made up of stories. It is a book of stories big and small, sacred and profane, uplifting and distressing, stories of hope and despair, life and death, egotism and self-sacrifice, stories of human beings at their noblest and most ignominious. The Bible is a world of stories in the world of stories, the world in which God is involved from beginning to end. Is it not a matter of course, then, that the world of stories at large and the world of stories in the Christian Bible should illumine one another to deepen our experience of God and how God deals with us?

In the world of stories the room of our faith is enlarged and our theological space expanded. To read stories of people—their myths, legends, folktales, and real-life stories—is a liberating experience. We have read Christian stories—stories of the development of the Christian church, stories of evangelical outreach and endeavor, stories of heroes of Christian faith, stories of missionaries and Christians. But these stories confine us to the world constructed by the Christian church. It is a "Christian" world that we encounter in those stories, the only world that, according to most of us Christians, is important to God, the world of the people saved from their sins and granted God's favor. The question is whether this is the only world in which God is active. Of course not. Our faith and theology have prepared us for the world the Christian church has constructed, but not for the world God has created.

There are stories outside the Christian church as well as inside it—stories of people around us, stories of the human community to which the Christian community is closely related, and stories of Asia, for example, to which Christians in Asia also belong. The world these stories represent is infinitely larger than the "Christian world." What a variety of stories this wide world of Asia contains!

There is the world of myths of creation and destruction, myths of how human beings and other living beings came to be. There is the world of legends about the birth of the nations in Asia and legends of gods and heroes who come and go. Besides the world of myths and legends, there is the world of stories that tell how fierce struggle for power brought about "homes in ruins and innocent people dead or scattered," to use a Chinese expression quoted earlier. There is of course the world of stories of faiths and religions, stories that testify how human beings can rise to the summit of their search for God and sink to the nadir of hell they create for themselves in the name of God and gods. Above all, there is the world of stories of how women, men, and children in various Asian countries and at various times in the history of their nations struggle against evil powers, how they suffer and die, and how they persist in their hope for a better world in which they may find the meaning to live.

The space these stories open up for us is immense, as immense as Asia. The stories Asia contains number as many as the inhabitants, who account for more than half of humanity. Can this reservoir of stories contain anything but a world full of surprises for us Christians? It is a world that arouses interest and curiosity, evokes empathy, and summons the spirit of adventure out of hiding in our Christian sanctuary. To go out of the space defined by the Christian church and to venture into the vast space of Asia is a great challenge. That vast space must be our theological space—the space inhabited by more than three billion people and home of many religions and cultures. This world of stories is the world of real people of flesh and blood, not the world of theological ideas and concepts. It is the world of tears and laughter, not the world developed by Christian minds and missionary enthusiasm. It is also the world in which men, women, and children commit sins and crimes against one another and in which they strive often in vain, but sometimes successfully, to reveal the divine light shining in the darkness of their hearts and in the depths of their community.

When we encounter stories in Asia in this way, stories to which we are not outsiders but insiders, not strangers but participants, stories that tell as much about ourselves as Christians as about our fellow Asians, we begin to realize how much the story of Jesus, that is, the story of his reign of God, is reflected in them, and how much they reflect the story of Jesus. We do not need to construct a theological framework to fit these two sets of stories together. We do not have to work out in advance theological norms and categories that legitimize whatever relationships may exist between them. Nor do we need to set up criteria that permit us to make a "correct" selection from both sets of stories in order to theologize about them.

What we need most is a theological mind not prejudiced toward stories indigenous to Asia and alien to the Christian church. We have to cultivate the theological imagination that can help us image God and perceive God's activity in the stories. We have to apply the same theological imagination to the stories in the Christian Bible, especially stories of the reign of God that Jesus told, not only in words and parables, but in the life he lived with the poor and oppressed of his time. Does not Jesus' life of suffering and death relate to the lives of millions in Asia—and for that matter, to those in the rest of the world—in the past, present, and future?

Such a theological enterprise is not what most Christians and theologians have been groomed for. It may be novel to us, but it was not novel to Jesus. Jesus in fact would be at home with this task, especially if we recall the reconstruction in the second chapter of how Jesus engaged in faith and theology. We can now present our task, which until now has been described in words, in visual form:

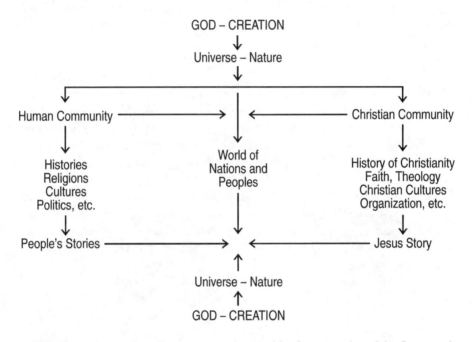

What we see in this illustration is the world of stories shared by Jesus and people. It is also the world in which the story of Jesus and the stories of people take place. Should it not, then, be the world in which we practice our faith and do our theology, the world in which the four arrows converge, the world of stories created by God, Jesus as humanity through the Spirit.

What takes place in the theological process described is a conversation between the story of Jesus and the stories of people expanding to God's creation. It is not a leisurely conversation over a cup of tea. It is not a theological debate over imaginary theological issues. And it is not an exercise to prove who is right. Yes, it is a *theological* conversation, but the conversation is theological because it relates to God as well as humanity, because God is called upon to bear witness to what has been going on in the universe and in our world—the world in which human beings struggle for hope in the face of hopelessness and for the meaning of life, always overshadowed by death.

The word *conversation* is in fact no longer adequate for such a theological exercise. The conversation can be so intense that the conversation partners find themselves running into one another. They interact in the stories, enter into one another's lives, worlds, and histories as they tell their stories—I find myself in your story and you find yourself in my story. My story becomes your story and your story becomes my story. I now believe that this would be the way Jesus would listen to stories told by the people of Asia, for instance. Is this not the way he listened to the stories of the poor and the disinherited of his day? Is it not also the way he identified himself with women and men weary in body and in spirit? An invisible bond thus formed between him and the people. Even if many of these people, including his own disciples, were to betray him, to denounce him before the authorities, and to desert him, they were soon to regain that spiritual bond. The content of their conversation with Jesus changed and the level of their engagement with him deepened when they realized they were in the presence of the risen Jesus.

It is the same bond that I am sure would be forged between Jesus and the people today, including Christians, in an interchange of stories. As the story of Jesus and stories from Asia interpenetrate, a theological space also opens for the stories in Hebrew Scripture. Stories from other parts of the world will come into play as well. What takes place, then, is a theological feast of stories—the story of Jesus, stories from Asia, stories in Hebrew Scripture, stories from the Christian community, and stories from the rest of the world, told as stories of God's dealing with humanity. What we encounter is a theological world of stories, or better, the divine-human world of stories. If our theology is to be *theo*-logy, do we not have to go about it in this *divine*-human world of stories? And if our Christology is to be *Christo*-logy, that is, an experience of encountering Jesus of Nazareth, the human being in whom "the Word of God became flesh," is there any other world in which to engage ourselves in Christology than in this divine-*human* world of stories?

To come to Jesus, to listen to what he said and to see what he did, to experience his suffering, to fathom the meaning of his death, and to be part of the glory of his resurrection, we as Christians must come and listen to those stories lived and told by women, men, and children in the world. We do not just listen to them. We must hear in them how God is speaking to us Christians. We must perceive in them the footsteps of Jesus. We must see in them what the reign of God meant to Jesus. This come-and-see process also has to be reversed. To see in these stories from different parts of the world the stories of God, we have to come and listen to the story of Jesus with much more intensity and sensibility than we have before. This is a dynamic process—not an either-or option of listening either to our stories or to the stories of Jesus, but a "both-and" process. It is this dynamic process that enables our faith to be rooted in the soil on which each of us lives and our theological efforts to become indigenous to the cultures into which we were born.

Stage Five: A Story from Taiwan— A Theological Exploration

We have reached the fifth stage of our theological exercise. After what we have done in the previous stages, we should be ready now to explore how stories may enable us to come to grips with *theological* meanings of suffering and hope in people's daily lives. Let us, then, come and listen to a story and, together with Jesus, engage with it theologically. It is a real story told by a young man from the Ami tribe in Taiwan,[10] a story of his aboriginal family having its innocent hope betrayed by the treachery and ruthlessness of the business world. The story is called "The Name of My Mother Is Distress."

The young man came from a large family of seven children, with two older brothers, two older sisters, and two younger sisters. The village in which the family lived was poor. The villagers, his parents included, worked hard and hired themselves out for hard labor. Still they could hardly make ends meet. The pressures of life, however, did not diminish their spirit of joviality. After dark the villagers would gather together to sip drinks, to chat, and to sing tribal songs. Their voices mingled with the sound of mountain streams and the singing of birds returning to their nests.

But happy days did not last long. Without warning the construction work was started in this quiet village. They were told that the village had been made a model village and model houses were being built for sale in them. Mortgage plans would be available. Everybody was excited. The old thatched huts would be replaced by new brick houses.

I was twelve years old when our dilapidated hut was torn down. It took half a year for the new house to be built. We were all happy. It was not a large house; still it had a living room, a kitchen, a dining room, four bedrooms, complete with a bathroom. The down payment was four hundred thousand yen, with an additional three hundred thousand yen[11] to be paid in seven installments within seven years. This was a huge sum.

Hardly had we enjoyed our new house for two months than Father woke me up in great haste one morning and told me that I had to leave home and go to work in a distant place. I was not happy. Father randomly took some of my clothes, put them in a small bag, and gave it to me. Presently I found myself among strangers. I sensed something wrong. All I could do was to scream and cry, but to no avail. I had no time to say good-bye to my schoolmates, to my mother, to my younger sisters. Tears flowing down my cheeks, I left home and set out on a journey on a bus, not knowing where I was going.

We stopped at every village on the way to pick up more people. The thought did not occur to me to escape. Before long we arrived at a harbor, led into a building filled with fishing nets and equipment. We were like caged birds unable to fly away. The old man from the city in charge of us told us, "I have purchased you at a price." I did not understand what he meant. During the two weeks we were trained to do our job, I at last realized we were sold to work on fishing boats.

For the next two and a half years we were on the sea working like slaves with little time for rest. From some of the friends I made on the fishing boat I came to know why my brothers had disappeared ten years ago. Like myself they were taken away from home to work on fishing boats. My sisters were sold to be prostitutes in the cities. My parents did not know all this. All they knew was what the business people from the cities told them: their children are going to make a lot of money to pay for their debts and mortgages for their new house.

My life on the sea continues. On occasion I am allowed to return home for a short while. My mother looks older and more haggard each time I come home, holding deep pain and distress in her heart and on her face. During my long absence she is entirely alone. My father, disappointed and at a loss, left her and returned to the village he had come from. My brothers had died on the sea and my mother does not know the whereabouts of my sisters. How I wish I could stay home and be with her! But thinking of so much debt still to be paid, I have to tear myself away to face the unknown fate on the sea.

What keeps my mother's company now are distress and this house—a model house in a model village, a modern two-story brick house.[12]

Each time the haggard mother and the only surviving son part may be the last time. And all this pain and distress comes from the brick house that once promised them joy and happiness.

This is a story familiar to countless families in the countries of Asia that have achieved the so-called economic miracle. Much inhumanity has been committed against helpless women, men, and children in the mindless pursuit of economic prosperity that shapes the policy and conduct of politics in this post–Cold War world. The irony is that the West, which has been shaped by Christianity and which for centuries has taught the world the Christian virtues of love and justice, is deeply involved in the network of power and money that creates, in countries far from its shores, story after story of a separated mother and son.

The story told by the young man from the Ami tribe in Taiwan is not a success story. It is a story of betrayal. The mother and the son who survived to tell the story are not vindicated. Their story and the stories of many others are stories of failure, stories of simple and innocent hope betrayed, stories of having become prey to the fast world of power and money. This particular story ends with the mother left alone at home with her pain and distress, while the young son, the storyteller, tears himself away to set out again for the fishing boat, to redeem the debt that dims their hope and overshadows their future. How would Jesus respond to such a story?

This story of betrayal recalls another story of betrayal in Hebrew Scripture. It is the story of Joseph sold into slavery by his brothers (see Genesis 37ff.). The story is not as simple as it appears. It is not just a story of how Joseph, innocent and unsuspecting, is betrayed by his own brothers and winds up in the country of Pharaoh as its ruler. It is a complex story that has far-reaching implications for the hagiography (sacred history) of Israel. This complex story of God's promise, which began with the emigration of Abraham from Mesopotamia to "the promised land," is interrupted by the long and tortuous sojourn of his descendants in Egypt, and at last reaches its zenith in the establishment of the Davidic kingdom in the promised land. The key to the story is the words the storyteller puts on the lips of Joseph in his emotional reunion with his brothers: "God sent me before you to preserve for you a remnant on earth, and to keep alive for you many survivors. *So it was not you who sent me here, but God*" (Gen. 45:7-8a; emphasis added).

What appears to be a story of betrayal and failure becomes a success story. It is not only the success story of Joseph, who becomes the second-most powerful man in Egypt, nor the success story of Israel in gaining the promised land, but *the success story of God* with Israel and, through Israel, with the nations. Success does not come cheaply, but with sweat and tears. In each case it is filled with trauma. There is no shortage of tragedy, as well as victory. But it is *success,* nonetheless. God's promise, as in the case of Joseph, is to prevail in the end—if not now or in the near future, then at the end of time. In the final analysis, the history of "the people of God" must be a success story. Did Jesus, a Jew, also take the history of his own nation in this way?

The history of Christianity is written as a success story, too. The Christian church picks up the thread left by Israel, repairs the story, and reconstructs it. Israel failed God, but the Christian church succeeded with God. Has not Christianity successfully transformed the West and its culture? Has not the missionary expansion of the churches in the non-Western world been one success story after another? This success of the Christian church with God and with the world translates into the success of Christians. Christians are those who have been assured of God's salvation. Their success in the world is the demonstration of how they have succeeded with God. How would Jesus react to this "success" story of the Christian church and Christians?

In contrast to the success story of Christianity and its adherents, the story of the tribal family in Taiwan is one of failure, lacking the happy ending of Joseph's story. The Taiwanese story ends with the mother and the son imprisoned in the house of debts and distressed by their bleak future. For them, and for many a woman and man in Asia, and, for that matter, in the rest of the world, there is no "exodus" from their "Egypt," not to mention the victory of entering the promised land. The stories of their lives as individuals and as a community lack the plot that runs through Christian stories, the plot that begins with God's promise and ends with its fulfillment, if not in this world then in the world to come.

The Christian plot is not entirely new. It is inspired by the way the people of ancient Israel interpreted their historical experiences. The Christian church has christianized the plot and then spiritualized it. God's call for Abraham to leave his home for the promised land is now the call to women and men to leave their "pagan" ways and to become members of the Christian church. The Exodus of the Hebrews from Egypt, the house of bondage, becomes the exodus from the religions and cultures unrelated to Christianity. As for salvation, it is granted only to those who repent of the sin of worshiping gods and idols.

What we have are two stories, a biblical story of Joseph and a story of a tribal family. These two stories are told in different contexts—the story of Joseph shaped by the faith that God would bring about the promise made to the nation of Israel, and the story of a tribal family, not framed by a faith in the divine purpose, but developed out of a tragic situation. The two stories also have entirely different views of what the world is like and of what life must be. The story of Joseph presupposes a God who elected a people to be special among the nations, but the story of the aboriginal family is not part of such lofty theology. This family struggles to survive in the harsh world of money and greed.

We are dealing with two theological worlds—the theological world, as represented in Joseph's story, and the "theological" world of the tribal family. They are very different worlds. One cannot understand the story of the tribal family in terms of Joseph's story and the theological framework it represents. Those notions of election, promise, exodus, salvation, and fulfillment—the notions central to Christian faith and theology—simply do not apply to stories like those of the tribal family. To explore the theological meaning of such a story we need a different theological framework. What would this framework be? Where do we find it? Having found it, how would we use it to explore theological meanings of the story of the tribal family on the one hand and, on the other hand, to reconstruct what biblical stories such as the story of Joseph really meant for the people of ancient Israel, and what they could mean for Christians today as part of a world of diverse religions and cultures?

These are not irrelevant questions. They are at the heart of what we believe as Christians and of what we do in our theological reflections in the part of the world not dominated by Christianity. The questions appear complicated and difficult, more so today because most of the "Christian" answers tend, on the whole, to be either indifferent or negative. Most Christian theologians and preachers may listen to the story of that tribal family with sympathy, but they may not *hear* what the story is telling us theologically. They are not able to tell us how to locate the events in their scheme of call and promise, exodus, fulfillment, and salvation. The simple fact is that the Taiwanese story cannot be placed in the traditional theological scheme of their faith and theology.

To listen to the story of that tribal family and to *hear* what it is telling us theologically, we must come and see how Jesus would listen to it, and how he would *hear* in it not only human pain and distress but God's pain and distress. This is the way he listened to the women, men, and children around him and *heard* their inner voices—voices of despair and longing, voices of pain and heartache. It is as simple as that. But to practice that kind of *theo-logical* listening and hearing is far from simple. As long as we are bound by the rules of the game called theology that we have inherited, it is almost an impossible thing to do.

But Jesus was able to do it. How? He was able to listen in this manner not because he had worked out a new theological methodology, a clever way to deal with stories, but because he was full of God's grace and truth (John 1:14) and "had *compassion* for [the great crowd], because they were like sheep without a shepherd" (Mark 6:34; also Matt. 9:36; emphasis added). That grace and truth of God enabled Jesus to hear God's story in stories of people's distress and suffering—stories that had no place in the official religion. The compassion he had for women, men, and children made him hear his own story in their stories of pain and agony—stories liable to be dismissed as not important enough for the theological traditions. That grace and truth of God made self-centered faith impossible. The compassion of God made the theological scheme of election and salvation irrelevant.

It is from Jesus that we must learn to listen to such stories as the story of the tribal family. It is not a ready-made faith that we learn from Jesus; he did not have such faith. Do we not see him strive to do God's will throughout his life? Do we not perceive him struggling to discern God's will in Gethsemane, until the last moment? Faith for Jesus is anything but ready-made. Nor do we come to him for a theological system that explains how God works in human community. Unlike most of us Christians, theologians, and preachers, Jesus did not have such a system. Otherwise how could he have said, for example, to a woman brought to be stoned for adultery, "Neither do I condemn you. Go your way, and from now on do not sin again" (John 8:11)?

We come to Jesus to learn more fundamental things—things without which theology is either empty discourse or heartless talk. We must learn from Jesus how to read the stories in the Bible and the stories in the world outside the Bible with compassion. We come to sit at his feet to *experience* how he touches, with God's grace and truth, the hearts and souls of men, women, and children who tell him their stories, and to learn to do the same with the stories we hear in the Bible and in our world. With theological erudition and sophistication at our command, we do not lack theological methods and systems. What we lack is God's grace and truth through which we can look at things and *see* them. We also lack that compassion without which we do not *hear* others' stories, even though we listen to them.

God's grace and truth and human compassion—these have to be the heart of our faith and the center of our theology. Jesus had them in plenty. That is why he was different from other religious teachers of his time. That is why he had to take issue with the religious authorities of his day. And that is why he was able to read God's story in the stories of people and to identify the reign of God in those stories. As we move into the world of stories to explore the meaning of what it means for people to live, to believe, to hope, and to love in the world of pain and suffering, we must try to listen with Jesus and to *hear* with him, to look with him and to *see* with him. In the company of Jesus we hope we will encounter *the story* behind stories and *the story* in stories—the story of God and human beings engaged in the search for life, faith, hope, and love.

Part Two

LIFE

*And can any of you by worrying add a single
hour to your span of life?*

—Matt. 6:27

A Legend

In about the year 563 B.C.E.[1] Gautama Siddhartha, later to be called Gautama
the Buddha (Gautama the Enlightened One), was born as the eldest son to "a
king of the Shakyas, a scion of the solar race," near the town of Kapilavastu in
what is now Nepal. Carefully protected from the world outside the palace, his
life had been filled with the luxury, pleasure, and enjoyment worthy of his royal
dignity until one day he, according to the legend,

> mounted a golden chariot, to which were harnessed four well-trained
> steeds with golden trappings, driven by a manly, honest, and skillful
> charioteer....
>
> The prince saw a man overcome with old age, different in form from
> other people, and his curiosity was aroused. With his eyes fixed on the
> man, he asked the charioteer.
>
> "Oh, charioteer! Who is this man with gray hair, supported by a staff
> in his hand, his eyes sunken under his eyebrows, his limbs feeble and bent?
> Is this transformation a natural state or an accident?"
>
> The charioteer, when he was thus asked, his intelligence being con-
> fused by the gods, saw no harm in telling the prince its significance, which
> should have been discreetly withheld from him: "Old age, it is called, the
> destroyer of beauty and vigor, the source of sorrow, the depriver of plea-
> sures, the slayer of memories, the enemy of sense organs. That man has
> been ruined by old age...."
>
> The prince, moved, asked the charioteer: "Will this evil come upon me
> also?" The charioteer then replied: "Advanced age will certainly come upon
> you through the inescapable force of time, no matter how long you may

live. People in the world are aware of old age, the destroyer of beauty; yet they seek [pleasure]."

[During his second excursion from the palace, the prince saw] a man whose body was afflicted by disease. He fixed his eyes on the man and asked the charioteer: "Who is this man whose abdomen is swollen and whose body quivers as he breathes? His shoulders and arms are limp, his legs are pale and emaciated. Leaning on another for support, he is crying out, 'Mother!'"

To this the charioteer answered: "Lord, this is the great misfortune called disease, developed from disorder of elements, by which this man, though he had been strong, had become disabled." Eyeing him again compassionately, the prince said: "Is this evil peculiar to him or is this [danger of] disease common to all people?" The charioteer replied: "Prince, this evil is common to all; yet the world filled with suffering seeks enjoyment, however oppressed it is by disease...."

[The prince, however, takes yet another ride out of the palace and saw] a man's corpse being carried on the road.... The prince asked the charioteer: "Who is the man being carried by four others, followed by persons in distress? He is well adorned, yet being mourned."

The charioteer, whose mind was overcome by the Shuddhadhivasa gods of pure soul, told the Lord what should not have been revealed: "This is someone bereft of intellect, senses, breath, and powers, lying unconscious like a bundle of grass or a log of wood. He had been raised and guarded with much care and affection, but now he is being abandoned."

Having heard the words of the charioteer, the prince became frightened and asked: "Is this state of being peculiar to this man, or is such the end of all people?" The charioteer then said to him: "This is the last state of all people. Death is certain for all, whether they be of low, middle, or high degree."

Though he was a steadfast man, the prince felt faint as soon as he heard about death. Leaning his shoulders against the railing, he said in a sad tone: "...Charioteer, turn back, for this is not the time for the pleasure-ground. How can a person of intelligence, aware of death, enjoy oneself in this fateful hour?"[2]

Chapter 4

Death Is Not
the Wages of Sin

The story in Genesis of the first human being is perplexing, as the one God personally brought into being meets a tragic end. The story begins: "Then the Lord God formed human being from the dust of the ground, and breathed into the nostrils the breath of life; and the human being became a living being" (Gen. 2:7).[1] It is an auspicious beginning. But the story takes an unexpected turn and concludes with a verdict that is final and irreversible. "You are dust, and to dust you shall return" (Gen. 3:19b). It is true that God formed us human beings "from the dust of the ground." It is also true that "we are dust." But within us, according to the biblical story, is something more than the dust out of which we were taken: "the breath of life" God breathed into our nostrils for us to become "living beings."

Why then should human beings return to dust? Why should that breath of life, which might have enabled us to become something more than dust, leave us? These must be some of the questions which this story from ancient Israel seeks to address. These are very human questions, arising from daily experience, that are relevant to each one of us. The moon waxes and wanes. Spring yields to summer, summer to autumn, and autumn to winter. As for human beings, we not only live but die. Why? Although our ancestors were not able to explain death biologically, they tried to explain it religiously.

For Christians the biblical story of Adam and Eve eating the forbidden fruit gives the straight answer. Similar stories from other peoples come up with a strikingly similar answer, though much less directly. But is the answer a right answer? Is it convincing, particularly today? Further, what led our ancestors to the answer? What is the theology that underlies their answer?

Our theme in Part Two is life—what it is and what it means. To grapple with life, we need to grapple at the same time with death and with what it means. For death may shed light on what it means to live. Is it not true that one cannot begin to live until one knows what it means to die? For us today as well as for our ancestors in the remote past—in fact for all human beings throughout the ages—the question of death is a religious question, a question about how we human beings understand ourselves in relation to God.

A Doctor's Testimony

If the biblical story of the human being created from dust and returning to dust perplexes and disturbs us, the following testimony of a doctor is no less perplexing and disturbing.

> The wife held the body of her husband and cried loudly. The young son, twenty-two years old, held his father's still-warm hand, letting his tears run down silently, his shoulders trembling. The brothers of Shimada, the man who had just passed away, were sobbing. His sisters, like his wife, were crying loudly. Only Shimada, his breathing and his heart having stopped, showed no sign of any movement. His death, announced by the doctor about ten minutes ago, was the undisputed fact. No amount of tears could change it. Still, these people could accept it only with tears.
>
> Having cried long enough, the wife stood up with resolution and said to her husband lying in front of her: "Let's leave. Let's go home. You don't have to suffer here in the hospital anymore." When his brothers and sisters heard what had just been said, they began to pack the things beside the bed. There was not much to pack—things he used during his stay in the hospital, things such as worn-out toothbrushes, half-used toothpaste, some soiled plastic cups, a newly opened tissue box, towels whose color had faded, underwear that would not be worn again, pajamas, and the teacup he liked best to drink from. They slowly sorted out these daily necessities.
>
> It was a long struggle against the fatal illness. Compared with it, packing these things took only a few moments. Tomorrow perhaps another patient would be lying on this bed, moaning in pain. That person certainly would not know that the patient who had occupied the same bed died yesterday. But all this had nothing anymore to do with the person who had just passed away. . . . [2]

This story is no fiction. This is just one of many stories of a doctor's daily encounters with death. It is one of hundreds of thousands of stories of death and dying, the stories that take place each day in hospitals, at home, at refugee camps, and on battlefields. How do such stories of everyday experience relate to the biblical story of death? This is the question we are going to explore.

What the doctor tells us is a story about death. It is typical and familiar. Still, it seizes us with a sense of helplessness. It moves us deeply, reminding us of the fragility of life, if not the senselessness of it. We are seeing the tears of those at the deathbed of their loved one. We are looking at the body that shows not the slightest sign of movement. And we find ourselves standing on the verge of the gulf that separates the living and the dead. "Let's go home," the wife says to her husband. But is home, without him alive, still home? Is the home that no longer carries his voice, his laughter, and his movements still home? Is home still home when it is no longer filled with his breath of life? His death has changed forever what used to be home. It has changed the relationships of the people with whom he shared life—his wife, his children, his brothers and sisters.

Death strikes at the very root of relationships. Life can be shared. It must be shared. A solitary life is a crippled life. An egocentric life turns human beings, oneself included, into means to an end—whether social status, political power, economic gain, or sexual gratification. But death, which is so close to life, which is a shadow of life, which accompanies life all the time, cannot be shared. It is a solitary experience. You may shed tears over the death of a friend, a relative, or a loved one, but you cannot die the death of that person. Death is heartless. Though you may sob bitterly and cry your heart out, still death stares at you devoid of emotion.

The doctor's account of the scene surrounding the death of a person named Shimada conveys not only the irreversibility of death but its impersonality. The packing of ordinary items such as toothbrushes, pajamas, and the teacup that used to belong to him heightens the havoc created by death. Even these things, while lacking motion and emotion, once were alive with motion and emotion as parts of the person now deceased. They too are discarded by death. They have to be packed, put away, disposed of, and eventually forgotten. Death has the power to render dead everything associated with the deceased person.

The man called Shimada passed away, but death has not passed away. The doctor, in his matter-of-fact account, seems to be making the point that nothing could stop death from occurring over and over again. Against death all becomes defenseless, including this particular individual called Shimada. Tomorrow, so the doctor tells us, another patient will occupy the bed vacated by Shimada, not knowing that Shimada had died on it the previous day. Although the doctor does not tell us, it is not difficult to surmise that perhaps the new occupant too will succumb sooner or later to a fatal disease, and after the prolonged pain and suffering will follow the former patient into the realm of no return.

With each death the doctor, like anybody else, encounters the tyranny of death, its invincibility. Even the most advanced medical science and technology have to give in to it at the end. Death devours the living. It stops time for the dead. It defeats finally every effort to withstand it. It is the only thing between heaven and earth that knows no defeat. It may give a respite to its victims, but it allows them no lasting victory.

We cannot but ask ourselves whether this was also Jesus' own experience when faced with death on the cross. In spite of what he thought and said about faith in life beyond death, was he not a victim who had to succumb to death? And his mother and other women at the foot of the cross watching him die—were they not overcome not only by extreme sorrow but by the sense of a helpless void? Jesus is said to have cried out to God, quoting Psalm 22, "My God, my God, why have you abandoned me?" These words of anguish and desperation could have been uttered by his mother and close followers also in their brokenheartedness and utter despair.

A Life-and-Death Matter

What is death, then? What does it mean? What sense does it make in relation to life? Or does it make no sense at all? If these are the questions implicit in the doctor's story, they are our questions also. They are, in other words, human questions—questions of all human beings, ancient or modern, Eastern or Western. It must have been to address such questions that the Genesis story referred to earlier set out to give an account of how death came to dominate life. But does the biblical story get it right? Or do we get it right? Does the story tell us what we should know about life and death? Or do we miss what it really wants to say to us? Has the way the church has interpreted it misled generations of believing women and men, putting a mask on death and keeping us from seeing its true face?

The human being, according to the biblical story, is the dust of the ground animated and enlivened by the breath of life from God. This is a remarkable theological insight that perceives the human being as more than mere dust, more than biological material. The breath of life comes from God. It belongs to God. It is a part of God. It cannot be other than God in God's own self. This is an extraordinary insight into the nature of the human being. It is also a profound statement about the relationship between God and human beings. The breath of life is God sharing God's life with us, God imparting God's own self to us, God giving up part of God for us. Human being is not *human* being apart from God. Human being is not human *being* when separated from God's being. And human being is not *living* being if it were not for the breath of the living God. Human being is Immanuel—God-with-us; no, not just God-with-us, God-*in*-us!

This is a lofty view of human beings, amounting to great self-awareness of what it means to be human. Entirely overwhelmed, a poet in ancient Israel confesses to God:

> You have made [human beings] a little
>   lower than God,
> and crowned them with glory and honor.
>
> (Ps. 8:5)

Recognizing the glory and honor of being human is a confession of faith in the greatness of God. This is a theological statement made by the theologian-poet who enjoys the well-being of life. But this, as we all know, is not the whole story. Our experience tells us that this human being God "crowned with glory and honor" returns to dust, deprived of that glory and honor, and ceases to have the breath God once breathed into them—is this not totally perplexing?

The euphoria is gone: we become God-not-in-us, even God-not-with-us. That breath of life God breathed into us is withdrawn. We are back to where we began—a lump of dust without the breath of life, a cold body without motion and devoid of emotion. How can the thought not be perplexing, even disturbing? The thought must have perplexed the storyteller who told the story. It must have disturbed the people of the community the storyteller was addressing. It should have disturbed the men and women throughout the ages who heard or read the story. And it should perplex, even disturb, us Christians today as well. After all, we are living human beings just like those who are not Christian. Like anyone else we have to face the fact that we are dust and to dust we shall return. Being Christian does not make us different from fellow human beings when returning to dust is the destination of our physical existence.

It is evident that the biblical story is not just bewildering. Nor is it a story told to tease us. It is not somebody else's story and irrelevant to us. On the contrary, though the story is addressed to people of the past, it is also addressed to us today. Though a story about the life and death of ancient human beings, it is no less a story of our life and death at present. It is the story of ancients, yes, but it is also our story. It is a life-and-death matter to them, but the story is also life and death to us. It is a story that has to be told in the first person, singular or plural, and not in the third person as if it is someone else's business.

What strikes us first in the Genesis story is a sense of sadness. One perceives a pathos of inevitability, an echo of fatalism. But this is not all. There are questions crying out: Why from dust to dust? The origin of humans from the dust of the ground can be explained because dust is the physical substance of human existence. But why do humans turn to dust? Did God breathe the breath of life into us for nothing? Was not the divine breath of life to make us into something other than dust? We are made from the dust of the ground. This is God's doing. This is God at work like a great sculptor. But why must we return to dust? This is an anticlimax, a distressing epilogue. Our end is no different from our beginning. Could this be God's doing also? Was this also intended by God at the outset? But how could God show lack of ingenuity, the God who began so ingeniously? Did the God who accounts for the emergence of living human beings also engineer our disintegration into dust? Is God the author of death as well as life?

Or, in terms more familiar to us, is God responsible for our death? Such questions could have been in the minds of the wife, the children, and the brothers and sisters of the deceased person in the doctor's testimony above. These people were not Christians, and did not express their deep sorrow in a Christian way. They may not even be religious in the sense of believing in one supreme God who created heaven and earth. But their tears pose a big question about the meaning of life, which has been overshadowed by the death of their loved one. Even the simple account of packing the things the deceased left behind—does it not contain complex questions about human beings and their destiny? The loud crying of the deceased person's wife and sisters, the trembling of his son's shoulders as the latter wept in silence, and the sobbing of his brothers—are not these expressions of sorrow and helplessness related to the theological question of who is in charge of the ebb and flow of life in the universe? Does it not reflect the utter vulnerability of us human beings for what death has done to countless lives, and for what it can also do to each one of us? Does it not make our joy over a newborn life hollow, cast a shadow over the life we live, and muffle the hope we cherish for the future? Whether the biblical story or the doctor's testimony, it is a life-and-death matter with which we have to deal.

How would Jesus reply to such questions? How did he deal with the matter of death as well as life? How did his reflection deepen his experience of God as the life-giving power? Or, like each of us, was he also racing against time, hoping to gain some glimpses of eternity in time, tasting a life immortal in the life mortal?

God as Source of the "Serious Command"

How are we to make any sense of life and death? How are we to deal with the fact of death, the daily experience with death, and the premonition of one's own death? Are these questions the beginning of religion? Is death what motivates human beings to recite incantations and to develop rituals in efforts to evade death, to trick it, or even to gain the upper hand over it? Human beings have been preoccupied with death since the inception of a most rudimental form of civilization.[3] In this scientific-technological age, our preoccupation with death not only has gone on unabated; it has increased. The profusion of literary output on death is proof. Scientists, biological and medical, have redoubled their effort to probe the mystery of life and death, above all death. There are even scientists who risk their professional reputation to delve into the esoteric sphere of reincarnation, a sphere once strictly confined to religions.[4] Death has become a hot subject not only for religion but for science.

Gautama Siddhartha, in the story recounted in the opening to Part Two, was perplexed and then terribly disturbed that a living human being could return to dust, with no life. Encountered with the fact of death for the first time, he had to ask his charioteer: "Who is the man being carried by four others, followed by persons in distress?" He then "became frightened" and asked again: "Is this state of being peculiar to this man, or is such the end of all people?" Learning that this is "the last state of all people," Gautama was overtaken by sadness. Rendered numb by fear and sadness, he mumbled, perhaps more to himself than to his charioteer: "How can a person of intelligence, aware of death, enjoy oneself in this fateful hour?" The legend has it that he lost no time in setting out on the long arduous road to become the Buddha, the Enlightened One, liberated from the fear and sadness that death inflicts on life.

The fact of death, the reality of it, perplexes and disturbs us. Although efforts have been made to show that death has been accepted as part of nature, that it is as natural as the setting and rising of the sun, human beings have not been reconciled to it deep in their subconsciousness. Does not the story in the third chapter of Genesis communicate this fact? The story seems to be saying that death is fateful to human beings. It interrupts life. It moves the present tense to the past tense. It turns what is to what was, turning what we are and what we have done into memories that will eventually fade away and disappear. The world will go on as if we never existed. Death changes us from a person to a body, from a living being to a lifeless corpse. It alters our relationship with God once and for all.

> The dead do not praise the Lord,
>   nor do any that go down into silence.
>   (Ps. 115:17)

Death renders the dead silent even before God. All prayers cease. There is no communication with God anymore. The dead cannot break that silence, and even God cannot break it. Such is the power of death.

Hebrew Scripture, however, is not much occupied with breaking the silence that death imposes on us and on God. It is a futile exercise anyway. But it tries to explain the reason for that silence. It does not try to answer the question of how to get the better of death, which is bound to be a fruitless effort. It seems more interested in the theology of death than in the overcoming of it. It wrestles with why death occurs instead of how to deal with it. In this way the Bible is consistent. Death in the biblical story is a theological concern just as birth is a theological event. One is told that the human being formed from the dust of the ground did not become a *living* being until God breathed the breath of life into it. God was responsible for the coming into being of human being. God is the source and origin of human life. Hence, birth is a *theo*-logical event.

If we need God for the birth of human beings, we also need God for death. This must be what the teller of the biblical story thought. Death, no less than birth, is a *theo*-logical matter. It relates to human beings, but human beings do not die for no reason. What is this cause, then? It must have something to do with God. The cause is not God's death. Of course not. Human beings have been dying ever since they appeared on the stage of God's creation. But God does not die. God *cannot* die. The end of God would be the end of creation, the end of hope for its renewal, and the end of a vision for its re-creation. For the sake of creation, for the sake of all things in creation, and for the sake of human beings, even if only to give an account of why human beings have to die, God must *be*.

If death is a theological matter, that is, related as much to God as to human beings, it cannot be dismissed as a natural phenomenon. How can death, the happening that disrupts the normal course of life, that reduces a person to a lifeless thing, that severs ties and relationships of family and community—how can death be natural? It is most unnatural, particularly when it concerns human life. This must be the reasoning that shaped the biblical story. The experience described in the doctor's testimony—not an isolated experience but a universal experience—must also be very much the experience that affected the making of the biblical story.

We know that other created things appear and disappear. We also observe that animals are born and die. This, we believe, is part of their nature. Human beings are born and also die. But we are aware of the fact of death, conscious of its certainty, and troubled by its inescapability. It may be that this very self-awareness makes us distinct from other created things. On the one hand we are, like everything else, part of nature, but we also *stand out* of nature. For this reason death cannot be something that just happens naturally. It happens, but it should not happen, because we are endowed with what other living beings do not have—the breath of life directly from God.

Why, then, does death happen? There must be a theological reason besides the biological reasons; that is, God must have played a part in it. But here is a troubling question: Why did God become involved in the death of human beings? This must be the theological question that inspired the biblical story. It is a very real question, not only for the biblical storyteller. It is an almost universal question that takes form in different languages and idioms, in the stories and myths of many peoples. The answer given in the biblical story is that death is a negative response of God to something negative that human beings did against God. The focus is shifted from God to the human being. God's response has its origins in a human being eating from the tree forbidden by God. "You shall not eat," we are told, "of the fruit of the tree that is in the middle of the garden." This is a strict order. It is a command of categorical nature, a mandate that allows no discussion. In contrast to the auspicious way the human being came to be a living being, God's command contains an ominous tone. The sky becomes overcast. The light dims. The joyous scene of paradise is now covered with gloom.

There is tremendous suspense here. What will happen next? Trouble or rescue? Grief or happiness? Anguish or serenity? Bad news or good news?

The news is bad. The order not to eat the fruit of the forbidden tree—the tree of the knowledge of good and evil—is followed by a warning of what would happen: "You shall die" (Gen. 2:17; 3:3). What is at stake here, the future of the tree or the divine order? It is the latter. "The story," contrary to the prevailing view, "is not interested in the character of the tree. The trees are incidental to the main point that God's command is a serious one."[5] But as the story unfolds, neither God nor God's serious command is blamed for humans' death. It is human beings who had trespassed the divine injunction that brought death upon them.

No one has sought to question the basic *theo*-logical premise of the story that the divine command combines with the divine threat of a death sentence. This premise "demonstrates God's seriousness in prohibiting access to the tree."[6] The focus of the story shifts from the tree to the command, then to the God who issued the command. Was the storyteller conscious of this development? We are not sure. If the storyteller was not conscious of it, then an important clue about the cause of human death inadvertently strayed into the story: death is closely related to God, through the strict order God instituted for a human being not to eat the fruit of the forbidden tree.

At this point an abrupt shift takes place for the second time in the story. It is a reversal of the first shift we identified. The cause of death shifts from God who instituted it to the human beings who brought it upon themselves by not obeying God's command. As we shall discuss, it is this second shift that has become central to the teachings of the Christian church on atonement—from Paul in the first century, to Augustine in the third to fourth centuries, to Anselm of Canterbury in the eleventh century, and to most theologians and Christians today.

Though the traditions of the Christian church may have already passed judgment on the biblical story, we are not yet through with it. Many questions remain. One of them, a fundamental question that seldom gets asked, is: Who is this God who issued that "serious command"? What is this God like? It is not difficult to answer. Behind this "serious command" is a serious God—a God who means what is said. In this "divine threat" one finds a threatening God—a God who cannot be trifled with. A serious and threatening God must be the God who dominated the storyteller and the community of women, men, and children who listened. This serious God must not be taken for granted. This God must be appeased with offerings and sacrifices, not only with the choicest crops and with animals without defects, but sometimes also with one's firstborn child.[7] To this God, one must pledge loyalty through prayers and vows. This is a no-nonsense God who rewards the virtuous with good and the wicked with evil. This God cannot be offended without serious consequences.

But is this God God in God's own self? Is it the true God? Such questions are implied in what Eve says to the serpent: "God said, 'You shall not eat of the fruit of the tree that is in the middle of the garden, nor shall you touch it, *or you shall die*'" (Gen. 3:3; emphasis added). The storyteller must have underlined the last few words with a loud voice to bring home to the audience the seriousness of the divine command. Implicit in Eve's response is not only a veiled discontent with God's serious command but an unspoken question about the God of the serious command. How can this God be the God who breathed the breath of life into us and made us living human beings?

There is another equally important question: Did God, the God who created human beings, give the order not to eat from the tree and warn us with a death penalty? This is precisely what the serpent, that crafty creature, insinuated to Eve, thus inducing her to commit the grave sin of eating the forbidden fruit. The serpent sowed—did it not?—the seed of doubt in her mind when it said to her: "Did God say, 'You shall not eat from any tree in the garden?'" (Gen. 3:1).

The serpent did not stop at sowing the seed of doubt in her. The serpent went further, and confided to her in no uncertain terms: "You will not die; for God knows that when you eat of it your eyes will be opened, and you will be like God, knowing good and evil" (3:4-5).

As we all know, this is a vital part of the story. Theologians who use the text have left no stone unturned in discussing the sinful nature of human beings in relation to God. But is this all the story says? Does what the serpent is made to say appeal to nothing but human pride, sinful nature, impiety, and rebellion? Perhaps there is something in the story that escaped our attention before; that is, what the serpent said to Eve might in fact have been raising a legitimate doubt or question as to whether the "serious command" came from God.

It has seldom occurred to Christians to ask such a question. Instead, we quickly look to ourselves for the reasons we have to die and why we deserve it. Death is the result of our folly in not taking God's command seriously. Since this is the case, we should not look elsewhere for the reason why we have to die, except to our sinful nature. Sin and death have thus become strange bed-fellows in the human mind. That sin and death are intertwined is the belief that has come to prevail not only in the communities of faith rooted in Hebrew Scripture and the New Testament, but also in the communities with different religious orientations and cultural traditions. Here is, for example, a story told by the native people of Poso, a district of central Celebes in Indonesia:

> In the beginning the sky was very near the earth, and the Creator, who lived in it, used to let down his gifts to human beings at the end of a rope. One day when the Creator lowered a stone, our first father and mother would have none of it and called to their Maker, "What have we to do with this stone? Give us something else." The Creator complied and hauled away the rope; the stone mounted up and up until it vanished from sight. Presently the rope was seen coming down from heaven again, and this time there was a banana at the end of it instead of a stone. Our first parents ran at the banana and took it. Then there came a voice from heaven saying: "Because you have chosen the banana, your life shall be like its life. When the banana-tree has offspring, the parent stem dies; so shall ye die and your children shall step into your place. Had ye chosen the stone, your life would have been like the life of the stone, changeless and immortal." The man and his wife mourned over their fatal choice, but it was too late; that is how through the eating of a banana death came into the world.[8]

An innocent myth? Far from it. The story, like the biblical story, is told to explain why death has become the human lot. It is a sober story, no less sober than the story in Hebrew Scripture.

These two stories—the biblical story and the story from Indonesia—differ in more than one way. The Indonesian story, like most myths and stories from

Asia, is not as intense and thick as the Genesis story. The fruit that brings death to human beings is a banana, a common tropical fruit in most Asian countries, and not the unspecified fruit in the biblical story. The names of the ancestors—"our first father and mother"—are not mentioned. In spite of such differences, the main motif in the two stories is strikingly similar: in both stories the motif is an incorrect decision. The two decisions result in death.

The two stories also convey fundamentally the same message: human beings, and not God, are ultimately to blame for their death. The Creator in the Indonesian myth does not issue a serious command, but the choice between the stone and the banana turns out to be a serious test set by the deity for the first ancestors. Still, like the biblical story, there is no attempt in the Indonesian story to make God accountable for the choice the ancestors made when they rejected the stone in favor of the banana. It was their choice, not God's. To emphasize this point, the first ancestors in the Indonesian story are said to "mourn over their fatal choice." It is their stupidity and willfulness that bring about their mortality.

But they show defiance, too. When they saw the stone the Creator had lowered for them on a rope, they were not pleased. In fact they became agitated, and did not bother to conceal their displeasure. "What have we to do with this stone?" they said petulantly. It may be this same petulant tone that we hear in what our biblical ancestors said to the serpent: "But God said, 'You shall not eat of the fruit of the tree that is in the middle of the garden, nor shall you touch it.'" Nor shall you touch it! This is a strong statement not found in the original command (Gen. 2:17). Why does the storyteller make Eve say it? In making this "slight alteration," the storyteller plants a big clue to where the story is heading: the storyteller is painting for the audience a picture of a God who is "a little harsh and repressive, forbidding the tree even to be touched."[9] Christian theology has not taken a God who is "a little harsh and repressive" to heart in the interpretation of the story. The biblical story to Christian theology has become the archetypical story of the fall of human being from God's grace. And death is the result of this fall.

As for the first ancestors in the Indonesian story, their petulance developed into a demand. "Give us something else," they said to the Creator. This was a fateful demand. They should have known better, for they got what they had demanded. The Creator cannot be defied without grave consequences. Choosing the banana over the stone, inadvertently the ancestors chose death. "Through the eating of a banana," concludes the Indonesian story, "death came into the world." This is a sad story. Like the biblical story, this Indonesian story tells us that human beings were their own undoing. We ourselves are to blame for our destiny. We bring upon ourselves death that terminates life. The Creator is not responsible. But how could the Creator not be responsible? Was it not the Creator who withdrew the stone and set the banana before our first ancestors? Was not the Creator at least morally responsible for the fatal choice they had made?

How would Jesus have responded to the Indonesian story of the deity offering a choice between the stone and the banana—the Jesus who asked if any one of his listeners would give a stone to their children instead of bread (Matt. 7:9)? There is no ready answer, for Jesus would not have known the Indonesian story. But the story of Adam and Eve eating the fruit against the strict order of God should have been familiar to him. It is in the first book of the Torah, the sacred scripture of his own religion. It is reasonable to think that some of his listeners asked him to explain the story. It is also plausible that in response to their request Jesus put into practice one of his basic phrases in interpreting the Hebrew Scriptures: "You have heard that it was said to those of ancient times ... but I say to you ..." (Matt. 5:21-22, for example). Unfortunately, the writers of the Gospels have left no record of what Jesus said on this matter. But he said and did other things that may help us know how he might have responded. We will take this question up in the last sections of this chapter.

Death Is Not the Wages of Sin

It is *not* my purpose to make God responsible for the death of human beings. Nor is it my intention to establish the innocence of human beings with regard to the reason for their death. Either way it is beside the point. To deal with death in the first manner is *theo*-logically wrong, for God is the God of life and not the God of death. Dealing with death in the second manner is *anthropo*-logically irresponsible, because death does testify to how human beings can bring destruction not only to themselves but to lives directly and indirectly related to them.

We have to cut open the tightly closed theological circle of sin and death. The official teaching of the Christian church may hold that death is the result of human sin in disobedience to God,[10] but at the deathbed of our loved ones, in our distress and grief, we do not remind ourselves of this fact. Nor is this what doctors and priests say to the dying patients to whom they are ministering. Linking death with what is known in religion as sin—is this not a case of how theology is often developed in total disregard of what we feel, of what we believe, and of how we conduct ourselves in real situations?

The assertion in Christianity that death is the wages of sin has a solid biblical basis. It comes from none other than Paul, perhaps the greatest theologian Christianity has ever had. In his letter to the Christians in Rome one reads: "The wages of sin is death" (Rom. 6:23). Ever since Paul penned these words, the Christian church has adopted the saying and made it an article of faith and teaching.

The fate of death is sealed. It has lodged in the heart of the Christian traditions and in the minds of Christian believers, bound to sin "like glue and lacquer" (*ru jiao ci qi*), to use a Chinese expression. The pairing is in fact more than just a close relationship. Death has not been viewed as a biological occurrence, but as a religious event. Human beings in this view die not because of illness or of the failure of physical organs, but because of rupture in the relationship between them and God. Death is, to use Paul's words, "the wages of sin." We have earned death by defying God's command. Death is, in other words, the punishment we deserve for the sin Adam and Eve committed against God. Generations of human beings, including ourselves, who have come after them, have inherited death as the wages of sin. Death as well as sin have become our human destiny.

In this matter of sin and death Paul's language is explicit and his theology leaves no room for doubt. He is consistent here, although on other questions he can come up with contradicting statements. That death is the wages of sin is the conclusion of what he in effect said earlier in the same Letter to the Romans: "Just as sin came into the world through one man [Adam], and death came through sin, and so death spread to all because all have sinned . . . " (5:12). Sin is the cause of death and death is the effect of sin! If this was true with Adam, it is also true with all human beings.

Concerning this matter, however, Paul made a serious theological error. The error is to define sin as human disobedience to God and to make it the basis of all we believe with regard to God, human beings, and nature. Sin understood in this sense has played a central role in the teachings and practices of the Christian church. There is the doctrine that God allowed Jesus to die on the cross in order to "atone" for human sin. Has not this "doctrine of atonement"—the doctrine that has shaped the way the church has understood itself, God, Jesus Christ, and even mission—been derived from the idea of sin as human offense against God? Has not Christianity in different forms—popular and elite, high and low, esoteric and exoteric, liberal and conservative, mainline and sectarian—been preoccupied with the question of how to be saved from sin that leads to death? God seems to have nothing else to do but to "rescue [us] from this body of death" (Rom. 7:24).

Anselm of Canterbury, for example, reasoned in the eleventh century: "The crux of the problem is why God became a human being in order to save humankind from death. . . . the restoration of human nature ought not to be left undone, and yet could not be done unless human beings paid what they owed to God for their sin. This debt was so great that only God was able to pay it, although only human beings ought to pay it."[11] This statement is typical of the theology known as the "judicial theory of atonement" that has dominated the Christian church for centuries. This kind of theology has been introduced to Asia and other non-Western regions. It has been translated into a theology of mission that focuses on the idea that Jesus' blood shed on the cross cleansed our sin, appeased God's wrath against us, and saved our souls from eternal death.

The theology of atonement, the idea of human beings having to appease God for sins committed against God and the understanding of death as divine punishment, is not original to Christianity. It is very much a part of the religious cultures and practices of most nations and peoples. Do we not find these ideas in the Hebrew Scriptures? Do we not come across them in the myths, folktales, and religious documents of our ancient ancestors, Eastern or Western? If these "judicial" ideas of atonement and practices of religious sacrifice point to the insecurity and fear deep in human consciousness, they may not represent what God must be in God's own self. Christian theology has refined these popular ideas and practices and focused them on Jesus as the Son of God, the second person of the Trinity—even as Godself. In dying on the cross Jesus paid, to paraphrase Anselm, a debt of sin so enormous that only God was able to pay it, despite the fact that it was human beings who sinned against God in the first place, beginning with Adam and continuing to each of us today.

Anselm continues: "Hence, it was necessary for God to assume a human nature into a unity of person, so that the one who with respect to his nature ought to make payment, but was unable to, would be the one who with respect to his person was able to."[12] If preachers and theologians no longer use such language to emphasize what God had to do to enact atonement for human sin and to have "God's honor satisfied," they continue to teach the idea of the "judicial" nature of atonement. And death, in theological classrooms, in Sunday school classes, and from the pulpit, continues to be taught as "the wages of sin."

Is this how Jesus regarded death? Is this how he envisioned his own death? Is this the way he actually experienced death on the cross? We will deal with such questions later when we explore how Jesus faced death—the death of others and his own death. But one thing is certain: *for Jesus death cannot be, and thus is not, the wages of sin.* There is no reason to believe that Jesus considered his death on the cross as a debt, as a ransom, or as a payment that God paid on behalf of human beings to redeem them from their sin and to satisfy God's honor. This is not the way Jesus experienced God. Nor is this the way Jesus understood God to behave.

The Phenomenal and the Ephemeral

Linking death with sin committed against God has come to dictate what most religious believers think and do. But in Asia there has been a tradition of viewing death differently from the prevailing religious teachings and practices. I am referring to Chuang Tzu, a very original thinker in China in the fourth century B.C.E. He not only developed the teachings of Lao Tzu, an older contemporary of Confucius (551–479 B.C.E.), and brought Taoism to its consummation, but exerted a profound impact on Buddhism, introduced to China in the first century C.E., and later on Zen Buddhism in particular. He is regarded by some as having surpassed Lao Tzu in his insights into human nature in relation to what is real and eternal, and what is temporal and ephemeral.[13]

In the chapter called "Bliss" in the *Chuang Tzu,* a collection of sayings attributed to him, one finds this episode:

Chuang Tzu's wife died and Hui Tzu went to offer his condolence. He found Chuang Tzu squatting on the ground and singing, beating on an earthen bowl. He said, "Someone has lived with you, raised children for you and now she has aged and died. Is it not enough that you should not shed any tear? But now you sing and beat the bowl. Is this not too much?"

"No," replied Chuang Tzu. "When she died, how could I help being affected? But as I think the matter over, I realize that originally she had no life; and not only no life, she had no form; not only no form, she had no material force (*ch'i*). In the limbo of existence and non-existence, there was transformation and the material force was evolved. The material force was transformed to be form, form was transformed to become life, and now birth has transformed to become death. This is like the rotation of the four seasons, spring, summer, fall, and winter. Now she lies asleep in the great house (the universe). For me to go about weeping and wailing would be to show my ignorance of destiny. Therefore I desist."[14]

Though one might be taken aback by the singing and beating of the bowl—merrymaking—at Chuang Tzu's wife's death, this is a thought-provoking story. What we encounter is not a cynic who takes a life-and-death matter lightly, definitely not a jester making fun of it, but a person who, in the midst of deep mourning for his wife's death, tries to grapple with the death that has deprived him of his lifelong companion.

The story portrays a man deeply saddened by his wife's death. But Hui Tzu, Chuang Tzu's scholar-friend and philosophical disputant, did not see his sadness. Hui Tzu was offended. "Is this not too much?" Hui Tzu confronted him and rebuked him. But this was Chuang Tzu's reply: "When she died, how could I help being affected?" He was not above human emotions. Despite his "theological" capacity to soar into heavens, to survey the mystery of the universe, and to commune with the Creator-Spirit, and despite his philosophical ability to descend to the depths of the earth and the oceans to test the limits of the human intellect, his wife's death brought him back to the reality of life. It made him realize how ephemeral human existence is.

Chuang Tzu is reported to have said: "Death and life are fate in action. Possessing all the constancy of night and dawn, they are nature in action, beyond the interference of human being."[15] Chuang Tzu was deeply affected by the realization that he is not the master of his own destiny. The destiny of all things and beings, including his own, is "beyond human interference." This is Chuang Tzu's admission of how limited and vulnerable we human beings are when it comes to the matter of life and death. It is his candid confession that human beings are ultimately powerless over their own destiny.[16]

Death and life are fate in action. How true! Such awareness is deeply rooted in the Chinese view of human destiny. It also underlies the Buddhist perception of the phenomenal world as ephemeral and impermanent.[17] But this is only a half-truth, and most of us, not only Christians but some Buddhists themselves, stop short at this half-truth, asserting that Buddhism teaches the negative view of life and the world and that it fosters fatalism.

But this is not entirely the case. There is much more to Buddhism than negativism and fatalism. "The material is no different from the immaterial," says the *Sutra of the Heart of Prajina,* one of the Buddhist Scriptures most loved and recited by Buddhists. It goes on to tell us that the reverse is also true: "The immaterial is no different from the material." Is there not a contradiction between the material and immaterial? Do these statements render these antonyms meaningless? The same sutra goes on to say in effect: "The material is the immaterial; the immaterial is the material."[18] This is very puzzling, to say the least.

The Chinese word for "the immaterial" is *kong (sunya* or *sunyata),* meaning literally "empty or emptiness." But *kong* is *not* nothing. It is the material transformed and sublimated. It is the material (*se*) grasped in its true nature. It is what is truly true, really real. That is why the immaterial is the material and the material is the immaterial. The immaterial is the true nature of the material. It is that truly true and that really real from which the material comes and to which the material returns. Perhaps one can say that the immaterial gets expressed in the material and the material gets resolved into the immaterial. To render *se zhi shi kong* and *kong zhi shi se* in the *Sutra of the Heart of Prajina* as "the phenomenal is ephemeral" and "the ephemeral is the phenomenal" is, thus, misleading. The fact is that the phenomenal is *not* ephemeral, transient, or fleeting. It can be lasting, enduring, and permanent if perceived in the depth of its being and from the perspective of the universal *xi* (energy, power, spirit), creating and re-creating all things in the world of phenomena.

If this is true with all things in the world, it is also true with human beings. That is why Buddhism can teach that "nothing has an ego" (*zhu fa wu wo*), that is, "nothing is independent of the law of causation," on the one hand and, on the other hand, that the true wisdom consists in "liberation from the law of causation." This liberated self is the true self, namely, "*atman* is *brahman* and *brahman* is *atman.*"[19] Applied to the matter of life and death, we perceive in this reasoning an effort not to deny the daily experience of living and dying, but to grapple with that which is real, permanent, and true in the midst of what is experienced as unreal, impermanent, and illusory.

Long before Buddhism made its way into China, Chuang Tzu already preoccupied himself with such "ultimate" matters of life and with the world in its deepest dimensions. "Life and death," he said, "are fate in action." What Chuang Tzu named "fate" is none other than what is known as "the law of causation" in primitive Buddhism. And as Buddhism sought to be liberated from the law of causation, Chuang Tzu, confronted with the death of his wife, set out to liberate himself from the "fate in action" that brings about life and especially death. "When she died," he said in response to his friend's rebuke, "how could I help being affected?" He must have spent many a sleepless night beside his wife's sickbed. He must have sought every possible means of cure for her. He fought "fate" to defeat death, but to no avail. His wife died. He must have cried his heart out. He was not unaffected by his wife's death.

Is death, then, a matter of fate in the sense of "the principle, power, or agency by which, according to certain philosophical and popular systems of belief, all events, or some events in particular, are unalterably predetermined from eternity"?[20] Is this what Chuang Tzu meant by "fate" (*min*)? Was he not advocating fatalism—defined as the "acceptance of every event as inevitable"[21]—when he said further: "Dying, being born, staying alive, perishing, failing, succeeding, poverty, riches, high caliber, low caliber, blame, praise, hunger, thirst, cold, heat—all these vicissitudes are the work of fate. They succeed one another in our presence day and night, but knowledge cannot determine their beginnings"?[22] If this is the case, there is nothing that one, even Chuang Tzu and most sages and religious masters, can do but subject oneself to the dictate of fate.

We should not, however, be too hasty in our verdict. We must try to understand what Chuang Tzu meant by the phrase "the work of fate" (*min zhi xing*). Everything hinges on what he meant by it. The word *min* (fate) in the phrase *min zhi xing* is "a noun indicating the conditioned situation, while *xing* (work) is movement. *Min zhi xing* thus means movement of the conditions decided apart from the human subject. If the human subject is not involved in this process of decision making (the work of fate), how can it affect the human subject?"[23]

This insight into the autonomous nature of the human subject or the self is subtle. Chuang Tzu beats "fate" at its own game, so to speak. He does acknowledge that we human beings cannot do anything about what happens in the world of phenomena, including such matters as life and death. But why should we do anything about them since they are in reality unrelated to us? The fact, Chuang Tzu wants to tell us, is that the human subject, the true self, does not belong to the world of phenomena and is not conditioned by it; even birth and death cannot touch it. "What is born and what dies, in short, are concerned with the physical aspects of human life, having nothing to do with the self."[24]

The human subject, the self, the true I, does not die! What dies are the phenomena that compose our physical life. "The real I is the transphenomenal subject, hence the death and life of the physical body do not change it."[25] Referring to a teacher by the name of Wang Tai, who "neither teaches nor engages in discussions, and yet after going to him knowing nothing, one returns filled to the brim," and who even earned the respect of Confucius, Chuang Tzu writes: "Death and birth are indeed the big things, but they can produce no change in him. Even were sky and earth to fall in ruins, he would not suffer any loss with them. He has seen how to become free from defects, so that he does not change with the rest of creation. He presides over the changes and preserves the stock that is his."[26]

From this point on the word *transformation* becomes of paramount importance. As Chuang Tzu tells us, "In the limbo of existence and non-existence, there was transformation.... The material force was transformed to be form, form was transformed to become life, and now birth has transformed to become death. This is like the rotation of the four seasons, spring, summer, fall, and winter." Does this not anticipate what Buddhism is to develop in depth later when it teaches that "the phenomenal is the real" and "the real is phenomenal"? To paraphrase this in Chuang Tzu's terms, can we not say that the phenomenal is transformed into the real and that the real is transformed into the phenomenal?

The process of birth and death may, then, be likened to the process of nature as in the change of seasons. Yes, the physical body does follow the natural process of birth and death. But the human being is not composed of a physical body only. There is, as we have seen, that human subject, that true self, that transcends the world of phenomena, that remains permanent in the natural process of birth and death, growth and decay. To distinguish this true self (*shi zai wo*) from the physical body (*xing qu wo*) is to gain the strength to live and the wisdom to face death. This strength and this wisdom are commonly expressed in the cultures in Asia deeply affected by Chuang Tzu's philosophical thoughts and by his deep insight into the nature of life and the world as *shi si ru gui*, meaning "looking upon death as going home."

This thought moves from the external world of change to the internal world that is not affected by change, from the phenomena of physical birth and death to the true self that is not subject to these events. This is how Chuang Tzu broke the cycle of birth and death (*po sheng si*), how he taught and practiced liberation from it. This must be why he was able to "sing and beat the bowl" after his wife's death. For him the true self of his wife was not dead. She was alive, more alive than she was when a part of his physical existence.

This body that lives after death—is this what Paul calls the "spiritual body" in his first letter to the Christians in Corinth? We are reminded of what he said about the resurrection of the dead in that letter: "What is sown is perishable, what is raised is imperishable.... It is sown a physical body, it is raised a spiritual body. If there is a physical body, there is also a spiritual body" (1 Cor. 15:42, 44). Does not one hear in these words a distant echo of Chuang Tzu?

Without knowing it, Chuang Tzu was preparing the religious ground for the entry of Buddhism into China some centuries after him. In this matter of birth and death, at least, "Chuang Tzu and Buddhism agreed without prior consultation."[27] Buddhism entered a land with rich and fertile religious soil. That it finally captivated the Chinese soul and mind and played a major role, together with Taoism and Confucianism, in the shaping of the religious consciousness of the Chinese people was no accident. Christianity too entered the same rich and fertile religious soil, but it refused to plant its seed in that soil. What it did was to try to replace Chinese soil with Christian soil it had brought from the West. The seed failed to germinate and take root. To this day Christianity has remained an outsider in the cultures penetrated deeply by Buddhism. This too was no accident.

The Glory of God

The question that interests us is this: How would Jesus himself have responded to what Chinese thinkers such as Chuang Tzu had to say about the ultimate problem of life and death? In the spiritual soil on which the vast majority of women, men, and children in parts of the world such as Asia toil and labor, hope and despair, live and die, would Jesus have found himself shaping their minds, souls, and spirits, not all by himself, but in the company of their sages, teachers, and religious masters? Would Jesus have brought fresh insights from his message of God's reign to enrich the ideas that had already been in China, for instance, for centuries, and in turn to be enriched by them?

Let us look at some of the stories in which Jesus confronted death. I am referring to the stories of Jesus raising a widow's son at Nain (Luke 7:11-17), Jairus's daughter (Mark 5:21-43; also Matt. 9:18-26; Luke 8:40-56), and Lazarus at Bethany (John 11:1-57). Studying these stories closely will tell us not only about how Jesus thought about life and death, but about the God with whom he related himself—to whom he wants all people to relate themselves.

"Jesus Had Compassion for Her"

The story appears commonplace, about a funeral of a young man at Nain, "a town in southern Galilee (modern Nein) about twenty-five miles from Capernaum."[28] Death itself, of course, is not commonplace. It plunges the loved ones of the deceased into the abyss. It strikes relatives and friends with a deep sense of loss. And it even brings a small town such as Nain to a momentary standstill as the townsfolk pause to see the funeral procession. But the work of the town still must carry on. People may not get used to such processions; still they have to accept them as an inevitable part of their daily life.

The funeral procession of the deceased young man at Nain is just one of those sober and yet commonplace stories that would not hold people's attention for long. The event would surely remain unrecorded in the town annals. But something happens to change this ordinary event to an extraordinary event, and to bring this brief episode to the pages of the Gospels.

Jesus, with his entourage of disciples and a large crowd, arrives in Nain just when "a man who had died was being carried out." That chance presence of Jesus turns the sad and sober procession of death into a drama of life and joy. Jesus touches the bier and calls the dead young man back to life. The people react with consternation, mixed with wonder. "Fear seized all of them," we are told, "and they glorified God."

If the story takes the entire town of Nain by surprise, it amazes us for other reasons. Whether by design or by accident, Luke, the storyteller, draws our attention to the grieving mother walking beside the bier in tears. Her distress is explained when Luke tells us that the dead young man is "his mother's only son." He lets us know further that she is also a widow. She is left with no one to support her. These snippets remind us of the doctor's testimony at the death scene of a man named Shimada, to which we referred earlier. Each small activity at the scene deepened the sorrow of his wife, son, and close relatives.

The sorrow that death forces upon the living is contagious. It creates a void in one's heart, depriving one of a vital force. Jesus, too, is deeply affected by the agony of the widowed mother. What is going on in Jesus' mind when he happens on the bier carrying the dead young man, accompanied by his mother in tears of sorrow? Is he reminding himself of the story in the third chapter of the Book of Genesis—the story that links death with disobeying God's command? Does he say to himself that this case demonstrates the inevitability of death, a result of the sin Adam and Eve committed against God? As Paul is to do later in his letter to the Christians at Corinth, does Jesus remark that death is the wages of sin?

No such thoughts cross the mind of Jesus. At least Luke does not give us reason to conclude otherwise. What we see is not Jesus in a theologically reflective mood, nor Jesus in a biblically stereotyped fashion. He has in fact never related himself to the Hebrew Scriptures in the way dictated by traditionalism. What takes hold of him instead, as Luke tells us, is "the compassion" he feels for the weeping mother. That compassion in his heart takes the form of words: "Do not weep." Then he proceeds to restore life to the young man.

Conspicuous in Jesus' attitude toward death and in his "theology" of death is that he does not relate death to sin or disobedience to God. The heart of death for Jesus is not sin but compassion. He has compassion for men, women, and children, such as this young man at Nain, who have to die; for the bereaved mother in mourning; for people helplessly watching their loved ones depart this world; and for the world death makes temporal and ephemeral. For Jesus it is compassion and not sin that empowers him to relate himself to death and to those devastated by the work of death.

The story of Jesus raising Lazarus from the dead (John 11:1-57) is also a powerful witness to Jesus' compassion, though the word is not found in the story. This time Jesus faces not the death of a stranger as in the previous two stories, but the death of someone to whom he is closely related. "Lord," he is informed, "he whom you love is ill" (11:3). The name of Lazarus is not mentioned, but Jesus knows instantly who it is. Jesus' compassion is rooted in his love. That is why his compassion amounts to more than pity, which can "sometimes connote slight contempt because the object is regarded as weak or inferior."[29] Jesus' compassion is his love in action. Rooted in love, it ennobles and empowers women and men touched by it.

As the story unfolds, we find Jesus at the house of Martha and Mary, sisters of the deceased Lazarus, in Bethany. Met by Mary and the Jews who have come to him weeping after Lazarus's death, Jesus "was greatly disturbed in spirit and deeply moved" (11:33). Jesus can hardly conceal the turmoil in his heart, turmoil he also experiences when faced with the death of men, women, and children in his company. He is disturbed in spirit and deeply moved by the pain death can inflict on people, by the suffering it causes human community, and by the despair it can bring to human beings.

The Lazarus story takes us even more deeply into the heart of Jesus. Jesus is told where Lazarus is buried, which is when Lazarus's death sinks into his mind and heart. "Jesus began to weep" (John 11:35). Jesus is deeply touched by the tragedy of death and by its relentlessness. His tears blend with the tears of Lazarus's sisters. The death of Lazarus brings Jesus and others together in the bond of tears and sorrow. It unites them in the communion of pain and suffering. From within this communion, with Jesus at its center, the power to live and to make life rises, awakening all to the reality of life eternal in the midst of life ephemeral.

Again in the Lazarus story, as in the stories of Jesus raising the widow's son and Jairus's daughter, no mention of sin is to be found. This is as it should be. For Jesus, death has nothing to do with what is known as sin against God; death is not inherited from our first ancestors. Yes, death poses an ultimate challenge to the meaning of life. It threatens humanity with extinction. It works to bury what human beings have achieved in the debris of the past. Jesus, like all of us, has to stare death in the face. But Jesus has not tried to legitimize death as something we deserve on account of sin. He has not attempted to justify death for the sake of God's honor and glory. Jesus does not need such a theology of death. If he does not need it, why should we need it? Why should the Christian church need it?

"The Child Is Not Dead but Sleeping"

This section begins with a closer look, in conjunction with the other two stories, at the story of Jesus raising Jairus's daughter. The incident probably took place at Capernaum on the northwestern shore of the Sea of Galilee. Unlike the story at Nain in which the death of the young man had already occurred when Jesus arrived on the scene, in this story Jairus the father seeks out Jesus and begs him to heal his daughter, who is "at the point of death," or "at her last gasp" (Mark 5:23).[30] This resembles the story of the raising of Lazarus, in which Jesus is also first told that Lazarus had fallen gravely ill. In both stories death occurs while Jesus is still on the way.

Why does this interval occur between the report of illness and death? In the Lazarus story, John, instead of having Jesus rush to Bethany straightaway, tells us that Jesus "stayed two days longer in the place where he was" (John 11:6), while Mark inserts a somewhat detailed account of Jesus healing a woman who suffers from hemorrhages (Mark 5:25-34). Evidently, there is a design in these delays. Is this because the storytellers want to convince the reader that death has actually occurred? Is it their purpose to demonstrate the power of Jesus over death, thus testifying to his divinity? Maybe. But is this the only explanation? Has something eluded our attention?

When Jesus finally reaches Jairus's house, he is greeted by "people weeping and wailing loudly" (Mark 5:38). It is a chaotic scene. Jairus's daughter had died at the age of twelve (5:42), and people are venting their uncontrollable sorrow, a spectacle common even today in Asian cities and villages. Jesus declares: "Why do you make a commotion and weep? The child is not dead but sleeping" (5:39). As soon as Jesus says this, people who had been weeping and wailing "laughed at him" (5:40). At first they must have thought they had misheard him. They are confused. And then they feel insulted. Is their loud wailing much ado about nothing? Be that as it may, the scene almost turns into a tragicomedy.

"The child is not dead but sleeping." This statement, it seems, and not the actual raising of Jairus's daughter with which the story ends, is the theological heart of the matter. It represents Jesus' theology of life and death, if Jesus had such a theology, in condensed form. The whole story revolves around the statement, and the meaning and message of the story has to be read in light of it. Without these words the story loses tension and intensity. Take away these words and the story becomes another story about the dead brought back to life. Remove these words and the story serves to illustrate and even to prove that Jesus is divine and endowed with divine power.

But the story is not about Jesus being either God or a human being. Nor does it concern God's intervention in the course of nature. It concerns the theology of life and death; it is a story about what it means for human beings to live and die, and to die and live. The words of Jesus give new meaning to the word *death* and invite us to regard death as a transition to a life no longer conditioned by it. Death, by fulfilling a task ordained by nature, consequently renders itself superfluous. Death dies and releases its grasp on life. Death is not "the last enemy to be destroyed," as Paul so passionately declared (1 Cor. 15:26), but a friend, as it were, who dies in order that others may live in the eternal embrace of God.

That is why Jairus's daughter, according to the story, is not dead but sleeping. What is the difference between death and sleep? Is the word *sleep* that Jesus uses a mere euphemism for death common in most languages and cultures? Or does he literally mean "sleeping" and seek to assure the people at the scene that the young girl is not dead? The answer must be neither. The girl is dead. The people know it for a fact, and Jesus does also. There is no need for Jesus to be euphemistic about the tragic reality of death or to give false hope to the people who have come to mourn, particularly to the child's parents.

But there is a true sense in which the dead are not dead. This is a negative statement, but how can it be stated in other than a negative way? We can of course choose to say that the dead are living. This is the basic belief behind the veneration of ancestors in Africa and Asia. Ancestors have crossed from the world of the living into the world of the dead, but they have not ceased to be. They have entered another mode of life. They are believed to return to the world of living to bestow blessings or to inflict misfortunes on the living, and are loved and feared at the same time. Even Confucius, an agnostic when it concerns gods, spirits, and the afterlife, when "offering sacrifice to his ancestors," is said to have "felt as if his ancestral spirits were actually present."[31] Ancestors for most Africans and Asians are not just dead. They are the living dead, that is, they are dead, yet living; living yet dead.

When Jesus declares that the girl is not dead but sleeping, he is not saying that the girl is among the living dead in the African or Asian fashion. Of course not. For Jesus, no less than for the people he is addressing, the girl is dead. But for Jesus, though not for the people, she is not dead in the sense of finished, gone, forever. In other words, death is not the final destination of life. It is not the end of a sentence. It is not the last act of a play. That is why the girl, even though dead, is sleeping.

"Sleeping" here is a metaphor, a figure of speech. The word does not indicate the kind of sleep we fall into at the end of the day, to wake up the following morning. The sleep in Mark 5:39 is a final sleep from which there is no waking again into everyday life. It is a sleep from which the dead wake into a totally different kind of life. We do not know what that life is like. Nor does Jesus know. But since "sleeping" is not the same as "dead," since it does not mean dead, it can be likened to the state of being in the womb of a mother in which a new life is nurtured, protected, and made to grow, develop, and mature.

The new life in the mother's womb has consciousness, even though it is undifferentiated consciousness. Its personhood is in the making. Its humanity is in formation. We can say that the new life in the mother's womb is in the state of sleep, though it is not an idle sleep, not an indifferent sleep, not an inert sleep. Just the contrary. It is a sleep that is filled with activity, energy, life-force, and promise. It is a sleep that provides all that is necessary for the creation of a new life.

We can say this and more about the new life in the womb of a mother. With our medical and technological know-how, we can observe life in the mother's womb. We can see the miraculous happenings in the womb and follow them at every stage, even every minute, along the way. We have no such know-how to observe the sleep of the dead. But if what we observe in the mother's womb is any clue, this much we can say about the sleep the dead have entered: it is a sleep in which a new life-force is at work to bring about a new life, a life that no longer needs the service of death for transition from one kind of life into another. It is a sleep in which creation of a new life is taking place, just as the creation of heavens and earth took place in the womb of God at the beginning of time.

"The child is not dead," says Jesus, "but sleeping." Would Jesus agree that the theology of life and death expounded above is implied in these words? Does he expect a theology of death and life to be developed from what he says in this particular situation? I do not know. But when we turn to the Lazarus story we not only hear, to our amazement, almost the same thing all over again, but are led even more deeply into Jesus' thoughts on death.

As we recall, Jesus set out for Bethany two days after he had been informed of Lazarus's illness. The next thing we hear is what he says to the disciples: "Our friend Lazarus has fallen asleep, but I am going there to awaken him" (John 11:11).[32] The disciples do not quite follow what this means. They are half-believing and half-doubting (*ban xin ban yi*), to use a Chinese expression. "Lord," they say to Jesus, "if he has fallen asleep, he will be all right" (11:12). This exchange between Jesus and the disciples is the storyteller's subtle way of preparing the reader for the real issue—the issue of life and death.

"Lazarus is dead" (11:14), Jesus says in response, thus making absolutely clear what he means by Lazarus having fallen asleep. Death is not just death and sleep is not just sleep. When death is perceived as sleep in the womb, in which a new life is created and from which a new life is to be born, death is less than death. It is not death. The word *death* as commonly understood does not exist anymore. Death is no more. Lazarus is not dead. He has fallen asleep to be born into a new life.

"You Would See the Glory of God"

The Lazarus story at this point fills the reader with anticipation. But the storyteller is not in a hurry. He lets the story move slowly but surely, letting events take their course. There is a distance of more than thirty kilometers to cover from "across the Jordan" (John 10:40), where Jesus had been, to Bethany.[33] Moving scenes depict his meeting with the tearful Martha and Mary, punctuated with what must be the author's deep thoughts on resurrection, perhaps projecting the death of Lazarus as a fait accompli. Even when Jesus is finally led to the tomb, the storyteller takes time to inform the reader how Jesus weeps for his beloved friend, and how Martha objects to his command to remove the stone that covers the entrance to the grave, again intimating that Lazarus is truly dead.

Then, and only then, does this "last and greatest miracle story in he Gospel of John" happen.[34] What is this miracle? The storyteller answers when he has Jesus say: "Did I not tell you that if you believed, you would see the glory of God?" (11:40). The sealed grave is not the glory of God, but the judgment of God. The dead buried in the grave do not tell of the glory of God but of the cruelty of God. The stone that keeps the world of the dead from the world of the living defies the glory of God and projects the darkness of God. The women and men mourning the death of Lazarus before the grave are not witnesses to the glory of God but to a God that needs the pain, suffering, and death of human beings to make up for the dishonor done to God.

The Genesis story of Adam and Eve links death with sin. God punishes them for their infringement upon the order God has given them. Ever since, fear of this God has been infused into the minds and hearts of generation after generation of believing men and women. There is always a God of darkness casting a shadow over the God of light. A God who is easily offended is never far from the God who forgives and saves. Preachers and theologians never let the women and men at an evangelical rally or at a worship service forget what an enormous price God has to pay for the sin they have inherited from Adam and Eve, and for the sin that they commit themselves.

But Jesus in the Lazarus story and in the stories of raising the young man at Nain and the daughter of Jairus, tells us a very different story about God. Jesus shows us a glorious God not overshadowed by darkness, who thus is able to overcome darkness. He shares with us the vision of the God whose love is not withdrawn because of the sin human beings are said to have committed. He bears witness to a God who is life itself, in whom there is no death, and for whom death does not make sense. It is into this God that the young man at Nain, the daughter of Jairus, and Lazarus have fallen asleep, to be created anew for a life with God and in God.

It is also into this God that we shall all fall asleep to be born again, into God in whom "there is no darkness"—and one may add, no death—"at all" (1 John 1:5). It is this vision of life in God that the same John, who told us the marvelous story of Jesus raising Lazarus, sees in "a great multitude that no one could count, from every nation, from all tribes and peoples and languages, standing before the throne and before the Lamb, robed in white, with palm branches in their hands" (Rev. 7:9). This is a glorious vision in which

> They will hunger no more, and thirst no more;
> the sun will not strike them,
> nor any scorching heat;
> for the Lamb at the center of the throne
> will be their shepherd,
> and he will guide them
> to springs of the water of life,
> and God will wipe away every tear from their eyes.
> (7:16-17)

This vision of life in God is a vision of faith, hope, and love. With a vision such as this we can return to the world in which we toil and labor to face pain and suffering.

Chapter 5

In the World There Is Suffering

To be awakened to the real meaning of death as life, to contemplate the eternal in the temporal, to realize the really real in the midst of the phenomenal and ephemeral, and to be inspired by a vision of life hereafter beyond the life here and now are the goals many spiritual seekers and religious practitioners endeavor to attain. But in spite of ourselves, seasons change, days and nights come and go, and the world of tension and conflict continues. We feel pain when pricked even by a tiny thorn, and we are hurt by unrequited kindness or love.

The changing seasons, the rising and setting of the sun, the demands of daily life, and the hurt felt in the body and the spirit—such things bring us back from detached contemplation to the life of the senses. Some great Zen masters are aware of this truth. Perhaps to be aware of it is part of enlightenment. Pai-chang (720–814), a Zen master in China during the Tang dynasty, is famous for one of the rules he laid down for his monastery, namely, "a day without work—a day without eating." He practiced what he preached. "When in his old age the monks took away his garden tools in order to spare his dwindling strength, he was true to his own directives and refused to eat until they would return his tools to him."[1]

There is a Buddhist story called "The Old Woman Burns an Ascetic's Hut." It speaks to this deep insight into our relatedness to the world that the ascetic has striven to transcend.

A long time ago an old woman provided for an ascetic for as long as twenty years. She used to have her twenty-eight-year-old daughter bring meals to him and wait on him.

One day when the young woman brought the meals to the ascetic as usual, she held him in her arms and asked him: "What do you feel?"

The ascetic replied: "Dry wood leaning on a chilly rock with no warmth after three winters."

When she returned home, she reported to her mother what had taken place.

Hearing what her daughter told her, the old woman became angry and said: "He for whom I have made provisions for twenty years is merely a man with no culture!"

She then drove the ascetic out from the hut and burnt it to the ground.[2]

What are we to make of this story? Is it a story of how the ascetic passed the last test and gained enlightenment? Is it an illustration of the Buddhist prejudice against women that sees them as an impediment to men's attainment of the Buddhahood?[3] Does the story imply that the old woman does not deserve the nirvana on account of her outrageous treatment of the ascetic? The story, however, is not intended to convey any of these ideas.

The moral of this Buddhist story consists of something else entirely. As the old woman sees it, the ascetic, after twenty years, should already have grasped the heart of the Buddha's teaching. He should have been liberated from preoccupation with his own self. What she tries to do, then, is to get him to return to family and society, to live in the world of love and hate, and to be a light to men and women submerged in "the sea of bitterness," or *ku hai*, as Buddhists characterize the world—to be "a man with culture." That is why she burns his hut, forcing him to leave it for the world of toil and labor.[4]

The perception of life and the world as full of adversities and sufferings is not limited to Buddhism. It shapes almost all religious beliefs and practices, and occupies a central place in most religious thought and teachings. This is no less true with Christianity. I believe it is at the level of the human experience of suffering that deep "human heartedness"—*agape* in Christianity, *jen* in Confucianism, or *bhakti* in Hinduism—can be fostered and genuine religious discourses developed. Does this not require of us Christians to look in more depth at the story in Genesis—describing our human lot to suffer—that we studied in the previous chapter?

Nikita's Story

To begin with, let us first listen to the story of Nikita Arteaga, a five-year-old girl from Petaluma, California, who when merely twenty-two months old was diagnosed with leukemia. Her life afterward was a heroic struggle against this "demon of ill health or curse of disease" (*bing mo*), to use a Chinese expression, involving her parents, relatives, friends, doctors, and nurses. What follows is an abridged version of the newspaper account:

Nikita Arteaga curled up like a newborn, pushing her nearly bald head up against her mother's chest, stroking her long hair. When she is very sick she is no longer five years old. She seeks solace in the past and in her mother's constant touch. On March 25 [1995], the day after Nikita tried to ride her new pink bike for the first time, her family got the news they prayed would never come—that Nikita had a second relapse.

Her bone marrow was packed with cancer cells. Her head had swollen and her legs ached so much she woke up screaming. Her doctors at Kaiser Hospital said Nikita had four, maybe six months to live. The cancer was also crowding out the platelets that cause clotting in her blood, making Nikita bruise easily. The half moons of pale skin under her eyes were blackened. There were faint blue circles on her arms. Even when Nikita fell asleep under her flowery quilt in the hospital, hooked up to tubes that dripped drugs into her heart, she folded her arms tight and grimaced.

Nikita has waited nearly a year for a perfect bone marrow match to be found—more than two million people have been screened through a global donor registry, with no success.

Most of all, her family is praying. . . . [5]

Sometimes Nikita showed signs of improvement. The family took her to visit some of her favorite cousins. She even wanted to go to Disneyland. Her parents were hopeful. "Maybe she's going to develop a cure for leukemia. Maybe God has intended for her to live to be 95 years old."[6] But Nikita did not live to be ninety-five years old. She succumbed to leukemia and died a few weeks later.

Nikita's story is the story of many children afflicted with incurable diseases. It is also the story of women and men engaged in life-and-death struggles against deadly viruses and cancerous growth in their bodies. Nikita's story, in short, is the story of human beings who, in spite of the spectacular scientific and technological culture of our time, have to fight life-threatening diseases such as cancer, heart disease, AIDS, or Alzheimer's disease, not to mention ailments from asthma to epilepsy, from flu to chronic pain. A world immune from lethal viruses? A life free from disease? Surely, this is a dream that will never come true.

A Disease Called Poverty

There is a disease called "poverty" in this postmodern world—a disease bred by the industrialization that created a global economy, which now dictates the life of peoples and the destiny of nations. This is particularly true in the so-called Third World, the latecomer and victim in a world in which the profit and prosperity of the rich and powerful, both in the East and West, make the rules. Farmland yields to factories. Forests cannot stop the march of bulldozers. As a result, people in rural areas, in a desperate effort for survival, migrate to the cities en masse, creating the chronic poverty that endangers the body, mind, and spirit, all in the ruthless race to profit from the free-market economy.

The seriousness of the Third World situation is apparent in a study done by the World Health Organization. "Rapid urbanization and the increase in urban population," it is reported,

are recognized as being among the major challenges for health development in the 1990s and in the decades to come. Between 1950 and 1980 the world's urban population increased from 701 million to 1983 million, or from 25 percent to 41 percent of the total world population; by the year 2000 this population will be 50 percent. Change has been particularly rapid in the South, where the scale of urban growth is unprecedented in human history and cities have experienced growth rates two to three times higher than those of industrialized countries in the past. Between 1990 and 2025, the total urban population in "developing countries" is projected to increase threefold, to 4000 million or 61 percent of the population.[7]

The reality presented in these statistics should cause great concern. This massive exodus of people from rural areas to cities radically upsets the ecological balance and seriously reduces the spiritual well-being of the human community. And it is going to defeat the prosperity and wealth achieved in the cities.

Proliferating in many urban centers in the Third World, continues the World Health Organization study, are slums in which "the poor are exposed to the health risks of modernization and suffer the consequences of social and psychological instability as the traditional support structures of the rural area steadily disappear."[8] When most of four billion people among the urban population of developing countries, if projections for the year 2025 are accurate, are condemned to destitute conditions, there must be something terribly wrong. These are symptoms of an industrial economy that has enriched the few at the cost of many. If as many as 61 percent of inhabitants in the urban centers are subjected to "malnutrition, infectious diseases, and degenerative diseases,"[9] the picture of the world as a global village of progress and affluence is nothing but a chimera.

What we see in the World Health Organization's study is not abstract and hypothetical. Each number represents a man, woman, or child who goes to bed with an empty stomach. Each percentage point stands for a group of human beings living in the poverty-stricken quarter of a city afflicted with "diseases of poverty." Imagine a city such as Calcutta, India, for example. "For the millions of exiles who crowded its slums, Calcutta," writes Dominique Lapierre in *The City of Joy*, a novel based on true stories, "represented neither culture nor history. For them it meant only a faint hope of finding some crumbs to survive until the next day."[10] Such extreme congestion and poverty give rise to health hazards. "In summer the proliferation of filth brought with it the risk of epidemics. Not so very long ago it was still a common occurrence for people to die of cholera, hepatitis, encephalitis, typhoid, and rabies."[11]

We human beings seem to be in an endless race against disease. In spite of notable successes, there are diseases that continue to defy human efforts to control and eradicate them. Even after cures are found for certain tenacious ailments, new ones wreak havoc. Are we safer, thanks to the progress in biological and medical sciences, from diseases at the end of the twentieth century than our predecessors at the turn of the last century? Not really. "New viruses and drug-resistant bacteria," it has been reported, "are reversing human victories over infectious disease.... Humanity once had the hubris to think it could control or even conquer all these microbes. But anyone who reads today's headlines knows how vain that hope turned out to be. New scourges are emerging—AIDS is not the only one—and older diseases like tuberculosis are rapidly evolving into forms that are resistant to antibiotics."[12]

This is a frightful picture. After the superhuman efforts of scientists to combat life-threatening viruses and bacteria, and the almost religious dedication to their eradication, these viruses and bacteria are returning with a vengeance, proving to be "new scourges" to postmodern humanity. The subtitle to the *Time* cover story quoted above—"Are we losing the war against infectious diseases?"— is more than just a rhetorical question. It is posed with the expectation of a pessimistic answer: Yes, we are losing the war against infectious diseases.

As with many other threats to quality of life, with regard to infectious disease developing countries are most at risk. "The danger is greatest, of course, in the underdeveloped world," *Time* observes, "where epidemics of cholera, dysentery and malaria are spawned by war, poverty, overcrowding and poor sanitation."[13] War is of particular concern in the Third World. Tribal wars turn people into ferocious animals that massacre one another. Civil wars result in ruined homes and family members dead or scattered. Ethnic and religious wars have caused hundreds of thousands of women, men, and children to starve, to contract disease, or to die in refugee camps. Wars in these and other forms pose deadly threats to the well-being of the human community in the underdeveloped world. Or it would be more accurate to say that such wars keep certain countries in the developed world "underdeveloped," and their people subject to the tyranny of epidemic.

The vulnerability of Third World countries is real. But it does not mean that the developed parts of the world can be safe from the attack of malicious viruses and bacteria. The fact is that the "microbial world knows no boundaries. For all the vaunted power of modern medicine, deadly infections are a growing threat to everyone, everywhere. Hardly a week goes by without reports of outbreaks in the U.S. and other developed nations."[14] There is neither east nor west, neither north nor south in the microbial world. The microbial world is also an ecumenical world, an *oikoumene* (a whole inhabited world) in Greek. In this world it makes no difference whether you are Buddhist or Christian, Jew or Hindu, Taoist or Muslim. We all cohabit the microbial world irrespective of gender, race, creed, or class.

This is a dangerous world in which we live and a precarious life we lead, perhaps more dangerous and precarious than the "primitive" times when our ancestors lived in caves and in isolated hamlets. But even this list of dangers has not exhausted the threats to the well-being of the global human community. We cannot but acknowledge that "hardly a day passes without news about a major or complex emergency happening in some part of the world. Disasters continue to strike and cause destruction in developing and developed countries alike, raising people's concern about their vulnerability to occurrences that can gravely affect day-to-day life and their future."[15] Each of us is hardly a stranger to disasters. If we ourselves are not caught, the devastation on the other side of the globe is immediately brought into our homes through television. The TV gives us a realistic sense of being among the victims. We are neighbors in a global village, even though most of us remain unrelated, or often hostile to one another on account of ethnicity, politics, or religion.

Thorns and Thistles

Indeed, the world in which we live is no disease-free Garden of Eden. Nor do we live in a paradise untouched by disasters, whether caused by whims of nature or created by human atrocities. This fact of life did not dawn on Gautama Siddhartha, the prince, until his first excursion into the city from his carefully protected life in the palace. Legend or not, his experience is a notable exception, for human beings for thousands of years, from Paleolithic times to today's technological culture, have known that life is hard. What is driven home to human beings is our vulnerability. We are vulnerable to the elements of nature. We are vulnerable to the invisible forces in the universe. We are vulnerable to the disease and pain that overwhelm our lives. We are even vulnerable to one another as human beings endowed with the ability to destroy one another in pursuit of power and greed, and in the name of the God or gods we worship. What is the true nature of this human vulnerability? The true nature of this vulnerability is suffering.

This vulnerability to suffering has haunted human beings. Philosophers reflect on suffering in order to get around it. Poets lament suffering, and sing about it in verses and hymns. Artists embrace suffering, and derive the power to create works of art that transcend it. As for religions, whether popular or official, human vulnerability engages the religious mind in search of deliverance. Types of deliverance differ from one religion to another. Buddhism, for example, faces suffering and trains the body and the mind to be detached from it. Popularized Taoism devotes effort to concocting an elixir of life to circumvent it. In Christianity we have both one of the most realistic accounts of suffering and, in retrospect, one of the most controversial. I am referring, of course, to the story in the third chapter of Genesis.

This Genesis story has been routinely understood as the story of the fall from God's grace. It is on this story of the Fall, as we have seen in our discourse on death, that the Christian church has constructed its edifice of beliefs and teachings, from creation to sin to incarnation to election to salvation. These beliefs and teachings of the church have been paraphrased, adapted, and even twisted from pulpits, in theological treatises, and in religious tracts to teach believers how to deal with the misfortunes of life. This was true in centuries past and it is also true today.

In *The Plague,* Albert Camus tells the very human drama of how the citizens of Oran, Algeria, fought the plague that suddenly struck them in the 1940s. Camus narrates tragic dramas of people dying from the plague, heroic dramas of a few doctors and medical personnel dedicated to fighting it day and night at the risk of their lives, heart-rending dramas of how the citizens of Oran were completely segregated from the rest of the world. In the midst of all these high dramas created by the plague, the church authorities organized a week of prayer to be concluded with a high mass on Sunday. Father Paneloux, a Jesuit priest, "a stalwart champion of Christian doctrine at its most precise and purest, equally remote from modern laxity and the obscurantism of the past,"[16] was assigned to deliver a sermon at the mass.

The cathedral was packed during the week of prayer. On Sunday, a huge congregation overfilled it. Mounting the pulpit, Father Paneloux, a celebrated churchman and learned theologian, "launched at the congregation his opening phrase in clear, emphatic voice: 'Calamity has come on you, my brethren, and my brethren, you deserve it.'"[17] Already rendered fearful, sad, and weak by the rampant plague, the congregation was not prepared for such theological bombast. But Father Paneloux went on in the same vein:

> Yes, the hour has come for serious thought. You fondly imagined it was enough to visit God on Sundays, thus you could make free of your weekdays. You believed some brief formalities, some bending of the knee, would recompense Him well enough for your criminal indifference. But God is not mocked. These brief encounters could not sate the fierce hunger of His love. He wished to see you longer and more often; that is His manner of loving and, indeed, it is the only manner of loving. And this is why, wearied of waiting for you to come to Him, He loosed on you this visitation; as he has visited all the cities that offended against Him, since the dawn of history. Now you are learning your lesson, the lesson that was learned by Cain and his offsprings, by the people of Sodom and Gomorrah, by Job and Pharaoh, by all that hardened their hearts against Him. And like them you have been beholding mankind and all creation with new eyes, since the gates of this city closed on you and on the pestilence. Now at last, you know the hour has struck to bend your thoughts to first and last things.[18]

This was the 1940s and not the premodern days of previous centuries. Do not sermons preached today sometimes still smack of the theology displayed in Father Paneloux's sermon? To some of his congregation "the sermon simply brought home the fact that they had been sentenced, for an unknown crime, to an indeterminate period of punishment."[19] As for Father Paneloux himself, he too was to die from the plague shortly after he had preached his sermon.

This is a pulpit eloquence conditioned by a myopic view of history and an arbitrary and thus dogmatic interpretation of the realities that confront human community. The speech turns God into a sadistic monster who satisfies God's insatiable hunger for love and devotion at the enormous cost of human lives. This kind of belief in God, preached from the pulpit and taught at Sunday school, in Bible study, and even in theological classrooms, has become part of popular Christian faith. Such facts are not only true of Christianity, but of other religions as well. But the heartening fact is that both within Christianity and other religions there have been efforts to reevaluate such traditional and popular beliefs about diseases and disasters. As far as Christians are concerned, we must begin with our biblical story of the Fall and explore it in relation to how human beings live, toil, and die in the womb of God's creation.

This brings us back to the story in Genesis 3:1-19. When we leave out God's command, human disobedience, and the divine punishments, the story presents quite a different picture. It even gives us a bundle of deep insights into the reality of life and the world—insights rooted in the lived experiences of men and women regardless of where and when they live. This is the genius of the story often ignored by the teachings of the Christian church exemplified in Father Paneloux's sermon.

This consideration leads to an important question as to the integrity of the story in Genesis 3:1-19. Most of us are used to reading the story as a series of happenings. First the serpent seduces the woman into resentment of God's command not to eat the forbidden fruit. This event is followed not only by Eve eating the fruit herself, but by her sharing it with her husband. Then comes God's discovery of the offense, leading to the couple's expulsion from the garden. The story ends with God's pronouncement of punishments to the offenders, first the serpent, then the woman, and lastly the man. What we have is thus supposed to be one story with a beginning and an ending—a story of how human beings have to go through hardships in life as the result of their "fall" from God's favor, which came about because they dared to question and defy the validity of God's command.

This way of reading the story assumes that it is all one piece, that it was composed as one uninterrupted story and meant to be treated as such. But is this assumption correct? Is not the story as we have it perhaps made up of more than one story? Are there not stories in the story? Can we not at least separate, for example, the story of the punishments from the story of expulsion from the garden? That is to say, are there not two originally separate stories woven into one story? There are strong indications that this could have been the case. "There is a remarkable difference in content," it is pointed out, "between the punishment of expulsion and the punishments in vv. 14-19. The former is firmly fixed in the structure of the narrative inasmuch as God put people in the garden—God drove people out of the garden. The punishments in vv. 14-19 on the contrary have no direct relationship with the offense: they describe factually the present state of existence of serpent, woman and man which by way of after-thought are explained as punishments."[20]

This is an observation of critical importance, particularly the observation that the idea of punishment is "an after-thought"; that is, it is a thought that gains attention *only after* the punishment links with the expulsion part to become one story. Taken as an originally independent piece, the so-called punishments are in fact no punishments at all. They are examples of the hardships human beings go through in life and some instances of trials they encounter in the world. These are accounts of how human beings fare in their everyday living. In short, "they describe factually the present state of existence" and have nothing to do with divine punishments.

The hardships to which the story of Genesis 3:14-19 refers is not told in a detached fashion, stated impersonally, or related in resignation. These and many other hardships and trials point up one fundamental reality of life in the world: the suffering and pain that accompany life from the cradle to the grave. Implicit in these accounts of hardships and trials is one deep-rooted religious question of why life in the world cannot take place without suffering and pain. This of course is a universal question that has motivated people in different places and times to search for answers. How does the story in Hebrew Scripture deal with this universal and, I must add, perennial question in its account of human hardships and trials? To engage with this question, let us first look into the part of the story that describes childbirth.

"In Pain You Shall Bring Forth Children"

Childbirth for women is accompanied by acute pain. They are called "pangs of birth" for good reason. Even today, when methods such as prenatal exercise, medication, and anesthesia are available, the experience is a great ordeal. The ordeal was much greater when such means were not available. It was not un-common for women to lose their life while giving birth. The biblical story is absolutely right. In pain, it says, women shall bring forth children.

But in spite of the pain and risks involved, is giving birth to a child consid-ered something to be avoided at any cost? Does it enter the woman's mind that childbirth is a punishment from God? Does it occur to any woman that child-birth carries the stigma of divine displeasure, due to the episode in which the first ancestors were expelled from the Garden of Eden? No such questions would cross the mind of the woman giving birth. None would enter the thoughts of those celebrating a new life.

But let not theologians, particularly male theologians like myself, dwell on birthing. Do not let church authorities, which have often consisted of male bishops, priests, and ministers, pontificate on a matter they are incapable of experiencing firsthand. Instead, let us listen to how an old woman in a small Bedouin community in Egypt, for example, tells what it means to give birth to a child. She has given birth to many children and acted as midwife for all her sons' children. This is what she says to the anthropologist who reproduced the story:

"Does the woman cry?" I had asked. "Does she scream?"

"If she has sense she doesn't cry. If she has a strong will, she doesn't scream. But if she's like these women," she had said, turning to her daughters-in-law, "she makes noise like this."

They had all laughed, these women who had given birth so often, as one of them mimicked for me the moans and screams of childbirth.

The old woman went on. "Then I say, 'Listen. Hold your breath.' This is so the kid comes out right away. When the kid comes out, I hold it face up. I hold the umbilical cord, like this"—she made the gesture of milking an udder and added, "If the afterbirth doesn't come out, I gently massage the cord, with my hand. This is birth as we do it. . . ."

When I asked if any of the other old women in the camp, Migdim for example, knew how to deliver babies, she snorted. "Once I came and found Migdim and the other old woman just sitting there with one of the twins lying on the floor next to its mother. I told them, "Why don't you lend a hand? You've given birth before. What's the matter with you? What are you being bashful about? Why don't you get close? . . .">[21]

"What are you being bashful about?" says the old mother to the hesitant Migdim and the other old woman. Birthing is the most natural thing in the world. There is nothing to be bashful about. It is a fact of life. There is nothing to be afraid of.

Notice the absence of any religious reservation about birthing in the old woman's account, this in a Bedouin community today that must share many of the ways of life and views of the world with ancient Israel. She tells what she knows matter-of-factly. Does this not give unexpected support to our view that the reality of life depicted in Genesis 3:14-19 has nothing to do with the story of the expulsion from the garden that preceded it?

The last idea that would occur to the old Bedouin woman is that birthing is a punishment from God inflicted on women. Just the contrary. When we listen to what else she has to say, we know at once why.

Midwifing has great recompense. I mean God rewards it. I swear to God, these hands here and these legs strain. And I won't even talk about what sometimes comes down on my hands. My arms will be swimming in blood. Only after the woman finishes and is fine, only then do they get me soap and hot water. I wash my hands and my body and my hair. I take off everything I was wearing.

"There's lot of blood? You don't get disgusted?" I can't help asking.

"No. Because it is a righteous act, you don't get disgusted."[22]

This personal account of an old Bedouin mother who taught herself to deliver babies must describe an experience common to women engaged in midwifery all over the world, even to doctors and nurses working in today's well-equipped hospital delivery rooms.

"Midwifing has great recompense," the old woman said. Then in order not to be misunderstood she quickly added: "I mean God rewards it." She gives a profound statement in a few simple words; a deep religious insight into what birthing means in a short sentence. Yes, the woman giving birth has to moan and scream with great pain. Yes, giving birth, to quote other women in that Bedouin community, "is as hard as war",[23] still it is a war with rewards from God. The entire event is a real-life drama. A new life in the mother's womb struggles to be born, and the mother bears the pain—the pain of the flesh of her flesh tearing away from her, the pain of the life of her life separating from her. But it is "a righteous act," according to the old Bedouin woman—righteous in the sight of God and before generations of humanity. Blood from the mother's womb is the testimony to that righteous act. How then could birthing with blood be disgusting to God, to the woman in labor, to the midwife, nurses, and doctors?

Look at the smile on the face of the mother who has just given birth. Is there a sweeter, more satisfied, and loving smile in the world? It is the smile of the same woman who has just gone through tremendous agony and pain. Is not that smile the greatest reward from God? Think of the smiles on the faces of the midwife, doctors, or nurses who have just delivered the baby. These are smiles of great achievement, smiles for having participated in bringing a new life into the world, smiles for having been able to be part of the mystery called life. And imagine the joy that news of the birth brings to family members, relatives, and friends. The newborn child becomes a bond between its mother and father, a tie that binds men and women that constitute the family and the community.

The joy is not a divine punishment for a "sinful" act committed in a remote past in the garden, but God's gift of a new life. As for the pain women have to go through, it is not a penalty for the sin of disobedience allegedly committed by Eve, the first woman, but a reminder that the life to be born is God's reward for the great labor exerted. Birthing, with all its moaning and screaming induced by excruciating pain, is not a divine curse.

Did not God have to bring forth life out of the womb of "the earth [that] was a formless void and darkness [that] covered the face of the deep" (Gen. 1:2)? Did not God's creation begin in pain? Is not the pain the woman experiences in pregnancy, and that culminates in the pangs of birth, part of the pain of the creation that came out of the womb of darkness? Did not God see "everything that God had made, and indeed, it was very good" (Gen. 1:31)? Is it not true that God, in crowning the labor of giving birth to the heavens and the earth and all things in them, "blessed the seventh day and hallowed it, because on it God rested from all the work that God had done in creation" (Gen. 2:3)?

As a matter of fact, in biblical cultures as well as in most other cultures it is barrenness, not birthing, that is regarded as divine punishment. Consider, for instance, the story of Sarah, Abraham's wife, who was taken by Abimelech, king of Gerar, to be his consort because Abraham had said she was his sister (Gen. 20:1-18).[24] As the result of God's timely intervention in Abimelech's dream, Sarah was returned to Abraham unharmed. But before the incident came to a happy end, Abimelech had to pay the price for what he had done. God "had closed fast all the wombs of the house of Abimelech because of Sarah, Abraham's wife" (20:18). The story of Jacob and his two wives, Leah and Rachel, also illustrates how a woman with no children was considered to be the result, if not of God's punishment, then at least of God's displeasure. This displeasure is what Jacob referred to when he angrily said to Rachel, the childless wife, "Am I in the place of God, who has withheld from you the fruit of the womb?" (Gen. 30:2).

The well-known story of Hannah (1 Sam. 1:1—2:11) also begins with the fact of barrenness. Hannah, one of the wives of Elkanah, became an easy target of taunt and disdain because, according to the storyteller, "the Lord had closed her womb" (1:5). But events were to take an unexpected turn. She was to be blessed with a child named Samuel, who later was to become the prophet and kingmaker. The story captures the gratitude and joy of Hannah in verses attributed to her when she dedicated her child to God at the Temple:

> My heart exults in the Lord;
> my strength is exalted in my God.
> My mouth derides my enemies,
>   because I rejoice in my victory.
>   (2:1)

These are words from the heart of a vindicated woman. Giving birth to a child is a cause of celebration. It is a victory. What a contrast these words make to Hannah when she "was deeply distressed and . . . wept bitterly" (1:10), praying to God to grant her a child!

This is the story of Hannah, but it is not hers alone. It is the story of women, both past and present, who have not been able to conceive. The story of stories that continues to be celebrated today not only by Christians, but by people all over the world, is the story of Christmas, the story of the birth of Jesus. In that story the words of Hannah many centuries before are heard again on the lips of a young woman called Mary, destined to become the mother of Jesus:

> My soul magnifies the Lord,
>   and my spirit rejoices in God my Savior,
> for God has looked with favor on
>   the lowliness of God's servant.
> Surely, from now on all generations
>   will call me blessed. . . . (Luke 1:46-48)

Giving birth to a child is a divine event as well as a human event. It is a "magnificat." It is a *magnificent* event, a result of God's blessing. How could generations before and after Mary not help magnifying God for each and every birth?

"The Magnificat of the Midwife" is a poem that brings into bright and colorful relief the event of Jesus' birth. These poetic verses, down-to-earth in language and sublime in meaning, dramatize this most human event of birthing into a miracle of life and sing the words to the glory of God.

> My soul proclaims the greatness and glory of God,
> and my spirit exalts in God my Savior,
> For God has permitted me to witness a holy birth,
> The Christ Child come into the world.
> When she who was chosen labored,
> I was by her side.
> I held her hand as she was seized by pangs of birth,
> Assuring her that she was not alone,
> And that this piercing pain would soon pass.
> I witnessed the crowning, Glory be to God,
> The moment new life emerged,
> Speaking softly to ease the mother's fear and apprehension.
> Helping to sever the cord, I raised the infant in my hands,
> Wiped blood from his wiggling infant body,
> And wrapped him tightly in soft cloth.
> At that moment, I could have sworn that angels were singing,
> And that the star-filled night shone on him alone.
> Never will I forget that night—
> That night when new life was born
> So quietly, so gently, in a dung-filled stable.
> Always will I remember
> That the birth of the Holy
> Comes in this way:
> With pangs of labor,
> With apprehension,
> With blood and with tears,
> Always giving way,
> In due course,
> As they did on this most wondrous of nights
> To hope,
> To faith,
> To love,
> And to Life.[25]

It is hard to find a commentary, an exegesis, or a theology that can surpass these verses on Mary's Magnificat.

Giving birth to a life is a human-divine drama in love. Love, not punishment, is the power that generates life. Birthing is a divine-human act of faith that brings joy and thanksgiving. Childbirth is an act of hope between human beings and God, hope that each childbirth represents a new beginning of God with human beings and human beings with God. Without such love, faith, and hope, how can we as women and men venture into life in and with God from here to eternity, a life full of toil and labor? Is not the entire life of Jesus such a journey?

"In Toil You Shall Eat All the Days of Your Life"

If women give birth to a child *in pain,* men are to provide daily sustenance also *in pain* all the days of their life (Gen. 3:17b).[26] It is interesting to note that the same Hebrew word (*'itsabon*) used for women's labor pain is also used to describe the work men have to do to earn a living. Although women's labor pain is unique to women, the pain associated with the toil of earning daily bread does not belong to men alone. In the cultures shaped by patriarchal system and structure, women toil much harder than men. Even in this postmodern world, in which more women are joining the labor force and assuming managerial responsibilities, most still have to cope with the double "labor pain" of childbearing and working outside the home to support their family.

What the biblical storyteller wants to suggest must be that in a society in which men were almost solely responsible for providing for the family, the pain from their toil and labor was not easier to bear than the pain women had to go through in childbearing. In other words, pain is the lot of all human beings, whether men or women. "By the sweat of your face," continues the storyteller, "you shall eat bread until you return to the ground" (Gen. 3:19). This statement applies to both men and women today and in olden days.

The biblical story is right. "In pain," that is, "in toil" (NRSV) and "by labor" (REB), "you shall eat of [the ground] all the days of your life." To live one has to toil. To be a useful member of a human community one has to labor. Life without toil and labor can be a boring life. Such is an unproductive life, a life "lived in the state of drunkenness and in the dream of death" (*zui sheng meng si*), to use a Chinese expression. Toil and labor is, of course, not limited to the physical part of existence. There are mental spiritual labors. Toil and labor stands for the entire range of human activity, physical, mental, moral, and spiritual. The terms encompass the creative force with which human beings are endowed.

In the remains of human civilizations since prehistoric times, be they flint stones used by our most ancient ancestors for hunting and farming, ruins of temples and shrines, engravings of animals on cave walls, paintings and sculptures by great masters both in the East and the West, theaters and playhouses, music, poetry, stories, spaceships, satellites, or computers, one sees the fruits of human toil and labor. Civilization begins not only at Suma,[27] but also in Greece, China, and Egypt. As inheritors of past civilizations and makers of modern civilization, how can we dismiss all creative efforts as nothing but as consequences of human defiance against God and the expressions of human hubris to be like God?

Toil as such has nothing to do with divine punishment. Labor is human vocation, and as such it keeps our body, mind, and spirit active and healthy, enables life to continue from generation to generation, creates well-being for family and society, and contributes to the maintenance of God's creation. This is what the poem "I Am a Child of Burma" tells us:

> If anyone asks you who I am,
> Just tell them, "I am a child of Burma."
>
> My sweat mingles with its soil and waters.
> With the peasants, I have tilled the earth,
> planted, nurtured and harvested the rice,
> and carried the produce to every village,
> so my brothers and sisters will be nourished.
> I have fished its waters and hunted its forests
> and I know every inch of its rich resources.
> The dusty paths which crisscross my motherland
> have been marked by my footprints,
> and its mountains, valleys and rivers
> have heard my voice.[28]

One can almost see in these lines the young Burmese poet with a hoe in his hand, working side by side with the farmers. One can hear him sing in these verses as he delivers the fruits of his toil to kith and kin. One dances with him with the rhythm of this song as he ascends to the mountains and descends to the valleys and rivers. Yes, "in pain we shall eat all the days of our life." And yes, "by the sweat of our face we shall eat rice until we return to the ground." But it is the pain of joy. It is the sweat of blessing. To toil and labor is not punishment imposed on human beings by God. Just the contrary. Work brings to those who toil and labor joy and blessing from God. Did not God create human beings "to till the ground" (Gen. 2:5) and "to be fruitful and multiply" (Gen. 1:28)?

"Thorns and Thistles"

Unfortunately, however, we have not yet heard the end of the poem. The Burmese poet still intones:

> If anyone asks you who I am,
> just tell them, "I am a child of Burma."

But this is not the same child of Burma that he once was. His verses take an abrupt turn. His song changes its tune. The rhythm of his poem shows signs of disturbance. He now muses pensively:

> My tears have flowed for those who suffer.
> My arms have held the children
> whose hungry bodies cry for their mothers' breast.
> With the peasants I have watched in grief

> as the rice withered in the hot sun,
> and the officials took the meager crop for tax.
> I have cried for my brothers and sisters,
> locked away in prisons, with no voice of defense,
> and death their only liberation.
> We have labored hard and long to build life
> and yet, each day, the hope of our hearts has faded into poverty.[29]

Our young Burmese poet is no longer on top of a mountain but at the bottom of a pit. He is not singing anymore, but sighing and lamenting. This is not an ode of joy. This is a dirge played under the thick cloud of darkness that has descended on him.

Instead of laughter, tears. Instead of busy marketplaces, crowded prisons. Instead of life, now death. The fields used to be lush with rice, but not anymore. Life was rich with enough food to go around and plenty of love to share, but now poverty has set in to weaken the body and enfeeble the spirit. Toil used to be a joy, but now it brings stress and pain. Fruits of labor once enjoyed have turned into bitter pills of suffering. What has happened? the Burmese poet asks. What has gone wrong? Why this tragic change in my country? Cannot something be done to bring freedom, justice, and love back to my people? He is desperate as "the hope of his heart fades into poverty."

"Thorns and thistles," the Bible says, "[the ground] shall bring forth for you" (Gen. 3:18a). "The ground" is the land the farmer cultivates to produce rice as Asia's staple food. The ground is the society we organize to ensure our health as individuals, as families, and as a community. The ground is the nation constituted to protect citizens from harm's way, to enhance our well-being, and to give us a role in the community of nations and peoples. The ground is this inhabited world we human beings share with diverse faiths and cultures. The ground is the entire creation God has entrusted to us—women, men, and children—to care for and develop, not only for human benefit but for the benefit of all creatures. But on this ground where there should be flowers and fruits, there are now thorns and thistles.

Thorns and thistles are those dark forces that maim and destroy the true, good, and beautiful. These forces are sinister, evil, and destructive. History tells us that human civilizations are never free from them. Human beings suffer because of them. Where do these evil forces come from? This has been one of the most puzzling and also most agonizing questions human beings have faced. These forces are as secretive as they are ferocious. They are as devious as they are brutal. They could also be as pious as they are immoral. They can create an oppressive government to take people's conscience captive. They can levy heavy taxes from law-abiding and hard-working men and women to enrich themselves and their cronies. These forces take on an even more sinister look when institutionalized into systems of religious beliefs and doctrines, hierarchies of power and authority, and when pretending to speak on behalf of God, but in fact while holding the hearts and souls of believers hostage to their own selfish interests and profane ambitions.

Let us have no illusion about what our toil and labor is able to achieve. We cannot afford to be complacent about civilizations we have built. We must face the fact that life, be it our own private life or life of humankind, is filled with conflicts—conflicts of light and darkness, truth and lies, love and hate. History, for that matter, is not any different. History, whether national history or world history, is where human beings never cease to find themselves playing the roles of victimizers and victims in turn. History, in sum, consists of stories of life and the world in which "if the good grows by a foot, the devil will grow by ten times as much" (*dao gao yi chu, mo gau yi zhang*), according to a Chinese saying, meaning that the force of evil always manages to beat the force of good. It does not have to be this way, but it has always been this way. Why?

This is the question of the Burmese poet. It is the question asked by religious thinkers, philosophers, ethicists, and by thinking women and men in all ages. It is also our question today. But no sooner have philosophers raised the question than they become engaged in metaphysical debates about the origin and nature of evil. When theologians and preachers talk about the question—and they talk about it a lot, almost too much, as if it is their sacred vocation to give an answer—they are more interested in defending the God of their belief systems and doctrinal traditions than in identifying themselves with the people undergoing terrible suffering through no fault of their own.

The fact is that God—the God who knows everything (omniscient), who is all-good (omnibenevolent) and all-powerful (omnipotent)—is more of an embarrassment to thinking believers, as they watch innocent children like Nikita in the earlier story suffer and die, than an explanation of why such children have to die with so much suffering. How are those of us who hold to the classical teachings of the Christian church about God, sin, and punishment to respond to the following statement about the Holocaust, for example?

> Any God who could permit the Holocaust, who could remain silent during it, who could "hide God's face" while it dragged on, was not worth believing in. There might well be a limit to how much we could understand about God, but Auschwitz demanded an unreasonable suspension of understanding. In the face of such great evil, God, the good and the powerful, was too inexplicable, as men and women said, "God is dead."[30]

God is not dead! you and I shout at the top of our lungs. We broadcast it from the rooftops of our church buildings. But how are we to explain the behaviors of God the statement describes?

In *The Brothers Karamazov*, the classic novel by Dostoyevsky, one comes across this brief exchange between Ivan and Alyosha Karamazov, the two broth-

ers, as they are engrossed in a lengthy discussion on the problem of the suffering
of innocent people:

> "Why are you telling me all this [stories of the suffering of the innocent],
> Ivan?" asked Alyosha.
>
> "I can't help thinking that if the devil doesn't exist and, therefore,
> human beings have created it, they have created it in their own image
> and likeness."
>
> "Just as human beings did God, you mean."[31]

With a writer's deep intuition and an artist's power of imagination, Dostoyevsky
has in this discourse said what most Christians, be they lay or clerical, dare not
even think: "Just as human beings did God, you mean."

We human beings, no matter whether Muslim, Buddhist, or Christian, have
"created God in our image and likeness." This is what Dostoyevsky is saying.
This is the premise with which thinking Christians, for example, must begin
to look more closely at many of the belief systems we have inherited from our
church and its traditions, including the problem of evil and suffering. As human
beings we are endowed with knowledge, power, and moral sensibility. These
among other qualities make us what we are as human beings. How otherwise
can we associate a being called God with similar attributes such as knowledge,
power, and moral qualities?

But what we are endowed with is limited in scope, extent, and volume. This
we know and acknowledge to ourselves. We also know that for God to be God
we cannot set limits to what God possesses. Hence concepts such as *omnipotent*
(all-powerful), *omnibenevolent* (all-good), and *omniscient* (all-knowing) are attributed to God. We do not in fact know what in actuality these concepts mean
when applied to God, for none of us is in possession of them and none of us has
seen God. Does this not mean that in a very real sense we have created God in
our own image and likeness, as Alyosha, learning to be a monk in a monastery,
responded to his brother Ivan, puzzled and at a loss?

As far as we are concerned, the problem arises as we try to relate this God we
consider to be all-powerful, all-good, and all-knowing to the evil and suffering
that mars each page of human history. It is a most serious problem, because it is
possible that the God to whom we try to relate may not be God in God's own
self. In other words, what we have been doing, from philosophers in their books
to theologians in their study to believers in the pew, is justifying the behavior
of the God of our own making against evil and suffering in the world, and *not*
God in God's own self.

Does God in God's own self need our defense to be God? Is that God in
need of our justification to remain God? In fact it is we human beings who have
to explain ourselves in the face of sufferings brought about by human evil. On
this point Ivan Karamazov is right. To Alyosha he said: "I can't help thinking
that if the devil doesn't exist and, therefore, human beings have created it, they

have created it in their own image and likeness." Ivan has said something not only right, but deep, despite his rebellion against religious traditions and social conventions. He does not attribute evil to God but to human beings. It is not God who needs to be justified, but human beings. It is not God who needs to be called to testify, but human beings. The origin of evil shifts from God to human beings. The question of why the innocent have to suffer is now not asked of God, but of human beings.

This shift of focus from God to human beings is of critical importance as we deal with evil and suffering. Thorns and thistles are not planted by God but by human beings. It is on this premise that we can begin to respond to the statement on the Holocaust quoted above. We can make our response not argumentatively but prayerfully, not by way of debate but with confession.

> God did not permit the Holocaust. How could God permit it? It was carried out behind God's back. But God did not remain silent while the horror of the Holocaust was going on. God was crying in the crying of those women, men, and children herded to the gas chambers. God was weeping in the weeping of those who watched helplessly their loved ones led away to be slaughtered. God did not hide 'God's face.' How can one fail to see God's face in the faces of those terror-stricken Jews fallen victim to the insanity of their fellow human beings? True, we cannot understand God, not because God did not or was not able to stop the Holocaust, but because God, in spite of being God, chose to weep, suffer and die as each Jew who wept, suffered and died. We do not understand this God, but we are able to retain our hope for the world because of this God.[32]

Can we say more? Perhaps not. Have we left something unsaid? Yes, there is much left unsaid. How can anyone exhaust what is to be said about God? How can anyone try to say more when trying to figure out God's relationship to such horrendous tragedies as the Holocaust or to the suffering of innocent children such as Nikita? Did Jesus say more than what we have said? This question will be examined in the next section.

My Name Is Legion

There is no shortage of pain in human life, whether one likes it or not. Whether suffering is nature's doing or our own doing—and it is much more the latter than the former—the world is abundant in suffering. This is the heart of the problem Buddhism addresses by referring to "the noble truth of suffering." "The Buddha was convinced that suffering overbalanced pleasure in human life so much that it would be better never to have been born. More tears have flowed, he tells us, than all the water that is in the four great oceans."[33]

We Christians tend to dismiss the Buddhist teaching on suffering as the ground of Buddhist denial of the world and of its withdrawal from it. Compounded with the doctrine of *karma*, Buddhism is said to have fostered the spirit of fatalism and the attitude of resignation in its believers. There is truth in this opinion, but do not most religions, including Christianity, possess, in one way or another, teaching and practice that deny the world? Does not Buddhism, again like other religions, including Christianity, also put compassion into practice when it engages in relief work, social projects, and reform programs? We should perhaps agree that "Buddhism follows the general lines of religious evolution from a more other-worldly to a more this-worldly orientation."[34]

The Buddha, it is said, was so overwhelmed by the enormity of human suffering that he taught: "Birth is suffering; decay is suffering; death is suffering; sorrow, lamentation, pain, grief and despair are suffering."[35] This is a very negative view on life and world. But does it not remind us at once of Job in our Hebrew Scriptures, and of his outbursts when beset with the calamities that struck him and his family? To the three friends completely horrified by what they had seen in him, Job burst into a heart-rending lament:

> Let the day perish in which I was born,
>   and the night that said,
> "A man-child is conceived."
> Let that day be darkness!
>   May God above not seek it,
>   or light shine on it. (3:3-4)

What a terrible thing to say, especially for someone like Job, who "was blameless and upright," and who "feared God and turned away from evil" (1:1)! Here is a blameless and upright man wishing that the day of his birth had never existed. Here is a believer who fears God calling upon God not to let light shine on that day.

Are these blasphemous words? Is this an impious utterance? But the picture is not of Job sitting in the house of worship praising God. Nor is this Job making offerings and thanking God for the wealth and prosperity with which he was blessed. This is the Job who lost his seven sons and three daughters in one day in a sudden desert hurricane, who had to be told that his "seven thousand sheep, three thousand camels, five hundred yoke of oxen, five hundred donkeys, and very many servants" (1:3) had been either killed or carried off by the Sabeans from North Arabia,[36] and who, afflicted with "loathsome sores ... from the sole of his foot to the crown of his head," was sitting among the ashes and scraping himself with a potsherd (2:7-8).

What a horrible picture! Actually, it is not the day of his birth that Job laments. He laments his enormous suffering, which makes him wish to be dead rather than alive. The author of this great drama of Job—was he or she an eyewitness to such tragedy or did he or she have to suffer from something like it?—shows Job making a death wish:

> Why did I not die at birth,
>   come forth from the womb and expire?
> Why were there knees to receive me,
>   or breasts for me to suck? (3:11-12)

These are strong words, but are they strong enough for a man such as Job and his miserable condition? They are bitter words, but are they bitter enough for someone like Job, on whom so much suffering has been inflicted? Again it is not birth, but life with its suffering, that he laments. Such experiences of life prompt Buddhism to identify suffering as the heart of the human problem, and to devote almost its entire effort to be free from it.

Whether the tragic drama of Job is the fiction of a literary genius or the creation of a deeply religious mind, these thoughts on suffering are not all that we come across in the Hebrew Scriptures. Even prophets, entrusted with the ministry of God's words, are not, when the going becomes rough, entirely foreign to the struggle of the soul we see in Job. One thinks of Jeremiah, the prophet active during the first half of the sixth century B.C.E., when Judah was precipitating toward defeat and captivity at the hands of Babylonia. His was a mission impossible. In vain he tried to exhort his people back to God, to help them perceive the different ways in which history was moving, and to counsel them to rebuild their lives in the land of captivity. But he had to suffer for all his efforts. He was branded as a traitor, and attempts were made on his life. At one point he felt so desperate that he gave vent to his lament in language much like that of Job:[37]

> Cursed be the day on which I was born!
> The day when my mother bore me,
>   let it not be blessed!
> Cursed be the man who brought the news
>   to my father, saying,
> "A child is born to you, a son,"
>   making him very glad.
> Let that man be like the cities
>   that the Lord overthrew without pity;
> let him hear a cry in the morning
>   and an alarm at noon,
> because he did not kill me in the womb;
>   so my mother would have been my grave,
>   and her womb forever great.
> Why did I come forth from the womb
>   to see toil and sorrow,
>   and spend my days in shame?
>   (Jer. 20:14-18)

These words terrify us. They shake us to the bottom of our being. They wake us from complacency.

How could Jeremiah, a prophet, curse the day he was born? How could he, a man of God, think of death in the womb when his life became tough? But in these curses of Jeremiah, as in the lament poured out by Job, we encounter the very human beings who have to struggle with life against all odds and who raise one of the most fundamental problems of life, namely, the problem of the meaning of life in the midst of suffering. Jeremiah's suffering is not unlike that of the Buddha, who also wrestled with suffering and taught his followers to find the meaning of life in the emptying of the self and in the compassion for *zhong-sheng*, that is, for all living creatures. As for the prophets such as Jeremiah and the author of the Book of Job, they urged people to turn to God for the renewal of their faith in God, of their love for one another, and of their hope for the future of their nation.

Jesus, too, is no stranger to suffering. The Gospel writers tell how Jesus associates himself with men, women, and children who suffer from social, economic, and religious discrimination. Lazarus, in one of Jesus' parables, lies at the gate of a rich man's house "covered with sores, [longing] to satisfy his hunger with what fell from the rich man's table" (Luke 16:20-21). Jesus must have been familiar with many such Lazaruses. In another scene at the Temple "a poor widow came and put [into the treasury] two small copper coins, which are worth a penny" (Mark 12:42). There must have been many a poor widow in the crowds that followed him. His life had also been touched by the innocent children who fell to the sword of Herod the king in an insane attempt to do away with the baby Jesus (Matt. 2:16-18). As he went about his ministry, he must have come across many children in rags—starved, abused, or even murdered.

If suffering has a name, it must be "legion." It comes in all shapes and forms. It occurs in different colors and shades. It takes place in all places, at all times, and at all levels of life. It can be physical, racial, sexual, mental, economic, social, political, or even religious. Indeed, its name is "legion"; that is, it stems from many reasons and gets manifested in many different ways. There seems no end to it. It affects us personally and as members of the global community. How is one to face suffering? What needs to be done to overcome it? How is one to turn suffering into a challenge to create a new meaning of life?

This brings us to the story of the Gerasene demoniac with the name of "legion" (Mark 5:1-20; also Matt. 8:28-34; Luke 8:26-39). This is an extraordinary story and an exciting drama. The story is told in so vivid a manner that it could almost be an account by someone who saw it happen. "There are many details in the story which, far from being embellishments of an originally bald statement, bear all the marks of reminiscence from an eyewitness."[38] The story tells at some length how Jesus healed a man "with an unclean spirit" (Mark 5:2) or "who had demons" (Luke 8:27), in the part of the Gerasenes close to the Sea of Galilee "in the partially Gentile territory of the Decapolis."[39]

We have what appears to be one of the miracle stories of the healing Jesus performed during his ministry. Healing is usually considered to be the way he demonstrated his supernatural power. But in between the lines the story tells us something much more down-to-earth, relevant to each of us at a deeper level of our lives. Implicit in the story is in fact a variety of causes that contribute to human sufferings Jesus encountered in human community; "the demoniac" in the story happens to be a particular case of those sufferings. These human causes, and not divine punishment, are the root of sufferings in the world. By having Jesus heal the demented man, the story conveys an important message: suffering can be healed, and the well-being of human beings and the world in which we live restored.

The man Jesus encountered lived, we are told, "among the tombs" in the cemetery. This "may be a sign of alienation."[40] A cemetery is built so the dead can be severed from the living. It is a realm of silence isolated from the noise of the world. It houses memories of relationships disrupted and terminated. It stores the past, detached from the present and separated from the future. It is a reminder that decay alienates a person from him or herself, and that the alienated person is no longer a person but a thing. The cemetery testifies that eternity is nothing but a cessation of time.

Such alienation generates anxiety in us all. Does such alienation represent the end of all things that affect us as living beings, and that affect the world which sustains our lives? It may be that the world of objects, or the objective world, does not exist at all. The world could be a figment of my imagination, or a projection of my thought. Nothing may have existed before I came into the world, and nothing may exist after I depart. Perhaps the only reality during the duration of my existence is this "I"; all the rest is mere illusion. But if I came from nothing and return to nothing, am I not also nothing? Is not this reality called "I" also an illusion? Now this is an idea that should worry us. This is anxiety of the most fundamental kind that sometimes gives us an aching void in the depths of our being. Is not Buddhism after all right when it teaches that

> Empty and calm and devoid of ego [*atman*]
> Is the nature of all things:
> There is no individual being
> That in reality exist?[41]

Perhaps there is some truth in this Buddhist wisdom, which sees through the vanity and unreality of the human self and all that the self has built around itself to create a false sense of security.

But one has to be very tough-minded to be at peace with this Buddhist view of life and the world as absolutely unreal. For mundane people, like most of us, what may be called "anxiety of being" creates fear—fear about our ultimate destiny and the destiny of the world. Is there perhaps nothing beyond the cemetery after all? One is haunted by the thought. Such fear of being gives rise to questions about the ties that bind us in different relationships—husband and wife, parents and children, brothers and sisters, relatives and friends. Perhaps these ties are not strong enough to last beyond our present life. They may not survive our death. The thought gives us deep despair.

From alienation to anxiety to fear to despair. How many of us can maintain peace and serenity in our hearts and minds when these factors take hold? Not many. The man who made his home among the tombs could be one of those threatened by "the fear of non-being," and he became violently demented. To compound the matter further, his alienation is not merely of a social nature. It has serious religious implications, too. That he is sick in the body, mind, and spirit and is driven to live among the tombs alienates him from the religious community as well, for tombs are regarded as "ritually unclean."[42] The man in this way became doubly alienated.

This is strange, is it not? One can be socially alienated for all sorts of reasons—race, gender, creed, class, or health—but does one have to be alienated religiously? A religious community should be one of the few places in which alienation is healed and health restored. Unfortunately, this is not always the case. AIDS, for example, has become a divisive issue in the Christian churches today. The practice of alienating the sick goes far back into the history of most religions. The sick are considered to be ritually unclean and cursed by God. They have no place in the religious community until their health is restored and they can become ritually clean again. One only has to recall the words about "the suffering servant":

> Surely he has borne our infirmities
>   and carried our diseases;
> yet we accounted him stricken,
>   struck down by God, and afflicted.
>   (Isa. 53:4)

Note carefully what the poet says. It is not said that "God" strikes down him "who has borne our infirmities and carried our diseases," but "we" who account him to be stricken by God. It is we who regard him as such and not God, and this makes all the difference.

It is well to remind ourselves again that "in the ancient world's way of thinking suffering as such indicated God's smiting and God's wrath," and that "this attitude was the orthodox, correct, indeed the devout one."[43] Did not Job's friends try to reason with him with such orthodox, correct, and devout attitudes, provoking his impassioned rebuttal? The fact is that most of us in the Christian church, even today, are apt to play Job's friends to those who suffer—if not in public, at least in private.

But by saying that it is "we" who consider the suffering servant to be struck down by God, the poet might be taking exception to that "orthodox" view, affirming neither that the servant is the target of God's wrath nor that his suffering has been brought about God. For those of us Christians who routinely relate Jesus to "the suffering servant" and who view Jesus' death on the cross as God's plan to have him bear our sins, we have a lot of rethinking to do. If it is not God who afflicted the servant with suffering as "we" thought God did, how can we take the cross to be God's judgment on our sins?

One of the most amazing things about Jesus is that Jesus, who lived in the "ancient world" in which the orthodox attitude to human suffering and divine punishment prevailed, is entirely free from it. This fact is evident in story after story of how Jesus healed the sick and comforted and empowered suffering men and women. The woman who had "been suffering from hemorrhages for twelve years" touches Jesus, who is surrounded by a large crowd. Instead of feeling ritually polluted, Jesus is "immediately aware that power had gone forth from him" to heal the woman of her disease (Mark 5:24-34; also Luke 8:43-48; Matt. 9:20-22). The story of Jesus healing the man born blind is a most beautiful example of how Jesus "deconstructed" the "orthodox" view and "reconstructed" what should be a theologically correct attitude to human suffering. To the disciples' question, "Rabbi, who sinned, this man or his parents, that he was born blind?" Jesus replied: "Neither this man nor his parents sinned; he was born blind so that God's works might be revealed in him" (John 9:2-3).[44] What are God's works of which Jesus speaks? These are the works of love and not of wrath, the works of healing and not of condemning, the works of acceptance and not of rejection.

The episode with the man who called himself Legion ends with him becoming sound and well, at peace with himself, with God, and with the world around him. The story tells us that healing of the body, mind, and soul of human beings and the world—which is what salvation essentially means—is possible because of God's involvement in our sufferings and God's mercy for those who suffer. This must be what Jesus means when he says to the man: "Go home to your friends, and tell them how much the Lord has done for you, and what mercy the Lord has shown you" (Mark 5:19). God's mercy and not God's punishment of the sin allegedly committed by our first ancestors is the heart of Jesus' healing ministry. It is this power of God's mercy that Jesus exercises to overcome human sufferings in his healing ministry.

"In the world you will have suffering," says Jesus in John the Evangelist's account. "But take heart! I have conquered the world" (John 16:33 [REB]). Suffering mentioned here refers back to "the persecution predicted in [John] 15:18—16:4a,"[45] the persecution the community of Jesus' followers is to undergo in the years ahead. This saying attributed to Jesus by the author of John's Gospel can, however, be expanded to include other sufferings as well. Jesus himself is not unfamiliar with persecution on account of what he says and does. Persecution is to lead him to his death on the cross. Is not the cross the suffering of sufferings? Does it not stand for all human sufferings, including persecution for the sake of what one believes? Does it not sum up what suffering can bring to a person—separation, humiliation, pain, bloodshed, even death?

But suffering can be endured and overcome, Jesus is saying, not by one's own patience, fortitude, or willpower, but by the mercy of God. In restoring peace to that violent demoniac, in enabling sick people to regain their health, and in empowering his followers to endure persecution—this is what Jesus means when he says, "I have conquered the world." Jesus is not indulging in the triumphalism that the Christian church is to indulge in later. There is no room in Jesus' faith for false triumphalism. "In the world," he reminds us, "you will have suffering." As long as you live, you will have suffering. As long as the world exists, there will be suffering. Let us make no mistake about it. Let us have no illusion about a life and world of no suffering. But where suffering is, there God's mercy is also. All we need to know, all we can know, is that without this faith in God's mercy, suffering in its all possible manifestations is utterly pointless and meaningless. Suffering, far from alienating us from God who is said to punish us with pangs of birth, toil, and labor for the dishonor done to God, should drive us ever closer to God, who in mercy and compassion embraces us with the power to heal and become well.

Ultimately, suffering is a matter of faith—faith in the God of mercy and not in the God of punishment. It is also a matter of hope and love. Paul, who is no stranger to suffering, is at his most profound when he writes in his letter to the Christians in Rome: "Suffering produces endurance, and endurance produces character, and character produces hope, and hope does not disappoint us, because God's love has been poured into our hearts through the Holy Spirit that has been given to us" (Rom. 5:3-5). Can more be said about suffering? Perhaps not.

Part Three

HOPE

The [reign of God] is like a mustard seed,
which, when sown upon the ground,
is the smallest of all the seeds on earth;
yet when it is sown it grows up
and becomes the greatest of all shrubs,
and puts forth large branches,
so that the birds of the air
can make nests in its shade.

—Mark 4:31-32

I Am Human

I am human, who'd dare say I'm not?
Who'd dare say I have no body? Then why do
you let me live like a dog?
Why do you let me die like an animal?

I am human, I am human.
You see my skin, you see my bones, you see my eyes,
you see my body, like yours....
I am asking for life, I'm human.

You see my children and they're hungry,
You see these fields which aren't mine,
You see these people who eat my bread!
I want to earn my bread, I'm human.

O earth, strange land, who rules you, you my realm?
Tomorrow, my earth, I want you to be mine,
I'm asking for justice, I'm human.

131

There is no work for my two hands,
Tomorrow will I take as tool plow or gun?
I need work, I'm human.

You see my heart, but do you hear it?
Your heart which beats, mine which strikes out,
A human heart at the heart of the world.
I need you to love me, I'm human.

And in my heart there rises a song,
A song as violent as a great wind,
A song which ranges far and wide like the wind.
I want my freedom, I'm human![1]

Chapter 6

Elusive Hope

Everything has a history. Events occur at certain times and in certain places. They are segments in a series of events, parts of the episodes and experiences accumulated in the past. In 221 B.C.E., for example, King Cheng of Ch'in in northwest China created a unified Chinese empire and made himself Shih Huang Ti, First Sovereign Emperor. This was a momentous event that was to have far-reaching consequences for the history of China. In 49 B.C.E. a Roman general by the name of Julius Caesar led his army across the river Rubicon in north-central Italy to engage in a battle against Pompey, another Roman general, defeated the latter, and made himself the sole ruler. This too was a decisive event in the history of the Roman Empire. To give just one more example of events that have shaped the destiny of peoples and nations, in 1949 the victorious Chinese Communist army rode into Beijing with Mao Zedong at its head. Thus inaugurated was the People's Republic of China which, after basking in glory for an initial few years, was to plunge its people into tragedies of almost unprecedented magnitude.

But generals and emperors alone cannot make history. While they take credit for what has been achieved, especially for the momentous events, one cannot forget countless women, men, and children who have had to forfeit their livelihood, their possessions, even their lives. A Chinese idiom says it well: "While a general achieves success and acquires fame, millions lie dead, their bones left to dry" (*yi chiang kong ch'eng wan ku ku*). It is these nameless millions, and not generals and emperors, who make history. They make history by being either victims or witnesses to the power of human beings to build and destroy.

We human beings make history, for better or worse. We are historical beings. We are history. And we become history. But we are not the sole makers of history, nor are we its sole owners. Is this not obvious as we have come to realize that we coexist with a host of other beings, animate and inanimate, organic and inorganic? Surrounding us are animals, birds, fish, and insects; grass, plants, and trees; air and light; mountains, rivers, and oceans; the sun, the moon, and the stars; earth, stones, and minerals. We are not the only inhabitants in the universe. We live with a host of others, and we breathe with them. We are dependent on other beings as much as, or even much more than, they are dependent on us. Each of these things and beings has its own history. Most of them, as a matter of fact, have infinitely longer histories than human history. These histories are so long that they are measured in tens of millions of light years or in geologic time.

Whether short or long, whether brief or lasting, history is history because it has a beginning and an end. It is a process, a duration of time. But more important, history is history not because it consists merely of dates and places, but because it is moved by a promise to achieve a purpose, even the most elemental promise and purpose of being alive and of carrying life forward for posterity. In other words, history itself has a history. It is a history of how a promise is made and unmade, how it is carried out and aborted, and how it reaches or fails to reach a destination. History consists of a series of promises and goals. At the heart of history is hope, the power that moves history from promise to reality, the energy that enables something to emerge from promise. History, then, consists of hopes conceived and miscarried, hopes realized and frustrated, hopes born and dead. History is, thus, the history of hope.

Hope, too, has a history. That is why we must speak about different kinds of hope—elusive hope, hope in struggle, power of hope, and prayers of hope. In Christianity the tendency is to dehistoricize hope, to unhinge it from the course of real life and to remove it from happenings in the world. Hope gets disconnected from our living experiences and disjointed from the daily experiences of others. To hope as one who believes in God and to hope as one who goes through life with its ups and downs—especially a life with more downs than ups—tend to become separated. In faith and in theology we speak of hope in the future—a future with no deadline, a future at the end of time, a future in which hope is to come true. This is what is called "eschatological hope" in Christian theology. But is not "eschatological hope" a hope eternally postponed? Is it not a hope that forever eludes our grasp? Is it not, in short, an elusive hope to which we have attached ourselves?

Instead of a hope eternally out of our sight and beyond our grasp, should we not speak of hope for the present? Should we not have a message of hope for people going through hardships in body and spirit? And is it not on the basis of the present hope that we take a critical look at the past hope and anticipate the future hope? What Jesus did, it seems, is to retrieve hope in God out of the past, to rescue it from the future, and to make it "up-to-date" and "timely" for the women, men, and children who looked to him. Is this not why he told people that the reign of God *is* theirs in the present tense, not in the past tense, not in the future tense (Matt. 5:3; also Luke 6:20)? Let us, then, start by discerning how hope can be, and often is, elusive in the realities of life and the world, just as in the preceding chapter we tried to come to grips with life and living in relation to suffering and death.

Shattered Dreams

Hope is for human beings what water is for fish. Taken out of water, fish die; in the absence of hope human beings lose zest for life and strength to live. This is a truism of course, but nonetheless true. Hope does not have to be a hope that moves heaven and earth; it can be a hope as elemental as not losing a job that earns you and your family daily rice. It does not have to be a hope as ambitious as that of turning an evil political system upside down; it can be a hope as modest as living in peace with your neighbors. It does not have to be an earth-shaking hope of replacing the present world of pain and suffering with a utopia of joy and laughter; it can be a simple and modest hope of working in agreeable situations and hospitable environments. But it is this simple and modest hope that is denied to many a woman and man.

Mediatrix Jane Quilim was a Filipino migrant domestic worker in Hong Kong. She set out for Hong Kong with high hopes but soon found herself in dire situations. She was completely disillusioned. Here is the story in her own words:

> I worked in a beauty parlor [in the Philippines] before I came to Hong Kong. My husband paints houses on a contractual basis. My salary helped augment my husband's income, enough to feed the whole family with three meals a day. I have five children. As work was getting scarce, and the value of wages seemed to be less and less, my husband thought of going to Saudi Arabia. But then we had no money to pay the [recruiting] agent.
>
> At that time also, I had a very good impression of Hong Kong. I based this on the magazines one of my customers used to bring to the parlor, showing the different views of Hong Kong and the interior designs of the houses. I also made as a basis the attitude of my Chinese friends/ customers. One of them convinced me to work in Hong Kong but I said I had no money to pay the agency fee. She offered me a "Fly-now-Pay-later" arrangement of 17,500 pesos....
>
> I accepted the offer and came to Hong Kong on February 12, 1986. On that very day, without allowing me to adjust even for a few minutes, I was given instructions one after the other. It was Chinese New Year.
>
> On the second day, I was given a list of instructions on what to do for almost every minute of the day from 5 A.M. to 9 P.M. But more often than not, I can only go to bed when the child is asleep or after a mahjong session.
>
> My first employer was very strict and watched all my moves. She can do this because she stays home most of the time. We had communications problem. We expressed things differently, communicated in a third language. Because of this, I used to cry when alone or sing my troubles away. Once she heard me singing, she stopped me, asking what I was trying

to prove. She asked why I was singing. I said to express my feelings and comfort myself. All the more she stopped me. She said it was like fighting back to her. . . .

She prohibited me from talking with other Filipinos without telling me why. Until one time, because I was eager to talk in my language and I felt excited to talk to another Filipino, she caught me talking to our Filipino neighbor. At once, she shouted and scolded me, saying they are "bad influence." Every Saturday, she would take me to her in-laws' house to work there.

I was thinking of terminating my contract but I also remember my debts and decide I should forget about termination. I will just continue my work despite the difficulties. Because with the "Fly-now-Pay-later" system, 100 percent of my salary was paid to the agency. And the total amount was equivalent to my four-months' salary.

After four months, however, my employer gave me a termination letter. I have not even sent anything to my family. I realized I just went abroad to help the agency make money out of my labor.

At that time I didn't know anything. I was terminated without notice but I was not paid anything in lieu of that notice. I just said YES to anything she said. I felt helpless.[1]

This seems to be a commonplace story of a Philippine woman domestic worker, exploited and helpless, "stranded in a foreign land, away from her kin" (*chu mu wu qing*), to use a Chinese expression. In 1991 there were about seventy thousand of them in Hong Kong. Many have a similar story to tell. If this is a story of one hundred, one thousand, or twenty thousand, the story is no longer commonplace. It is a story crying out to be heard, one story among many stories of exploitation taking place internationally, nationally, and locally.

Mediatrix Jane Quilim's plight did not end with the termination of her employment. In order to pay off not only the debts she owed to the recruitment agency, but to send home money her family badly needed, she found another employer. She did not fare any better the second time around. She was forced to work for half the pay in the contract, was treated with contempt by her employer, and finally was dismissed without prior notice. When she reflects on what happened to her, she says: "Looking back, I feel my dreams are shattered. I want to go home, but I still need to earn a living."[2] With the shattered dreams her hope to provide a decent living for her five children was gone, too.

Scarce Work, Low Wages

Life begins with hope. It is greeted with a promise. Hope and promise go hand in hand. Hope is a promise made, and promise is a hope anticipated. This is how parents, for example, welcome their newborn child to the world. Is not hope, then, a basic desire that moves life? Is it not an elemental human right to which each human being is entitled? Are we not born with it? It is one of the most primitive and basic instincts of human beings, of our ancestors of the remote past and of we who live in today's "civilized" world. This desire or instinct continues throughout our lives. Are there parents who do not wish their children "to become dragons and phoenixes" (*cheng long cheng feng*) as most parents in Asia do, hoping that they will excel in what they do, get on well in the world, and become somebody? There are, in short, scarcely any of us who do not hope to achieve a goal—to be a fine craftsperson, a good professional, a successful businessperson, a productive farmer, a distinguished scholar, an acclaimed artist, a respectable politician?

In the process, however, many hearts are broken, many tears shed, many ideals corrupted, and many lives ruined and wasted. Are not most tragedies of life we have seen and experienced attributable to hopes unfulfilled and promises broken? But we humans are incorrigible when it comes to hope and promise. Despite setbacks and failures, we continue to hope and to make promises. What is left for us as individuals and as a community except hope, particularly when the going gets rough?

This is the case for Mediatrix Jane Quilim of the Philippines. For her and for hundreds of thousands of migrant workers from the Philippines it is the hope for betterment of life at home that drives them overseas. According to the Consultation on Asia Labor Migration held by the Christian Conference of Asia (CCA) in 1991, "there were already over 3.5 million Filipino migrant workers all over the world."[3] The number has since risen to at least four million. This is approximately 6 percent of the nation's total population of sixty-six million. The proportion is significant. The question is why do so many Filipino women and men have to hire themselves out abroad, in most cases, for low-paying jobs in inhospitable situations and under unfavorable conditions?

To make a long story short, the reason relates, first and foremost, to the uphill struggle for the majority of people in the Philippines to make ends meet. The Philippines challenges the notion of "economic success" that supposedly has made Asia a developed region on par with Europe and North America. It debunks the prevailing notion that the world economy has created the so-called Pacific or Asia-Pacific Century in which Asia plays a major economic role. There are, to be sure, some exciting statistics. "For the 1985–90 period," it is pointed out, "the real GDP [the gross domestic product] of the developed countries of North America, Western Europe and the Pacific was estimated to have grown by 3.1 percent."[4] Note that the Pacific region (Asia) is mentioned in the same breath with Europe and North America. Most notably, even the socialist nation of China has been making spectacular strides in economic development. Its GDP is said to have grown by 8.3 percent in recent years.[5]

This, unfortunately, is

only one side of the development coin. The fact is that the gap between the developed and the underdeveloped countries remains wide: in 1985, by World Bank reckoning, 71 percent of the world's poor population were Asians. In 1988, per capita income (expressed in 1980 dollars) for the developing countries of East Asia was only a tenth of that of the developed countries; for South Asia, the proportion was merely 2.5 percent.[6]

What this tells us is that Japan, the big dragon, and the four little dragons of South Korea, Taiwan, Hong Kong, and Singapore alone do not make Asia. That a few nations become prosperous while others remain in economic hardship, both within Asia at large and within particular countries, is a grave injustice.

While world economic systems have proven unjust to the great majority of women, men, and children in Asia, the ASEAN—the Association of Southeast Asian Nations, consisting of Indonesia, Malaysia, the Philippines, Singapore, and Thailand—has also failed in its intents and purposes. When it came into being in Bangkok in 1967, it declared that one of its aims would be "to accelerate the economic growth, social progress and cultural development in the region through joint endeavors in the spirit of equality and partnership in order to strengthen the foundation for a prosperous and peaceful community of Southeast Asian nations."[7] As in most declarations, national or international, political or religious, this ASEAN Declaration says all the right things about working toward economic prosperity in the spirit of equality and partnership. On paper it reads quite well. It has all the quality of pious religious talk.

True, economic prosperity has been achieved by some ASEAN member nations, notably Singapore, but not in the spirit of equality and partnership, leaving the Philippines, for example, to send millions of its men and women overseas to strive for economic survival. This is another raw example for how economic prosperity, be it personal or national, cannot be achieved in the spirit of equality and partnership. The sad fact, today as yesterday, is that efforts toward economic prosperity pit nations against each other, divide human community, and corrupt human relationships.

Jesus is right when he says: "What does it profit [people] if they gain the whole world, but lose or forfeit themselves?" (Luke 9:25; also Mark 8:36; Matt. 16:26). In the course of attaining economic prosperity, the world, Asia included, has not attained equality or enhanced mutual relationships. We in the world today are in danger of attaining economic prosperity but losing the ability to be truly human to one another. This is exactly what Jesus warned two thousand years ago. But his warning has all too often fallen on deaf ears amidst human efforts to outdo one another in power and wealth.

After almost thirty years, the ASEAN not only has not achieved its aim, but has not moved closer to it. The prevailing reality is that "income inequality in the ASEAN region is relatively high for developing countries, with 45–56 percent of incomes accruing to the top 20 percent of families. The bottom 40 percent, generally the poverty group, are clearly marginal, and appear to be making little progress." It is to this poverty group of 40 percent "at the bottom of the social order" that growth has to be directed. But what happens is that "growth has contributed primarily to [a] relative increase in welfare for middle- and upper-income households."[8]

Such observations give us a different picture of what Asia is like economically. Though we may speak of Asia in glowing terms as offering great opportunities for economic development, especially for those nations who are economic powers, we are blind to the misery and destitution the drive toward global economic prosperity is creating for almost half the population of Asia— and for more than half of the world's population, if Africa and Latin America are taken into account. We are committing moral as well as economic injustices against men, women, and children at the bottom of this "global village."

Since most economists speak and act as high priests of the world economy, politicians stake their political fortunes on the voters' economic well-being,[9] and most Western tourists only get to see sights developed for tourism and shop at commercial centers displaying every sign of "Asian prosperity," one normally does not find out how most people fare economically. Economists and politicians are more like impressionistic painters than painters of realism. To know why millions of men and women from the Philippines in this "prosperous Asia," in "this region of economic opportunity," have to suffer inhuman treatment in other countries for the sake of economic survival, we need to look elsewhere.

One problem is the enormous debt that Asian countries such as the Philippines have incurred—debts that are the price for "economic development" that inevitably includes transactions in costly weapons of war. Is it not ironic that a country can be impoverished as the result of "economic development"? But this is what happens. Heavy borrowing creates millions of migrant workers who earn their living overseas and who are used as pawns to pay off national debt. We are told that

> when the debt crisis erupted in 1988, the developing countries of the Asia-Pacific region owed 17.7 percent of the total third world debt. By 1988 this had gone up to 22.8 percent.[10]

This debt situation is bad enough, but it is not the whole story. There is also what is called "the cost of borrowing." In 1982, it is pointed out that

> 19.6 percent of the third world's total debt service was paid by the Asia-Pacific developing countries. By 1988, this had risen to 28.9 percent. In interest alone the region was paying in 1988 over two times what it had been paying in 1982.[11]

As the saying goes, there is no such thing as a "free lunch." The developing nations in Asia are so burdened with debts and interest that "economic development" has proven a curse rather than a blessing. The fact is that the Asia-Pacific region is now paying *more* to its creditors than it is receiving in loans. In 1988, for every US dollar that came into the region as lending, US $1.18 was shelled out as interest and principal payments on external debt.[12]

It is the rich few, whether the lending nations, transnational corporations, or the rich and powerful within the developing countries, that amass colossal profit, while the majority of average citizens find themselves unsuspecting pawns in the course of repaying ever-growing national debts.

What this scenario means for countries such as the Philippines is obvious. But it is not obvious to tourists of the Philippines; most of them do not see such problems in the carefree children playing in the alleys and in the smiling faces of the people. To politicians the situation is not obvious either; they refuse to admit it as they wine and dine with the rich. But the worsening economic crisis is evident to those who have the eyes to see, the ears to hear, and the hearts to feel. It takes an economic meltdown, which developed in Asia in 1997, for some to notice. The meltdown has taken the world by surprise, causing the rich and privileged to scramble desperately for a way out of the crisis. In the midst of this economic crisis, it is the poor who have to bear the brunt.

Listed below are some of the critical facts that, even way back at the start of the 1990s, did not bode well for the average working women and men of the Philippines:

- the balance-of-trade deficit ballooned to a staggering U.S. $4.1 billion in 1990 from $2.5 billion in 1989. The trade deficit for the first two months of 1991 reached $683.4 million.

- the foreign debt stood somewhere between 28 and 30 billion pesos while local accumulated public debt exceeded 350 billion pesos.

- the budget deficit at the end of 1990 had reached 60 billion pesos.

- the government at the beginning of the 1990s was implementing new tax measures, both direct and indirect. It is through indirect taxes (like the sales tax) that the toiling masses or workers and peasants in the middle social strata are made to pay taxes constituting a greater percentage of their earnings than that paid by the ruling elite. Thus they are further victimized and consigned to misery and want.

- unemployment was at 10 percent among the labor force of 25 million, with 33 percent underemployed.

- 80 percent of the population of 60 million fell below the poverty line.[13]

This is a grim picture. What we see is a debt-ridden country with the masses of working men and women bearing the brunt of the national economic crisis.

That in Asia, a part of the world considered in the early 1990s to be a place of unlimited economic opportunity, exists a country with 80 percent of its population living below the poverty line is hard to understand. But it is a fact. It is a fact for Mediatrix Jane Quilim. Her income from a beauty parlor where she worked, combined with the earnings of her husband as a housepainter, used to be "enough to feed the whole family [including five children]." But not anymore. As she tells us, "Work was getting scarce, and the value of wages seemed to be less and less." This is her personal economic crisis. She worked very hard, and she did not create the crisis herself. In all probability she did not know that the national debts incurred by her government were to blame. Even if she had known, what use would the information have been to her?

What does hope, then, mean for her? As the Philippines is the only country in Asia that can be called a "Christian" country, having been converted to Christianity during Spanish colonial rule, she is presumably a Roman Catholic Christian. Sunday after Sunday in church she must have listened to the good news called the gospel, heard God's blessings promised over and over to her and her children, and had her hope kindled and rekindled by sermons urging her to trust and hope in God, if not now, then by the last day when the Lord comes again. But all this talk must have meant very little when she had to face the harsh realities of life. Going overseas to work as a domestic helper seemed the only way out. It might have fulfilled her hope of earning enough to feed her family.

Fly Now and Pay Later

For people such as Mediatrix Jane Quilim struggling to make ends meet, the dream of a trip overseas is irresistible. What inspires the dream is the hope to earn enough to provide their children with a decent life. Hope for them is a project, neither a philosophical idea nor a religious concept, much less a theological design. Like most of the struggling poor, Mediatrix Jane Quilim had no clue how to get her project of hope started. Where was she to get the funds needed for the trip overseas? Her project of hope was frustrated before it had even gotten started. By accident, however, she was told about what is called "fly now and pay later," a scheme supposedly designed to enable people like her to fulfill their longing. She was excited. She felt as if her family had a future. She convinced herself and her husband that this was a chance she could not miss. Eventually she enrolled herself in the "fly now and pay later" scheme and set out on a journey of hope to Hong Kong.

But what is this "fly now and pay later" scheme? It is a scheme that allows a prospective migrant worker to borrow a sum of money from private or state recruitment agencies to start the process of working abroad. It sounds innocent and helpful, but it is anything but innocent and helpful. What happens in fact is that the state and private recruitment agencies and moneylenders link together to exploit the helpless migrant workers. The agent fees are "set at a ridiculously high 20,000 pesos though the amount permitted by law is 5,000 pesos."[14] For Mediatrix Jane Quilim the fee was as much as 17,500 pesos!

Needless to say, all this has disastrous effects on the workers who "end up paying four months to a year of their basic wages as costs of agent fees, getting necessary documentation and bribes."[15] Excited by the prospect of a trip abroad for the first time in their lives and the anticipation of improving their impoverished life, most of the aspiring migrant workers are not aware of what they are getting into.

Mediatrix Jane Quilim was no exception. She was a loser and fell victim to all parties. First, she had debts to pay the moneylender and the recruitment agency. She was not able to send any money back to her family and realized too late that she "just went abroad to help the agency make money out of my labor." Second, she had to endure ill treatment from her employer in Hong Kong. To add insult to injury, she was dismissed without reason. Third, she did not know that she was only a pawn helping her government pay off debt and a victim of the domestic economic problems besetting her country.

Hers is not an isolated case. It is not merely an incident that occurs to migrant workers from the Philippines. What we encounter here is a global phenomenon.[16] There are stories, at once moving and tragic, of the fortitude of Chinese laborers brought to California more than a hundred years ago to build railways in dangerous situations. Separated from their families and cultures, they were ill-paid and treated like slaves; many of them died dreaming of returning home with riches "to bring glory to their families and ancestors" (*rong chong yao chu*), as a Chinese saying goes. Migrant workers in Switzerland, mostly from Spain and Italy, are prohibited "from changing employers or sector of the economy and from bringing their families with them. Those who refuse to accept this separation and have their wife and children join them live in appalling living conditions and constant anxiety."[17] An Italian mother recalls how a migrant worker, when ill, was told: "You're here to work, not to be ill. You can go back where you came from if you want to lie around, but you can't do it here."[18]

Let My People Go?

Do not the stories of Mediatrix Jane Quilim and many other migrant workers in different countries and continents remind us of the Israelite people, reduced to slave laborers in ancient Egypt? Are not these stories modern versions of the Israelite migrant workers toiling under pharaohs? More than three thousand years separate one set of stories from another, but they all tell how human beings treat fellow humans. Many centuries have elapsed since the Israelite people had to submit to inhuman treatment at the hands of Egyptian rulers, but those who hold power today do not seem to deal better with those under their control.

One cannot help recalling how African Americans had to endure two hundred years of slavery in America. The history of slavery in America is a history of horror and shame. It is made even more horrible and shameful because the slave owners in this case were not ancient Egyptians, whom most Christians would call "pagans," but Christians themselves. The history of countries shaped by religions such as Hinduism and Islam is not kinder. What is the problem? What is wrong with human beings? Why have religions, including Christianity, not been able, with so much emphasis on salvation, to act as signs and examples of how human beings should treat one another and how history must be shaped and developed?

The fact is that people of different religions, and even those within the same religion, have continued to persecute, oppress, even kill one another. Salvation for some becomes damnation for others. Is this not a supreme irony? Is this not ultimate sacrilege? Salvation is of course related to hope. Is there not something wrong in what religions teach and propagate as the hope of salvation? Have religions distorted the meaning of salvation and hope? Is this deficiency among religions one of the reasons why hope for some becomes despair for others, just as salvation for some often proves to be condemnation for others?

Each religion, we acknowledge, is not free from the tendency to construct its own history on the basis of difference from, even hostility toward, other religions. At work at the heart of each religion often seems to be the law of separation and hostility, and not grace, reconciliation, and harmony. Otherwise, why have almost 80 percent of wars fought in human history been related to religion? Why has the cooperative work of religious believers for peace and well-being always been difficult? Why is a religion often divided within itself, illustrated, for instance, by the divided churches and confessions within Christianity?

There is another question that should disconcert us: Why do we almost always have to write the history of our own religion and construct our beliefs and teachings at the expense of other religions? Not one religion is free from such practice. But Christians seem the worst offenders. We have consistently promoted what we believe in opposition to what others believe. This is what we have always done in relation to Islam, Hinduism, or Buddhism. We are particularly unscrupulous when it comes to Judaism. We have gone about rewriting what the people of the Hebrew Scriptures believed and practiced on the premise that the hope of salvation they forfeited has come true with Christianity. As to whether they really forfeited salvation or not, whether we have done complete justice to countless women, men, and children in the Hebrew Scriptures who died not only in despair but in hope, is seldom asked. If hope for them was illusive, it could be illusive for Christians as well.

"Why Did You Bring Us Out of Egypt?"

Let us first turn to the Book of Exodus. In it we read one dramatic story after another of how the people of Israel are liberated from life "engulfed in deep water and burning fire" (*shui shen huo re*), to use a Chinese expression; that is, they are liberated from a life of deep distress and from the abyss of suffering in the land of bondage. But the focus of these stories quickly moves from a group of people to one particular person. It does not take us long to realize who the hero is in these dramas of liberation. It is as if the entire Book of Exodus were written to tell how Moses became the leader of liberation and the founder of the nation later to be called Israel.

From beginning to end Moses is portrayed as the protagonist who gave birth to the Exodus stories. He shaped and changed them, built and dismantled them. Moses becomes the guiding spirit of the movement toward freedom and the chief architect of the nation founded on the Ten Commandments he is said to have received directly from God. From the story of how he came to be the commissioned leader of the liberation movement (Exodus 3) in the unusual encounter with the burning bush to the story of how he personally received the Ten Commandments from God on Mount Sinai (19:10—20:21; also 34:1-9), the focus gradually but decidedly shifts from the people to Moses, from those who are led to the one who leads, from the ruled to the ruler. Divine authority is built around his leadership, even around himself.

What developed in the process is opposition between the people, increasingly forced to play a passive role in matters concerning their own material and spiritual well-being, and Moses their paramount leader whose words are law. Followers had to obey the words he received from God, who "used to speak to Moses face to face, as one speaks to a friend" (33:11).[19] There are indications that opposition had been brewing. One only needs to read the story of the people, tired and hungry in the desert, complaining to Moses: "If only we had died by the hand of the Lord in the land of Egypt, when we sat by the fleshpots and ate our fill of bread; for you have brought us out into this wilderness to kill this whole assembly with hunger" (16:3). The people even quarreled with Moses when they were dying of thirst. They were bitter and scarcely concealed it: "Why did you bring us out of Egypt, to kill us and our children and livestock with thirst?" (17:3).

There must have been many other incidents that did not find their way into the Book of Exodus. But these two verses alone make us suspect that the situation of the people of Israel in the wilderness, after their escape from Egypt, was anything but rosy. A Chinese expression such as *yuan sheng chai dau*, meaning "complaints can be heard everywhere," or *yuan qi chong tian*, meaning "the resentment soars heaven high," can accurately describe what was happening. Events came to a head when the people, in Moses' long absence on Mount Sinai, made a golden calf to worship in place of Yahweh their God. The result was as tragic as it was traumatic. A great purge took place. Moses rallied around himself the sons of Levi and commanded them to kill their brothers, friends, and neighbors in the camp. As many as three thousand people were said to be put to the sword.[20]

We have been taught to read these stories siding with Moses. As for the people who harassed Moses their leader, they got what they deserved. Moses, the man of God, was always right. It was the people who erred. To contradict Moses is to contradict God. To complain against the leader is to complain against God. To rebel against the hero Moses is to rebel against the Lord. This is the theological formula that has shaped our reading. But is this all there is to it? Do we always have to read stories in the Bible from top down, from the perspective of the "men of God," who are always in the right because God confided in them? Are the people always ignorant, discontented, ungrateful, and rebellious? Should we not have given more thought to the question the people put to Moses in desperation: "Why did you bring us out of Egypt to die of hunger in the desert?" Should we not pay more attention to the people, faced with thirst, hunger, and death, with the shattering of their dreams and hopes? In our theological reading of the Hebrew Scriptures, we have not always noticed how elusive hope was for the people in the desert and the desperation of having to face thirst and hunger, possibly leading to death. There is no room for an elusive hope in our theology. The people who died in despair in the desert have been unaccounted for in our theology, which is dominated almost completely by the promise of the land. But this future hope itself proves elusive, as we shall see.

Because we have always approached the Bible with a set of predetermined theological ideas and religious teachings, we have not been able to notice subtle changes taking place—changes of focus from those on the top to those at the bottom, from those who lead to those who are led, from those who rule to those who are ruled. When the focus shifts, questions very different from those with which we are familiar begin to emerge and issues different from those that used to concern us start to engage our attention.

Suppose we read these stories to which we just referred, for example, and place ourselves among the people—not with Moses. Let us imagine ourselves in the wilderness under the scorching sun. Let us place ourselves among the people wandering in the desert, looking for an oasis. Would we not think their hunger a just cause for complaint? Is not their thirst a legitimate reason for questioning Moses' leadership? Would not Moses' long absence in such difficult times cause them worry, fear, and even panic? Such questions make us wonder whether storytellers have told their listeners and readers all that happened during the journey through the desert. Or perhaps they have inserted stories about people's complaints, even revolts, hoping in secret that future readers may turn their attention to the countless men, women, and children without names who toiled, suffered, and perished under the one supreme leader whose name we know so well.

This shift in focus has enormous implications for our understanding of biblical stories. What concerned the masses of Israelite people most in the wilderness were food and water. These are the necessities of life. They desperately needed the "bread of life" and the "water of life." Their hope, their expectation, was as simple as that. It was not an unreasonable expectation. Nor was it an exorbitant hope. Moses, as portrayed in these desert stories, did not understand this fact. He even got impatient with the masses. "Why do you quarrel with me?" he said. "Why do you test the Lord?" (Exod. 17:2).

But Jesus understood basic needs. He was so aware of these basics of everyday life that he even taught his disciples to pray: "Give us each day our daily bread" (Luke 11:3; also Matt. 6:11). Do we not recall how Jesus saw to it that "a great crowd" which had come to hear him in an out-of-the-way place was properly fed before they set out on their journey home (Mark 6:32-44)?[21]

Another incident also provokes us to think. Jesus and the disciples were passing through grainfields (Matt. 12:1-8; also Mark 2:23-28; Luke 6:1-5). "His disciples were hungry, and they began to pluck heads of grain and to eat" (Matt. 12:1). It so happened that it was the sabbath, and the Pharisees who saw the incident took issue with Jesus. But Jesus quickly came to his disciples' defense, reminding the accusers of two past incidents. "Have you not read," he asked them, "what David did when he and his companions were hungry? He entered the house of God and ate the bread of the Presence, which it was not lawful for him or his companions to eat, but only for the priests. Or have you not read in the law that on the sabbath the priests in the temple break the sabbath and yet are guiltless?" Jesus never wavered from his stance when it came to the matter of choice between satisfying people's needs or what was proscribed in the law.

If Jesus had been one of the Israelite people struggling to survive in the desert, he would not only have supported their complaints against Moses but perhaps taken an active part in alerting the leadership to the dire situation. This makes one wonder how Jesus read these stories in the Book of Exodus. He must have read them very differently from the way they had been read by the religious authorities. That his heart always went out to those in pain and suffering prompts us to believe that he would have sided with the hungry and thirsty people in the desert rather than with their leader, who would invoke divine authority and punishment at the slightest provocation.

But religious leaders are prone to act differently from Jesus. They are trained to side with God against people, not knowing that God supports the people. They believe that they have the ears of God, while what people say in distress smacks of mischief and lack of faith. They convince themselves that their task is to make God's will known, not realizing that there is no way of knowing God's will if they do not see what people face in the rough-and-tumble of the world. Many people of all religions, including Christians, have had to contend, like Jesus, with religious leadership, often with terrible consequences. Jesus was put to death for his opposition.

Though sad, this is a historical fact we have to face. Many men and women have suffered at the hands of religious authorities for what they believed and did in response to their conscience. Should this fact not prompt us to take a fresh look at the way we have traditionally viewed Moses and his leadership as he led the Israelites on their journey toward freedom? Should we not consider the countless people who died with their hope unfulfilled? Should our hearts not go out to those women, men, and children, deprived of food and drink, who had to face uncertainty and danger in the wilderness and who were unable to get excited about the hope of gaining the promised land in the distant future? They did murmur against Moses, asking: "Did you bring us out of Egypt to kill us?" Do we hear just the insolence and ingratitude in these words? Or do we hear something else? That the people dared to question and challenge their "divinely sanctioned" leader, their "national savior," seems to speak volumes. Their situation could not have been more terrible. Were they perhaps justified in taking steps against him?

"Who Made You a Ruler over Us?"

What this discussion means for us theologically is disturbing. We are conditioned to view the drama of the Exodus almost solely on the basis of what Moses is said to have been commissioned by God to do, that is, to lead his people out of bondage in Egypt. A great vision is envisioned for the people and an exciting future prepared. What they have in store is the hope of new life in the land of freedom and plenty, a hope promised by none other than God. The main plot of the story has already been prepared—the plot that leads from Egypt through the wilderness to the destination, in the land flowing with milk and honey. Is this illusion or reality? Of course it is reality. Is this a promise or a fantasy? Without question, it is a promise. Is it a hope or a daydream? It is, beyond a shadow of doubt, a hope. How can it be a daydream when the vision has been disclosed to the religious authorities by God?

The faith of the Exodus storytellers must have been shaped by the official theology of who God is and what God wills, constructed by the leaders and teachers of their religious community long after that memorable event. The leaders and teachers were many generations removed from the event and had no personal experience of it. It is their faith in the God they worshiped in "the land of promise" that formed the basis of the Exodus stories. Still there are, as indicated above, episodes that reflect what people said and did to question and even challenge their leadership. But most of us, Christians and theologians, have almost totally neglected to take these episodes into serious account. We have accepted the official theology that shaped most of the stories in the Hebrew Scriptures. But this is not all we have done. We have adapted the theology, refined it, expanded it, and developed it into a comprehensive "Christian" theology of God's saving activity. The result is that the episodes reflecting people's reactions to what had been prescribed by their religious authorities are either played down or judged to be evidence of their disobedience to God, even of their rebellion against God.

The underlying theological assumption is that, from the very beginning, what the Christian church has taught as God's promise has been progressively fulfilled in Christianity. Armed with such a theological premise, most of us Christians and theologians have constructed a theology of history for Christianity, for the people of the Hebrew Scriptures, and for all the nations and peoples of the world. This grandiose theology of history embraces the entire span of time. It is "Christian" to its very core.

But the question is whether the theology is as grandiose as it claims, as comprehensive as it assumes, and as convincing as it professes, especially to people unrelated to Christianity. When Christianity was on the march in the heyday of Western political hegemony, the theological premise was not questioned. Nor did it occur to most Christians to question the premise. But when Western political hegemony finally came to an end, when we realized that we Christians do not live in a world shaped and dominated by Christianity, the opportunity to hold the view of life and world created by that "grandiose" theology of history also ended. This is a theological realism that faces Christian churches and Christians today. Many of us still find it difficult to adjust.

But it is also a fact that this grand theology of history has not remained unquestioned and unchallenged. It has been pointed out that even the official theology that shaped the faith of the Hebrew Scriptures—that the history of ancient Israel was from the very beginning inspired by God's promise of land and prosperity—was anachronistic, that it applied a theology developed later in time to what had taken place much earlier. If this is the case with Hebrew Scripture itself, how much more anachronistic is it to apply the Christian theology of hope and promise to the experiences of ancient people of Israel, such as those in the Exodus from Egypt?

To disentangle the later theology of promise from what actually happened to people in earlier times, we have to note that "the promises [to ancient Israelite people] had an extraordinarily long life span. References to the promises, however, are far from uniformly distributed. Among the prophets they appear first in Jeremiah and Ezekiel; in the Psalms they are rare. They are very frequent, however in Deuteronomy [written in the seventh century B.C.E.], where the recollection of the promise of the land, given to the fathers, is more frequent than the land promise passages in Genesis 12–50."[22] That is to say, the theology of promise was the product of "royal theology" in the seventh century, adapted and developed particularly to be the central religious-political ideology during the reign of King Josiah. This royal theology of promise got extended all the way back to the times of "the fathers" and became the theological principle underlying the history of "the patriarchs."

If this is how the theology of promise came into being, it is no wonder that "for all the references outside Genesis 12–50...fulfillment does not come to the fathers themselves but for Israel. The later period had no interest in promises that had been fulfilled for the fathers themselves."[23] Even when the faith of Abraham received special mention and commendation (Gen. 22:15-18, for instance), "we can recognize clearly the interests of a later period, for which

Abraham's obedience now becomes the model of obedience and faith."[24] Does this not mean that we can only make use of the theology of promise with extreme restraint, that we should not allow it to govern the happenings in Israel before the seventh century B.C.E., not to mention the history of the nations and peoples outside the influence of Christianity?

What has been said is particularly relevant to the familiar story of Abraham's call, a story that launches the migration of an obscure tribal family in Mesopotamia into the theological orbit of divine election and promise. "Now the Lord said to Abram," begins the storyteller known as the Yahwist, so named because of the preference for Yawheh as the name for God, "'Go from your country and your kindred and your father's house to the land that I will show you. I will make of you a great nation, and I will bless you, and make your name great, so that you will be a blessing. I will bless those who bless you, and the one who curses you I will curse; and in you all the families of the earth shall be blessed'" (Gen. 12:1-3). What is contained in this passage has been *chin ke yu lu*, literally "golden order and jade law"—namely, the "golden rule"—for the theology of how God came to be related to Israel first and later to Christians in a way unparalleled in human history.

This is a brilliant theology, a theology that grows out of its center to all nations and peoples, even to the whole earth. That in the eighth century B.C.E. such a "global" or "ecumenical" theology had already come into being is amazing indeed. But when one realizes that the storyteller called the Yahwist was telling stories against the background of the great empire built by King David and now bedecked in glory and luxury under the reign of King Solomon, such theological development may not be surprising after all. This is an obvious example of how a theology cannot be taken at face value. Every theology, ancient or modern, Eastern or Western, has to be assessed and appreciated in relation to the religious-cultural and social-political situations in which it comes to be formulated.

As to the theology of election and promise highlighted in the story of Abraham's call in Genesis 12, it is "a literary composition of the Yahwist to introduce the patriarchal history" not belonging to "the patriarchal period."[25] There is, in actual fact, nothing strange in this observation. Theology is always contemporary. It is situational, and takes place within a certain framework of time and space. In this sense theology, any theology, is particular. But there is always a tendency to endow a particular theology with universal significance, extending its frame of reference in a particular time and place to all times and all places. History cannot escape such theological generalization. Theology, just as any other mental and spiritual adventure of humanity, consists of ideas, prognosis, and wisdom more of hindsight than foresight. It often projects its hindsight onto what took place a long time ago. That is why with regard to history, theology tends to commit the error of getting time upside down. It is thus no surprise that what had gone on long before the tenth century B.C.E. in ancient Israel also came to be part of the theology of election and promise formulated much later in time.

The question the beleaguered people in the desert put to Moses, "Why did you bring us out from Egypt?" begins, then, to gain an importance it had not received before. The leadership of Moses is questioned. People do not accept without question what he has offered, be it the promise of a land of plenty or a future full of blessings, even freedom. His authority, said to be divinely endowed, is challenged. The tragedy of the golden calf incident could be seen as an expression of that challenge. To regard the incident as nothing but people resorting to idolatry is to miss a critical point. What people challenged was not Yahweh their God, but Moses their leader. What they tested was not the authority of God but the authority Moses claimed to have received from God.

The brutal way in which the people were crushed in their protest is ample evidence of how the authority represented by Moses had to be maintained at any cost. It is not difficult to imagine that the authority of God, always seasoned with love and mercy, suffered in the eyes of people. The people learned that God is to be feared rather than loved. God is to be kept at a distance and not to come too close. God is high and mighty rather than accessible and compassionate. The storyteller shows how people became very afraid of the stern and judgmental God when they say to Moses: "You speak to us, and we will listen; but do not let God speak to us, or we will die" (Exod. 20:19).

Even a passing acquaintance with the history of religions will tell us that fear for the awesome deity is not unique to the Israelite people. It is a universal experience. Story after story from the pages of the history of religions tell us that instead of making God less frightful, religious authorities tend to make God even more fearful and inaccessible. In the Gospels we see how Jesus set himself against such religious authorities and made every effort to endear God to people, teaching them to call God "Abba," father, mother, parent.

Moses' leadership was not questioned for the first time at Mount Sinai. There was at least one precedent in Egypt. Ingeniously, the storyteller seems to have planted a story in the Exodus accounts to foreshadow how the relationship between Moses the leader and the people was to become strained. According to the story, Moses, a hot-blooded youth brought up as a prince with all splendor and pomp in the Pharaoh's palace and full of the sense of justice and chivalry, killed an " Egyptian beating a Hebrew, one of his kinsfolk" (Exod. 2:11-12). He must have been secretly proud of what he had done. He was able to do something for his people despite the fact that he had been part of the royal establishment that enslaved them.

The next day, he came across two Hebrews fighting each other. He intervened, believing what he had done the previous day should have gained him acceptance. But to his dismay, what he encountered was hostility. One of the quarreling men said to him: "Who made you a ruler and judge over us? Do you mean to kill me as you killed the Egyptian?" (Exod. 2:14). Moses was taken aback. This was not what he expected. Was this an isolated incident? Is it nothing more than a passing episode in the whole drama of the Exodus? The storyteller tells us that the incident frightened Moses. He had to flee the scene and also Egypt, the land that had adopted him. He returned later to lead his people out of Egypt, but as we have seen, his leadership did not remain unchallenged.

The story of his death on Mount Nebo, after he was denied entry with the people into "the promised land," gives us a lot to think about in this connection. Here the storyteller again seems to suggest skillfully that Moses was not accepted by the people or by God without question. "Moses, the servant of the Lord," we are told, "died there in the land of Moab, at the Lord's command" (Deut. 34:5). Thus ended the life of Moses, an uninspiring end to a life that had begun with fanfare and excitement. The solitary figure of Moses fading away on Mount Nebo, overlooking the promised land across the Jordan, induces deep feelings and empathy. The hope of a promised land had eluded him. As he looked across the vast land, perhaps what most occupied his mind was the women, men, and children without number who had died not knowing when their suffering would end. At death Moses finally found his place among the compatriots to whom he had brought not freedom but pain, not hope but despair, not life but death.

In Moses dying alone on Mount Nebo, and in his countless compatriots who died with the vision of freedom and the hope of a new land forever out of reach, we have glimpses of men, women, and children with their vision of life destroyed and their hope shattered. In them we feel the pain and suffering of Filipino migrant workers in Hong Kong such as Mediatrix Jane Quilim. Above all, the ancient Israelites, including Moses, remind us of Jesus with his followers at the Last Supper, facing an imminent death that was going to undo what he had done. What was utmost in the minds of his followers in those dark hours? For that matter, what occupied Jesus in his thoughts and prayers?

We have not taken such questions to heart in our faith and theology. But it is in these questions that we can more seriously wrestle with the hope we hold and cherish, not only as Christians, but as vulnerable human beings like Moses and the Israelites, like Jesus' followers two thousand years ago, like migrant workers all over the world today, and like Jesus himself. We have all been too ready to dwell on hope, a hope God promised to us in the indefinite past and that God is going to fulfill in an indefinite future. Ours tends to be a theology of hope that addresses God, but not pressing human questions.

If we avoid these questions, we do not provide a theology of hope but a theology of illusion. When we turn our eyes and minds from tragic realities of life and history, we are engaged not in a theology of truth but in a theology of deception. When we conduct our theological business on the premise that hope is theologically "proleptic," a hope for the future to be realized only at the end of time, then we are engaged in a theology of chimeras. Often in our theology we have confused illusion with reality, taken fantasy for truth, and substituted chimeras for hope.

Bricks without Straw

We must now retrace our steps from the theologically highly charged scene at Mount Sinai, from the exciting events surrounding the Exodus, to the scenes of Israelite people toiling in harsh conditions as Pharaoh's slave laborers. This is the setting in which the drama of the Exodus begins. The Pharaoh and his cronies "set taskmasters over [the Israelite people] to oppress them with forced labor. They built supply cities, Pithom and Rameses, for Pharaoh" (Exod. 1:11). In all probability the forced labor mentioned in these two cities "went on under the first two kings of the Nineteenth Dynasty, Seti II (about 1310–1290 B.C.E.) and his son Rameses II (about 1290–1224 B.C.E.)."[26]

The dates and places introduced at the outset of the Exodus story have received extensive archaeological, historical, and chronological study. But curiously, the story itself, without which there would have been no Exodus, has been treated in passing as a piece of background information. The reason is not difficult to guess. Theology in both Judaism and Christianity is not as interested in men, women, and children who suffered under forced labor. The interest is greater in developing the faith and theology of how God is related—first to the people of Israel and then to Christians—to God's covenant people and in the special privileges set apart for these special groups.

This idea has come to be known as "covenant theology." But this has been a theology that discriminates. In the case of Christianity, the theology has not only discriminated against people who are not Christian, but even against Jewish believers. As for the people who suffered and perished doing Pharaoh's slave labor, they have not been the subject of our theological concern. By bypassing them in our theology of covenant, we have done them an injustice. They are no more than a means to an end in our theology. It has not occurred to us to grapple theologically with their suffering and death, for their own sake as people and not for the sake of our "high" theology of promise, hope, and covenant.

These laborers deserve every bit of our theological attention. With the reappearance of Moses as the divinely appointed leader who would lead them to freedom, their already hard life was made even harder. In response to Moses' demand to let the people go, however, Pharaoh decided to make the laborers' lives more unbearable, even impossible. He ordered the supervisors not to provide straw for the bricks the laborers made. "Let them go and collect their own straw," he commanded, "but see that they produce the same tally of bricks as before; on no account reduce it. They are lazy, and that is why they are clamoring to go and offer sacrifice to their God. Keep these men hard at work; let them attend to that. Take no notice of their lies" (Exod. 5:7-9 [REB]).

In the Pharaoh's words there is a curious echo, almost word for word, of what the Italian migrant worker (see p. 142) was told by his employer: "You're here to work, not to be ill." More than three thousand years separate these two incidents, but they tell the same story of how human beings treat one another. Ancient Israelites in Egypt had to make bricks with the straw they had to collect for themselves. They were punished for not being able to produce the same amount of bricks as when they had been provided with straw. In the testimony of another Filipino migrant domestic worker in Hong Kong the echo is even louder and more distinct. She was ordered one evening by her employer "to buy two bowls of instant noodles with her own money. When I served it to her, she gloated and said it is just right that my money should be spent for them as punishment for my slowness. She then told me to clear the table. Suddenly, she picked up the soup and threw it at my back. . . ."[27]

It is hard to believe that the story of ancient Israelites in Egypt is still repeated in today's world—the world that has made leaps and bounds in standards of living, the world supposedly far better enlightened about ethical values, rights, and the integrity of individual persons. Perhaps human beings in essence have not changed much, despite all the moral teachings and religious endeavors. Have we not seen incredible atrocities committed in this twentieth century? A Chinese saying has sadly got it right: "Rivers and mountains are easier to change than human nature" (*chiang shan yi kai ren xin nan yi*).[28] The world in which we live today, just like the world thousands of years ago, is still one in which "the strong prey on the weak and the weak fall victim to the strong." Do not these realities make us think more realistically about what religion can do? Has not religion, including Christianity, from time to time played an active part in this game of the strong preying on the weak?

Death of the Firstborn

If our theology of hope and covenant has done injustice to the countless Israelite people who suffered and perished under Pharaoh and during the dangerous and desperate trek in the wilderness, it has done even more injustice to the innocent children of Egyptian families. On the eve of the Israelites' escape from Egypt, the last and tenth plague struck. It was a brutal and tragic plague that inflicted untold miseries on Egyptian parents and their families. What happened, if it happened as told in the Exodus story, was nothing less than a crime against humanity.

Moses said to the people: "Thus says the Lord: About midnight I will go out through Egypt. Every firstborn in the land of Egypt shall die, from the firstborn of Pharaoh who sits on his throne to the firstborn of the female slaves who is behind the handmill, and all the firstborn of the livestock" (Exod. 11:4-5). This is the last act of the drama that the audience sympathetic to the oppressed had been waiting for. What had to happen was at last going to happen. After all that Pharaoh had done to make the people of Israel suffer, he would get what he deserved. This was the price he had to pay for refusing to let the Israelites go free. This is the punishment he would get for setting himself against Yahweh, the God of Moses, and Yahweh's people.

The people of the Hebrew Scriptures long after the Exodus read the story in this way. And this is how generations of Christians have read the story. But is this not a horrible story? Is this not a terrible tragedy for the Egyptian families? Pharaoh treated the Israelite people harshly. He put them through unbearable suffering. Many of them died from the hard labor he imposed on them. He had Hebrew baby boys killed as soon as they were born. As the Chinese would say, "the list of his crimes is long enough to reach heaven" (*zui e tau tian*). Indeed, he deserved punishment for the terrible things he had done to the Israelite people.

But what do the Egyptian firstborn have to do with Pharaoh's atrocities against Hebrew slave laborers? The firstborn of the Egyptian slave females, and even Pharaoh's own firstborn, are totally innocent. They are victims of Pharaoh's cruelty and atrocities as are the Israelite slaves. What had been done to them was not less unjust than what had been done to the people of Israel. With regard to killing the firstborn of the livestock, the story becomes absurd. Why do these animals have to bear the brunt of what Pharaoh had done?

The inclusion of the Egyptian firstborn in the massacre—for this act is a massacre—may be excusable if this were a fairy tale and not to be read as a historical account. It could be acceptable as religious fiction meant to teach the faithful not to set oneself against God and what God commands. It could even be a story with a moral lesson, warning the reader against the practice of tit for tat. But we Christians have always read the story as a historical narrative, as an event that actually took place. The story forms part of the struggle of the Israelite people for freedom. But, far more important, the tale forms part of the story of how God chose a particular people to be "a great nation" in whom "all the families of the earth shall be blessed" (Gen. 12:2-3).

In other words, what happened to the firstborn of Egypt belongs to the history of the "chosen" people of God. This makes some of us feel very unsettled. That the massacre of the innocent forms part of the history of "a great nation" has been a theological matter of fact to most Christians. We stay behind closed doors with the people ready to depart from the land of oppression and slavery, holding our breath, waiting for the angels of death "to pass over our house."

But should we not stop to think that this incident may have been a mistake? If we are theologically enterprising, should we not ponder deeply what the death of the firstborn would have meant to God when God was setting the people of Israel free? If we are not to be naive in our practice of faith and theology, do we not find ourselves asking why these innocent firstborn had to die in order for the Israelite people to be free? We may even go further and ask whether it was morally right for these innocent children to have been involved in the struggle for liberation. And there is always a question that we have to ask if we are to look for God's truth: Did God really tell Moses that God would bring about the death of the firstborn to make way for the Israelites' freedom?

We Christians have been too hasty, if not too callous, in passing over the account of the death of the firstborn in the Exodus narrative. We have been theologically insensitive to it, giving it no more than a fleeting thought as an episode in the "triumphant" departure of the oppressed people of Israel from the land of the oppressive Pharaoh. Such hastiness and such insensitivity have too often been part of the history of Christianity. The triumphant church has too hastily condemned those who question what it has taught to be true. It has alienated and even disposed of those who dare to question its authority. When it moved to the parts of the world with many cultures and religions, it has been insensitive to what people believe and how they live, creating divisions in the communities to whom it professes to bring reconciliation, peace, and salvation.

We have made many mistakes in the name of our faith and committed many theological errors. The world today, no longer dominated by the nations shaped by Christianity, has made more and more of us aware of these mistakes and errors. We have listened to the story of Mediatrix Jane Quilim, a Filipino migrant worker in Hong Kong. We have also heard the stories of migrant workers in many parts of the world, including Europe and North America. They tell us something we have not taken seriously before. They remind us that our theology has tended to serve those who are successful, prosperous, and powerful, and not those who are powerless and helpless. Millions of people such as Mediatrix Jane Quilim have reasons to say that the Christian theology of hope does not apply to them, that all they have is an elusive hope, a hope that slips through their fingers.

When we return to stories such as the massacre of the firstborn in Exodus, the book on which we have built our theology of promise and hope, we begin to hear the voices of those firstborn murdered in the struggle between Pharaoh and Moses, between the masters and slaves. What are these voices saying to us? Have we ever tried to listen to these voices? What questions are these voices asking us? But have we ever paid attention to these questions? These voices, in fact, are posing a serious question to the Christian theology of hope: Is it God's will to let the Israelite people go free at the expense of the firstborn of Egypt, who have nothing to do with what Pharaoh has done? Why does Israelite freedom have to be won at the cost of innocent infants? Why does God have to be unjust to the firstborn to do justice to the suffering people of Israel? How are we, in short, going to justify our theology of hope to the firstborn of Egypt?

We cannot justify our theology of hope to them. There is no justification for it. We have to admit that our theology has been built on a wrong premise— the premise that God chooses some and reject others, that God saves some and condemns others, that God blesses some and curses others, that God, in order to make some live, makes others die. This statement may oversimplify the theology most of us have learned and that we continue to learn, but it has been the basic tenet of our faith and theology nevertheless. But is this God of our theology of hope the God who created heavens and earth? Is this God the God who brought *all* nations and peoples into being? Is this God the God of Jesus?

This is not the God, we must insist, who created heavens and earth and all things, including all human beings. Above all, this is not the God that Jesus has shown us in what he said and did. In spite of this God of creation, and in spite of this God of Jesus, we Christians have developed a faith and theology that turn God into a God of prejudice, chauvinism, and even apartheid. How can we explain to the firstborn of the Egypt why they had to die for the Israelite people to be set free? We cannot justify the way in which we have understood God to have harmed them and a great number of men, women, and children in history. God, in our theology, brings hope and salvation to a small group of people at the expense of a real majority of humankind.

What we can tell those firstborn of Egypt and what we must tell them is simply this: the God said to have decreed their death is not the God who created all human beings, including them. To great numbers of people we have to say: the God who allows them to die at the hands of those who have done what they have done in the name of God is not the God of Jesus. Was not Jesus himself murdered by those who always had the name of God on their lips? Was he not crucified by them in the name of their God?

None of what can be said to the firstborn of Egypt can undo what was done to them. Our candid admission, already so belated, is not of any help to them who died not knowing why. But as we become aware of the injustice contained in our faith and of something fundamentally abnormal in our theology, particularly in the way we have theologized about God and about how God deals brutally with people outside of our "Christian" world, we cannot but read more carefully this part of the Exodus story.

This is what we must do: We must pause when we reach the end of the third verse of the eleventh chapter in the Book of Exodus. This is important. We must not let ourselves be carried away in the excitement of reading how the Israelite people were instructed to take silver and gold from their Egyptian neighbors (11:1-3). This was a dishonorable thing to do, to say the least. It was a deceitful thing to do, too, because the Israelites took advantage of whatever friendship and goodwill that still existed between them and their Egyptian neighbors. Here the storyteller slips, intentionally or inadvertently, a footnote into the story: "The Lord gave the people favor in the sight of the Egyptians." One can almost perceive glee on the storyteller's face!

But we must not get carried away by the discovery of this insertion. Instead, we must slow down when we begin the next paragraph, and read it word by word, sentence by sentence. Even a comma, a colon, or a period is not to be passed over. There should not be "passovers" when we read stories, and Bible stories are no exception. To pass over certain sections of the story is to disregard them. This is what happened to our Christian theology of the Exodus.

The massacre of the Egyptian firstborn has no place in our theology. We have passed over it and virtually disregarded it. We have not even heard "a loud cry throughout the whole land of Egypt, such as has never been or will never be again" (Exod. 11:6).

It was a cry of the mothers who had given birth to their firstborn. It was the cry of the fathers who had worked hard to provide home for their precious offspring. It was the cry of the brothers and sisters who had lost their siblings. It was the cry of the grandparents who had to witness their grandchildren dying in their own blood. And it was the cry of the farmers whose livestock were butchered. The whole of Egypt wailed in pain and anguish. But the Israelite people were too busy getting ready to get away to hear it. The generations of Jewish leaders and theologians were too occupied with their own dream of divine promise to notice it. As for Christians and theologians, we have had too much on our theological plate in sorting out the chosen from the unchosen, screening the saved from the unsaved, and setting Christians apart from pagans to be bothered with the loud cry of the Egyptian mothers, fathers, brothers, sisters, and grandparents—the cry "such as has never been or will never be again."

But the ingenious hand of the storyteller remains active. The official version of the Exodus story has to be told, and, yes, the song of Miriam, sister of Moses, has to be duly recorded.

> Sing to the Lord,
>> for the Lord has triumphed gloriously;
>> horse and rider the Lord has thrown into the sea.
>>> (Exod. 15:21)

The Exodus is the great triumph of the Lord, the great victory of the Israelite people, and a moment of great glory for God.

But the storyteller also remembers the loud cry in the land of Egypt. The cry remains in his memory. It resounds in his heart. This is perhaps—I have to stress the little word *perhaps,* because I go not by what is written—the reason why the storyteller begins in Exodus 11:4 by saying: "Moses said [to the people]..." The storyteller then, and only then, goes on to tell us, "Thus says the Lord: About midnight I will go out through Egypt. Every firstborn in the land of Egypt shall die, from the firstborn of Pharaoh who sits on his throne to the firstborn of the female slave who is behind the handmill, and all the firstborn of the livestock" (11:4-5).

Moses said. This is how the storyteller continues the story in 11:4. It is Moses who reported what the Lord had said to him regarding the firstborn in Egypt. Most of us have never noticed something important here. And we have not suspected that the storyteller may be communicating covertly something he cannot say overtly: "Moses said, 'Thus says the Lord...'" The text says, *Moses said,* and not *the Lord said. Moses said* what he had heard the Lord say. Moses is the principal speaker in 11:4, not God.

Beginning with the phrase "Moses said," the story departs from the earlier pattern. Until this moment, the storyteller almost always has God take the active role in speaking to Moses. God called to Moses out of the burning bush and spoke to him (Exod. 3:4). "The Lord said to Moses" what God would do to Pharaoh (Exod. 6:1). Each plague, from the first to the ninth, begins with the statement, "Then the Lord said to Moses,"[29] and is followed by the account of how God would punish Pharaoh and his people. But when the storyteller gets to the story of the firstborn, the format changes. The direct speech of God to Moses becomes indirect speech communicated by Moses to the people. It is no longer, "the Lord said to Moses," but, "Moses said." Moses tells the people what God said to him.

Is this change in the form of speech from the direct to indirect address intentional or accidental? It could have been intentional. After nine terrible plagues, the storyteller seems to hesitate. He is not sure whether the action is God's doing. Is the most horrible thing he will tell a direct command from God? Or is the command from Moses? Is the command what Moses understood God to have said? One wonders whether such thoughts were in the storyteller's mind when he prefaced the account of the last catastrophe with the phrase "Moses said," instead of the earlier statement, "Then the Lord said to Moses." At least there is a lapse in the train of the storyteller's thought. Is it a lapse he has left discreetly behind? Is he letting us ask whether God had really promised to carry out those atrocious acts, or whether Moses speaks on his own behalf?

We are led to wonder whether the slaughter of the firstborn was in fact carried out by the Israelite people and later attributed to God. It is conceivable that a natural catastrophe or epidemic devastated a large part of the land and its population, prompting the Israelites to conclude that these events were divine punishment for what Pharaoh and his officers had done to them. It has been suggested that at least some of the disasters and plagues could have actually taken place around the time the Israelite people left Egypt. But the slaughter of the firstborn is different from all the catastrophes that preceded it. Could this final tragic act be nothing more than a fiction created by the storyteller either to enliven the story or to heighten its dramatic quality?

In any case, one wishes that an atrocity such as the slaughter of the innocent did not take place. Fiction or not, it is immoral to attain one's hope by inflicting suffering on others. It is religious sadism to gloat over the pain and misfortune of others as part of the fulfillment of divine purpose. A theology that falls short of moral integrity is not theology. A theology that smacks of sadism does not deserve the name. But does not the Christian theology of promise and hope, developed from the story of the Exodus, at least make us very uncomfortable? Do we not have to ask whether the story of the Exodus taken at face value can be the basis of our theology of promise and hope, a theology that has taken up the central place in our life and faith as Christians?

These same questions have to be directed also to the theology of liberation that has flourished since its appearance in Latin America in the beginning of the 1970s. It has awakened the oppressed part of humanity, ethnic minorities and those socially, economically, and politically exploited and discriminated against, including women. It has inspired these groups to strive for human rights, and in the case of Christians, to develop their own theologies over against the theology of the dominant society and culture. It is an explosive, soul-searching theology, and has turned the theological world upside down. A theological genie has been let out of its long imprisonment in the bottle manufactured by the traditional, authoritarian, male-dominated church hierarchy. Christian theology will never be the same again. This is a cause for celebration.

But there is a nagging question. The Exodus story has served as the cornerstone for liberation theology of almost all colors and shades, the story representing the liberation of the enslaved people of Israel from the land of Egypt. Those of us who have embraced liberation theology and promoted it in a variety of settings have identified ourselves with the oppressed people of Israel. We have accepted the official version of the Exodus story and applied it to our own theological efforts. In the process two ideas have eluded us.

In the first place, we have not recognized that the official version of the Exodus story has been adopted by the theology of the traditional church to develop its theology of promise and hope—a theology that discriminates against the disinherited, minorities, women, and people outside the Christian church. Has not liberation theology parted company from such theology? Second, those who embrace liberation theology have identified themselves with the Israelite people who suffered under Pharaoh. This of course is right. But what about the ordinary men, women, and children of Egypt, those who also suffered from the dictatorship of Pharaoh and who fell victim to Pharaoh's refusal to let the people of Israel go? What about the firstborn children murdered so the Israelite people could set out on their march to freedom? Liberation theology, just like the traditional theology from which it has tried to dissociate itself, has no place for them.

If traditional theology and even liberation theology have no place for the murdered children, would Jesus have a place for them in his heart and in his experience of God as the loving Abba—father, mother, or parent? Most certainly he would. In the Gospels there is no record of Jesus retelling the story of the Exodus. But the Gospel writers have left us many stories of how Jesus' heart goes out to disinherited people. He also has a tender spot in his heart for children. It is possible that he would not have accepted the official version of the Exodus story, let alone the official theology of promise, hope, and election based on it. His vision of the reign of God is far removed from the official theology of God, which favors a particular people and confers special favors and privileges on them.

But an incident related to the birth of Jesus has a curious similarity to the incident in the Exodus story with which we have been engaged. I am referring to the massacre of infants by King Herod in what can only be called an act of insanity—an act aimed at doing away with baby Jesus as a potential rival to his kingly power. As Matthew's nativity story tells us, the infant Jesus had been hastily sent away before Herod was able to lay his hand on him. Incensed, Herod "sent and killed all the children in and around Bethlehem who were two years old or under" (Matt. 2:16). This was a senseless and gruesome massacre, no less so than the massacre of the firstborn of Egypt some 1,300 years before.

The tragic incident inspires the author of Matthew's Gospel to quote the prophet Jeremiah:

> A voice was heard in Ramah,
>   wailing and loud lamentation,
> Rachel weeping for her children;
>   she refused to be consoled,
>   because they are no more.
>   (Matt. 2:18)

Who could be consoled after such an atrocity committed against innocent children? The mothers whose children were murdered mercilessly before their very eyes could not. Their wailing must have reached heaven and shaken the earth.

Do we not hear in the wailing of these Jewish mothers the wailing of the Egyptian mothers whose firstborn were massacred? Do we not see hearts broken and rent just like the hearts of the mothers in Egypt? Jewish infants and Egyptian firstborn—are they different in God's eyes because the former were the children of promise while the latter were not? Jewish mothers and Egyptians mothers—should the loud cry of the former be the subject of our theological anguish, whereas the loud cry of the latter is no more than a whisper in our theological essays?

Jesus must have heard the story of the massacre of the firstborn in Egypt as a part of the Exodus drama. He must have been pained by it. What about the story of the massacre of the children in Bethlehem shortly after his own birth? He may not have heard it himself. It might have been a story circulated among his followers long after his death. It could have been a story created to enhance the drama surrounding his birth. But suppose he had heard about the incident—he would surely have been horrified. That many an innocent child died because of him! That many a mother wept and wailed for their children only because they happened to be born around the time he was born! That the death of these children were supposed to be part of the saving purpose of God he had come to fulfill!

Jesus would have found it difficult to be at peace with the story. He would have decided that it was impossible to justify the death of these children as something that God had predetermined as part of God's saving purpose. He would have no use for a theology of hope that means despair for others. He would have opposed a theology of life for the elect that becomes a theology of death for the nonelect. He would have nothing to do with a theology of joy for a small group of humanity that turns into a theology of lament for the majority. If he would not have been party to the theology of liberation that failed to take account of the murdered Egyptian firstborn, he would not have been party to any Christology or soteriology developed by the Christian church, with him at the center, that completely "passed over" the children who died under Herod's sword.

What would have been Jesus' theology of hope? How would he have treated the subject of hope in his daily contacts with the women, men, and children who had little to hope for? How would he have gone about reconstructing the theology of hope, taking into the heart of his theological endeavor the elusive hope with which people around him had to live? Since he himself lived with the prospect of death, the genuine possibility of murder and assassination, how did he keep his faith in the God of hope? How was he able to hope at all? For Jesus and for most of us, hope is not a philosophical idea to be debated, but a challenge to be faced in a real life. Nor is it a theological concept unrelated to our topsy-turvy world. For Jesus as well as for most of us, hope struggles to be born out of the world of frustration, sorrow, despair, and death. Hope, to be true, has to be born in the midst of pain. It is to this pain of the birth of hope that we now turn.

Chapter 7

Ethics of Hope

Jesus has decentralized life and faith from the temple and recentralized it in people. It is people who live their lives and practice their faith. Jesus liberates people from what the temple has come to stand for under the religious authorities: religious legalism and political intrigue. He makes it clear that the temple itself is not the hope of the people, nor is it the hope of their nation. He remembers that the Temple built by King Solomon was burned to the ground by the Babylonians. He knows that the Second Temple, reconstructed by those who had returned from exile in Babylon, was pillaged by Antiochus Epiphanes. What stands in front of him is the Temple rebuilt by King Herod the Great. Does he foresee that it is also going to be destroyed? His premonition is to come true when Jerusalem falls to Roman troops commanded by Titus, and the Temple is razed.

But the destruction of the Temple does not mean the end of people's hope. In actual fact, the Temple, controlled and managed by the religious hierarchy, had been a false hope. What it had offered was an illusion of hope. It had stood in the way of their hopes and aspirations. It had, ironically, stopped them from entering the kingdom of heaven (Matt. 23:13). It had deprived them of "the weightier matters of the law: justice and mercy and faith" (Matt. 23:23). It had deceived them with a beautiful appearance that concealed "greed and self-indulgence" (Matt. 23:25). Between the hope preached by the religious establishment and the hope cherished by the people there is a great chasm. The chasm is often so great that the two hopes are diametrically opposed, like south from north or north from south.

What can shorten the distance between people and hope? A theology of hope that dwells on hope as a future occurrence, as an "eschatological" event? More faith in God who offers hope that "passes all our understanding"? Faith in the all-knowing God and in hope that one day will be fulfilled may help detach us from the pressing problems of life, but will it help us find the "justice, mercy, and faith" that Jesus talked about? Does such faith enable us to live the reign of God, not in heaven in the future, but on earth in the present? These are some of the questions theologians of hope, preachers of God's kingdom, and Christians who have to live in hope in the midst of heartbreaks, conflicts, and despairs cannot avoid.

162

We do not need more theology of hope; we have had plenty already. We are so used to preaching on hope that it ceases to bring excitement. But is hope without excitement still hope? Is hope richly dressed, but meagerly related to life, still hope? For hope to be hope, it has to address the present as well as the future, perhaps the present more than the future. For hope to be hope, it has to be "contemporary" as well as "proleptic," perhaps more contemporary than proleptic.

Hope should not become outdated either. Who wants an outdated hope? An outdated hope is good only for personal reminiscence, historical memory, and theological nostalgia. Paul is almost right when he says that "hope that is seen is not hope" (Rom. 8:24). But hope cannot remain perpetually hidden. A hope eternally tucked away in the time to come may tantalize our theological curiosity but cannot fill the void in our heart and the emptiness of our spirit. Hope that is unseen has to become seen to be a *real* hope. And the hope that is seen, in order not to become outdated, has to become a hope unseen that gives birth to a hope that is seen—hope that can fill the hungry stomach, lift up the downtrodden, and bring justice and freedom to those deprived.

Hope not seen and hope seen have to be in creative tension. What connects one with the other is the power intrinsic to hope. What is this power? Is it a theological power—power that emanates from our faith in God? Yes. But it also has to be an ethical power—power that enables human beings to live in this world of *wu chang,* a Buddhist term meaning the ever-changing world. As a matter of fact, there is no theological power that is not at the same time an ethical power; and there is no ethical power that is not a theological power. If the ethical power of hope receives particular emphasis here, it is because it has received less attention in some of the theologies of hope. We must therefore deal with the ethics of hope.

The ethical power of hope empowers us to reconstruct lives ruined by hatred, greed, and violence. That ethical power also allows us not to become cynical about or resigned to the powers of evil. It strengthens our faith in God who, as the very source of our faith, is much closer to us than we are to ourselves. Hope is not just power. It is *ethical* power, power to change the situations that degrade individual persons and corrupt human community. Hope as an ethical power is related to God's saving power, the power that works within us, that gives us courage to live, and that changes our lives and the world around us. It is this ethical power that will be the focus of our continuing engagement with hope.

Incense Sticks Named "Hope"

Hope, used as a verb, besides meaning "to long for" or "to dream about," also means, among other things, "to cherish, to count on, to sweat it out, to hang in, to take heart."[1] These verbal expressions have to be in the present tense. They refer to what one does to bring about what one longs for or dreams about. Hope is present already as one "hangs in there and sweats it out." To put it another way, there will be no hope if one does not hang in there and sweat it out. Hope is not just a word, but an action. It does not consist merely in waiting, but in doing. It is a seed sown in the ground of the present. It is this kind of hope that we encounter in the following story.

We are about to hear a story told in the first person. It is a testimony of Kannan in India, who hangs in there and sweats out his hope in a life filled with frustrations and adversities. It seems as if he was born a stranger to hope.

The name my parents gave me is Kannan. But it is usual for everybody to call me "Hey, cripple." I belong to a very poor family. . . .

My father is a coolie. I am the eldest of eight children. It was impossible for my parents to bestow any attention on us children since the battle for the belly took most of their time. I was struck by polio when I was three months old. My father, who was totally ignorant of polio preventives, tried his level best to help me. Some suggested that if my leg was washed with hot rice water it may be restored. But we ate only once a day and that, too, was the cheapest available rag (millet). Only very few times we could afford to eat rice. According to some other people's suggestion they buried me waist-deep in dry sand from morning until noon for six months. My parents, who had to be away at work then, used to ask other little children to watch over me. Sometimes these children used to desert me and go away. In spite of all this, my deformity remained the same.

With someone's help I was admitted to a small school. The feeling that I was not like others was a torture to me. Other children always made fun of me, calling me "cripple." . . . No one considered me as a human being. I was broken-hearted. I had to leave school to help the family and did all sorts of jobs. I gathered firewood in small bundles and started selling them door-to-door. I started selling peanuts and bananas street by street. Sometimes, knowing I am a cripple, people used to bolt away with my money and the goods. Even buses used to avoid me and pass me by.

More than the disability in my body, society made me a cripple also inside. This was death to me. Like me, there are thousands of poor handicapped today who die inwardly like this. What else can we expect in slums, where there is great poverty and ignorance? . . .

We are not people. The pitiable condition of expecting other people's charity has killed our sense of self-respect and has brought us to a condition of less than animals. Superstitions such as "it is our fate," "it is God's curse on us," do not allow us to become people. We are poor. No good thing ever reaches us, including the International Year of the Disabled. There is little hope for people like us.

Therefore, we, the poor slum handicapped, joined together and with the help of a group started to organize. We are now 1,200 people in eighteen slums. "Our disability is in our bodies, not in our spirit"—"we have every right to live equally with others." With these convictions we help each other. We share what we know. In a small training place those who know bag-making, book-binding, tailoring and other handicrafts share our skills and also our profits. We have named the incense sticks we make *"HOPE."* We go in procession to the government and demand our rights. We spread knowledge about polio prevention and employment possibilities and understanding about the causes of our poverty and degradation. We aspire to gain our dignity and our rights through our struggle without expecting anyone's pity or charity. . . .[2]

The language in which the story is told sometimes gets broken in grammar and syntax. Does it not reflect how deeply the heart of the storyteller is broken and how severely his soul is injured? But this is not the whole story. There is something more in Kannan's speech—the power to change the conditions imposed on people like him and to create possibilities out of impossible situations. I would like to call that power "the ethical power of hope." The story, eloquent in its simplicity, is a powerful testimony to it.

"My Father Is a Coolie"

One phrase says it all: "My father is a coolie." The father of the young storyteller is a coolie. The term *coolie* originally comes from "Hindi *kuli,* an aboriginal tribal name," or from "Tamil *kuli,* wages," meaning "unskilled laborer or porter in or from the Far East hired for low or subsistence wages."[3] It is a pejorative term, almost as pejorative as the word *slave.* As a matter of fact, the history of the "coolie trade" is closely related to that of slavery. The trade "began in the late 1800s as a response to the labor shortage brought on by the worldwide movement to abolish slavery. The majority of those contract laborers were shipped from China to developing European colonial areas such as Hawaii, Malaya, and the Caribbean."[4] This was another trade of human bodies instituted by the "Christian" West for economic gain and development.

The way the coolie trade was carried out was not any better than the slave trade. "Conditions in the depots where the laborers were stored awaiting shipment, and the vessels in which they sailed, were cramped and inhumane, resulting in much sickness, misery, and death."[5] There must be countless stories of the suffering these men endured on their way to an unknown destination. There must also be as many stories of those who died of maltreatment and sickness, without reaching their destination.

The irony is that what is started as a Western colonial institution, bringing shame and indignity to laborers from Asia, became a social institution in India and China, causing the poor to suffer misery and inhumanity. Society depended on their services as much as they depended on the job for their survival. The rich relied on them to maintain their lifestyle of affluence and self-importance as much as the laborers relied on the rich for the subsistence wages to maintain their rock-bottom life. Once a coolie you were always a coolie. You were condemned to the very bottom of society. You had no rights to claim deserved wages for your labor and service, not to mention rights as a human being. You had no rights except the charity bestowed on you by the society and by your masters.

Coolies abounded in the China of feudal and semicolonial days and in India, which remains a caste society. Our young storyteller has the misfortune of having been born to a coolie's family, condemned to a life of hardship and destitution. "The battle for the belly," as he graphically puts it, "took most of the time" of his parents and their eight children. His lot is bad enough, but when he was three months old he came down with polio. Medical treatment was out of the question. He was subjected to a crude folk treatment, which proved futile. All his life he has had to put up with insults from others and with self-pity brought about by his physical deformity. He was made a "cripple" not only in the body but, more painfully, in the soul and the spirit.

"We Are Not People"

Born to a coolie's family and made a "cripple" by polio, Kannan is treated by society as a "nonhuman," a "nonperson," a "nobody." He was an object of ridicule at school. Innocent children can be cruel to children different in physical appearance and ability without knowing the hurt they are causing. They show contempt to those from less-fortunate families, not realizing they are wounding hearts. Kannan had to leave school because he could not take the ridicule and contempt from his classmates.

But leaving school did not leave him in peace. To help his parents with some rupees, he went "selling peanuts and bananas street by street." The sight of a crippled child selling peanuts and bananas excited the fancy of street urchins. He was entirely helpless when they "bolted away with [his] money and goods." The sight of him utterly desperate and helpless might have seemed as funny as it was pathetic. But these were not only his plights. Being a cripple from the slum seemed to turn the whole society against him. He recalls sadly that "even buses used to avoid me and pass me by." He says of himself and people like him: "We are not people." Deep down in his heart is the hopelessness that saps the courage to live and debilitates life.

We are not people. A person forced to say this is a person without hope. A community that places a human being in such a condition is no longer a fellowship built on *communion*, which involves the sharing of thoughts and emotions and intimate relationships with deep mutual understanding. A society that can afford hope only for the rich, the privileged, and the healthy is an immoral society. Such a society has no sympathy for those who toil and labor as "coolies." The "coolies" may have instrumental value, providing menial services at society's beck and call, but they are not viewed as having human value. A society that thrives on their hardship is a morally degraded society. A society that allows some people to enjoy riches at the expense of those who cannot earn enough to stave off hunger is morally bankrupt.

Thanks to a reduction in recent years in military confrontations between East and West, the focus of the world economy has shifted visibly from a military economy to a consumer economy. Economic development has diverted from military complexes to consumer complexes. The world has become a gigantic market where sellers and buyers transact goods and money, and where profit is the only thing that matters. Profit is the god of the market. Many nations in the world today, including some of those in what is called the Third World, have learned to worship this god.

The importance of economic prosperity is not lost to politicians. Economic prosperity has become almost the single most important factor in politics; the issue is often at the center of political campaigns. If aspiring to high elected office, you disregard the state of national economic health to your detriment. The political establishment has tied itself to the economic machine, with issues such as human rights around the world, for example, becoming secondary. Bill Clinton's victorious U.S. presidential campaign in 1992 was driven in part by a campaign slogan that helped keep the candidate's mind on the pocketbooks of the people: "It's the economy, stupid!"

World economic statistics show that many nations have achieved wealth in a remarkably short time. Even countries subjected to the colonial rule that once exploited their human and material resources, in some cases for centuries, have come to the forefront of world economic development. But as we all know, everything has its price. Economic development has made many societies rich and prosperous. At the same time it has made them morally vulnerable. Human hope is now defined in terms of industrial outputs. It is measured in relation to the average per-capita income. It is conditioned to the rise and fall in stock markets. It is determined by the growth in gross national products. Hope can be bought and sold in nations today. It has become a merchandise that ebbs and flows in value in domestic and international trade.

In a world in which economic factors reign supreme, hope has lost its independence. It is attached to stocks, subsumed under commodities, relative to the volumes of transactions in goods and products. Hope depends on favorable or unfavorable trade relations. With its independence gone, hope no longer commands unquestioned authority. Making the world a more friendly place to live has ceased to be an ideal. Hope does not relate to a vision for a community in which some men, women, and children do not have to say: "We are not people." Hope has become less and less human. It has become an item for computation, something found in strategy files for economic growth and development. Hope has been taken from human beings and relocated in the impersonal world of economic competition and survival.

The quality of hope has also changed. It is no longer a human force that enables us to aspire to that which is true, good, and beautiful, but a material force that sucks us into the world of things. Subjected to forces of economy, it ceases to inspire the best in human beings—self-sacrifice, for example—but produces selfishness and greed. Hope for a large number of people in the world today is not a spiritual power, renewing them for the arduous demands of love, justice, and peace. Human beings have become an "economic animal," motivated by the uncanny instinct to go after prey—economic gain. The rest of life seems less important. Crippled coolies such as Kannan can be ignored or disposed of if regarded as a hindrance to the growth of the national economy and to the prosperity of the few.

A Family without Hope

Kannan is aware that he is not alone in his misfortune. There are many others in his slum area inhumanely treated and socially ostracized. "In one family alone," he says, "there are five or six who are deaf, blind, crippled or mentally retarded."[6] Nature seems to have been particularly cruel to that family. How can there be hope for a family with five or six children afflicted with deformities? Having to scrape for a living, how could they afford medical care?

Hope is not to be found in the vocabulary of such a family. It is an entirely foreign notion, a luxury as utterly inaccessible as medical care. Kannan calls to mind the case of a twenty-year-old woman related to his family. She was "mentally retarded and stunted in growth from birth." Her condition was congenital. Who or what was at fault? Her parents? Their unhealthy diets? The polluted slum environments? The herb medicine from the quack doctor her mother took during her pregnancy? No one knows. But one thing is certain: dire poverty, below-subsistence wages, poor diet, and lack of medical care all contributed to the birth of a deformed child.

The birth of such a child ends whatever hope the parents might have had. It deprives them of already scant resources for living. It is a burden added to the heavy burden of life they bear. Birth of a child brings some hope, if the child grows up to be one additional member of the family labor force. But when a child is born deformed, this minimal hope is gone. For twenty-one years this physically and mentally disabled woman was never taken out of her house. She was left alone in her own excreta. Her parents were able to clean her only once a week. How is one to talk to such people and their families about hope? How is a religion to preach to them about hope? To speak to them about "eschatological" hope, to preach to them about hope in the future, in the world to come, in the life hereafter—is this not unethical, even immoral?

"God's Curse on Us"

If hope has become a material entity in a world increasingly dominated by the free-market economy, what has the world of religion done? Religions are expected to equip men and women with the power of hope, not only to deal with the transiency of life, but to empower them to create meaning in the complex world of endless struggle and competition. As the story of Kannan testifies, his own religion has failed him. His own religious community has discriminated against him and left him to struggle for mere survival. And his own people, the caste women and men, who give much devotion to their gods, treat him as a nonperson, as one who does not count in Hindu society.

Hinduism, into which Kannan was born, has a very long history. It is the world's oldest surviving religion, with roots dating back in India to prehistoric times. It has given the world fine religious writings such as the Vedas, the Ramayana, the Mahabarata, and the Bhagavad Gita. These writings not only represent the Indian religious mind at its deepest, in search of the origin and destiny of the human being, but belong to the richest heritage of the human spirit in its quest for meaning on earth and beyond. Although India, according to its constitution, is a secular state and has a mostly Hindu population, Hinduism plays the dominant role in religious, social, and political life. Perhaps it is not too off the mark to say that India is Hinduism and Hinduism is India. What one encounters in that great subcontinent of Asia is Hindu India.

With its immense diversities and differences in ethnicity, language, and religious expression, with magnificent manifestations of its fertile mind in the arts, literature, and philosophy, and with the gap between the great wealth of the few and the extreme poverty of the many—a gap that is scandalous and even obscene—India defies description. Still, the religious literature referred to above offers us glimpses of the best and noblest in India. The Vedas, for example, is "the oldest Hindu scripture, older than the sacred writings of any other major religion"[7] in the world, having originated "approximately between 2500 and 600 B.C.E."[8] In these Vedas one comes across a "Hymn of Creation":

1. Non-being then existed not nor being;
   There was no air, no sky that is beyond it.
   What was concealed? Wherein? In whose protection?
   And was there deep unfathomable water?

2. Death then existed not nor life immortal;
   Of neither night nor day was any token.
   By its inherent force the One breathed windless;
   No other thing than that beyond existed.

3. Darkness there was at first by darkness hidden;
   Without distinct marks, this all was water.
   That which, becoming, by the void was covered,
   That One by force of heat came into being.

4. Desire entered the One in the beginning:
   It was the earliest seed, of thought the product.

> The sages searching in their hearts with wisdom,
> Found out the bond of being in non-being.

5. Their ray extended light across the darkness:
   But was the One above or was it under?
   Creative force was there, and fertile power:
   Below was energy, above was impulse.

6. Who knows for certain? Who shall here declare it?
   Where was it born, and whence came this creation?
   The gods were born after this world's creation:
   Then who can know from whence it has arisen?

7. None knoweth whence creation has arisen;
   And whether he has or has not produced it;
   He who surveys it in the highest heaven,
   He only knows, or haply he may know not.[9]

These verses of creation truly astonish us, having come from India some millennia ago.

The hymn is dedicated to creation, to things and phenomena, natural or otherwise, that one can see, touch, feel, and smell. To them is sung the hymn of praise. But how did all these things come into being? Above all, how did human beings come to be? How did the creation take place? How did creation itself happen? There must have been a "desire," a "creative force," a "fertile mind," "the One in the beginning" that gave birth to creation and all things in it. Does one not hear echoes of this Vedic hymn of creation in the creation story of the Hebrew Scriptures, or, for that matter, in the creation stories and hymns of other ancient peoples? Human spirits of ancient times seem to call one to another in the depths of the creation.

But the hymn of praise to creation turns into a hymn of awe. The religious mind that responded to creation in poems of sublime beauty realizes that what one is confronted with is a mystery—a deep mystery beyond human comprehension. "Who can know from whence [creation] has arisen? "The gods born after this world's creation" would not know. If the gods do not know, how could human beings, born after the gods, know? The only one who knows is the One who caused creation to come into being and who "surveys it in the highest heaven." But perhaps even that One "may know not."

This is not agnosticism. Our ancient ancestors were too awed by the mystery of creation to be agnostic. Their hearts were too much in tune with the spiritual forces of the universe to give room to impiety. Overwhelmed by the mystery, all they could do was to be silent. Saying that even the Creator who has brought our surroundings into being may not know the origin of creation is not skepticism about the wisdom and power of the Creator, but an acknowledgment of human beings' utter ignorance about God.

The "Hymn of Creation" reminds us of the Book of Job, a literary master-piece that explores God's incomprehensibility in the face of human suffering. Toward the end of the laborious but fruitless theological harangues of Job's friends, who try to force him to admit his culpability for the tragedies that had struck him and his family, God says to Job "out of the whirlwind":

> Who is this that darkens counsel
> by words without knowledge?
> Gird up your loins like a man,
> I will question you,
> and you shall declare to me.
>
> Where were you
> when I laid the foundation of the earth?
> Tell me, if you have understanding.
> Who determined
> its measurements—surely you know!
> Or who stretched the line upon it?
> On what were its bases sunk,
> or who laid its cornerstone
> when the morning stars sang together
> and all the heavenly beings shouted for joy?
>
> (Job 38:2-7)

These are words from someone overwhelmed by the mystery of creation and awed by the infinite expanse of time and space. The work is the product of a deeply religious mind and heart, speaking not out of desperation, but out of a profound faith in God the Creator in spite of all the travails of life.

"Where were you when I laid the foundation of the earth?" This is a final and decisive question. You may try to theorize about the order of the universe. You may try to give theological reasons for what you perceive, based on your limited experience. But faced with the question of the foundation of the earth, asked about the beginning of creation, you have to admit that you are completely ignorant. The reason is obvious: You were simply not there! If you were not there, if you were not an eyewitness of how creation came into being, you can only confess your awe and wonder. This is what the author of the Book of Job and those who composed the creation hymn of the Vedas confessed.

What we encounter is a profound ignorance of a deeply religious and spir-itual nature. We human beings do not know the divine truth behind what we can see, smell, hear, and touch. What we see may not reflect the reality in the innermost part of the divine being. What we hear may be a distortion of the voice of truth in the mind of God. What we touch may keep us from perceiv-ing the compassionate heart of the all-loving Mother-Father God. And what we comprehend may be originating in ourselves, and not in that Being beyond our comprehension. But religion, especially organized and established religion, has always directed our spiritual aspirations and religious sensibilities, not to that creating, all-loving, yet incomprehensible God, but to what we can see, hear, touch, or comprehend with our senses and minds—that is, rituals, doctrines, canons, and even taboos.

A religion, when substituting its rituals, doctrines, canons, and taboos for the creating, loving, and incomprehensible God, becomes a crisis to itself and a danger to its adherents. A religion may make a clear distinction between what is acceptable and what is not, whereas for God what is acceptable to the religion may be unacceptable, and what is unacceptable to the religion may be acceptable to God. Religion may draw a line between what is true and what is not true. But to God what is true for the religion may be untrue, and what is untrue to the religion may be true to God. In many instances organized religion allows no doubt as to what is sacred and what is profane, what is holy and what is secular. It divides people between us and them, between those who are favored (saved) and those who are not. But chances are that, for God, what the religion considers sacred and holy may be profane and secular, and what the religion rejects as profane and secular may be sacred and holy. It is also likely that God does not separate us from them and them from us, or divide those who are saved and those who are not saved.

How could God the Creator function with such petty dichotomies without ceasing to be God the Creator? Is God still the all-loving God when God discriminates against one group of men, women, and children, as a religion tends to do on grounds of religious affiliation, racial origin, gender, sexual orientation, class, or caste? Is God in alliance with certain religious communities and believers over against others? Is God prejudiced against those who are economically deprived and physically disabled such as Kannan, our storyteller? In short, is God the God of hope for the privileged only? Are people like Kannan left without hope from society and also from the God of his own religion?

As Christians we read in the Bible that the God of Jesus is not like the God just described. His God is not a dichotomous God—a God who divides what God has created in nature and in human community into hostile camps. Did not Jesus exhort his followers, "Love your enemies and pray for those who persecute you, so that you may be children of your God in heaven" (Matt. 5:44-45; also Luke 6:27)? His God does not judge according to one's religious affiliation or sectarian loyalty; his God is solely concerned whether one's heart is in the right place.

Jesus made a statement that shows his deep insight into human nature and, by inference, his most penetrating critique of what goes on in the name of religion: "It is not what goes into the mouth that defiles a person, but it is what comes out of the mouth that defiles" (Matt. 15:11; also Mark 7:15). How true! Are not divisions within a religion and conflicts between religions often results of inflammatory words that come out of the mouths of the religious authorities and fanatical believers? This statement can be applied to all religions, including Christianity.

Religion is an effort on the part of human beings to translate the spiritual quest for God into images, symbols, forms, and teachings that are more accessible to human devotion and to the human mind. But when these images, symbols, forms, and teachings are detached from the faith in God in us but beyond us, and become ends in themselves—objects of human faith and devotion—religion is beset by corruption. This is what happened to Jesus' own religion. He took upon himself the task to reshape his religion so that it could once again serve God and people in need.

The spiritual quest and the philosophical search we encounter in the Vedas are no exception to this almost universal course—from adoration of the Creator God, to formulation of rituals and teachings in the service of that adoration, and finally to the replacement of devotion with loyalty to human religious constructions. In the Vedas, such as the Rig Veda below, we do come across efforts to put religious devotion to work in daily life and to wrestle with ethical expectations of that devotion.

1. The gods inflict not hunger as a means to kill:
   Death frequently befalls even satiated men.
   The charitable giver's wealth melts not away;
   The niggard never finds a man to pity him.

2. Who, of abundant food possessed, makes hard his heart
   Toward a needy and decrepit suppliant
   Whom once he courted, come to pray to him for bread:
   A man like this as well finds none to pity him.

3. He is the liberal man who helps the beggar
   That, craving food, emaciated wanders,
   And coming to his aid, when asked to succor,
   Immediately makes him a friend hereafter.

4. He is no friend who gives not of his substance
   To his devoted, intimate companion:
   This friend should turn from him—here is no haven—
   And seek a stranger elsewhere as a helper.

5. The wealthier man should give unto the needy,
   Considering the course of life hereafter;
   For riches are like chariot wheels revolving:
   Now to one man they come, now to another.

6. The foolish man from food has no advantage;
   In truth I say: it is but his undoing;

No friend he ever fosters, no companion:
He eats alone, and he alone is guilty.

7. The plough that cleaves the soil produces nurture;
   He that bestirs his feet completes his journey.
   The speaking *brahmin* earns more than the silent;
   A friend who gives is better than the niggard.[10]

These words speak to our hearts as well as to our minds. They enrich the treasury of wisdom human beings have been inspired to utter throughout the ages.

In tone, words, and even in ethos these verses of the Rig Veda from ancient India do not sound foreign to the Christian ear accustomed to the wisdom taught by the sage who composed Proverbs in the Hebrew Scriptures.

Do not withhold good from those to whom it is due,
   when it is in your power to do it.
Do not say to your neighbor,
   "Go, and come again, tomorrow I will give it"—
   when you have it with you.
Do not plan harm against your neighbor
   who lives trustingly beside you.
Do not quarrel with anyone without cause,
   when no harm has been done to you.
Do not envy the violent
   and do not choose any of their ways.
                              (Prov. 3:27-31)

Such proverbs are moral maxims developed from long experience. They are words of wisdom containing profound religious truth.

Do not rob the poor
   because they are poor,
   or crush the afflicted at the gate;
for the Lord pleads their cause
   and despoils of life those
   who despoil them.
                              (Prov. 22:22-23)

For the sage of Proverbs moral concerns are not a matter of expediency; they are divine imperatives because they belong to God's nature, to the God who stands with the poor and defends them. God, however one may describe God, is a moral God.

What we have in Proverbs is *theo-logical ethics,* ethics developed from theology and theology translated into ethics. Such ethical reasoning is what

constituted the heart of the message of the prophets. It is this prophetic tradition that Jesus inherited, and he pressed hard the religious authorities of his
day to face the ethical implications of what they believed and taught. In what he
said and did, whether in the controversy with Jewish religious leaders or in his
teaching and preaching before the men and women who followed him, he called
upon hearers to grapple with the ethical consequences of their faith.

In this matter Jesus is very serious. He sounds urgent, for he is not dealing
with a matter that can be postponed or deferred. Take the story of Zacchaeus,
for instance (Luke 19:1-10). Noticing the anxious Zacchaeus in the tree, Jesus
offered to stay with him, a chief tax collector hated and shunned by his own
people. Jesus accepted him without condition. This acceptance sent Zacchaeus's
life in a completely different direction. He offered to make amends of wrongs
he had done. This was a dramatic turn of events, but Jesus' proclamation was
even more dramatic. "Today," he declared, "salvation has come to this house!"
Today, and not tomorrow. On the spot and not somewhere else, in the synagogue or at the Temple. This very moment and not at the end of time. What
made Zacchaeus's hope of salvation real was his decision to practice his faith
in response to Jesus' message. What Zacchaeus practiced was an ethics of hope,
realized not only in his own life but in those lives he had exploited before.

Has Christian theology grasped the urgency of hope Jesus' presence generated? The answer cannot be certain. Theology and ethics have been divorced
and have gone their separate ways. The result has been disastrous: there is not
much ethics in theology and not much theology in ethics, leading to the poverty
of both. With regard to the theme of hope, there has in recent years been too
much of a theology of hope and too little of an ethics of hope. Hope, as said
earlier, is separated from the present in theological thought and eternally postponed. Does not the sage of Proverbs also tell us that "hope deferred makes the
heart sick" (13:12)? Surely it does. Does it not also make the hearts of Kannan
and of women and men like him sick? Surely it does. Hope deferred also makes
God's heart sick, because God pleads the cause of the poor.

For the Rig Veda, ethics is also grounded in theology. Although the Vedic
hymns "were composed for an audience primarily occupied with earthly goods:
health, long life, many sons, abundant cattle, wealth,"[11] they do not extol earthly
goods at the expense of God or gods. The hymn quoted above begins by saying,
"the gods inflict not hunger as a means to kill." God is not vindictive. God does
not terrorize with disaster helpless men, women, and children. God is a Being
that can be trusted, rain or shine. The longing for such a God is the heart of
human religious activity, ancient or modern, Eastern or Western. This is the
unsophisticated and unindoctrinated part of faith and an innate part of human
beings as *homo religiosus*. This longing predates established religions, including
Christianity and Hinduism.

But as organized religions develop, this loving God becomes less loving. This
God of compassion grows less compassionate. What emerges is a God or gods

grown more remote from worshipers, more unapproachable by believers. All the while religion works to extend the distance between the loving God and the longing people. It takes upon itself the role of a matchmaker between God and people. It has made itself indispensable in this role by building structures of religious hierarchy and the bureaucracy of the priesthood. Meanwhile, it has packaged and repackaged God, made and remade God to resemble its own likes and dislikes rather than God in God's own self.

This God, created by religion, has frightened many believers and alienated others. "The Roman Catholicism of my childhood," recalls a former Roman Catholic nun, "was a rather frightening creed. James Joyce got it right in *Portrait of the Artist as Young Man:* I listened to my share of hellfire sermons. In fact hell seemed a more potent reality than God, because it was something I could grasp imaginatively."[12] Are not Christians in Protestant churches also brought up on sermons about the eternal damnation of "infidels" in hell and the everlasting bliss in paradise for those who have accepted Jesus as their personal savior? Buddhism too spreads fear of hell with its vivid and lurid—almost too vivid and too lurid—descriptions of how those who have committed evil suffer unspeakable torment and pain in hell. Is there a religion that is free from religious terror committed against believers?

Kannan tells us that he too is a victim of a religion turned into terror. In his case that religion is Hinduism. Crippled and living in the slum, he and people like him are made to say that what they suffer is not only "our fate," but "God's curse on us." To attribute one's misfortune to fate is bad enough, but to believe it to be God's curse is even worse. *Curse* is a word loaded with vindictiveness, hate, and anger. When personal misfortune, physical deformity, and a poverty-stricken life are believed to be the results of God's curse, the God you worship is an angry and vindictive God filled with hate.

Is this God the God who "inflicts not hunger as a means to kill" in the Vedic hymn? It cannot be. A God who curses is not God. A God who has to be vindicated does not deserve to be God. A God who hates—how can that be the God who gave birth to all things? Such a God does not exist in reality, but only in human imagination. It is a religious fiction created by those who hold power over people's spiritual well-being. The real God has no taboos. There is nothing in the real God to repulse human beings. Between the real God and human beings there are no taboos. The God surrounded by taboos and protected from human approach may be the God of a religion, but cannot be God in God's own self.

"There Is No Hope for People Like Us"

Cursed by God, one becomes totally hopeless. One may be able to endure physical pain and may get used to the derision of society. But how can one endure the pain of heart caused by the belief that one is cursed by God? How can one resign oneself to the idea of being abandoned by God? And how can one grow accustomed to a God who "drops stones on you who have fallen into a well" (*lo jing xia shi*), to use a Chinese idiom?

For innocent members of a religion God is their last hope. They are not versed in erudite teachings and doctrines. They are not educated about the meanings many religious images and symbols are supposed to tell them. Even though they may dutifully perform rituals and pay dues, they are ignorant of the theological underpinnings of worship services and religious ceremonies. They recite prayers, worship at temples and churches, carry out religious duties, and placate and please their God to obtain favor, to be protected from illness, misery, perversity, or calamity.

Religion for ordinary believers takes place in earnest between worshipers and God, between human beings and the divine being, between the frail, finite, mortal women and men and the powerful, infinite, immortal God. The physical parts of a religion—temple, church, sanctuary, images, and icons; organizations such as orders, bureaucracy, and the priesthood; spiritual exercises such as worship, prayer, and meditation—should help ordinary believers come closer to God.

God is the heart of their faith, the center of their life, and the sum total of their hope. To be alienated by God causes anxiety. To be left alone by God makes them feel uneasy and empty. To be abandoned by God drives them desperate. To be cursed by God is to become an outcast both socially and religiously in a culture shaped by religion. A prayer from Africa, offered to Imana, the great Creator of Ruanda-Urundi, helps illustrate the closeness believers feel to God:

> O Imana of Urundi (Ruanda), if only you would help me! O Imana of pity, Imana of my father's house (or country), if only you would help me! O Imana of the country of the Hutu and the Tutsi, if only you would help me just this once! O Imana, if only you would give me a rugo and children! I prostrate myself before you, Imana of Urundi (Ruanda). I cry to you: give me offspring, give me as you give to others! Imana, what shall I do, where shall I go? I am in distress, is there room for me? O Merciful, O Imana of mercy, help this once![13]

This prayer of extreme distress must have been in the hearts of tens of thousands of Rwandan victims of the recent fierce tribal war between the Hutu and the Tutsi, triggered by the assassination of President Juvenal Habyarimana.

Imana, the Creator God, "is honored but not feared, as the creator God has no power to harm."[14] Does not the most "primitive" and thus the most authentic belief in God lie in the depths of human religious consciousness? Is it not almost universal in established or popular religions? But somewhere along the way the God who is not feared becomes a fearful God, and the God who has no power to harm obtains enormous power to harm. This change must have happened even before religious activities became organized by religious institutions. But the transformation of God into a fearful God came especially to be part of organized religion. Religion as it gains structure loses innocence. It becomes a buffer state, so to speak, between God and believers, claiming to be able to do things beyond its limits. This is when religion becomes an idolatry and takes the place of God, making itself the object of people's devotion and loyalty.

A religion that infringes upon divine precincts begins to do many things in the name of God—instituting religious laws, setting up hierarchies of power and authority, developing doctrines and canons, engaging in heresy hunting, waging wars, and even renaming God in God's name. Such a religion, instead of alleviating guilt and bringing peace, causes anguish and fear. How else is one to explain a prayer to God as desperate and hopeless as this "Sumero-Akkadian Prayer"?

> In ignorance I have eaten that forbidden by my god;
> In ignorance I have set foot on that prohibited by my goddess.
> O Lord, my transgressions are many; great are my sins.
> O my god, (my) transgressions are many; great are (my) sins.
> O goddess, (my) transgressions are many; great are (my) sins.
> O god whom I know or do not know, (my) transgressions are many;
>   great are (my) sins.
> O goddess whom I know or do not know, (my) transgressions are many;
>   great are (my) sins;
> The transgression which I have committed, indeed I do not know;
> The sin which I have done, indeed I do not know.
> The forbidden thing I have eaten, indeed I do not know;
> The prohibited (place) on which I have set foot, indeed I do not know;
> The lord in the anger of his heart looked at me;
> The god in the rage of his heart confronted me;
> When the goddess was angry with me, she made me become ill.
> The god whom I know or do not know has oppressed me;
> The goddess whom I know or do not know has placed suffering upon me.
> Although I am constantly looking for help, no one takes me by the hand;
> When I weep they do not come to my side.
> I utter laments, but no one hears me;
> O my god, merciful one, I address to thee the prayer,
> "Ever incline to hear me";
> I kiss the feet of my goddess; I crawl before thee.[15]

The God addressed in the prayer is an oppressive God, a God of despair and not a God of hope. Such a prayer reveals the dark side of a religion that threatens people with God's anger and punishment.

No religion is free from representing God in this way, not even the religion of ancient Israel. There are psalms in the Hebrew Scriptures that extol the glory of God, celebrate God's majesty, give thanks to God for God's saving love. But there are also psalms that give vent to distress, frustration, uncertainty, and fear.

> O Lord, do not rebuke me in your anger,
>   or discipline me in your wrath.
> For your arrows have sunk into me,
>   and your hand has come down on me.
>
> There is no soundness in my flesh
>   because of your indignation;
> there is no health in my bones
>   because of my sin.
> For my iniquities have gone over my head;
>   they weigh like a burden too heavy for me.
>
> My wounds grow foul and fester
>   because of my foolishness;
> I am utterly bowed down and prostrate;
>   all day long I go around mourning.
>   (Ps. 38:1-6)

We do not know what troubles the psalmist. Whether tragedy or illness, the psalmist takes the suffering as an indication of God's anger and punishment.

But does God cause human beings to suffer? And having caused suffering, does God let it be known that the suffering is also God's punishment? But in the Sumero-Akkadian prayer there is confusion as to what transgressions have been committed. In the Hebrew psalm, although the psalmist says, "I confess my iniquity; I am sorry for my sin" (38:18), one is not quite sure who has committed iniquity and sin. For immediately after the confession the psalmist says: "Those who are my foes without cause are mighty, and many are those who hate me wrongfully" (38:19). Is it not evident that the iniquity and sin for which the psalmist prays for God's forgiveness have in fact been committed by the psalmist's enemies?

The psalmist of the Hebrew Scriptures and the suppliant of the Sumero-Akkadian prayer have both got things wrong. If common belief leads them to think that illness or misfortune is the divine punishment for sin, they must reject this thought as untrue. They must have enough faith to say that their God, who is love, does not punish them. On the contrary, God is standing by their side, in pain and in love, embracing their sick body and frightened spirit. If their religion has taught them that they deserve God's displeasure and punishment for what they have done, they must muster enough courage to say that their God is not a vindictive God. If they are accused of iniquity and sin they have not committed or do not remember having committed, they have to raise their voice and protest. They must be able to say that a religion that identifies their suffering with God's anger and punishment is wrong, that it is a morbid and oppressive religion.

It is religion and not God that is against worshipers. It is religious institutions and not the divine order that commit believers to suffering. For us to be free for one another and particularly for God, we may have to free ourselves from religion—from the religious institution that makes us fearful and that humiliates us in front of God, from a religion that compels our psalmist to implore God at the end of his prayer: "Do not forsake me, O Lord; O my God, do not be far from me" (38:21). The God of your religion may forsake you, but the God who created you will never forsake you; the God of your religion may be far from you, but the God who gave birth to you is never far. This God who never forsakes you and who is never far is your hope, and not the religion that teaches you to be religious lest God forsake you and stay far away.

By the same token, the Sumero-Akkadian prayer does not have to end with these words: "I kiss the feet of my goddess; I crawl before thee." Kissing someone's feet is an expression of servitude. This is what religious authorities demand, not God. Crawling before someone is an act of humiliation. Again, this act is what those who hold power over you expect, and not God. The true God, the God who created you, nurtures you, and protects you from harm's way will not treat you like a servant, a minion, a slave, a criminal. That God will not ask you to crawl before God to humiliate, shame, or degrade you. It is the religion that has taken the place of God, that has control over you, that demands you to perform such acts of humiliation.

No wonder Kannan and many men, women, and children like him suffer under oppressive religious establishments and traditions. They bear "God's curse" on their bodies. Cursed by God, they are also cursed by their fellow human beings. Kannan recalls that "this was death to me," that "there are thousands of poor handicapped today who die inwardly." Dying inwardly can mean only one thing: spiritual death. Physical death does not have to bring about spiritual death. The body dies, but the spirit lives on. But when the spirit dies, even though the body is still alive, the person dies with it. The person who is physically alive but spiritually dead is said to be *xing shi zou rou* in Chinese, namely, "a walking corpse." The religion that makes people, particularly the poor and the disabled, feel they are as good as dead not only does injustice to human beings but to God, and not merely betrays people, but God.

For a religion not to be a source of despair but a source of hope, inner transformation is necessary—transformation from a religion of injustice to one of justice, from a religion of fear to one of assurance. Religion has to go back to its roots, recover what is true and good there, and reconstruct itself in response to the call from the past and to the demands of the present. In Christianity this is called "reformation"; a reformation took place in Europe in the sixteenth century. But for a religion to have a future, reformation has to take place not once, but twice, three times, or any number of times. Religion is an incorrigible thing, much like politics. It quickly succumbs to the temptation of power, becomes susceptible to greed. Before it knows it, it has allowed itself to serve the rich and the powerful, and to do disservice to the poor and the powerless. It readily yields itself to authoritarianism, dictating believers' lives with rigid teachings and doctrines, antiquated ideas and beliefs.

Judaism of Jesus' time badly needed reform. Jesus took upon himself the task of bringing about inner changes in his own religious tradition. The cost, we all know, was high. He paid for it with death on the cross. The Christianity founded on this Jesus also needs reforms. Mention has already been made about the Reformation of Christianity in Europe in the sixteenth century. Buddhism is also no exception. In China and Japan it had to be rescued at times from compromises with political powers and from indulgence in avarice, in order to remain true to the spirit of its founder and to practice the self-sacrifice exemplified by the Boddhisattvas.

There should, in short, be no room in religion for a God who curses human beings. Hinduism, to which Kannan, our poor and disabled storyteller, belongs, is no exception. One has to be reminded that

> the Vedic gods have an intimate relation of love with human beings. Every individual has the right to be loved by the gods and also to love the gods in return.... The gods love human beings, and human beings are referred to as desirous of loving gods (Deva Kama). The god Agni has been referred to as one of the most affectionate gods who loves human beings as a father loves his son or as an elder brother loves his younger brother. Agni has been called a father, brother, and even a son. Even the battle-god Indra is regarded as an affectionate god. These very tendencies are responsible for the path of devotion (Bhakti Marga) which appears in its full bloom in the Bhagavad Gita.[16]

How does the God of love turn into the God who discriminates, who takes the side of the privileged against the dispossessed? Is not religion—the religion that comes to represent the interest of the ruling class—responsible?

The fact is that the religion with which Kannan is familiar has left him to cope with his own misery. The society to which he belongs does not treat him as a human being. And the strangers he meets outside the slum take advantage of him, a poor cripple who cannot defend himself from their ridicules and exploitation. Where can he turn for help? Not to his parents; they themselves are helpless. Where can he seek relief from his hardships? Not in society. Society is either indifferent to him or turns against him. Where can he have his hope rekindled—hope to live as a human being, hope to be free from anxiety, and hope to overcome death of the spirit? Not from his religion. It is his religion that created outcasts like him. Kannan seems to have exhausted all his resources, material and spiritual. He seems to be trapped in the fate decreed for him from eternity. He seems destined to endure the curse of God until the end of his life.

Ethics of Hope

But fortunately for him, Kannan was able to turn around before he had reached the end of his rope. Lucky for him, he did not have to give up in despair but was able to have his hope rekindled. It was not society that enabled him to be human again. Nor was it religion that empowered him not to give in to the death of his inner self. He realized that he could not expect society to give him back his humanity. He also became aware that he could not depend on religion to rejuvenate his hope to live as a respectable and useful human being. Like freedom, hope has to be earned, and not received as charity. Like justice, hope has to be won, and not picked up ready-made. Like love, hope has to be nurtured, and not had without feeling. For hope to be hope, it has to be a motivating power that changes what you are supposed to be to what you have to be. Hope is something closely related to all aspects of your life, both external and internal. It provides energy to turn what cannot be seen into what can be seen, what is in the future to what is present, what is envisioned to what is real. In other words, for hope to be hope, it has to be an ethical power for change.

Hope as an Ethical Power

Hope as an ethical power is self-transforming. It makes us aware of the power working in us to change us. It awakens in us the desire to overcome obstacles that inhibit our growth toward becoming a full-fledged human being. It empowers us to break the chains that bind us—chains of self-pity, resignation, and submission. For Kannan, our storyteller, that ethical power of hope makes him realize "the pitiable condition of expecting other people's charity" that "killed our sense of self-respect and brought us to a condition of less than animals."

Charity can be shown without love, and it often takes that form. Such charity may enhance the self-respect of the charity giver, but it diminishes the self-respect of the charity receiver. Charity can be administered impersonally, and often is. In both Eastern and Western society, charity organizations proliferate. They grow into machines that dispense charity as if it were a commodity. Charity contributes to the charity giver's false sense of spiritual well-being, but it often suppresses the spirit of the charity receiver to strive for self-improvement. This is what Kannan and many in the slums like him came to realize. Hope as an ethical power made them realize the unethical nature of small charities thrown at them, which served to humiliate them, to perpetuate their pitiful condition, to keep them subservient forever as coolies and slaves, or even to be rid of them.

We are reminded of Jesus' parable of the rich man and Lazarus (Luke 16:19-31). Poor and covered with sores, Lazarus had to fight with the dogs for the scraps of food discarded by the rich man and his guests. He lived literally like an animal, if not worse than an animal. He died without self-respect, perhaps like many of Kannan's contemporaries in India, believing it was his fate to be

cursed by God. But Jesus repudiates this popular belief. At this point his parable moves from realism to symbolism, from depicting what is often the case in
human community to what human community must be. Jesus shows us a scene
of bliss in paradise, with Lazarus in Abraham's arms and the rich man in hell
suffering extreme torments. In the parable all this happens after their deaths.
But Jesus tries to emphasize the ethical power of hope that turns the experience
of human community on earth from suffering to joy, adversity to happiness, hell
to paradise. If hope does not have ethical power, it is not hope. This was one of
the ideas Jesus tried to bring home to his listeners.

The ethical power of hope inspires, motivates, and compels us to take action.
In Kannan and his friends that power began to stir them up and make them
restless. Hope has to be *ethical* precisely for this reason. Ethics is concerned,
among other things, with "normative inquiries about the principles, standards,
or methods for determining what is morally right or wrong, good or bad."[17]
But is this all there is to ethics? Ethics, like philosophy and theology, deals too
much with principles and standards, and too little with what these principles and
standards can do to enable us to practice right instead of wrong, good instead of
bad. History tells us and our experience confirms that more wrong than right,
and more evil than good has been committed in human community.

We do not have to bring up horrendous tragedies such as the Holocaust, the
tribal massacres in Rwanda, or the ethnic cleansing in Bosnia. Just take the case
of Kannan our storyteller. The moral standards prevailing in India teach people
not to treat others like animals because they are poor and disabled, but Kannan
and people like him are still treated horribly. The religious principles advocate
that God is all-loving and good, but the principles are shunned as if this loving
and good God can also cast curses. In the society of India, as in any other
society, people are taught from early in their lives not to wrong others but to do
good, but they can still despise, ridicule, and even exploit unfortunate women
and men such as Kannan.

What is the problem? How is one to resolve the obvious contradiction between what "the law" demands and what is actually practiced? Here is an insight
that partially addresses our concern:

> A normative basis is not sufficient unto itself, since the tradition does not
> address all aspects of reality. Scientific theories which attempt to inter-
> pret empirical facts must be added. Both theories and facts are essential in
> ethics because they give understanding and empirical grounding to those
> in situations in which ethical decisions must be made. Without theo-
> ries and facts, norms wander around in confusion, unable to inform the
> situation."[18]

Norms, theories, and facts are closely related. The importance of this interrelationship cannot be emphasized enough. To illustrate the interrelationship, we
are invited to

consider poverty in the Third World. Approximately five hundred million people are seriously malnourished in a world with more than enough food to go around. This is a fact. The numbers, however, only indicate magnitude. Economic and political theories are necessary to give meaning to the numbers and suggest alternative courses of action. Norms, such as Christianity's concern for the poor, make these numbers a scandal and are the basis for selecting among competing economic theories an alternative course of action.[19]

This statement represents an effort in the right direction. Theology and even ethics have been too preoccupied with norms and assumptions. Norms and assumptions have shaped theories that explain realities. In the world today, such high-handed methods no longer work. Theology and ethics have to face the facts of how people live and suffer, letting these facts develop theories and shape norms and principles.

But this procedural change is still not enough. Even theories and norms constructed on the basis of facts and realities, that is, informed by what is really happening to men, women, and children in their struggle to live, are often powerless to change the prevailing situation. The idea of a just world economic order is one example. It is based on the recognition that the prevailing world economic order is an unjust one, that it is making rich nations richer and poor nations poorer. Lack of moral integrity on the part of those who profit from the unjust economic order has to be exposed. But an economic order that can do justice to the poor is not likely to be put in place anytime soon. Norms and theories derived from facts do not have the power to change the situation.

The situation just described is much like the interaction between Jesus and a rich young man (Mark 10:17-22). The man approached Jesus and asked, "What must I do to inherit eternal life?" He confessed that he had done everything expected of him as a responsible member of the society and religious establishment. He must have struck Jesus as a sincere person, for Jesus looked at him and "loved him." He had not come to test Jesus, nor to grind a theological axe. He was not instigated by Jesus' opponents to make life difficult for Jesus. To this honest, earnest, and devoted young man Jesus said: "You lack one thing; go, sell what you own, and give the money to the poor, and you will have treasure in heaven; then come, follow me." This was too much for the young man. "He was shocked," Mark tells us, "and went away grieving, for he had many possessions" (10:22). The rich young man had mastered the principles of his religion. He was at home with the religious norms he had learned. Still, he was shocked when Jesus told him to put into practice those moral principles and religious norms.

If norms and principles developed independently from facts will not change the world, nor will the norms and principles reconstructed on the basis of facts and realities. Those norms and principles possess no ethical power to change the world. The hope they offer to people is an empty hope, without moral conviction or ethical power. Political hope offered by ambitious politicians tends to be this kind of hope. Most of the hope preached from the religious pulpit—hope in the future, hope in the promise of God, hope to come at the end of time—is this kind of hope. This empty hope cannot redress the suffering of Kannan and people like him. It cannot help them live as human beings. It only allows them to live at the mercy of gods and other human beings.

For hope to be ethical, it has to create new meaning in a life that has been devastated by physical disability and human abuse. An ethical hope is creative hope, a hope that gives birth to a new human being and that creates a new community. This is exactly what happened to Kannan and his friends. This is the turning point in his story. He tells us how "the poor slum handicapped joined together and with the help of a group started to organize. We are now 1,200 people in eighteen slums." Their hope is no longer in the charity society that gives and withholds at will. It does not depend on the religious institution that preaches hope but dispenses despair. Their hope, the real hope that brings change to their lives and to their community, comes from joining together as a community. Isolated, they are helpless victims, but together they are a community with a purpose. Scattered, they are objects of taunt and abuse, but together they gain power as subjects of their own life and destiny.

A City of Hope

They are, Kannan is proud to tell us, "1,200 people in eighteen slums." You may laugh at one individual with impunity, but you cannot laugh at 1,200 people. You may mistreat one pitiful person, but you cannot mistreat 1,200 persons organized to defy you. A lone individual, disabled and handicapped, is bound to be defeated and disposed of. But 1,200 persons together are no longer disabled or handicapped. United in the body, heart, mind, and soul, they—each of them—become whole persons, not to be made fun of, slighted, or abused. This is what Kannan means when he says: "Our disability is in our bodies, not in our spirit." This is a declaration that they are fully human, even more human than those who are able in body but disabled in spirit. This is also the statement of their hope. What offers more hope than a revitalized spirit in reconstructing a life that was crushed and a community that had lost its moral integrity?

The statement of Kannan's group is a penetrating insight that makes clear what makes a human being human—not the appearance but the soul, not the external beauty but the inner beauty, not outward pretensions but the strength that reflects the freedom of the spirit. These words of Kannan remind us of what Jesus once said to his disciples as he was sending them out on a preaching mission: "Do not fear those who kill the body but cannot kill the soul; rather fear those who can destroy both soul and body" (Matt. 10:28; also Luke 12:4-5). The spirit that is not disabled can empower the body to overcome its physical limitation and to serve the purpose of life. The soul that survives the violence done to the body can be reunited with the body to give birth to new life. The spirit and soul together can re-create a body ravaged by illness and unite women and men in building a new community.

In this community of 1,200 people from eighteen slums hope becomes a present reality. Hope is not an abstraction in the temple but a presence in their midst when they help each other. Hope is manifested, becomes visible, touchable, and graspable when they share the skills of bag making, bookbinding, tailoring, and other handicrafts as well as profits from their labor. If hope is not an abstract idea, it is not religious jargon either. The hope grasped by 1,200 disabled men, women, and children from eighteen slums is a "material" hope—hope that can be handled with their hands and that can be tasted in the food they have earned by working together as a community.

This community of 1,200 also makes incense sticks they call "HOPE"—hope in capital letters, hope in bold letters. As the incense stick of hope burns, "smoke of hope" fills their workplace. Hope is not odorless; they can smell it. It is not something outside them; they inhale it and let it fill their whole being. They become people of hope—hope on their persons, hope inside and outside. They themselves become hope to themselves, to one another, and even to future generations. Their hope is as vivid as the pulse in their veins. It is as real as the bags they make. It is as solid as the books they bind.

They are determined that their hope has to be extended to others. Hope is genuine when it kindles hope and becomes contagious to others. A hope that does not inspire others is selfish hope, and selfish hope is false hope, a hope gained at the expense of others. A hope that does not kindle hope in others is barren hope. A barren hope only yields despair, resignation, and death of the spirit. Hope that is not contagious does not grow, multiply, and spread. It becomes less vigorous, grows dimmer and dimmer. At last its fire is extinguished, reduced to a heap of ashes.

This is not the kind of hope with which Kannan and his friends lighted their incense sticks. Theirs is a hope that grows, expands, and reproduces. They "go in procession to the government and demand our rights." They "spread knowledge about polio prevention and employment possibilities and understanding about the causes of our poverty and degradation." The actions that they have taken and continue to take manifest the ethical power of their hope. They are not contented with the hope they have found for themselves. They do not light the incense sticks of hope in their workplace and forget what is happening to other unfortunate souls in the streets.

The hope they have found not only changes them but others, even the society around them. In their hope is this ethical power to change. They may be ignorant about principles, theories, or the theology of hope. But they can practice the ethics of hope. Their ethics of hope consists in the realization that they have rights to live as human beings like anybody else, especially like those who treat them as less than human. Their hope comes from the awareness that their physical disability is preventable and that they have the responsibility to make people aware. Their hope teaches them that their misfortune and poverty have causes deeply rooted in society, politics, and religion, and have nothing to do with their God. Above all, their ethics of hope enables them to reach this resolution: "We aspire to gain our dignity and our rights through our struggle without expecting anyone's pity or charity." This in essence is the ethics of hope.

The ethics of hope constructs tomorrow on the foundation of today. It builds tomorrow's promise on the hope striven for today. Hope consists of movements of the human spirit toward God, who is in us and around us. In the presence of this God in and around us our ethics of hope becomes our prayer of hope, the prayer that God's will be done on earth as in heaven.

Part Four

FAITH

So I [Jesus] say to you, Ask, and it will be given you; search, and you will find; knock, and the door will be opened for you. For everyone who asks receives, and everyone who searches finds, and for everyone who knocks, the door will be opened.

—Luke 11:9-10

Peruvian Magnificat

I SING TO THE LORD
FOR THE LORD IS GREAT

To the Lord I sing my praises,
Joyful in my Savior God;
The Lord has called me to remembrance
Poor, exploited as I am.

Friends around me all are saying
"You're the servant-girl of God!"
The Lord is good, and God's compassion
Always reaches to the poor.
And we know that the Lord is greatest,
For the Lord brings the boastful down,
Raises up the oppressed people,
Puts the bosses in their place.
God gives bread to those who have none,
Casts aside the millionaire;
As Jesus said, God always struggles
With the people, at their side.[1]

Chapter 8

Faith in the World
of Divided Loyalties

In the previous section we emphasized the "present-ness" of hope, its "con-temporaneousness." Hope is *con-temporaneous*. It is conceived in time and hinged to time. It moves in time and with time. As time is time because it does not stand still, nor does hope stand still. As time gives birth to time, so does hope give birth to hope. And as time realizes itself by creating new times, hope also realizes itself by creating new hopes.

In this sense there is always something new with the hope that lives in time and moves with time. It is our experience that a hope that is new, a hope that is to grow out of the present hope, is beyond what we can see. Often it is beyond our grasp, even beyond our anticipation. For this reason a sense of suspense always accompanies hope. The suspense can be small or great, depending on the nature of the hope. To be able to bear it, we have to have faith. Faith is a power that enables us not to be crushed under the weight of the suspense of hope. The greater the suspense, the greater our faith must be. Hope without faith is like a car without an engine to get it started and to perform the function for which the car is made.

Suspense always has an element of unpredictability. A hope that can be predicted is deprived of excitement and wonder, is missing vitality. In this sense and in this sense alone we agree with Paul when he says that "hope that is seen is not hope" (Rom. 8:24). A genuine hope is not like a letter box that receives letters with correct addresses and postage. Often neither its itinerary nor its destination is clearly marked. To be able to cope with the unpredictability of hope and even to be excited by it, we need a faith that makes us not fear or turn away from it.

Since hope can be unpredictable, it often takes us by surprise. Hope and a sense of surprise go hand in hand. A hope that does not surprise us is a routine hope. Is a routine hope still hope? Is it not another word for sterile life, a status quo society, and a stagnant world? If this is the case, a teacher of ancient Israel is undoubtedly correct when he intones that "a generation goes and a generation comes, but the earth remains forever," or that "what has been is what will be, and what has been done is what will be done; there is nothing new under the sun" (Eccl. 1:4, 9).

But there is always something new under the sun, and we are often taken by surprise by what takes place in ourselves and in the world. For hope to be hope it has to have the wisdom to discern something new in our routine lives and to apprehend change in a world that seems indifferent to new seasons and generations. Faith is this wisdom that makes it possible for us to perceive elements of surprise in hope.

If hope can come true, it can also be defeated. How many of us have started with high hopes only to have the castle built on them crumble? Maybe the hope we have set is unrealistic. It could be that we have not thought through ways to attain our hopes. Our failure may be caused by our misjudgment and miscalculation, but there are also social and political factors beyond our control. Hope, in a sense, is a bet. The higher the bet, the greater the risk, especially considering that we are not in command of all necessary information or circumstances.

In spite of the uncertainty, we human beings continue to hope. Why? Is it because we are incorrigible? Is it because we are always driven by ambitions for achievement? Is it because built within us is the desire to transcend ourselves, to reach beyond the present and to test limits of our finitude? Any of these reasons is possible. But when our hope is not just for personal gain and advancement, there must be something else that motivates and inspires us. When we hope for justice to prevail in society, for love for our neighbors—even for our enemies—or for peace in the world, we need something other than selfish hope. As we know too well, hopes directed to such selfless goals will be frustrated and defeated again and again. What do we need besides hope? What enables us not to be frustrated when the going gets rough, not to accept defeat when the hope for a world of justice, love, and freedom seems nowhere in sight? It is faith.

Hope without faith is like a husk without rice, a body without the spirit, a reverie unrelated to reality. Hope not empowered by faith is like a house built on sand, to quote Jesus. "The rain fell, and the floods came, and the winds blew and beat against that house, and it fell—and great was its fall!" (Matt. 7:27). What is this faith? How does it function in our life and in the world? What power does it have? These are some of the questions we want to explore.

Three Loyalties

The "Holy" Land has been in the news not since the birth of the state of Israel in 1948, not since our television sets started bringing into our living rooms stories of conflicts, bloodshed, and death between the warring parties and religions, but since Abraham and his family left their home in Mesopotamia some 3,500 years ago to seek a new home in Palestine. God said to Abram, later to be renamed Abraham, "Go from your country and your kindred and your father's house to the land that I will show you. I will make of you a great nation, and I will bless you, and make your name great, so that *by you all the families of the earth shall bless themselves*" (Gen. 12:1-3).[1]

Abraham did not become a great nation, but many generations later King David built a great empire. Storytellers and historians of ancient Israel believed that becoming a great nation was a blessing from God. As to whether by this nation "all the families of the earth" were blessed is an entirely different matter. The conflicts that have destroyed countless lives and families in Palestine throughout history make it difficult for us to take that statement of faith at face value. A firsthand account from that land of promise and despair makes us ponder deeply the claims of different but related faiths, which have turned Palestine into anything but a "holy" land.

> As a Palestinian Quaker woman, a native of the Holy Land, I have been confronted all my life with structures of injustice. As a Palestinian, I have lived under military occupation since 1967. As an Arab woman in a male culture, I have no equality with my brothers. And as a pacifist in an area of military conflict, I am often misinterpreted as being passive or submissive or accepting of injustice. . . .
>
> Living under military occupation has made me go through deep self-searching, and I have been confronted with three loyalties. The first loyalty is to Christ, who calls us to love our enemy. The second loyalty is to our fellow-men or women in need or trouble, to aid them in whatever way we can. The third loyalty prevents us from being willing to aid our invader. In our situation, no one can set the rules for us to follow, but what we can do is to testify that, in our experience, the spirit of God leads us into the truth and gives us the needed guidance in every situation.
>
> We have gone through circumstances of great privation, anxiety and suffering. All these seemed at times to weaken our sense of dependence on God. But when I know that wherever I am, whether in affluence or in poverty, whether I have personal liberty or not, God has a service for me to render, I feel a sense of both hope and joy.[2]

The story is about faith in a world of divided loyalties and of religious and political conflicts.

For most of us Christians faith has not been the issue; the divided loyalties are the issue. Does this woman not find her Christian faith is also an issue as she tries to cope with being Christian, Arab, and Palestinian? Is her situation unique, or do those of us in Asia, for example, also find ourselves in a world in which our Christian faith conflicts with other loyalties? Such questions invite us to examine our faith and to sort out its negative and positive relations with neighbors with diverse religious allegiances and political commitments.

Loyalty to Jesus

My "first loyalty," says our Palestinian Christian woman, "is to Christ, who calls us to love our enemy." Stop, readers, and take note. She does not merely say her loyalty is to Christ, period. Even if this were all she had to say, it would be, though brief, an excellent statement of faith. Is it any different from saying that Jesus is Christ? This is what Christians have confessed from the inception of the Christian church to the present day. Her faith statement reminds us of one of the earliest Christian hymns, known to us as the christological hymn (Phil. 2:5-11). The hymn ends by professing that "every tongue should confess that Jesus Christ is Lord." My first—not second, not third—loyalty is to Christ. Such a profession of faith will certainly win theological approval. The expression of primary loyalty will receive commendation from the church authorities.

There is no doubt that Jean Zaru, a Palestinian Christian woman from Ramallah and the author of the above faith statement, is a theologically literate person, even a sophisticated one. She was a member of the Central Committee of the World Council of Churches and a vice president of the World YWCA.[3] She must be acquainted with creeds in the history of Christianity and confessions of faith enunciated by contemporary churches. Above all, she knows how central Christ is for all these creeds and confessions of faith. This Christ of the Christian church must be also central to her life and faith. Is it any wonder that she, reflecting on conflicting loyalties posed by her situation, expresses her loyalty to Christ, first and foremost, almost spontaneously?

But "[my] first loyalty is to Christ" is not all that she says. It is immediately followed by a phrase to qualify "Christ." It is to Christ *who calls us to love our enemy* to whom she commits her first loyalty, and this qualification changes not only the tone of what she says but the content, not only its form but its substance. "[My] first loyalty is to Christ"—this can be merely the rhetoric of faith. It may not carry much meaning, express a conviction, or demand a commitment. For many of us Christians, are not the confessions of faith we recite in church, be they the Nicene Creed or the Apostles' Creed, mostly mere words? Did we not cease to think about their meaning long ago?

The word *Christ* has become, strange though it may sound, a word full of questions. Who is Christ—a king anointed to restore the kingdom of David, a Messiah appointed to establish the kingdom of God on earth to replace all nations and kingdoms? Who is Christ—the founder of Christianity who has entrusted the keys of God's kingdom to it, the head of the Christian church represented by popes, bishops, and ministers, most of them still male? Who is Christ—the Savior of my soul and the only Savior of the world, a Savior who saves those who, like us, believe in God and who judges those who don't? Who is Christ—an object of Christian cult, a magical name to invoke in times of difficulty and danger, a religious word that evokes Christian piety?

But is this Christ Jesus? Is this Christ the Jesus of Nazareth who walked the earth two thousand years ago? Is this Christ the Jesus who once said that "foxes have holes and birds of the air have nests; but the Son of Man has nowhere to lay his head" (Matt. 8:20)? Is this Christ the Jesus who came "not to be served but to serve" (Matt. 20:28)? Is this Christ the Jesus who was prepared to "undergo great suffering, and be rejected by the elders, the chief priests, and the scribes" (Mark 8:31)? And is this Christ the Jesus who prayed in the Garden of Gethsemane: "Abba, Father, remove this cup [of suffering and death on the cross] from me; yet not what I want, but what you want" (Mark 14:36)?

For most of us Christians this Jesus is not Christ. This Jesus is too down-to-earth for our liking. This Jesus is too disturbing and too demanding for us to emulate. This Jesus calls into question how we regard and worship him, so much so that he may not look with approval at our worship services and our elegant liturgies. This Jesus questions too much the ways in which most of us live for ourselves to make us feel comfortable in his presence. And this Jesus says things so true that we wish they were not true, and does things so right that we wish they were wrong. In short, my Christ, your Christ, and the Christs of most Christians are not necessarily Jesus himself, the son of Mary and Joseph. Our confession of faith in Christ as the Savior of the world, unfortunately, is not always the same thing as following the Jesus who lived and died for the reign of God among the destitute and the disinherited.

Does not this tell us that our confession cannot stop at the noun *Christ?* Does it not remind us that we cannot show our loyalty to *Christ* pure and simple? In this matter, brevity is not a virtue and silence is not gold. We must go on to say in what kind of Christ we confess our faith. We must explain to which Christ we show our loyalty. Our confession is not finished until we have made these declarations. The church, high or low, can confess its faith in Christ; it has done so for two thousand years. Christians—Orthodox, Catholic, and Protestant—have pledged their loyalty to Christ, fought one another for Christ, and even on occasion have become martyrs for Christ. But we are all too aware, from the history of Christianity and from our own experience, that the Christs (note the plural!) we have fashioned and to whom we have pledged our loyalty often cause us to be divided among ourselves and to be unfriendly, even hostile, to people outside the Christian church.

I do not really know if the Palestinian Christian woman who crafted that splendid statement of faith was aware of this background. But I do know that her statement of faith does not end with Christ. Whether this is a conscious theological effort on her part or merely accidental, again I do not know. But that is not important. What is important is that she goes on to tell us who Christ is for her, to what kind of Christ she is prepared to pledge her loyalty. "[My] first loyalty is to Christ," she says, "*who calls us to love our enemy*" (emphasis added).

Is this not a flash of theological insight? Christ for her is not just any Christ; it is the Christ "who calls us to love our enemy." I may not agree with Christ as a victor, not only over sins but also over people of cultures and religions outside of Christianity, but how can I disagree with you when you commit yourself to the Christ "who calls us to love our enemy"? You may disengage yourself from my Christ as a revolutionary intent on fighting against injustice and oppression, but how can you not embrace my Christ "who calls us to love our enemy"? We Christians from different confessional backgrounds and traditions may refuse to enter into communion with one another at the Lord's Table, but can we not rally around the Christ who "calls us to love our enemy"? After all, did not Jesus say:

> You have heard that it was said, "You shall love your neighbor and hate your enemy." But I say to you, Love your enemies and pray for those who persecute you, so that you may be children of your Father in heaven. . . .
>
> (Matt. 5:43-45)

This is one of Jesus' sayings most Christians through the ages have held as an ethic noble but unrealistic, ideal but impracticable.

But Jesus, as we all know, practiced what he exhorted others to do. According to Luke, Jesus prayed to God to forgive his opponents and enemies who conspired to bring about his death. "Father," he said, addressing God, "forgive them; for they do not know what they are doing" (Luke 23:34). Jesus knows that some Pharisees are teaching people to love their neighbor and to hate their enemy.[4] But he says something very different and striking.

Loving one's neighbor and hating one's enemy seems sensible. Can a society function normally without this code, ancient Jewish society and almost all human societies throughout the world included? Can a society still have law and order if people do not protect their own interests against intruders, swindlers, or murderers? If nations do not oppose invaders and aggressors, how can they maintain their national dignity and territorial integrity? If human beings do not defend themselves against thieves, crooks, and plunderers, how can they preserve the civilizations they have built? Archaeologists in fact tell us that there has been no shortage, in East or West, of those who plunder and destroy human achievements, among them kings and emperors—political leaders turned warmongers.

The injunction to love one's neighbor and hate one's enemy, it is evident, is not wisdom particular to ancient Israel. The saying can be found written in books of law and elsewhere, and has been practiced ever since human beings emerged from the obscurity of history. It is a universal law in the sense that it is rooted in the human instinct for survival. It is something, to use modern scientific jargon, coded in our DNA. From the survival of our own individual selves to that of our families, tribes, communities, nations, and even the world, love of self or self-love is the basic law of life and history.

But Jesus wants to have this "law of human nature" drastically changed. "You shall love your neighbor"—this is the first part of the Jewish law and the universal law of human conduct. Jesus does not challenge that. It would be insane for him to do so. Neighbor does not just mean the person living next door. Neighbor is not just a sociological concept. It symbolizes the bond of love that starts from loved ones in the immediate family and expands to relatives in extended families and circles of friends. Without this bond of love there may be a family but no home, a society but no community, a country but no nation or people.

The problem we face in the world today is the weakening of this bond of love. If Jesus were with us today, he would exhort us to strengthen this bond of love.

Jesus is not taking issue with love of neighbor. He does not ask us to hate our neighbor and love our enemy. He is not demanding us to turn our neighbor into our enemy in order to make friends with our enemy. Yes, he does go on to say that if you love those who love you and greet only your brothers and sisters, you are doing what everyone else does (Matt. 5:46-47). In all these interactions your faith is not tested. Even without particular reference to faith you can perform all these duties to family and neighbor. But there are situations in which your faith in God will be tested—situations in which you are confronted with your enemies. What are you to do? Hate them, fight them, and if possible destroy them? Or accept them, care for them, and work out a bond of love with them?

Confronting our enemies is an option we hope and pray we do not have to face. But when we face it, we are to accept them, care for them, and work out a bond of love with our enemies. Jesus would rather we love our enemies not because we are particularly pious, noble-minded, or altruistic. We are none of these things. Love of enemies is, Jesus is saying, what our faith demands. That must be why Jesus does not just say, "love your enemy," leaving us confused or frustrated as to what to do. He follows his exhortation with these words: "...so that you may be children of your Father in heaven." These words do not make the injunction to love one's enemy easier to practice. The heart of the matter must have to do with what "enemy" refers to in Jesus' mind. He could not be referring to "enemy" as a general concept. He must have specified who the enemy is in his discourse with his listeners. It may even be that he did not actually use the word *enemy*, but that the word was supplied by the Gospel writers, Matthew and Luke. What Jesus meant by "enemy" must be those people who oppose you, who try to do you harm, who plot evil things against you.

Jesus had people who opposed him, who hated what he was saying and doing, who plotted to bring about his downfall. They were the religious authorities represented by chief priests, Pharisees, and scribes. Luke seems to be referring to these groups when he has Jesus exhort his followers to love their "enemies," saying further:

> Do good to those who hate you,
> bless those who curse you,
> pray for those who abuse you.
>   (Luke 6:27-28)

Is it not obvious that by "enemies" Jesus refers to certain people with whom he has to deal—those who hate, curse, and abuse him?

It becomes even more obvious when we recall some of the things Jesus said in the Beatitudes. He specifically mentions that one is blessed when "people hate you, and when they exclude you, revile you, and defame you" (Luke 6:22; also Matt. 5:11). Jesus himself has had plenty of encounters with such people.

Besides being very much occupied with his followers and crowds of people, Jesus' thoughts are also taken up with his religious opponents who "hate him" for what he has to say about them, who "exclude him" because he often does outrageous things such as healing sick persons on the sabbath, who "revile" him and accuse him of "having Beelzebul, and by the ruler of demons [casting] out demons" (Mark 3:22; also Matt. 9:34), and who "abuse" him, trying in one instance to "hurl him off the cliff" (Luke 4:29).

Jesus is even more specific in his teaching as to how to deal with enemies. "Do good to those who hate you," he says. How did he deal with such enemies? What was his response to them? Did he try to avoid them as much as possible, as most of us would do in order to stay away from trouble? Or did he try to be pleasant with them even though he resented them in his heart? This is not how he conducted himself; to do so would have amounted to what he himself called hypocrisy. What he did was to reason with enemies, to make them realize they misrepresented the law, and to let them see how they abused people.

Jesus also said that one should bless enemies. What did he mean? Did he bless those who cursed him, the religious leaders who called him a blasphemer of God? Both *blessing* and *cursing* are strong words, particularly the latter. To curse someone is to detest them, to declare that they have fallen out of favor with God, to treat them as a heretic, and to excommunicate them. To bless enemies is to declare that they are accepted by God, that they are in favor with God, and that they are treated as children of God.

Jesus did bless those who cursed him. We remember those heart-rending words with which he addressed himself to them. "Jerusalem, Jerusalem," he lamented, "the city that kills the prophets and stones those who are sent to it! How often have I desired to gather your children together as a hen gathers her brood under her wings, and you were not willing!" (Matt. 23:37). Jesus got into heated arguments with his religious opponents. He knew they were not going to let him get away unharmed. Still, Jesus wanted "to gather [them] together as a hen gathers her brood under her wings." In pouring his heart over them in this way, was not Jesus in fact saying a blessing over them?

Jesus also asked for prayer for enemies. For Jesus prayer is not merely words. His prayer is a communion with God in the deepest parts of his heart and being. In prayers he communes with God, exposes himself to God, and puts himself in the hand of God. In the presence of God in prayer, he has to be completely honest with God and with himself. He does not flatter God, as many of us do in prayer, piling one ornate and high-flown word upon another, perhaps making God feel embarrassed. When he exhorts us to pray for those who abuse us, he means asking God to grant us the power of grace, not merely not to seek our enemies' downfall, but to commend them to God's care.

In prayer such as this the depth of our faith is surveyed and its strength is tested. Jesus himself must have often prayed for those who hounded him. On the cross he is heard to be praying to God to forgive his murderers. To pray for others, especially for those who abuse you, is to put your life on the line. This is when prayer ceases to be mere words, but one's true self before God. Prayer in such cases puts your life at risk in front of those who abuse you, who take advantage of you, who even try to kill you.

We now begin to understand how the Palestinian Christian woman and her fellow Palestinian Christians put themselves in a serious situation when they give their first loyalty to Christ who calls them to love their enemy. They are not saying this in a peaceful environment, but in an environment filled with tension and hostility. They are not reciting these words in a church service surrounded by choruses singing to the glory of God, but in the land of deafening gun sounds and bomb explosions. They are not repeating these words in a society in which peace and harmony prevail, but in a society torn apart by religious and political conflicts. The environment makes their prayer a completely honest prayer, a deadly serious prayer, and a really dangerous prayer.

To be loyal to Christ who calls them to love their enemy is *to do good* to those extremists, whether Arab, Palestinian, or Jew, who hate them for their efforts toward peace, *to bless* those who despise them because they are obstacles to territorial claims, and *to pray* for those who expand their national borders by taking land away from them. As one practices this prayer, one has to learn that love of enemy is not a matter of simple charity one does to gain a good feeling as a Christian. Nor is it a philanthropic generosity one can afford out of affluence. One is committing oneself to a faith in a world of political conflicts, religious contentions, and military confrontations.

Are this Palestinian Christian woman and those Palestinian Christians who share her faith and conviction getting themselves into an impossible situation? Is what they say nothing but empty words? Like many other Christians elsewhere, are they being less than candid in their prayers, less than honest in the presence of God, and less than serious about the faith they have learned from Jesus? These are fair questions.

Such questions take us back to the situation of Syria, Palestine, and Lebanon during the First World War. In 1914, the year the war erupted, the entire region was invaded by locusts and epidemics. Within three years, 350,000 had died of hunger and disease, as much as 10 percent of the region's population. In Jerusalem, it was reported, three hundred Jews died every month.[5]

But also reported was what some Arabs did to help the starving Jewish immigrants. For the Jewish immigrants in the region of Galilee, Arabs provided six thousand bushels of wheat to relieve their hunger. How much six thousand bushels of wheat were worth can be estimated with the knowledge that, at that time, wheat and gold coins had the same value by weight.[6] Although this was long before the Palestinian-Israeli conflicts developed into full-scale wars, the tension between the native Arabs and the European Jews who had immigrated to Palestine had been mounting since the end of the eighteenth century.

History does not necessarily solve conflicts between warring parties; often it is the cause of them. In history one can always find justification for conflict and war. But we should not give up on history so easily. Reflecting on causes and the development of conflicts, one becomes aware that history is not always treated justly. To carry out national interest, to expand territorial boundaries, and to achieve domination of other nations and peoples stories of how rival parties used to live in peace and to help one another are suppressed, even banned. But when caught in national and international conflicts, such as our Palestinian Christians, do we not have to go back to uncover stories from the "good old days" in which we and those with whom we are now in conflict helped one another in times of suffering?

There are many stories of how people with different political backgrounds and religious convictions work together in situations of division and conflict. And Palestine is no exception. Without such stories we human beings would be condemned without hope or future. The world would be a battleground in which evil forces always win at the end. But this is not the history we experience and not the world in which we live. True, there are always conflicts of interest. True, there will be always those who ruthlessly exploit others, but they do not write the final chapter of history. Neither do those who resort to violence build the world of the future.

Loyalty to People in Need

Justice, peace, and freedom will be always fragile. They will have to be won again and again. In this struggle against violence and terror, there are always women and men committed to love their enemies, that is, to "do good to those who hate them, to bless those who curse them, and to pray for those who abuse them." This is the heart of their faith shaped by their loyalty to Jesus: "Until we surrender to God as Jesus did, and until we reach that stage where we can forgive those who have offended us, we will not have peace, and we will not have liberation."[7] If this belief exists in Palestine, it also exists in other parts of the world. These people are the real builders of history and the true makers of the world, even though their names are not recorded in history books.

This kind of faith—faith that responds to Jesus' call to love one's enemies—works miracles. In this kind of faith the line between enemies and friends becomes obscured, the wall between those who hate us and those who like us begins to be removed, and the rift between those who curse us and those who bless us does not seem final. Hostility between those who abuse us and those who cherish us can be overcome, and separation between "we" and "they" can be dissolved. Our loyalty to Jesus who calls us to love our enemies enables us to see in "enemies," if not friends, then at least women, men, and children in need and in trouble. This is a real breakthrough in our psyche, in our attitudes to those outside of us, and in our ways of dealing with those who inflict pain and suffering on us.

Is this a sentimental faith? Is this the kind of faith to which we pay lip service at our worship in church? Is it professed for publicity's sake, enabling the world outside to believe that we are "good" people and that our enemies are "bad" people? There is no shortage of sentimental faith among Christians who live their lives and practice their faith in a racially, culturally, and politically homogenous community. But for those Christians, like Palestinian Christians, who have their faith tested each day in a racially, politically, and religiously heterogenous community and in an atmosphere of division and conflict, a sentimental faith will not help. It will only make them passive and inactive. A sentimental faith is a false faith. At least it is not a faith in the Jesus who calls us to love our enemies.

Is this faith cherished by many Christians utopian, especially when the world, including Palestine, seems to be heading for destruction? Unlike sentimental faith, utopian faith is not necessarily a world-denying faith. Some of those who hold it are genuinely troubled by the evils they see, and their hearts ache for victims of human atrocities. But they come to the conclusion that this world is not reparable, nor is it redeemable. They become thoroughly disillusioned. They project another world, another era, and another creation that will replace the present age in some future time. It is at this point that sentimental faith and utopian faith become strange bedfellows, passive and inactive in their relation to the present world. A utopian faith is an illusive faith that has little to do with faith in Jesus, who exhorts us to do good to those who hate us.

What, then, is an alternative to these faiths, a faith neither sentimental nor utopian? Should it be a militant faith, a faith that bursts out into soul-stirring hymns at evangelical rallies, hymns such as "Onward Christian Soldiers"? Military metaphors in this hymn are obvious. The hymn vividly, and one must add, crudely, portrays one side of Christian spirituality—self-centered, restless, assertive, and combative. Christianity that once dominated the world outside the West has been known for its aggressive spirituality, posing, in Asia for example, a striking contrast to more contemplative spirituality that seeks communion with the divine, the human, and the natural. This is one of the reasons why Christianity is still regarded as a Western religion in most Asian countries. Professing a militant religion in a situation of conflict is like adding fuel to flame.

This influence is keenly felt by some Palestinian Christians today. They try to dissociate themselves from the militant Christianity that came to replace the Christian faith they have had for almost two thousand years. Finding themselves victims of years of political and religious colonialism from the West, some of them are even prompted "to declare, as Christian Arabs, that we are not a part of the Christianity that helped plunder five continents, enslave people in many regions, and wipe out people and civilizations in North America and Australia, and [that] is now threatening the Palestinians with a similar fate."[8] This is a strong indictment, but it is painfully true. This statement alone shows how thinking Christians today need to be engaged in a reunderstanding of our

Christian past and in reconstructing Christian faith and theology in a world of divided political, cultural, and religious identities and commitments.

When parties in conflict and warring factions begin to see people in place of abstract, impersonal "enemies," when they begin to perceive human beings in place of those they hate, curse, and abuse, some very different realities start to come into view. They are no longer faced with enemies to liquidate but men, women, and children in need and in trouble. For Christians it is the loyalty to Christ "who calls us to love our enemy" that leads to loyalty to "fellow-men or women in need or trouble," whether Palestinians or Jews. On January 22, 1988, heads of Palestinian Christian churches in Jerusalem issued their first unified statement in over one thousand years in the midst of escalating tension and conflict.

> [We] take our stand with truth and justice against all forms of injus-
> tice and oppression. We stand with the suffering and the oppressed, we
> stand with refugees and the deported, with the distressed and the victims
> of injustice, we stand with those who mourn and are bereaved, with the
> hungry and the poor. In accordance with the Word of God through the
> prophet Isaiah, chapter 1, verse 17: "Learn to do good, seek justice, correct
> oppression, defend the fatherless, plead for the widow."[9]

For those of us familiar with statements on justice, peace, or freedom that have been made by ecumenical Christianity, there is little new in this statement. What is important, however, is not whether it is new or not. It has to be appreciated as the first joint statement leaders from different churches in Jerusalem were able to make in over one thousand years. What is more, it was the ever deepening tragedy of Israeli-Palestinian conflict that compelled this unprecedented action.

What Christian leaders in Jerusalem did is a cause for thanksgiving. In that conflict-torn land, in that land of the origin of their faith, they were at last able to profess their faith and to take action together. At the same time, that it had taken a thousand years to make such a joint profession of faith makes us realize once again that the history of Christianity is more a history of division than unity. The forces that divide churches—doctrinal disputes, compounded with social and political issues—are always stronger than the forces that unite churches in Jesus. And it is almost always external forces, what some of us may call "secular" forces, that compel churches and Christians to stand together in faith and action.

This joint statement by Christian leaders in Jerusalem is a statement of faith. It is even a confession of faith. The heart of it is these few words: "We stand with . . ." Faith is not doctrine. It is not church order. It is not liturgy. It is standing with others. For more than a thousand years, and especially in the past few decades, Christians in Palestine have been taught to stand apart from one another. In many cases they are even taught to stand in opposition to one another. Of course this is not the case with Palestinian Christians only. It has also been the case, for example, with Christian missions in Asia and Africa. The history of Christian mission has been the history of Christian converts standing apart from, even standing in opposition to, one another. It has been the history of standing apart from people of other faiths, even from the communities in which the missionaries themselves live.

But living in a situation of conflict, Palestinian Christians have at last realized that the Christian faith that came to them fashioned and packaged by the West is not quite the same as the Christian faith that originated in the land of their birth two thousand years ago. They are embarrassed by their Christian faith because it came to be "related so closely to the faith of our oppressors and their supporters."[10] The Christian faith that embarrasses them is also the faith that "has often come back to us fragmented and in the form of religious colonization."[11]

How many Christians outside the so-called Holy Land, and how many of us who have made pilgrimages or sight-seeing tours, know the plight of Palestinian Christians? Like their fellow Palestinians, they have been subjected to Western colonialism and the partition of Palestine imposed on them in 1948. But they also suffer from religious colonialism. The faith of their colonizers came to them fragmented, that is, confessionally divided and denominationally competitive. That faith taught them to regard Muslims, their kith and kin, and Jews, their brothers and sisters with whom they share the Hebrew Scriptures, as enemies. The faith of their colonizers divides and sows hostility between them and the men and women to whom they are related historically, ethnically, and religiously.

That faith that separates Christians or that requires Palestinian Christians to stand apart from their neighbors of other faiths cannot be the faith Jesus practiced in his ministry of God's reign. The faith of Jesus, the faith that has been theirs for two thousand years, and not the faith brought by the denominationally separated and politically motivated Christian churches and groups in the West, is the faith that stands with the people with whom they have shared religion, culture, history, and land. To be aware of this fundamental fact of Palestinian Christian faith is the beginning of their renewed efforts toward peace, justice, and freedom.

To stand with is "to be on the side of." This fact can become complicated when we make a change in the ones with whom we stand. The change brings about a realignment of relationships. This is precisely what Palestinian Christian leaders in Jerusalem were doing when they made their joint statement. "[We] take our stand," they said, "with truth and justice." Truth and justice always sound right, though the truth and justice asserted by those in a position of power cannot be the same as the truth and justice those without power strive to gain. Truth and justice have to be related to particular issues, concerns, and situations, or one cannot know if what is claimed is really true and if what is defended is truly just.

It must be for this reason that the statement of the Palestinian Christian leaders goes on to say whose side they are on. "We stand with the suffering and the oppressed," says the statement. It also declares that Palestinian Christians "stand with refugees and the deported, we stand with those who mourn and are bereaved." The reference to the suffering, the oppressed, the deported, the bereaved, to refugees and to those who mourn, shifts the focus from organized religions to believers, redirects Christian concern from the burden of the past to the well-being of people at present, and alters the ways in which people in conflict should treat one another. The statement recognizes that conflicts have inflicted suffering on Palestinians and Jews alike, that most of them are victims of the fighting. Suffering does not have religious and ethnic boundaries. It affects each of the victims no matter what they believe and regardless of their religious identities and political convictions.

The faith that enables Palestinian Christian leaders to say they stand with the suffering and the oppressed thus has important implications. It implies that they stand not only with Christians like themselves, but with Muslim Arabs bearing the brunt of the conflict. It implies that they also stand with Jews who suffer from conflicts with Palestinians, and who are oppressed by extreme members of their own religion determined to carry out their religious and political agenda regardless of cost. Can such faith be maintained? Is it possible in the actual situation of conflict? There is no easy answer to these questions.

But let us listen to the following story told by a Palestinian Christian woman about her father.

> One day in 1977 he came from the center of the town of Ramallah [on the West Bank] feeling completely disturbed. He had just seen two Israeli soldiers holding the hair of an eight- or nine-year-old boy and smashing his face against the wall. After telling us what he had seen, he said, "These cannot be Jews." Obviously he was experiencing a dilemma: either God is wrong in considering Jews as a chosen people or else these soldiers were not Jews. It was easier for him, it seems, to deny the Jewishness of the soldiers than to think that God was wrong. In this sense he was reasserting the theological meaning of a "chosen people": people who do not willingly and consciously harm others. He was defending Judaism from the behaviors of these soldiers.[12]

Such a story does make us think. Whether the boy being brutalized is Arab or Jewish is not important. What strikes us is that the father, as an Arab Christian, feels prompted to defend and not condemn Judaism after witnessing the brutal behavior of the Jewish soldiers.

It is the suffering Arab Christians themselves have gone through and the suffering of others they have witnessed that prompt them to cross the boundary between religion and politics. We begin to understand why a Palestinian Christian can say: "While I carry the sufferings of my people the Palestinians, I ache also for the sufferings of my brothers and sisters the Jews."[13] A *Palestinian*

Christian calling Jews "brothers and sisters"? A Palestinian *Christian* aching also for the sufferings of the Jews? Is this not strange? But this is the faith taught by Jesus.

The Palestinian Christian leaders in Jerusalem go on to pledge in their statement of faith that they "stand with...the hungry and the poor." Nowadays this sounds commonplace, almost platitudinous. Statements issued by Christian groups and churches at the local, national, regional, and international levels condemn the world economic order run by transnational corporations, deplore the widening gap between the rich and the poor, expose the complicity between the First World economic powers and the authoritarian regimes in the Third World. These declarations are not merely pious talk. They do express the conviction that something is fundamentally wrong with the existing economic order.

But conviction is one thing, commitment is another. Christianity, with the exception of the earliest stage of its history, has been a wealthy religion. From the fourth century onward, when it became wedded to the Roman Empire, it has been rich in prestige, power, estates, and worldly goods. From time to time it has to be reminded that Jesus—himself poor—lived, worked, and died with the poor. But Christianity in Europe and later in the Americas remained a rich religion. Outside the West, Christianity has also become a religion of middle- and upper-middle-class Christians. Certainly Christianity as a whole cannot say it "stands with the hungry and the poor."

Yet Christian churches in Palestine today, despite the history mentioned above, have not become rich churches. As a minority religion caught in the political and religious conflicts between Muslims and Jews, between Palestinians and Israelis, most of the churches are poor. In faith and in reality they can say that they stand with the poor and hungry. The churches are not only materially poor; they are also poor when it comes to social prestige and political power.

But Palestinian Christians are rich when they find themselves on the side of the poor and the hungry. They are rich because they are able to overcome the religious and political barriers that separate them from others. A Palestinian Christian woman engaged in social work says: "As a social worker at a humanitarian relief and development agency, whose mandate is to the poor and needy, I have been working with the oppressed of my country. We help the unprotected, the dispossessed, the injured, the sick, and the handicapped in cities, villages, and refugee camps, regardless of their sex, creed, or religion."[14]

Is there not something amazing in this personal testimony? Serving the needy people in the conflict-ridden land is hard. It takes faith, courage, and compassion. But what is amazing is that the service is rendered to men, women, and children "regardless of their sex, creed, or religion." Is this not a rich experience of faith, making Palestinian social workers spiritually rich? Is not such faith imparted by Jesus of Nazareth?

The faith that inspires Palestinian Christians to stand with the poor and the needy is rich in another way. One of the things they have learned, as they deal with people who suffer, is that "the Christian faith is not about pitying the poor, needy, and oppressed."[15] At first this is difficult to understand. Is it not part of human nature to have pity for those who are poor, unfortunate, or suffering? Is this not a feeling that makes us feel good psychologically?

But faith is not just psychological, not merely a way to feel good. Faith involves changing an oppressive situation or an unjust system. "The Christian faith," writes an Arab Christian woman, "is rather about helping people change their conditions. It is about helping change the structures so that *all* people become partners in enjoying life and in acquiring the means to life."[16] Faith is a commitment to change the conditions and structures that make *all* people—Arabs, Israelis, and Palestinians—suffer into conditions that make *all* people—Muslims, Jews, and Christians—enjoy life!

Faith is faith because it moves beyond ourselves to those outside us. Faith incorporates an awareness of others—not as adversaries who oppose us, but as human beings like ourselves with hope and despair, with needs and expectations, with worries and fears. Faith is faith in God, of course. It is not faith in other human beings. We worship God, but we do not worship human beings. To worship other human beings is idolatry, and is no different from worshiping objects such as trees or animals. Nor do we worship ourselves. This is self-idolatry. This is to elevate ourselves above ourselves as human beings.

Self-worship can affect founders of religious sects. When a *jiao-zhu,* the Chinese term for the head of a religious sect, begins to consider him or herself a *jiu-zhu,* that is, a savior, this presents the danger of apotheosis—making oneself into God. The beginning of apotheosis is the beginning of demonization. You begin to hear people whispering to you that you will be like God (Gen. 3:5).

That suggestion may be a whisper at first. It may not be more than just a way for people to say how much they respect, adore, and believe in you. That whisper grows louder among your followers and within you. Eventually the idea grows that you will be like God, that you are God. The process of self-divinization is complete. But the process of demonization is also initiated. Human beings cannot become something other than human without tragic consequences. For a human being to be God is, in fact, to be a devil. There is always this "satanic possibility" in religions, including Christianity.

Faith, basically and unreservedly, is faith in God. But it must be remembered that faith in God does not become "awareness of God" or "experience of God" until it becomes "awareness of others"—including human beings. This perspective of faith is often lost in situations of conflict. Politics separates devotees of the same religion, even worshipers of the same God, into rival factions and opposing camps. When politics is compounded with racial factors, the divisions in faith become even more serious. For most of Christianity's history the "white" God and the "white" Jesus have predominated. Gender has also played a prominent role in Christian theology. God is cast in the image of the male, and the church is organized with male priesthood at its center.

But people of different faiths and religions have come to realize that faith that divides people on account of politics, race, gender, or class is false. It is not only false; it is demonic. For Palestinian Christians, who have endured many tragedies as the result of religious and political conflicts, faith cannot continue in the Holy Land as an instrument of division. They seek "to address the common humanity of Jews, Muslims, and Christians living together in a land made holy only by their absolute commitment to peace and justice."[17] This is a statement of faith based not on correct doctrine but on a common life that calls for peace and justice.

Common humanity is the heart of the matter. World religions, including Christianity, profess to know the truth for all—what is good for people everywhere, the secret of eternal salvation. They talk about "all human beings," show interest in "people everywhere," and occupy themselves with "individual persons" regardless of where they are from. But in the faith they hold and the religion they practice there is often no room for "common humanity." This is a contradiction. Why do religions commit such contradictions? The reason is that what is "common" may threaten what is held to be "exclusive." It is also assumed that an effort to come to terms with what is common in humanity may undermine what each faith claims as "unique."

The world has suffered long enough from religions claiming exclusiveness and uniqueness. Trying to do justice to their claims, they have done grievous injustice to common humanity. In an effort to expand their influence over others and to win them over, they have done serious harm to what human beings hope and pray for—peace, justice, and freedom. As far as Palestinian Christians are concerned, it has taken a half-century of conflict and bloodshed in their own backyards to realize this. But it is still not too late to begin taking seriously that we human beings are made for, and not against, one another.

Jews, Muslims, and Christians are human beings before they are Jews, Muslims, and Christians. Jews, Muslims, and Christians live together as neighbors even though they practice their faiths separately. Jews, Muslims, and Christians share common humanity. Jews and Muslims are closely related because of similarities in history, culture, and sacred scriptures. "Blood," says a Chinese proverb, "is thicker than water" (*xue nong yu shui*), meaning that no relationship is tighter than a blood relationship. Jews, Muslims, and Christians have been bound in this relationship as long as one can remember.

Palestinian Christians, compelled by their tragic situation and inspired by the faith that goes back two thousand years, are at last saying what is of utmost importance for all parties in Palestine and all Christians and churches outside Palestine. Many of us Christians, taught to be loyal to our creeds and confessions, have to listen attentively to this Palestinian Christian woman:

One tradition among Christian women from Jerusalem was that any woman who could not conceive went to Hebron (an Islamic town) to kneel under the tree of Abraham (a Jewish symbol) and pray to Christ in order to have children. For my mother, who believed in the practice, being a Christian, a Muslim, and a Jew at the same time, this was not a contradiction; rather, it was part of her being human. What was alien to her thinking was to be purely a Christian, or purely a Muslim, or purely a Jew. Unlike the behavior of Western Christians (whose main concern seemed to be smaller and more divisions, and more precise and narrow definitions of who is what), her Christianity was an expansive one that included all others.[18]

Such reflection will outrage many Western, Asian, and African Christians, those who believe that theirs is the "purest form" of Christianity or who maintain that theirs is the only way to gain acceptance of God and hence eternal life.

What this Palestinian Christian woman is saying about her mother, and I believe about herself, is that she, as a Palestinian woman, is genetically Jewish and Arab. In this she is reclaiming the history of her people, relocating the origins of her life, and reorienting her politics. As a Christian she is rediscovering how her faith relates to the faiths of the people with whom she has shared much history and culture. To her amazement and also to her relief, she has realized that she is not a category unto herself; she is not that different from her Muslim and Jewish neighbors.

She is able to describe her thoughts as a "breakthrough" in her faith and in her heart—a breakthrough made possible by her "breakaway" from what she had seen to be the prevailing "behavior of Western Christians [or Christians shaped by Christianity from the West] whose main concern seemed to be more precise and narrow definitions of who is what." By insisting on "more precise and narrow definitions of who is what," Christianity has disrupted the life of Christian converts in their natural cultural habitats and caused difficulty in their relations with people of their own country.

Let us not dismiss the reflection of the Palestinian Christian woman as "syncretistic." The word as used in many Christian circles, open or closed, has become pejorative. But is there a religion which is not syncretistic? Was not Christianity itself a syncretistic religion from the start—a combination of Jewish, Greek, Roman, and folkloristic influences? Much of Christian faith and theology has been heavily influenced by religious thoughts, philosophical investigations, and worldviews that date to periods before and after Jesus.

It is the nature of religion to be syncretistic, evident in view of the interrelatedness of religion and culture. Religion and culture give birth to, shape, and change each other; they rise and fall in each other's company. Culture by nature also is syncretistic as it assimilates other cultures and makes its way into other cultures. There is no such thing as a "pure" culture, a culture that is sui generis in origin, development, and achievement. If there ever was a "pure" culture, it died a long time ago. For a culture lives, grows, and develops by active and creative responses to other cultures.

If, then, there is no such thing as "pure" culture, how can there be "pure" faith or religion? If there is such a thing, it exists only in the minds of believers and religious leaders who either are ignorant of the development of their own faith, or who have chosen not to take facts as facts. The word *syncretistic* does not have to be judgmental. It is rather a "descriptive" word, describing what a religion must be. Historians of religion use the word in this manner. There is no reason why Christians and theologians must use it pejoratively and judgmentally.

If the Palestinian Christian woman we quoted is "syncretistic" in her Christian faith, so be it. It is time for Christians, like that Palestinian Christian woman, to realize that we are syncretistic by nature and to learn to be creatively syncretistic in what we believe and practice. This is what some Palestinian Christians have decided to do as they pledge their loyalty to those who suffer from the military conflicts that have been wrecking their land, their community, their economy, their well-being, their life. A "pure" faith that divides a community, creates conflicts, and resorts to violence is an impure faith. It is not only impure, it is criminal. It has nothing to do with the God it confesses and defends, and it betrays God and innocent believers. It is, put simply, unfaith.

Loyalty to Country

Loyalty to Jesus—this is the first loyalty. Loyalty to the needy and the oppressed—this is the second loyalty. The faith shaped by these loyalties, as we have seen, disowns militant sectarianism, fanatical ideology, and the Christian identity that separates Christians from brothers and sisters of other faiths. The faith taught and practiced by Jesus of Nazareth has given Palestinian Christians the confidence that they can be at once Palestinians, Arabs, and Jews, that being Christians they have a lot in common with Muslims and Jews in matters of life and faith.

Third comes loyalty to country. Considered by itself, it sounds like narrow nationalism or like a call to national defense against outsiders. Taken out of context, such loyalty may make one wonder whether Palestinian Christians are having a lapse in faith—turning back to the divisive Christianity imported from outside, going back on what they said about caring for the suffering, and making no distinction between Christians, Jews, and Muslims. There is a real dilemma here between faith and practice, a contradiction between what one believes and how one practices what one believes, and a struggle between what the heart feels and what the realities of life dictate. There is no easy way out of the dilemma.

Faith as loyalty to Jesus, as loyalty to the needy and suffering, is tested by the contradiction. It is a crossroads for faith. For Palestinian Christians the test becomes particularly acute because loyalty to country follows loyalties to Jesus and to the needy, regardless of the latter's religious traditions and political backgrounds. They know they cannot retreat from their first two loyalties. They also know that loyalty to their country has to be dictated by their loyalty to Jesus and the needy.

Most Christians outside the West have had to face the same test since Christianity was introduced to us. In many instances we find ourselves choosing between the religion of our adoption or the country of our birth. This, however, is a false alternative. But for a long time we did not know we had chosen incorrectly, having assumed that the pledge of loyalty to Christianity meant we had to let go of a pledge to our country.

Is this the choice Jesus of Nazareth, who was born a Jew, lived and labored as a Jew, and died as a Jew, would have demanded of us? Would this be the kind of choice he would have asked us to make, the Jesus who declared, "Do not think that I have come to abolish the law or the prophets; I have come not to abolish but to fulfill" (Matt. 5:17)? He was so devoted to his tradition that he could not ignore its distortion in the community of his day. He was so immersed in the true spirit of his own religion that he could not put up with corruption among the religious hierarchy. He was so passionate about the destitute, the dispossessed, the politically oppressed, and the religiously discriminated and about their well-being that he identified himself with them and did not hesitate to announce that the reign of God belonged to them.

This Jesus would not demand that we dissociate ourselves from the country of our birth. He would not ask us to separate from our people who are not Christian, no more than would he tell Palestinian Christians to be disloyal to their country and people. Surely he would approve of the faith of Palestinian Christians such as Jean Zaru, the faith that inspires them to believe that loyalty to their country involves loving its people and its way of life. By "country" they refer to the Palestinian state that is to emerge out of the conflicts between Palestinians and Israelis. By "people" they mean all Palestinians who are Arabs, the majority of them Muslims. By the "way of life" they mean the Muslim as well as the Christian way of life. Jean Zaru also writes:

> I kept asking myself, if we say there is something of God in every person, why is it often so difficult to see that presence of God in others? Why is there so much evil and suffering in the world? For many years I struggled with this Christian truth, that we are made in the image and likeness of God. I was happy to learn that the belief in the divinity seems to be part of all religions. "The kingdom of God is within you," said Jesus. "You are the temple of God," wrote Paul. "He who knows himself knows God," said the Prophet Mohammed, and this is echoed by many Sufis.[19]

The meaning of this confession for Christian faith is important, especially for Christian faith in situations of conflict. It poses challenges to all religions in a world of divided loyalties.

In this statement of faith we encounter a Christian asking honest questions— questions most Christians do not ask because they are embarrassing. They have not been able to learn answers to these questions in church or even in theology classrooms. Christians hold that "there is something of God in every person," Zaru tells us. Lest this not be evident, she clarifies it by quoting Jesus and Paul. Translated into Jesus' language, the statement means: "The reign of God is within you." In Paul's words, it can be rendered: "You are the temple of God." Here Zaru may be taking a leap of faith by making the "you" in Jesus' and Paul's sayings, particularly in the latter, say more than they were originally intended.

But is faith still faith when it is bound by prescribed terms, and when it does not expand from its immediate frame of reference? Faith that remains within familiar boundaries has little more to say beyond what has already been said. Faith that treads carefully marked routes does not encounter new landscapes. Faith wary of diverting into unfamiliar territories may be safe faith, but it is not a faith that trusts in the God of wonder and surprises. This is not the faith Jesus had and practiced. He, for one, would not object that Zaru hears in Mohammed an echo of what he and Paul had said.

We should begin to understand why some Palestinian Christians can now say without hesitation:

> I am a Palestinian Arab Christian, but also, as intensively and dramatically, a citizen of Israel. I have Jewish friends, whom I respect and appreciate. They are both Israeli and foreign Jews. I was not born in Israel but in Palestine, before a part of it became the new state of Israel. I have learned from my life experience in Israel that whenever you meet with two Jews or two Palestinians, you have to face at least three opinions, each one's and their common opinion. I have learned that Jews and Palestinians are both right. None is absolutely right. Both survive under the heavy burden of the past. Aware of but not responsible for or accountable for the horrors of anti-Semitism in the Western world, the Palestinians are attempting to launch publicly the needed dynamism of solidarity and the vital embrace of reconciliation. Both Jews and Palestinians need to become emissaries of a solution to stop the vicious cycle of mutual corruption and self-destruction.[20]

Is this not another confession of faith, although its language and form have little in common with most historical creeds and confessions? This is a genuine confession of faith because it is made in response to a particular *status confessionis*, a confessing situation—the situation of conflict between Jews and Palestinians.

Two words play a key role in this statement: *solidarity* and *reconciliation*. The word *solidarity* reminds us of the joint statement of Palestinian Christian leaders in Jerusalem. In that statement they declared that they "stand with" the suffering, the hungry, and the poor regardless of the religious and political commitments of the ones who suffer. They pledge to be in solidarity with such people. Solidarity means taking steps to work toward reconciliation. Confession of solidarity becomes a confession of faith in action when it is translated into efforts toward reconciliation. The political reconciliation between Palestinians and Jews is still filled with uncertainties and crises. But religious reconciliation has to begin. It is an act of faith on the part of Palestinian Christians to serve the cause of reconciliation in solidarity with other religious groups.

Politically, the peace process has been going off and on for many years. It has been treacherous, torturous, and bloody. Even one of the major players—Israeli Prime Minister of Israel Yitzhak Rabin—was not safe from danger and even death on this road to peace. On the historic occasion of signing a peace accord with Yasser Arafat, chairman of the Palestinian Liberation Organization (PLO), on the South Lawn of the White House on September 13, 1993, Rabin declared: "We say today in a loud and clear voice, enough of blood and tears. Enough."[21] These words from an old warrior moved many to tears and raised the hope for peace. But extremists from his own community took exception to his words. For them not enough blood had yet been shed. Hardly two years after those memorable words, Rabin was felled by an assassin's bullet as he sang with 100,000 people who had gathered to celebrate the prospect of peace on Kings of Israel Square in Tel Aviv.[22]

Political and military conflicts in the "Holy" Land will continue, as will pain, suffering, and death. But the peace process has already begun, though it has lost one of its chief architects. The process cannot be reversed; not even ruthless political forces and extreme religious obsessions can thwart it forever. At the heart of the peace process must be Christians, Muslims, and Jews in Palestine, united in their hearts by their faith in God and by their commitment to the love, justice, and peace of that God.

Testifying to the Spirit of God

Faith experienced and practiced by Palestinian Christians has highlighted the importance of loyalty. For Palestinian Christians who live in conflict, loyalties to Jesus, to suffering people, and to the land are considered the most important. This does not exclude loyalties to church, family, or community. But these others will be shaped and practiced in relation to the three primary loyalties.

In the world today, whether inside or outside Palestine, *loyalty* can be a confusing concept. Like Palestinian Christians, we all live in a world of divided loyalties. Science, technology, communications, and economics make us conscious as never before of living in a globalized world. But loyalty seems to have become a rare commodity. Ours is a world manipulated by those who have the know-how, the means, and the power to change it according to their whims, aims, or interests. It is a world in which fierce competition and ruthless exploitation take place. It is a world that creates wealth and power for the few and poverty, helplessness, and envy for the many. If the many cherish no loyalty for our globalized world, nor do the few. For the few, it is not loyalty that motivates their actions, but the opportunities the world offers to achieve economic and political objectives.

If there is no common loyalty to the globalized world, there is, strangely, almost fanatical loyalty to one's personal well-being, which comes at the cost of public well-being. Loyalty is granted to a political party not because it stands for justice, but because it can be a means to position and power. Exclusively defined religious groups that exert strict control over their members' minds and bodies and that create division, alienation, and disruption in the family and in society have loyal followings. In the history of the world and in the history of religions we have seen more than enough havoc created by this kind of loyalty.

It is thus a very strange world in which we live—a world in which the word *loyalty* inspires neither respect nor interest, but excites blind obedience and results in destruction of self and other. *Loyalty* is a word that only makes some shrug their shoulders, generates indifference, and produces apathy. The word even smacks of bad taste, especially for those who have seen much evil committed in its name by political leaders and religious authorities. In our postmodern culture the word has lost integrity and moral power. It is no longer a credible word.

But Palestinian Christians have restored loyalty to their faith, insisting that Christian faith, if it is to be authentic and credible, has to be practiced through loyalty to Jesus, to the needy, and to country. Faith that is not loyal to Jesus and to what he stands for is opportunistic. Faith that is not loyal to the needy and the suffering is cold. The faith that shows no loyalty to one's country, that does not prompt it to strive for the well-being of people, is a faith in complicity with evil powers of this world. *Loyalty*, combined with faith, has once again become a respectable and theologically important word.

Faith, defined today as loyalty in a world of conflicts, cannot be practiced according to the rules laid down by the church, which are based on models of faith developed in the course of its history and on teaching and doctrine formalized in the traditions of the past. But faith practiced as loyalty has helped Palestinian Christians grasp its meaning. "In our situation," Jean Zaru writes, "no one can set the rules for us to follow, but what we can do is to testify that, in our experience, the Spirit of God leads us into the truth and gives us the needed guidance in every situation."[23] This must be the faith not only for Palestinian Christians, but for all Christians living in the world of divided interests and loyalties.

"No one can set the rules for us to follow." This is an important announcement, but, as a matter of fact, is not such a novel idea. Increasing numbers of African American, feminist, and Asian and African Christians and theologians have decided not to follow the Christian faith as defined by the male-dominated churches in the West and the Christian theology as developed in the cultures and contexts unrelated to them. Still, it is exciting to know that Palestinian Christians have joined the movement of those who will not let rules of faith brought from elsewhere dictate their beliefs.

The Palestinian Christians now follow the Spirit of God, and not the rules of faith and theology set for them. "What we can do is to testify that, in our experience, the Spirit of God leads us into the truth." This, in the last analysis, is the heart of faith. What, then, is faith? Faith is the response to the Spirit of God, which recruits men and women to engage in rebuilding human community. Faith is active participation in the work of God's Spirit and, at the same time, is a confession that derives its vision and strength from the grace of God.

Chapter 9

Our Faith and God's Grace

Living in the world of conflicts, divisions, and divided loyalties, we need faith that enables us to be open to the Spirit of God, that gives us the courage to respond to its call, and that inspires us to be part of what it is doing to restore human relationships in community. Without people with such faith history becomes nothing but tributes to the achievements of dictators and conquerors. Without women and men with such faith, we will face a bleak world with no dreams, visions, and hopes.

But the problem is that faith does not always meet faith. It is our experience that faith is more likely to meet unfaith, loyalty has to reckon with disloyalty, and solidarity is broken by betrayal. The problem is not just unfaith, disloyalty, and betrayal committed by others, but by ourselves as well. Just like the disciples of Jesus, we may be the ones that are unfaithful and disloyal to him, betraying him and his cause. Faith and unfaith, loyalty and disloyalty, solidarity and betrayal coexist both in us and in others.

Before...but Now...

Is this why we need God's grace to be able to continue in faith? Is this why we cannot talk about our faith without at the same time talking about God's grace? Does this mean that faith without God's grace is not really faith but self-assertion, that God's grace without our faith is not grace but God's self-imposition on us? How then are our faith and God's grace related to one another? How is our practice of faith changed and how is our experience of God's grace reshaped by ways in which our faith and God's grace interact with each other? The following personal reflection from a social worker in Hong Kong sets the stage for our engagement with such questions.

> I perceive God not only as the God of forgiveness but also the God of justice who disapproves of injustice. I have become more sensitive to the question of justice. Before, I did not realize that injustice has permeated my environment. Whenever there was injustice done to me, I rationalized it as God's will and accepted it in acquiescence.
>
> Before, I believed that only the church as a community is naturally and automatically deserving the favor of God. But now I realize that if the

church fails to serve the people in humility, she is like the prodigal son. During my early days of conversion, Christian faith for me was something that makes people happy. Now I see that to follow Christ means much more than that. One has to bear the cross and pay the price. Happiness and peace have to be built on justice.

Faith for me is no longer defined solely in terms of a God-person relationship, but its richness has also to be sought in a person-to-person relationship.

There is a key issue with which I am struggling at present. In my own context, the majority of the masses are "pagans" who have not received the grace of salvation. On the other hand, the masses are a "people" struggling for humanity with God on their side. How should I reconcile the two apparently paradoxical realities?

Living with people means struggle; both to struggle with them and to sustain an inner struggle within one's self. Through these struggles one experiences new dimensions of spiritual renewal, and I believe that God is calling all of us to undergo that renewal.[1]

This reflection bears the title "Perceiving God Anew." It is conversational, as if the author is sharing inner thoughts with an intimate friend. It reads like a prayer, filled with a sense of relief and renewed commitment, said to the newly perceived God in a private chamber.

Because the language of this personal reflection is plain and simple, it shows the sincerity of the person who made it. Because the tone is low-key, even subdued, it seems to harbor deep thoughts. Because it is meditative, it enables us to come in touch with a heart open to God and to people. In this reflection, couched in a plain, subdued, and meditative language, one perceives a soul comforted and strengthened by the faith that God is present with women and men who try to make sense of their lives in the world of hardships, anxieties, and injustices. The conflict between our faith and God's grace is resolved. It is not an either-or question—either our faith or God's grace. Our faith is not true faith if it gets separated from God's grace. Nor is God's grace genuine grace if it takes a dim view of our faith.

This reflection has theological importance, namely the insight that faith and grace are mutually interactive, that grace needs faith as much as faith needs grace. How did the author of this short reflection come to understand faith and grace in this way? To find an answer, we need to explore the background that gave rise to the reflection. We need to know where our author comes from before we can appreciate the theological shift that has taken place.

The author is a social worker and not a theologian. This is important. Theologians, especially theologians trained in the "good" theological traditions of the past and who continue to work within the norms prescribed by those traditions, are too sophisticated to express faith in such a plain fashion. Those theologians who conduct their business many heartbeats away from the din and cry of the people in the street cannot imagine how simple believers have to struggle between the faith they profess in church and the life they have to live in the world. But Christians such as this social worker live, work, and practice their faith in a much less sophisticated way. This is perhaps why they can come up with profound theological insights.

This social worker who is able "to perceive God anew" is a converted Christian. This is another important point. What one encounters in this social worker is a very different kind of converted Christian. Normally, conversion turns the converted persons to earnest Christians, often more earnest than the Christians who have inherited Christian faith from their parents. At the same time, they tend to become ardent critics of the religion from which they got converted, more ardent in their criticism than many other Christians. But the social worker is quite different. What one reads in this personal reflection is an openness to the world beyond the Christian church and an effort to perceive God's presence in that world. This observation has important implications for reconstructing the relationship between our faith and God's grace.

Our reconstruction of that relationship is facilitated by the way the social worker from Hong Kong highlights the change that has taken place in her faith. One repeatedly comes across in the reflection the phrasing, "before... but now..." The contrast between what was "before" and what is "now" is clear. This contrast reminds us of the way Jesus sometimes prefaced his teaching: "You have heard that it was said... but I say to you." To be able to realize the contrast between what one was taught to believe "before" and what one learns to believe "now" is the beginning of perceiving God anew. To move from what was upheld as valid and true "before" to what should "now" be so regarded is a critically important step forward in faith and theology.

We learn from the past but should not get stuck in the past. We explore the past not to be enslaved to the past but to be set free from it. We study the past not to repeat the past but to surpass it. In researching the past we become aware of how different we are at present, and are often compelled to strike out on a new path. In faith and theology as in the arts, science, technology, or even business, there is no room for laziness, spiritual or intellectual.

The social worker is right. One must know what came "before" in the Christian church and the beliefs and practices it taught. But what is demanded of Christians always is to know how our faith must be shaped and practiced "now." This personal reflection on faith thus does not remain personal. It becomes a public theological statement that challenges us to reconstruct our faith and theology in the world today.

Faith as Justice Opposed to Injustice

"Before," we are told, "I did not realize that injustice has permeated my environment." This is a candid admission, but how strange! The Christian faith that speaks so much of God's justice does not make Christians aware of injustices in their community, nation, or even in the church in which they worship the God of justice. But can the faith that cannot enable Christians to see the connection between God's justice and the injustices prevailing in society profess to speak on behalf of God? Can the faith that does not make Christians sensitive to injustices committed around them claim to transform the world? Is the faith that is blind to the fact that injustice also permeates the church itself the faith for which Jesus lived and died?

It does not take an extrasensitive mind to know that there is much injustice in the world. There is, as a matter of fact, more injustice than justice. This is simply a fact of life. But the social worker from Hong Kong, despite having gone to church Sunday after Sunday, and reading the Bible every day, "did not realize [it]." Many Christians in Hong Kong, devoted and dedicated like her, were not aware that for over a century British practiced a form of racism against the Chinese in Hong Kong, treating them as second- and even third-class citizens. Christians did not want to know that they had achieved economic prosperity at the expense of their human dignity.

Since it became a fait accompli that Hong Kong would return to Chinese sovereignty, which occurred in 1997, there has been soul-searching among some Hong Kong Christians. "After colonial rule for over a hundred years Hong Kong lacks the political structure of democracy. Participation in the decision making of the government is limited to a handful of big business people and power elites. As for most citizens of Hong Kong, they either have no opportunity to participate in politics or lack the motivation, intention, or urgent need for it. Looking back, we know that in the '50s the church in Hong Kong was engaged in refugee relief work, in the '60s and '70s in building schools and social welfare work, but basically, it 'attached' itself to the colonial government, playing no prophetic role."[2]

How could the church, which speaks so much of God's justice, be blind to the injustice done to the masses of men and women in Hong Kong, people with political rights and human dignity in short supply? Nowadays we deride the Japanese for being "economic animals." But was not Hong Kong also reduced to being an "economic animal" by its colonial government? If the church was blind to it, then the faith the church imparted must have been the root cause of the blindness.

What is that faith, then? "Whenever there was injustice done to me," says the social worker from Hong Kong, "I rationalized it as God's will and accepted it in acquiescence." This statement conceals the kind of Christian faith that prevailed and continues to prevail among many Christians, not only in Hong Kong but in Asia. It has also conditioned the attitude of many Christians living outside Asia—the attitude that excludes political and social concerns from the church, regarding those concerns as contradictory to the practice of Christian faith.

The problem is the concept of "God's will." What is God's will when injustice is done to you personally? Is it God's will for you to endure in silence? To accept it as a test of your faith? To turn it into a witness to God's love? Perhaps. The history of Christianity contains many examples of Christians who have faced injustice in such ways. But this is not what the social worker from Hong Kong would have us understand by accepting injustice "in acquiescence" to God's will. Not at all. For most Christians in Hong Kong and in the rest of Asia, God's will is nothing but their unwillingness to face injustice done to them, to learn its cause, and to seek to remove it. The concept of God's will in this case is a cop-out from the conflict in an effort to *da shi hua xiao shi, xiao shi hua wu she,* a Chinese expression meaning "reducing a big trouble to a small one and a small one to nothing." This may be a prudent way to deal with problems of life, but it does not resolve the cause of conflict and remove the acts of injustice. Is this what God wills, the God of justice who, even according to the traditional teaching of the church, does not condone sin and evil?

To accept injustice, done to you personally, in silence is to avoid facing it. The moral integrity of your faith is compromised. This is bad enough, but accepting without protest injustice perpetuated by a political system, a social structure, or a religious organization is even worse. That kind of injustice affects not only a few individuals, but many people, even an entire community. It can never be the will of God for injustice to continue. The God who is just, the God who is justice, demands that injustice that dehumanizes human beings be removed from the world. How can Christians acquiesce in injustice?

Faith cannot be separated from justice. Faith that turns its back on grave injustice such as racism is not faith. Faith as part of the institution of sexism is a distortion of faith. Faith that profits from terrible injustice such as apartheid is unfaith. And faith that attaches itself to injustice incorporated into colonial rule is a caricature of faith. It is not God's will that you acquiesce in it. This is what has dawned on the social worker in Hong Kong. *Now* faith for the social worker is something drastically different. Faith is faith in "the God of justice who disapproves of injustice."

This is a radical change. Faith "before" and faith "now" part company. They do not just go separate ways; they go in opposite directions. Not until one in faith takes the step to face injustice, to stand up to racism, to dismantle sexism, to say no to colonialism—and to authoritarian rule—does one know God's will. As one in faith does not know God's will, one does not know how much one has to depend on God's grace. God's grace can even get in one's way when one tries to substitute one's will, convenience, prejudice, and compromise for the will of God.

When one with faith looks away from injustice, one does not need God's grace for support. Faith at that moment becomes a human effort. But when one in faith faces injustice, one realizes how weak one's faith is and how much one needs God's grace to make it strong. As a person, faced with grave injustice of varied kinds, chooses to condone the injustice, God's grace becomes superfluous because one has already decided what to do. But as one with faith questions grave injustice and works against it, one realizes that one has to have every ounce of God's grace. What has been said applies to the church as well. When the church finds itself a part of unjust systems such as colonialism—because it has much to gain from it—why does it need God's grace, though it goes through the liturgical motions of invoking God's grace? In fact, it does not need God's grace. The reason is quite simple. Its needs for maintaining security, conducting religious activities, and carrying on ministries are already provided by the powers that be. But when the church finds itself at odds with the powers that be and challenges their legitimacy and authority, it is left with nothing but God's grace to rely on.

Faith as justice opposed to injustice has to be empowered by God's grace. It has nothing to depend on but God's grace. There is no political alliance it can form to strengthen its opposition to injustice. The fact is that the political alliance it may seek would be party to the very injustice to which it is opposed. For faith to be on the side of justice, for it to advocate the cause of justice, for it to maintain the integrity of justice, what can it depend on except God's grace? God's grace gives peace in the midst of turmoil. It imparts strength in the struggle against injustice. It never fails even when everyone and everything else fails.

This is the faith of the prophets in ancient Israel. Justice, as they understood and practiced it, "is not an impartial ministry to one's fellow human beings. It is not equivalent to giving every person his or her due." Justice is done "to be just," or better, "to be in the right" with others *and* with God.[3] The crux of the matter is the conjunction *and*. That is to say, faith demands not that we be in the right *either* with others *or* with God, but *both* with others *and* with God.

Faith practiced as justice in this both-and way cannot be haphazard. It often requires us to take sides. To avoid taking sides forces us to take the wrong side, not the side of God but the side of the powers and interests of this world. To be in the right *both* with the world *and* with God ought to keep us from being in the right with the world while being in the wrong with God. Oftentimes we may even claim to be in the right with God while being in the wrong with the world. Is not this why the ministry of the prophets in ancient Israel was eventful, provocative, even controversial? Listen to what Isaiah the prophet says about the moral depravity, conceit, and corruption of those in power in his day:

> Ah, you who call evil good
>   and good evil,
> who put darkness for light
>   and light for darkness,
> who put bitter for sweet
>   and sweet for bitter!

> Ah, you who are wise in your own eyes,
>   and shrewd in your own sight!
> Ah, you who are heroes in drinking wine
>   and valiant at mixing drink,
> who acquit the guilty for a bribe,
>   and deprive the innocent of their rights!
>   (Isa. 5:20-23)

The poem laments the involvement of the high and mighty in injustice. It indicts those corrupted by the power they hold. It is an outburst on behalf of people who have to bear the brunt of this arrangement. The faith that takes the powers to task in this way must be strong. But God's grace, which empowers that faith, must be even stronger.

Our faith and God's grace thus work hand in hand to perpetuate the light of truth, goodness, and beauty in a world polluted by power, greed, and self-interest. In moments of loneliness, weakness, and despair we are very much in need of God's grace to maintain our faith in the service of justice. God, who has no way of manifesting God's justice in the world except through those who are willing to take risks with God, counts on us not to give up, not to give ground, and not to give in.

This kind of faith and this kind of grace are what we witness in the ministry of Jesus. Abandoned by his friends as well as his enemies, Jesus is sustained by God's grace all the way to the cross on Calvary. The early Christian community drew strength from what Jesus prayed when the powers of this world were closing in: "Abba, Father, . . . remove this cup from me; yet, not what I want, but what you want" (Mark 14:36; also Luke 22:42). Left alone by the world, he stakes his faith on the God of grace. Is there a more sublime picture than this—Jesus embraced by and secure in God's grace? John the Evangelist shows theological insight when he puts these words in the mouth of John the Baptizer, with regard to Jesus: "From his fullness we have all received, grace upon grace" (John 1:16).

Faith as Freedom for Both Men and Women

The social worker from Hong Kong who engages us with her reflection on faith tells us further how she had been led to understand Christian faith. "During my early days of conversion," she says, "Christian faith for me was something that makes people happy." If happiness is what people pursue in their daily lives, it is also what religious believers, Christians among them, seek in their religious devotion and activities. Be happy! is the message of some popular preachers and evangelists. Sunday worship has to exude a sense of happiness with flowers, colorful costumes, and the preacher's beaming smiles. Why not? There is no reason for Christians to wear long faces at worship and to indulge in self-mortification.

Does not the heart of Jesus' message in the Sermon on the Plain exhort listeners to be happy? We read in the Beatitudes:

> Happy are you who are poor,
>   for yours is the reign of God.
> Happy are you who are hungry now,
>   for you will be filled.
> Happy are you who weep now,
>   for you will laugh.
>   (Luke 6:20-21)[4]

Even Jesus, who experienced deprivation of comforts in his ministry and who was never free from threats on his life, talked about being happy. Perhaps on account of the kind of life he lived and the mission he took upon himself, he needed happiness—if not external, then internal.

But Jesus is not selling a gospel of happiness, a gospel without pain and tears. The poor and dispossessed women, men, and children who listened to him, the undernourished and hungry, people wronged and taken advantage of because they are too powerless to fight back—it is such people to whom Jesus is bringing the message of happiness. The happiness he is sharing is the happiness that has to be won, the kind that would come true only when they decide not to accept the conditions of their life as preordained by God, when they are able to stand up and declare that they are entitled to human dignity, and when they are determined to strive for their rights. The happiness Jesus encourages is the happiness created by the effort to work toward change.

This kind of happiness is categorically different from the happiness promoted by many religious organizations today. Behind the latter is concealed a lot of unhappiness. Often it is a happiness achieved by ignoring the unhappiness of others. The social worker from Hong Kong was entirely unaware of this dimension to religion when she first converted to Christianity and joined the church. She did not know that the happiness pursued in her church had little to do with the happiness Jesus shared with people. She was not aware that the happiness the church was offering had not been gained by doing justice to all members of the church, women as well men, for example.

The Christian church in Hong Kong is not alone in practicing this religion of happiness, and in fostering faith linked with it. Behind the facade of happiness many people—at least half the members of the church—are not happy. They are women, of course. Most churches in Asia, whether or not they have been shaped by the traditional Confucian society, which treats women as inferior to men, are still dominated by men. While Asian society continues to extol traditional virtues of women and laments their effort to be free from traditional roles, the Christian church is not fundamentally different. Faith for women is not freedom, but burden and discrimination.

Am I overstating the case? Am I exaggerating it? Let us listen to the poem "Burdens," written by a woman Christian from Sri Lanka:

> Lo! Because I was born a woman
> Many a heavy burden on my shoulder was laden
> It was from you O God I thought
> and did carry the weight to date
> without fuss or fret
>
> But today I am but confused
> Is it burden that you instilled?
> Nay! It was burden thrust upon
> because I was born a woman
>
> The burden my mother carried
> She handed me down so furried
> The sea of reason that was hers
> I soon myself carried
>
> Women a symbol of patience and virtue
> the Goddess who protects family so true
> The rhythm went on and on
>
> to my parents a faithful daughter
> to my kith and kin a dutiful sister
> To my husband a virtuous wife
> To my children the Goddess of life.
>
> God, I am confused today.
> Love your neighbor as thyself you said
> and showed the way
> But have I forgotten to love the "me" in the "you"?
> Is this why I am confused so?[5]

"God," she says, "I am confused today." The poem was written in 1995, five years from the beginning of the twenty-first century, and not in the nineteenth century, not in the 1950s, not even in the 1980s. Many Christian women throughout Asia, not to mention many more women outside the Christian church, are also confused.

For men in the church there is no confusion. Does not the Bible say that "to make [the man] a helper as his partner" God took a rib from man and made woman (Gen. 2:18-22)? Reflecting the practice of the earliest Christian community, Paul, the alleged author of the Pastoral Letters, directs women in church to "learn in silence with full submission" and does not permit them "to teach or have authority over a man" (1 Tim. 2:11-12). But this is not all. The story of the Fall depicts Eve, the woman, succumbing to the temptation of the snake and eating the fruit of the forbidden tree, even giving the fruit to Adam, the man, to eat (see Genesis 3). This story, more than any other story in the Bible, has helped male theologians portray women in an unfavorable light, contributing to miseries and tragedies for women. The pastoral letter we have already quoted refers to that ancient story: "And Adam was not deceived, but the woman was deceived and became a transgressor" (1 Tim. 2:14). This seems to have sealed the fate of women. Down through the centuries they have borne "many a heavy burden," mourns the Christian woman from Sri Lanka.

This woman and millions of women in Asia today are still confused. They have been taught to believe that God punished them for the sin of disobedience allegedly committed by Eve, their Christian archetypal ancestress. The fact is that not God but men are responsible for their sufferings. It is not God but feudal society and patriarchal religion that have taught them they are inferior to men. Nor is it God but men with power, whether in society or in church, who refuse to recognize their full humanity and to treat them with full human dignity. Inheriting these tremendous burdens from centuries past, they have either "forgotten to love" themselves in God or felt guilty about asserting their full humanity in church as well as in society.

But the time of *ping fan* has arrived for women in Asia. The expression relates to actions taken to exonerate the men and women accused, charged, tortured, imprisoned, and executed during the Cultural Revolution in China (1966–76) for crimes they had not committed. The time to redress the miscarriage of justice suffered by women all over the world for centuries is here.

In the Christian church *ping fan* for women means no more and no less than faith as freedom—freedom from the sin and guilt imposed on them biblically and theologically and freedom to enjoy being children of God, to be proud of themselves as women endowed with gifts that will enable them to be artists, scientists, writers, carpenters, and last but not least, ministers and priests, bishops and archbishops, as well as daughters, sisters, wives, and mothers.

With this faith as freedom, all Christians, women and men, can begin to learn to seek "happiness" with justice, to use the language of the social worker. *Before* happiness in church was happiness without justice. But *now* the happiness they begin to seek in church, and in society, is happiness with justice. Their faith in God is *now* faith in the God, not of enslavement, but of freedom, who exists for both men *and* women at the same time.

This is how the social worker from Hong Kong has come to "perceive God anew." The God conceived anew is different from the God of the old days. *Before* God was "God the Father," period, but *now* God is God the Father *and* the Mother, the Mother *and* the Father. This does not mean that God is sexually conditioned. God is not sexually conditioned. God who is the Mother and the Father, the Mother and the Father, is God related at once to male and female on an equal basis and who, at the same time, is not conditioned by human sexual determinism. When you are a man, biologically you cannot be a woman. When you are a woman, biologically you cannot be a man. But God as the Father-Mother and the Mother-Father is not subject to such biological conditions.

This is an analogical way of speaking about God. How else can we speak of God? But when we apply this analogy to God, we are saying that this Father-Mother God, this Mother-Father God, cannot be God the Father without at the same time being God the Mother, that God cannot be God the Mother without at once being God the Father. This analogical language also underlies the faith that just as God is free for men, God is also free for women. This is the freedom of God uncorrupted by discrimination against one sex or another.

Christian faith is, then, the freedom to be female and human as well as to be male and human. It is such newfound faith that inspires another Christian woman from Sri Lanka:

> I believe in God who brooded over the waters
> who brought forth creation in beauty and harmony
>
> I believe in God, active in my land
> bringing order and peace from chaos and destruction
>
> I believe in God whose mighty acts of creation and liberation
> give hope to the poor, the oppressed and women
>
> I believe in Jesus who was conceived in the womb
> of a simple village girl making her burst into song
>
> I believe in Jesus who allowed himself to be touched
> by a bleeding woman, marveling at her faith
>
> I believe in Jesus surrounded with women
> who appeared to Mary on that first Easter Morn
>
> I believe in the Holy Spirit the Women in God
> active deep in our land, strengthening women and all life
>
> I believe in the Holy Spirit active in every person
> calling us out of our passivity to a fuller life.[6]

There is something fresh in such expression. It discloses a dimension of Christian faith suppressed for a long time.

The "creed" dutifully follows the conventional "trinitarian" structure, but what it says is anything but conventional. God gives hope to the poor, to the oppressed, *and to women*. Jesus, instead of being offended, *marvels* at the faith of the bleeding woman who touched him. The Holy Spirit is *the Women in God* active in every person, male or female. Presumably, the "creed" could go on to talk about the church and its responsibilities, ordination, baptism, and the Eucharist, all from women's perspectives. It could even develop into a full primer of

Christian theology. The "creed" shows us at least what Christian women believe and think, and to what they aspire when they experience faith as freedom.

Faith as Confidence in a Big-Hearted God

We have stressed that faith for us is freedom to be human, man or woman, woman or man. This leads to a vision of God being free to be God, which may sound rather obvious, even a matter of course. If God is not free to be God, can God still be God? If God's freedom to be God were not taken for granted, would God still deserve the name of God? And if God's freedom to be God were questioned, would God still be worthy of our worship and service? It has to be pointed out that there is a vast distance between what God in God's own self must be and what we believe God to be, a distance so vast that what we say about God remains on the verge of being blasphemous, if we claim it to be literally true. Moreover, there is a strong suspicion that what the Christian church has taught about God reflects more what it wants God to be and do than what God in reality is and does.

Are we, then, saying more about ourselves as human beings than about God-self when we make God a part of all events, from the creation and end of the world to the salvation of our souls? Maybe. This is the story of a theologian, a former Roman Catholic nun quoted earlier: "Despite my years as a nun, I do not believe that my experience of God is unusual. My ideas about God were formed in childhood and did not keep abreast of my growing knowledge in other disciplines. I had revised simplistic childhood views of Father Christmas; I had come to a more mature understanding of the complexities of the human predicament than had been possible in kindergarten. Yet my early, confused ideas about God had not been modified or developed. People without my peculiarly religious background may also find that their notion of God was formed in infancy. Since those days we have put away childish things and have discarded the God of our first years."[7]

Although this description rings true for many of us Christians, not everyone would agree. In fact, one can overhear loud protests rising from some Christian quarters. But do we not have to admit that we have retained many childish beliefs about God that we learned in church in our early years? We may also have to concede that we sometimes make contradictory truth-claims for God, claims that contradict common sense and that create unnecessary tensions and conflicts in the world—the world, we also believe, that "God in Jesus Christ" came to heal and reconcile.

One such truth-claim happens to be close and dear not only to Christians but to adherents of other faiths—the claim about salvation. Perhaps no issue has caused more controversy among Christians, and between Christians and people of other faiths, than this issue. It is understandable that people get excited about a question that deals not with passing phenomena of this world but with the eternal destiny of individual believers. One can make concessions on many matters, but not on a matter of such everlasting importance.

Needless to say, uncompromising assertions about salvation—that one is saved solely through Jesus Christ, for example—have become more questionable in Asia, where Christianity, which is usually a minority religion, has to coexist with the more homemade religions such as Buddhism, Hinduism, and Islam. The assertion has also proved confusing to an increasing number of thinking Christians, who have begun to learn to tell the difference between what the church teaches and what God does for humankind.

Apparently, the social worker from Hong Kong is one of the growing number of thinking Christians in Asia today. The thoughts and reflections she shares regarding a fresh perception of God are revealing. "There is a key issue with which I am struggling at present," she says. "In my own context, the majority of the masses are 'pagans' who have not received the grace of salvation. On the other hand, the masses are a 'people' struggling for humanity with God on their side. How should I reconcile the two apparently paradoxical realities?" A good question, but as long as one tries to put the new wine, that is, a fresh perception of God, into the old wineskin, namely, the faith and theology from the church of the past, there will be no answer.

The question raised is not new. It is as old as Christianity and is a question that Christian converts in Asia have had to face ever since Christianity arrived a few centuries ago. But the question has been treated either as an expression of weak faith or as a cunning device of the devil to sow seeds of doubt in good Christian hearts and minds. The fact is that the question can no longer be dismissed in such a high-handed fashion. For the social worker from Hong Kong, a convert to Christian faith, the question presents itself as "a key issue" that demands explanation.

But the question does not need a "great" theological mind to tackle it. It does not require that we stand the gospel on its head and view the world upside down. An answer is already contained in what the social worker continues to say about her dilemma. "The masses," she says, "are a 'people' struggling for humanity with God on their side." This, judging from the way it is said, is a matter-of-fact statement, but for those Christians who regard the masses as " 'pagans' who have not received the grace of salvation," this is a heretical statement. What she says sounds tentative and is not intended to be a firm theological pronouncement, but it contains a deep theological insight. The social worker may not be acutely aware of it, but with such a reflection she is *now* on the way to faith in the "God perceived anew," in contrast to the faith in the God of the church she joined as a convert.

As a social worker, the author has many interactions with people outside the Christian church. The women, men, and children she deals with five or six days a week are far more numerous than the members of the congregation with whom she gathers for worship service just once a week on Sunday. Her responsibility as a social worker demands that she stay in close touch with the people in her charge, usually those who are faring poorly in the affluent world of Hong Kong. She sees them as human beings who struggle to cope with life, to survive in the competitive world of a capitalist society, to make do with little in one of the financial capitals of the world. She listens to their big worries and small joys, shares their frequent failures and occasional successes, and stands by them when they have nowhere to turn when in pain and suffering.

At first all she had to do were her assigned duties as a social worker. But as time went on, duties became responsibilities that demanded her personal involvement. Then before she knew it, her responsibilities had become a ministry. And as she goes about her ministry, she perceives that her clients "are struggling for humanity with God on their side." This is a perception of far-reaching theological significance and consequences. God on the side of people outside the Christian church? God with women and men who are not Christians? God involved in their struggle to live a decent life, to improve their standard of living, to solve their family problems, to be accepted in society as human beings and not rejected for what they do not possess materially? Then it dawns on the social worker that such people have encountered what I would call a big-hearted God, whose grace of salvation is abundant enough to spill over into the world beyond the Christian church.

For the social worker this must be a truly astonishing change in perception. It is astonishing because it is not what she learned in church before. For many Christians with whom she worships, "the majority of the masses" she serves as a social worker are "pagans" who remain outside of God's salvation. They are not eligible for eternal life in God. This may be what most Christians with whom she worships maintain. But is God's grace of salvation such a grudging thing? Does not God's salvation extend to the people, Christian or not, who struggle to live as human beings in adverse economic, social, and political situations?

Such a thought must have been going on in the social worker's mind as she tried to relate what she had been taught to believe in church with what she did as a social worker, as one who perceives God's presence among people in their everyday struggle. If God's salvation is defined strictly in terms of individual Christians attaining eternal life, it is a very limited kind of salvation because it excludes most of the people in the world. It is also irresponsible salvation because it leaves them to fend for themselves both in this life and in the life hereafter. Surely God would have little to do with this kind of salvation.

There is a further question. If God's grace of salvation, even salvation understood as eternal life for individual souls, is available only to Christians and not to people outside of the Christian church, is it not a prejudiced kind of grace? Is a prejudiced king of grace still grace? Does not this kind of grace make God small-hearted? Is this a God big-hearted enough to create heavens and the earth, *all* living beings, and "pagans" as well Christians? Obviously, there is a stark contradiction between the belief that God's grace of salvation is available only in the Christian church and the belief that God is the Creator of the whole universe. Sadly, those evangelists and Christian believers intent on the salvation of their souls to the exclusion of others are either not aware of the contradiction or choose not to be bothered by it.

Since we have been exploring the change from "faith before" to "faith now" that the social worker from Hong Kong has gone through, let us take a closer look at Christianity in Hong Kong. On that tiny four-hundred-square-mile former British crown colony, now a "special administrative region" in China, as many as six million people live practically shoulder to shoulder. After more than one and a half centuries of rule by Britain, the head of whose monarchy is the head of the Church of England and, thus, a defender of the Christian faith, only 8 percent of the total population, according to a 1991 survey, are Christians, including about 250,000 Roman Catholics and 230,000 Protestants. Of the Protestants, 80,000 are from mainline denominations or are members of the Hong Kong Christian Council, 100,000 are evangelicals, and 50,000 are from independent congregations with no denominational affiliation.[8]

This is not a flattering record. With the political and religious powers wielded by colonial rulers, one expects that Christianity would have become the religion of most colonial subjects. Why did this not happen? Missiologically, aggressive claims that the churches in Hong Kong make for God's salvation could have detracted from Christianity's appeal. Other reasons could have been the churches' narrow and restricted view on God's activity in the world, and their tendency to align themselves with ruling powers, in this case the British colonial authorities. These and other factors have made the churches in Hong Kong less than faithful to the gospel of Jesus on the one hand and vulnerable to social and political changes on the other.

> For Christians from the mainline denominations [in Hong Kong], their Christian education was very minimal and hence, their faith very infantile. Their leaders, both lay and ordained, are just far too busy in meetings and administrative work. You will be utterly astonished to learn that the churches in Hong Kong are running a very huge business enterprise. Together, they provide more than 60 percent of the social welfare work, more than 40 percent of the school[ing] and about 20 percent of the hospital beds in Hong Kong. These leaders have little or no time to do any reading and thinking. Their pastoral work is extremely shabby, to say the least. But the most damaging is the fact that financially, this ecclesiastical social service empire has to rely on government funding as well as on huge donations from the business tycoons. Gradually, most denominational leaders and senior clergymen have become a part of the establishment. They stand to gain to uphold the present system which favors the rich and the powerful. The prophetic voice of the church is, therefore, extremely weak.[9]

This is a familiar story, not peculiar to Hong Kong. It is the story of Christianity ever since it became a strange bedfellow of the Roman Empire in the fourth century. The same story has been repeated, almost ad nauseam.

But the story is particularly poignant in Asia today as most Asian nations and peoples have taken upon themselves the colossal task of nation-building after colonial powers were forced to abandon their former colonies. The irony for Christians in Asia is that they are left with the colonial-missionary past, whose shadow will not go away. Even though the power and influence of Western Christianity are almost spent, especially in Europe, Christians in Asia have little to hold onto except missionary legacies from the past, irrelevant in the East and West. This is the case with the churches in Hong Kong. It is also true in many churches in countries that have gained political independence.

A history of Christianity in Asia, written in the wider context of the history of Asia, is no longer to be deferred. A theology of Christian mission, not just piously paying tribute to missionaries' three-pronged strategy of evangelism, education, and medical ministry, but developed on the basis of biblical and theological insights related to our historical and cultural experiences as Asian Christians, is no longer a task to be taken up in our spare time. It is not just a matter of bringing Christians in Asia up-to-date about changes that have shaped and continue to shape our political-economic and cultural-religious lives as Asians. It is no less than the task of reconstructing Christian faith and theology to be accountable to the big-hearted God, the God who is also on the side of the people "struggling for [their] humanity."

What is faith if not confidence in this big-hearted God? This big-hearted God has to replace the small-hearted God we have inherited from the past. The big-hearted God is the God of the entire creation, while the small-hearted God is the God of human creation. The big-hearted God is the God of the whole of humankind, whereas the small-hearted God is the God of "Christendom." The big-hearted God is concerned with the totality of our well-being, comprising body and soul, matter and spirit, life here and life hereafter. The small-hearted God, however, only takes care of that part of life called soul, spirit, and life hereafter. The big-hearted God hears the cries of the people dispossessed and in suffering, but the small-hearted God only listens to the prayers of the rich and the fortunate. Let us make no mistake: the God of Jesus is the big-hearted God and *not* the small-hearted God.

Does it need to be stressed that the big-hearted God creates in us a big-hearted faith? A big-hearted faith is the faith that, to quote Paul, makes us confess: "There is no longer Jew or Greek, there is no longer slave or free, there is no longer male or female" (Gal. 3:28). We know that most of the time this is just rhetoric for many of us Christians, even for Paul sometimes. But that we cannot live up to its high ideal does not invalidate it. The faith that enables us to say the words is a big-hearted faith. The faith that inspires us to practice it is also a big-hearted faith. This big-hearted faith, the faith confident in the big-hearted God, should inspire us to paraphrase Paul and say: in the big-hearted God there is no longer Christian or Jew, there is no longer Buddhist or Hindu, there is no longer Muslim or Confucianist. Our search for the truth of God, our experience of the saving grace of God, and our practice of Jesus' reign of God on earth as in heaven begins with a confession of faith in the big-hearted God.

God's grace of salvation and the masses struggling for their humanity with God on their side are, after all, not "paradoxical realities" as the social worker from Hong Kong supposes. They are "paradoxical" for Christians who still believe that God's grace of salvation is reserved only for members of the Christian church. But once our salvation is understood as part of, and not the whole of, God's purpose of creation, then there is nothing strange about God on the side of people "struggling for [their] humanity." It would be strange only if God were not on their side. It would surely be "paradoxical" if God, who created the universe and to whom all human beings owe their life, were to be found only on the side of Christians. Such "paradoxical realities" did not originate in God. They originated in the Christian church that mistook the Western domination of the world as an opening for the world's christianization.

Faith as Spiritual Renewal

From a small-hearted God to a big-hearted God—this is an enormous leap in our perception of God. Faith as confidence in the big-hearted God—this calls for a change deep in our spirit. God on the side of people struggling for their humanity—this is faith in a different God from the one perceived to be doing special favors for Christians. Such a God calls for profound changes in what we as Christians today think, believe, and do.

To respond to such changes requires spiritual renewal. It requires that we make our spirit responsive to God's Spirit working in the world, sensitive to needs and aspirations of people outside and inside the Christian church, and open to new ways in which God is active. The world, including Asia, from ancient times to the present, has had no shortage of noble spirits and indomitable souls. It is these spirits and souls that enable us to rebuild our lives and histories on the ruins left by human tragedies and natural disasters. Verses from Rabindranath Tagore of India sing to the Asian spirit renewed for the august task of creating a new day:

> Where the mind is without fear and the head is held high,
> Where knowledge is free,
> Where the world has not been broken up into fragments by narrow
>   domestic walls,
> Where words come out from the depth of truth,
> Where tireless striving stretches its arms toward perfection,
> Where the clear stream of reason has not lost its way into the dreary
>   desert land of dead habit,

Where the mind is led forward by thee into ever-widening thought and
     action,
Into that heaven of freedom, my father [and mother],
Let my country awake.[10]

One feels in these lines the Asian soul soaring in defiance of the gods of destruction. One perceives the spirits of Asian people rising above the ruins created by
demonic powers of annihilation. One is drawn deeply into the hearts and minds
of women and men in Asia who believe in the God of mercy, compassion,
and love.

Who is this "thee" who leads the mind "into ever-widening thought and action"? It must be the God who created both the heights and the depths, whose
thought we mortal beings cannot surmise, and whose actions we finite humans
cannot forestall. Who is this "thee" who keeps "the clear stream of reason" from
getting lost in the "dreary desert land of dead habit"? It must be those men
and women who dare the dictatorship of old habits to bring about a world of
new habits. Who is this "thee" who saves the world from being broken up into
"fragments by narrow domestic walls"? It must be those visionaries and martyrs
who keep the world from total fragmentation. Who is this "thee" who enables
even the poor and the disinherited to hold their heads high and to keep the
country awake for freedom? It is the men, women, and children determined
not to submit to the fate decreed by gods and to oppression perpetuated by the
powerful.

What we see in this language is the human spirit inspired by the divine Spirit
to work toward the advent of a new day. What we encounter is the Spirit of
God empowering the spirits of men and women not to yield to self-pity, complacency, or resignation. What moves us is the divine-human Spirit engaging
the world in the construction and reconstruction of human community that can
manifest God's love, justice, and freedom. This is a never-ending enterprise that
engages both God and humanity. The God perceived to be in partnership with
human beings, be they Hindus, Buddhists, or Christians, in such an enterprise
must be a big-hearted God who knows no national barriers, who allows no fa-
voritism on account of ethnic identity, and who does not judge people according
to their faiths and religions.

This renewal is no easy enterprise. It is not something we can do halfheart-
edly. It requires our full attention and demands our full commitment. As the
social worker from Hong Kong concludes: "Living with people means struggle;
both to struggle with them and to sustain an inner struggle within one's self.
Through these struggles one experiences new dimensions of spiritual renewal,
and I believe that God is calling all of us to undergo that renewal."

What are the "new dimensions of spiritual renewal"? What forms does such
renewal take? What demands does it make of us? The social worker does not
tell us. But it is not hard to guess the answers. If there are new dimensions of

spiritual renewal, there must be old dimensions from which to learn. We, like the social worker, know the old dimensions of spiritual renewal, from which we can come up with new dimensions.

First, let us point out that spiritual renewal is human renewal, and that faith as spiritual renewal is faith in the possibility, even the necessity, of human renewal. Spiritual renewal cannot be separated from human renewal as if the two had nothing to do with each other. But most Christians seem to believe that what is called "spirit" is something quite different from our biological self. As a result, what is regarded as "spiritual" is positioned against what is "physical" or "corporeal." This dualism of spirit versus body, between the spiritual and the physical, has created unhealthy, and often pathological, attitudes toward life and world among many Christians.

Such a division of our human self is entirely unfounded. This is not what the Bible tells us. We recall the story of God forming a human being from "the dust of the ground" and breathing into the nostrils "the breath of life [*ruaḥ* in Hebrew, meaning also wind, spirit]" enabling it to become "a living being" (Gen. 2:7). The human being was from the beginning a "spiritual" being, a being animated and brought to life as a being "of the spirit." This is a tremendous theological insight into the very nature of human being. It is a profound perception of how the human being is spiritual and physical all at once. The observation reflects how human beings are related to God and to one another both physically and spiritually.

Implications of this constitution of the human being are obvious. Spiritual growth and human growth are interwoven. Spiritual growth is not truly spiritual if it does not bring about human growth. Nor is human growth genuinely human if it is not accompanied by spiritual growth. This is what human being ought to be according to its original nature. But as we know, what *ought to be* is not always what *is*. For some religious believers to be "spiritual" is to disdain what is "human." There are also those who do not acknowledge the spiritual nature of human being in their pursuit of "human" fulfillment. Neither attitude does justice to the human being is as a spiritual-human, human-spiritual being.

Since a human being is a spiritual-human and human-spiritual being, how can spiritual renewal and human renewal not take place at the same time? If to be human is to be spiritual and to be spiritual is to be human, how can a human being be renewed spiritually every day without being renewed as a human being? It may be that our ancient ancestors, Eastern or Western, knew this fact better than those of us today, who have been shaped by the dualistic understanding of human nature as matter and spirit, or as body and soul. In *The Great Learning*, from China of the fifth century B.C.E. and reflecting the teachings of the Confucian school, one finds these words:

> If you can one day renovate [literally, "become new each and every day"] yourself, do so from day to day. Yea, let there be daily renovation.[11]

The key word in this saying is the Chinese word for "new" (*xin*), used as a verb (to renovate or renew). The saying can be rendered more literally as: "If you can become new each and every day, do so from day to day. Yea, let there be daily renewal."

Is this merely a moral teaching designed to enhance the control of rulers over their subjects in a feudal society? Granted that such a thought cannot be ruled out entirely, the saying does not serve merely as a political tool. Coming from the Confucian school, it relates to the development of human persons. We also read in the opening section of *The Great Learning:*

> The ancients who wished to illustrate illustrious virtue throughout the kingdom, first ordered well their own States. Wishing to order well their States, they first regulated their families. Wishing to regulate their families, they first cultivated their persons. Wishing to cultivate their persons, they first rectified their hearts. Wishing to rectify their hearts, they first sought to be sincere in their thoughts. Wishing to be sincere in their thoughts, they first extended to the utmost their knowledge. Such extension of knowledge lay in the investigation of things.[12]

This is a vision of a human community of perfect order, able to regulate the macrocosm of the state and the microcosm of the individual subject.

In this projection of society, public politics and private ethics work in harmony to create an ideal state. Of course the vision has remained a vision, not only in the history of China but in the history of all nations. Such an ideal state has never come. But it does stir our minds to realize that, already in ancient China, such a political philosophy engaged thinkers and philosophers.

What is of particular interest is the statement about rectifying the hearts and being sincere in thoughts. The heart is the center of each person, family, community, and nation, even the whole universe. All lives in the entire creation are unified in and have been generated from the cosmic heart. This is an important insight of the Confucian philosophy of life and universe, especially the philosophy of neo-Confucianism.

What, then, is the heart? It is "the metaphysical part of our nature, all that we comprehend under the terms of mind or soul, heart, and spirit."[13] It influences the whole of our being, including our outer being and inner being, both our physical being and our spiritual being. It holds the secret of the well-being of individuals, families, states, and the universe. It is important, then, that it be rectified, renovated, and renewed. To rectify the heart is to rectify our mind. To renovate it is to renovate our soul. And to renew it is to renew our spirit. In this teaching from ancient China we glimpse how Chinese thinkers attached great importance to "spiritual renewal," and saw how it was essential to life in the world. Such renewal must have been a struggle not only for teachers and thinkers but for those, rulers and common folks alike, they sought to inculcate.

The social worker from Hong Kong is right: spiritual renewal is a constant struggle. It is a struggle for people and a struggle within oneself to be true to the true human nature created by God. It is not something that takes place automatically. You cannot expect spiritual renewal to occur while waiting for God to renew your spirit. Nor is renewal purely subjective, happening in isolation from the people and the world around you. Spiritual renewal presupposes involvement in the daily struggle of people, sharing their pain and suffering, their joy and happiness. It becomes a reality as you work with them to improve the conditions of their lives, to deal with problems that vex their families, to fend off the forces that do them injustice, and to connect with them as their spirits are strengthened to go on.

Your own spiritual renewal presupposes the spiritual renewal you experience with people with whom you live and work. Spiritual renewal is a communal experience before it becomes a personal experience. Renewal happens in the community of women, men, and children in real-life situations before it happens in the depths of your spirit, in your private chamber. The same can be said of the church. Spiritual renewal said to have taken place within a church where Christians gather to worship is genuine and credible insofar as it resonates with people outside of the church in their struggle to cope with their adversities, to survive in an exploitative society, to strive for justice in the world, and to find meanings that sustain them in their efforts to keep faith in God, trust in humanity, and hope in the generations to come.

Faith in God's Grace

This is a lot to ask for from human beings, Christians or not, believers or not. Life and the world, both out there and inside us, test our faith and fortitude. There are those of us who fail, and who are discouraged and disillusioned. But there are also those who face the tests and grow in faith and maturity. What makes the difference? What is the secret? Let us look closely at some of the realities we go through in life and explore how our faith plays a role.

Faith in Future Generations?

We do stake our faith in the generations to come. This faith has become in Asia almost a religion in itself, particularly in societies influenced by Confucian culture. The Chinese expression *chuan zong jie dai* (continuing the family line by producing a male heir) has been central to the culture that defines almost everything Chinese people think and do, from ethical teachings to moral codes to social behaviors and customs. Those who have suffered most in this culture that idolizes male heirs are the wives who are not able to produce a son to continue the family line. Many tragic tales are told of women who are not able to give birth to a son, thus implicating their husbands in a heinous sin in traditional Chinese society, namely, the sin of having committed an unfilial act.

This scenario is not very different from a reading of Genesis 3 that sees Eve as implicating Adam in the sin of disobeying God.[14]

There is a saying that has been a household word in China for as long as one can remember: there are three unfilial acts, of which having no male offspring is the greatest. Many a woman has met her tragic fate, and many a family has gone through endless heartbreaking turmoil, because she cannot fulfill the duty of producing a male heir for her husband's family. When this virtue of filial piety gets closely connected with ancestor rites, the ritual practice of honoring ancestors, it is practiced almost as a religious duty. The practice of filial piety falls principally on the eldest son in the family. With no male heir to perform this duty, the parents are left without anyone to take care of them. In Chinese society there is no greater disaster. This is still reflected in popular culture in China today, in which many parents are willing to do anything, even killing female babies, to ensure having a son under the one-child-for-one-family policy enforced by the government because of pressures from population growth.

But even if a family is blessed with a male to continue its life into the next generation, hope thus created does not always fulfill the parents' expectations. The son may turn out to be a failure, squandering family fortunes and bringing shame to his parents and ancestors. There is a saying in Taiwan, based on observation of the ups and downs of the rich and famous, that family fortunes will not last more than three generations. There are of course exceptions, but this saying, unfortunately, is often true. Sometimes it does not even take three generations for "the family to collapse and [for] its fortune [to be] washed away" (*qing jia dang chan*), according to a Chinese expression.

In spite of all these complications, we continue to stake our faith in future generations. Most parents will still do their utmost to help their offspring get ahead in the world. The present generation will strive to be the bridge for generations to come, helping to improve the standard of living and to expand the frontiers of human knowledge and experience. But we cannot deny that this is all too fragile a faith we human beings cherish. Faith—the higher it is, the more grandiose it is, the more ambitious it is—often mocks and makes a fool of us. It teaches us how limited we are as human beings and makes us aware that we are not really the masters of our own life and destiny.

It is important to know this dark side of faith. Whether in our mundane life or in our religious life, we dutifully avoid this dark side, pretending not to see it. Faith is faith, we think, precisely because it has nothing to do with the dark side of life. Faith, by definition, must include everything that is good, bright, and full of promise. But the fact is that faith, if left to its own devices, would turn against us. It would leave us dead and cold at the end of our life and terminate our hope for the life to come.

Faith, then, is not everything. We must not idolize it. Faith, like anything else in the world, cannot be self-made. It does not contain in itself the power that enables us to rise again when we fall, that gives us courage when we are in despair, and that promises us life when death stares at us. Faith is not the first principle, so to speak, of life and history; it is not a prime mover of what we human beings have achieved or for what we are going to achieve.

What makes faith faith is grace—God's grace. It is God's grace that makes faith what it can be. It is God's grace that makes faith true faith. Human faith without God's grace can become human hubris, making human beings the center of the universe. Human faith that dispenses with God's grace can turn into the sheer human drive to dominate others politically, socially, or economically. In religion, faith that replaces God's grace is an empty promise offered to those who are successful in the world but who are not at all certain, and who even are fearful, about the life hereafter.

What makes faith genuine faith is God's grace. Faith may turn into an illusion, but God's grace never will. Faith is not ultimately reliable, but God's grace is reliable at all times from here to eternity. Faith may cease, but God's grace will never cease. Faith cannot be decisive, ultimate, and absolutely certain, but God's grace can. We live by God's grace and not by our faith. Put another way, we live by our faith insofar as we live by God's grace. We dare to believe not because of faith itself but because of God's grace. Faith may fail us and it does fail us, but God's grace never will because it is *God*'s grace.

Trust in Humanity?

If it is true that human faith is unreliable, the same is true of our trust in humanity. Perhaps there is nothing more difficult than trusting human beings, and that includes each and every one of us. In sober and honest moments we have to admit that we do not live up to others' expectation of trust and that we cannot trust ourselves. Buddhists say the world is an illusion. Idealist philosophers also tell us that objectivity is nothing more than our own subjectivity. Neither Buddhists nor philosophers of idealism are entirely correct. That I exist is a fact, especially when I touch my nose and hear my own breathing, although the fact that I have an illusion about myself and about the world around me is another matter.

But it cannot be denied that we live in the world of deceptions, and we ourselves are part of this deceptive world. This is true in politics, business enterprise, religious community, and in the world of our inner selves. This unreliability of what we human beings say and do may be what led Lao Tzu, a legendary thinker in ancient China, to say in *Tao-te Ching* (Classic of the way and its virtue):

> Eliminate sageliness, throw away knowledge,
> And the people will benefit a hundredfold.
> Eliminate humanity, throw away righteousness,
> And the people will return to filial piety and compassion.

> Eliminate craftiness, throw away profit,
> Then we will have no robbers and thieves.[15]

This sounds paradoxical. But is it?

"Sageliness," as meant by Lao Tzu, is "a particular characteristic, that of broad and extensive learning,"[16] essential for "an ideal ruler or an ideal human being." But Lao Tzu teaches that one should throw away sageliness and knowledge. By the same token, righteousness—to be right in moral conduct, just in judgment, and fair in human relationships—seemingly should be practiced as a cardinal virtue if we want to build a humane community. But Lao Tzu tells us to throw away humanity and righteousness. Is not all this puzzling and contradictory? What does he really mean? What is he trying to tell the people of his time, who lived in the times of "warring states" (the fifth to the third century B.C.E.), when princes and rulers were engaged in nothing but power struggles?

As Lao Tzu sees it, ambitious rulers would resort to anything, including knowledge and learning, to achieve their political purposes and territorial ambitions. They are interested in a humanity of the conquerors and not of the vanquished. Righteousness belongs to the prerogative of the victors. What is promoted as sageliness and knowledge is in fact "craftiness," the dubious art and skill of outdoing one's opponents. And what is declared as humanity and righteousness is in fact profit in disguise. All these supposedly positive characteristics make already suffering people suffer even more, rendering their already unbearable life more unbearable.

Lao Tzu is right. When all these ideals are thrown away, "the people will benefit a hundredfold...and return to filial piety and compassion." If this was true in the time of Lao Tzu, it is no less true today. If this insight into the nature of human beings and the world shows us a mind deeply in tune with the supremely compassionate mind of God the Creator, it also shows how the same insight has empowered men and women in history to strive for a better world intended by God. In contrast to craftiness and preoccupation with profit, Lao Tzu teaches people to

> Manifest plainness,
> Embrace simplicity,
> Reduce selfishness,
> Have few desires.[17]

These words reverberate, across the span of time, into the minds and hearts of many people who today live in a world of complexities, avarice, and cravings.

How can we trust humanity, each other, and ourselves in such a world? If trust was difficult in Lao Tzu's time, it is no less difficult today. Do we then sit around and watch nature devastated by our greed, human community wrecked by our selfishness, and our own selves consumed by endless desires and cravings?

We have reached the point at which we should realize that we have become the victims of our own greed, selfishness, and desires.

We are all victims of our moral perversity and wrongdoing. Victims are victims because they cannot extricate themselves from harms, abuses, wounds, and even deaths, whether self-inflicted or inflicted by others. To use religious language, we cannot save ourselves. This is not just pious religious jargon. We human beings are in desperate need of the power of grace and compassion to deliver us from our moral numbness and the violence we do to ourselves, to one another, and to the environments that we share with other creatures. This grace, this compassion, is God's grace and God's compassion.

If we have learned something from history and from the predicaments we have created, it is that our trust cannot be in humanity but in God, that our help comes not from ourselves but from God. It is when we have learned to trust in God that we can restore our trust in humanity. Paradoxically, as we "throw away" (in Lao Tzu's words) our humanity, corrupted by greed and power, then we gain true humanity—the humanity rooted in love and compassion, that is part of the entire created world, and that is deepened and enriched by God's grace.

Keeping Faith in God?

There is much talk about faith in God but there is little faith in God. This is true not only in the human community at large but also in the church. The age in which we live makes it difficult for us to keep faith in God. We must ask how much we hear and learn in church makes it easier for us to keep faith in God. The world has ceased to believe in a ready-made God, a God who is the answer to human problems dividing individual persons, families, societies, and the world.

There is much faith in God, but there is little faith in that faith in God. God is almost our last resort. We believe in what we are able to do, hoping that we do not have to resort to God. God is like a footnote, showing that we may refer to God but that God has no vital part to play in our business. Our culture today is one of faith in ourselves and one that keeps God as a backup, so to speak, or on reserve. Our culture has not done away with God, but it does not believe that God is involved in human affairs, whether private or public.

This sounds cynical, but what we see and experience today does militate against our faith in God. The world today is as barbarous, or even more barbarous, than former times. Modern barbarism has become sophisticated. It has increased its horror hundreds and thousands of times, as we have seen in the atomic bombs that ended World War II and in large-scale killings in tribal wars. When we see women, men, and children dying of the hunger and disease that racial conflicts and ethnic wars have brought on them, one's faith in a God of love and compassion is severely tested. One reasons that God is not as benign, active, and powerful as God is made out to be at church services and at evangelical rallies in huge stadiums.

But we do believe that there ought to be something more powerful than all the atrocities and tragedies we experience and witness. That kind of faith enables us to build a new life and a new world. What works in us is not just power, but the power of grace that comes from God. As Yoko Makashi, a Japanese painter, has said, likening human life to a river: "At one time the river will slowly flow under warm sunlight; at another time it will angrily roll down in stormy weather. And the river will do nothing but continuously flow, soon to be swallowed into the great ocean. The existence of humans also is like this stream of the river. They glitter white and become lost into darkness, then again float, become entangled, hail each other, and still run gushing out lives."[18]

Makashi's is a story of struggle and pain, involving struggles with her husband, who suffered from manic-depressive illness and died a tragic death. "I came to realize every time," she recalls, "the importance of human life, as well as the very slight difference between life and death, the real existence of God living in no other creature but in humans, and the God in humans responding to the Universal God."[19] As a human being she is only aware of God in humans. But this is not all that she says. The God in her enables her to respond to "the Universal God," God in every other creature in nature. God within her is the Universal God, and the Universal God is God within her.

It is this God who inspires her to paint until that God emerges from the depths of darkness that surround humanity and creation. Her vocation as an artist who has gone through suffering and pain is "to paint pictures until she perceives God apparent in her works."[20] If this is her vocation as an artist, should the vocation of Christians and particularly of theologians be less? Do we not have to struggle to practice our faith in God and to write about it until God, in God's grace, appears in what we do?

The testimony of Yoko Makashi continues: "When harmony conquering the dualities of light and darkness comes close to the surface of my canvas, my work is almost complete, bringing me wholehearted relief and emancipation. At such a satisfying time, I unexpectedly feel as if I had devoted myself to something and let myself be annihilated."[21] What a profound theological insight! Her father was a Buddhist and her mother a Christian. She experiences a deep perception of a relationship with God through the painting she, as a Buddhist-Christian painter, does.

The experience of God is an experience of self-annihilation. But annihilating our own self in God is the fulfillment of the experience. Put differently, death of our own self in God is the resurrection of our self in God. This is faith at its deepest. When gripped by this kind of faith, we experience it as the grace of God. It is our faith, but it is the grace of God. Faith is ours, but it is ours because it is enabled by God's grace. This is also what the social worker from Hong Kong has come to realize in her daily work among the less-privileged men and women in her charge. It is this same grace of God that gives new life to many women and men both within and outside Christianity.

Chapter 10

The Heart That Believes

God's grace makes our faith what it should be—faith given birth, nurtured, and empowered by the grace of God. As Christians we know this to be true. This is what Jesus showed us in what he said and did. But are we aware that this concept is not alien to other religions such as Buddhism? A Buddhist tale illustrates the concept beautifully.

The Parable of the Raft

"Monks, I will teach you Dharma—the parable of the raft—for getting across, not for retaining. Listen to it, pay careful attention, and I will speak. It is like a man, monks, who going on a journey should see a great stretch of water, the hither bank with dangers and fears, the farther bank secure and without fears, but there may be neither a boat for crossing over, nor a bridge across for going from the not-beyond to the beyond. It occurs to him that in order to cross over from the perils of this bank to the security of the farther bank, he should fashion a raft out of grass and sticks, branches and foliage, so that he could, striving with his hands and feet and depending on the raft, cross over to the beyond in safety. When he has done this and has crossed over to the beyond, it occurs to him that the raft has been very useful and he wonders if he ought to proceed taking it with him packed on his head or shoulders. What do you think, monks? That the man, in doing this, would be doing what should be done to the raft?"

"No, lord."

"What should that man do, monks, in order to do what should be done to that raft? In this case, monks, that man, when he has crossed over to the beyond and realizes how useful the raft has been to him, may think: 'Suppose that I, having beached this raft on dry ground, or having immersed it in the water, should proceed on my journey?' Monks, a man doing this would be doing what should be done to the raft—for getting across, not for retaining. You, monks, by understanding the parable of the rafter, must discard even right states of mind and, all the more, wrong states of mind."[1]

241

Buddhist Scriptures are full of delightful stories and thought-provoking parables, very much like the Gospels of the New Testament. "The Parable of the
Raft" is one of them. "Common to all schools of Buddhism,"[2] the parable has
much to teach us about faith, not in what we are and what we do, but in the
divine grace that enables us to be what we are and to do what we do.

Life is often compared to a journey to stress its transitory nature. We are
told, for example, that "here we have no lasting city, but we are looking for the
city that is to come" (Heb. 13:14). That life is transient is an essential part of
the Buddhist perception of life, too. Nothing in life is permanent and nothing
in it lasts forever.

> Everything changes, everything passes,
> Things appearing, things disappearing.
> But when all is over—everything having appeared
>   and having disappeared,
> Being and extinction both transcended.—
> Still the basic emptiness and silence abides,
> And that is blissful Peace.[3]

Faith and practice in Buddhism revolve around the view of life as a journey in
transition, undergoing change, and as a step to eternal bliss and peace in nirvana,
not only in the future but in the present.

What is this faith that enables us to transcend the life of change on the
one hand and, on the other hand, that gives us the power of peace to be of
service in this topsy-turvy world? Such a question has engaged Christians for
two thousand years. It has also preoccupied Buddhists for many centuries. Most
of us Christians are accustomed to the idea that in Christianity, particularly
within the churches of the Reformed traditions, we do not depend on faith as
works as an effort to gain God's acceptance. Buddhists, however, do just the
opposite, trying to gain deliverance from suffering through faith as works.

But is this not too simplistic a generalization of Buddhism and Christianity?
Is this not a caricature based on ignorance? It is a fact that within some "Reformed" Christian circles there is also emphasis on what we are and on what
we must do to gain God's favor, similar to what Buddhists do to become meri-
torious in the eye of the Buddha. At the same time, it is also a fact that many
Christians, Reformed or not, throw themselves upon the love and mercy of God,
saying like the tax collector in Jesus' parable, "God, be merciful to me, a sinner!"
Jesus hastens to declare to his listeners that "this man went down to his home
justified rather than the other," referring to the Pharisee who thanked God that
he was not like the tax collector (Luke 18:9-14).

Jesus makes it clear in this parable that you are accepted by God not because
of who you are and what you have done but because of God's mercy. Such
faith is not entirely alien to other religions. In Buddhist Scriptures, for example,
there is the story of how Sunita became Buddha's disciple. Sunita, the street

sweeper and scavenger, "poor and of humble birth, 'one for whom no one cared, despised, abused,' accustomed to bend the head before most people, saw the Buddha accompanied by a number of monks enter into Rajagriha near his place of work." As the scene unfolds, the story has Sunita tell readers what happened:

> I laid my baskets and my yoke,
> And came where I might due obeisance make,
> And of his loving kindness just for me,
> The chief of human beings halted upon his way.
> Low at his feet I bent, then standing by,
> I begged the Master's leave to join the Rule
> and follow him, of every creature Chief.
> Then he whose tender mercy watcheth all
> The world, the Master pitiful and kind,
> Gave me my answer: Come, Bhikhu! he said.
> Thereby to me was ordination given.[4]

The is a moving story. It moves us not only with its poetic beauty but with the Buddha's mercy of which it tells so exquisitely.

Does not the story remind us of another from a totally different setting? It is the story of Jesus and Bartimaeus, a blind beggar in Jericho (Mark 10:46-52). Hearing that Jesus was in town, Bartimaeus shouted at the top of his lungs: "Jesus, Son of David, have mercy on me!" People tried to stop him, but Jesus said: "Call him here." The scene seems to follow the scene in the Buddhist story. "Throwing off his cloak," we are told, "[Bartimaeus] sprang up and came to Jesus." These words vibrate with the joy of having been accepted by Jesus. The story ends with Jesus restoring sight to him with these words: "Go; your faith has made you well."

Faith made Bartimaeus well, enabling the blind man to see again. His faith moved Jesus to restore his sight. Is this faith totally different from the faith that made the street sweeper lay aside his baskets and his yoke, that prompted the scavenger to bend his feet low before the Master, and that moved the Master, in his loving-kindness and tender mercy, to accept him, a street sweeper and scavenger, as a member of his religious community? There is no mention of faith in this Buddhist story, but faith is implied. It is not only implied, it is assumed. What is this faith? What are Christians to make of it? And what does it do for those Buddhist believers who may, very much like Paul the Apostle, moan: "Wretched human being that I am! Who will rescue me from this body of death?" (Rom. 7:24)? It may be that the Buddhist parable of the raft, though calm in tone and tranquil in emotion, points to ways in which some deeply devout Buddhist souls have found peace and bliss, ways not entirely alien to Paul or, for that matter, to some pioneers of faith in the history of Christianity.

A Raft Fashioned out of Grass

Our attempt to explore the insights of the parable of the raft in relation to faith takes us back to the Heian Period (794–1185 C.E.) of Japan. The period was marked by the appearance of two great Buddhist monks—Saicho (or Dengyo Daishi, 767–822), who founded the Tendai sect of Buddhism in 805 on his return from a year of study in China, and Kukai (or Kobo Daishi, 744–835), who returned from China in 806 to found the Shingon sect. Both sects were founded at the new capital of Kyoto.

Though introduced to Japan from China only two hundred years before, Buddhism had already grown into a religion difficult for average men and women to understand and follow. Even for Kukai, a precocious student of Buddhism, it was anything but an easy path. As he himself recalled later in life: "Three vehicles, five vehicles, a dozen sutras—there were so many ways for me to seek the essence of Buddhism, but still my mind had doubts which could not be resolved. I beseeched all the Buddhas of the three worlds and the ten directions to show me not the disparity but the unity of the teachings."[5] This is not an unfamiliar story, not only for Buddhist devotees but for believers of other religions as well. To find a solution to the bewildering complexity of Buddhist teachings, Kukai went to China. But the Buddhism he brought back from China did not turn out to be more accessible to ordinary women and men in the street.

The Precious Key to the Secret Treasury, a condensed version of his masterwork, *The Ten Stages of Religious Consciousness,* speaks for itself. In his work he tried to "simplify" Buddhist doctrine, only to succeed in making it even more complicated and difficult to follow. The work reinforced the idea that Buddhism, with its numerous scriptures and abstruse teachings, was beyond the reach not only of lay people but scholars and monks such as Kukai himself. He begins *The Precious Key* with a candid admission:

> From the deep, dim, most distant past,
> A thousand thousand tomes we hold
> Of sacred texts and learned lore.
> Profound, abstruse, obscure and dark,
> Teachings diverse and manifold—
> Who can encompass such a store?

Who, indeed, could "encompass" such a vast inventory of Buddhist Scriptures? Who could exhaust such a plethora of teachings and doctrines, developed by many Buddhist schools?

> Yet, had no one written such,
> And if no one read what they have told,
> What should we know, what should we know?
> However hard they strove in thought,

The saint today, the sage of old
Would still be lost, have naught to show.[6]

One can perceive frustration in these lines. If a learned monk-scholar such as Kukai felt lost in the midst of "abstruse, obscure, dark, diverse and manifold" teachings, how could uneducated and uninformed laywomen and men have been expected to find their way?

This was a thought in the right direction. Kukai set out to present Buddhist teachings in a more systematic and intelligible way.

Did he succeed? Not very well. Did he make Buddhism more accessible to people? Not entirely. His words are his own witness:

Alas, people are ignorant of the treasures they possess, and in their confusion consider themselves enlightened. What is it but utter foolishness! The Buddha's compassion is indeed profound, but without his teaching how can they be saved? The remedies have been provided, yet if people refuse to take them, how can they be cured? If we do naught but spend our time in vain discussion and vain recitation, the King of Healing will surely scold us for it.

Now there are nine kinds of medicines for the diseases of the mind, but the most they can do is sweep away the surface and dispel the mind's confusion. Only in the Diamond Palace do we find the secret treasury opened wide to dispense its precious truths. To enjoy them or reject them—this is for everyone to decide in one's own mind. No one else can do it for you; you must realize it for yourself.[7]

The road to the secret world of the Buddha is long and hard. There are immense volumes of scriptures to study, most of them hard and difficult. Submission to rigorous discipline of the body and the mind is demanded of those who seek to gain access to the truths.

Obviously, this is not something to which ordinary men and women can aspire. As if to make them despair even more of their chances to gain glimpses of what is real and true, they are told that no one else can help them, that they have to do it for themselves. This is a religion teaching that "salvation" must come through one's own efforts, without help from outside oneself. Who is capable of such incessant study and of the austere life necessary to attain enlightenment? Not people who are preoccupied with hardships and worries of everyday life, but only those who can afford the luxuries afforded by time and wealth. It is not even certain whether those with the time and stamina can attain enlightenment.

It was only a matter of time before this school of Buddhism founded by Kukai was to become closely associated with the ruling families and aristocrats, then corrupted by the influence and wealth it had gained. The aftermath led

to the establishment of what is known as the Pure Land sect, which emphasizes salvation by faith in the Amida Buddha and by total dependence on the
Buddha's mercy.

As for Saicho, the other pillar of Buddhism in the Heian era, he was no
less emphatic about the importance of study and discipline, particularly discipline. On Mount Hiei in Kyoto he founded the Tendai school, the Buddhist
sect based on *The Lotus of the Wonderful Law* he had studied in China. In one
of his writings one finds a beautiful passage in which he uses the relation of the
lotus and water to describe the heart of Tendai teaching:

> In the lotus-flower is implicit its emergence from the water. If it does
> not emerge, its blossoms will not open; in the emergence is implicit the
> blossoming. If the water is three feet deep, the stalk of the flower will be
> four or five feet; if the water is seven or eight feet deep, the stalk will
> be over ten feet tall. That is what is implied by the emergence from the
> water. The greater the amount of water, the taller the stalk will grow;
> the potential growth is limitless. Now all human beings have the lotus of
> Buddhahood within them. It will rise above the mire and foul water of
> the Hinayana and Quasi-Mahayana, and then through the stage of the
> boddhisattvas to open, leaves and blossoms together, in full glory.[8]

Those who have seen lotus-flowers blossom in rivers and in ponds will grasp
at once the imagery painted here. The passage also brings before one's eyes the
image of the Buddha sitting on the lotus-flower in the posture of meditation.

All human beings have the lotus of Buddhahood in them, says Saicho. This
is derived from one of Buddha's principal teachings. This is what distinguished
the teaching of Buddha from the Hindu teachings of his day; his teaching
dwelled on Buddha-nature in all human beings regardless of class, if not of
sex. (The struggle of women to be full members of the Buddhist community is
a long story, common to all religions, including Christianity.) The question here
is how one can emerge from the water and bring the lotus-flower of Buddha
nature in oneself to full bloom. According to Saicho, "the way that one may
attain Buddhist perfection is to follow the way of Buddha by leading a life of
moral purity and contemplation. Indeed, it was this emphasis on moral perfection rather than the more metaphysical aspect of the Tendai philosophy which
most conspicuously appeared in his teachings."[9]

Kukai was preoccupied with the mastery of Buddhist doctrine developed in
copious scriptures and diverse texts. Saicho stressed the importance of moral
perfection as the way to become aware of the Buddhahood that is in each person. Neither seemed to realize that not many people are capable of achieving
mastery of Buddhist scriptures or moral perfection. Instead, they provided a
counsel of despair to women and men for whom moral perfection or mastery of
Buddhist texts was well beyond their dreams. These gifts are reserved only for
a select number of people, who dedicate all their time to study and meditation.

But even for these professional students of Buddhist schools, one must question whether any is capable of achieving the goal, even after years of study and discipline at temples and monasteries isolated from society and detached from people in the world.

Are not all these learnings and self-discipline in fact "the raft made of grass"—the raft the traveler made to cross the river from "the hither bank with dangers and fears" to "the farther bank secure and without fears"? Is not the raft merely a temporary measure? Is it not wrong to view the raft as something of eternal importance? Immense learnings and austere self-discipline cannot be all that conducive to enlightenment. These learnings and self-discipline are, as a matter of fact, not different from the raft; they have no permanent place in one's search for the truth.

Is not the raft only a means to an end? Is it not to miss the mark entirely to view the raft as an end in itself? By the same token, these learnings and self-discipline are means to achieve the end of eternal bliss. If practiced as if they were eternal bliss itself, would it not be to mistake the means for the end? If the raft becomes a hindrance rather than a help in the continuing journey, would not these learnings and self-discipline also become a hindrance rather than a help to one's journey of faith?

These are questions Shinran (1173–1262), founder of the Shin sect of the Jodo (Pure Land) Buddhism in Japan,[10] found himself asking more and more as his stay on Mount Hiei elapsed from months to years. He was no idle seeker of religious truths, lazy and inattentive. For twenty years, from the age of nine to twenty-nine, he pursed the way of salvation on Mount Hiei, the headquarters of the Tendai Buddhism founded by Saicho. "In view of the extensive knowledge of Buddhist scriptures that Shinran demonstrates in his writings, there can be little doubt that he applied himself very hard to scriptural studies, especially those in the Tendai and Pure Land tradition as transmitted on Mount Hiei. It is also highly likely that Shinran engaged in various other forms of Buddhist practice and meditations to which he could have been exposed during his twenty years of life in this eclectic center of Buddhism."[11] In Shinran's words, "I, the Bald-headed Fool Shinran, in the year 1201 rejected rigorous religious practices and took refuge in the principal vow [of Amida Buddha]."[12]

These may not be all the reasons that turned Shinran from the Buddhism of salvation through *jiriki* (self-power) to salvation through *tariki* (Other Power, power of Amida Buddha). As he plunged ever more deeply into the effort to perfect himself as a monk and to attain salvation, the more he realized that the task in which he was engaged was impossible. He had to admit that "I am one for whom any practice is difficult to accomplish."[13]

If he as a monk, entirely dedicated to the study of scriptures and to the practice of disciplines, found the whole exercise so difficult, how much more difficult it must be for the masses of men and women. He goes on to say: "But it is hard for the foolish and ignorant, who are ever sinking in birth-and-death, to perform acts with the mind of meditative practicers, for this is to cease thinking and to concentrate the mind. It is also hard to perform acts with the mind of non-meditative practicers, for this is to discard evil and practice good."[14] This was a dilemma for Shinran, for which no solution was in sight.

Who is "the foolish and ignorant"? Shinran himself. In his writings and in his conversation with others he calls himself "fool."[15] Whose is "the mind of non-meditative practicers"? It is the mind of women and men entirely preoccupied with everyday life, with no time for meditation. Shinran identifies himself with them. Turning away from faith in salvation through one's own effort to faith in salvation through the power of the Buddha compelled him to turn away from the religion of the elites that prevailed in his day to the religion of the masses—of men, women, and children regarded as hopeless and lost by the religious establishment and priestly hierarchies. If the religious teachings and doctrines, however true and profound, could not be of help to them, were these teachings not like the raft made of grass in the parable? The raft, since it is made of grass, is fragile in the extreme. It may be able to take a few people, rich and privileged, across the river, but it would surely sink when masses in need of getting across climb onto it. Would this not result in a great disaster?

If teachings and monastic disciplines proved to be useless to Shinran in achieving enlightenment, did they help him to overcome his worldly passions and unholy desires? Again he had to acknowledge that they were no more helpful to him in achieving moral perfection than in attaining enlightenment. This is what he had to confess years later:

> I now truly realize! How wretched I am! Ran, the stupid bald-headed one, deeply submerged in the wide ocean of desires and cravings, confusingly lost among the huge mountains of worldly fame and interests, has no aspirations for being counted among the elite of the definitely assured group and feels no pleasure in approaching the really true experience. How deplorable! How deplorable![16]

Shinran felt trapped between his arduous efforts to succeed in his monastic training and his frustrations from struggle with his own worldly desires. He was disillusioned, embittered, and broken.

This does not sound altogether unfamiliar to us Christians. It reminds us of the agony of Paul the Apostle, expressed from the deep recesses of his heart and spirit when writing to Christians in Rome:

> For we know that the law is spiritual; but I am of the flesh, sold into slavery under sin. I do not understand my own actions. For I do not do what I want, but I do the very thing I hate.... For I know that nothing good dwells within me, that is, in my flesh. I can will what is right, but I cannot do it. For I do not do the good I want, but the evil I do not want is what I do.... Wretched man that I am! (Rom. 7:14-24)

This is a confession most sincere and at the same time most desperate. It shows us Paul when, all at the same time, he was most remote from God and nearest to God.

In this confession Paul tells us a religious paradox: God is never as close as when we are deeply aware of our unworthiness and helplessness. As long as we feel we are strong, we do not need God. While we think that we are capable of moral perfection, God is superfluous to us. If we have every reason to believe that we are invincible, even immortal, God is a mere substitute for our own selves. But at times when we look deeply into ourselves, or gaze far beyond us into space so immense and time so infinite, we may realize that we are in the presence of God's grace despite ourselves.

If Shinran's experience reminds us of Paul the Apostle, it also makes us recall Martin Luther, an Augustinian monk, who founded Protestant Christianity after being excommunicated by the Roman Catholic Church. Just a year before his death, he wrote:

> Though I lived as a monk without reproach, I felt that I was a sinner before God with an extremely disturbed conscience. I could not believe that God was placated by my satisfaction. I did not love, yes, I hated the righteous God who punishes sinners, and secretly, if not blasphemously, certainly murmuring greatly, I was angry with God, and said, "As if, indeed, it is not enough, that miserable sinners, eternally lost through original sin, are crushed by every kind of calamity by the law of the decalogue, without having God add pain to pain by the gospel and also by the gospel threatening us with God's righteousness and wrath!" Thus I raged with a fierce and troubled conscience.[17]

The passage depicts a highly charged spirit, making every effort to excel in learning and in moral perfection, who ends up in dire agony and despair, on the verge of rebellion against the religious traditions to which he has surrendered body and soul.

"Wretched man that I am!" Paul lamented. "I raged with a fierce and troubled conscience," Luther confessed. "How deplorable! How deplorable!" mourned Shinran. That Shinran, a Buddhist monk from Japan in the twelfth century; Paul, a Jew converted to Jesus more than a thousand years before him; and Martin Luther, who lived in Germany about 350 years after Shinran, went through religious experiences so much alike is astonishing. Their stories are almost variations of the same story. Surely this cannot be accidental.

What is also amazing is that out of those profound experiences these three personalities became the pioneers and founders of new religious movements—Paul, beset with opposition from fellow Jews, becoming the first Christian missionary to the Gentiles; Martin Luther, his ties to the Roman Catholic Church violently severed, laying the foundation of Protestant Christianity; and

Shinran abandoning the raft of the official Buddhism of his youth and venturing into a new world of Pure Land Buddhism.

What we encounter in these three pioneers of religious traditions and path-finders of the human spiritual journey is perhaps more than just coincidental. What we encounter must be the Spirit of the God of love and compassion work-ing among men and women in different nations, inspiring them to seek God in diverse human situations, and opening their hearts and minds to the desperate cries from their fellow human beings. How else are we to explain such close parallels between these three religious forerunners, who otherwise are complete strangers to one another? If Shinran can be called "a Japanese Luther,"[18] cannot Paul be called "Jewish-Christian Shinran" and Luther "a German Shinran"?

Leaving the Raft Behind

It has to be pointed out, however, that similar religious experiences do not al-ways result in similar teachings and doctrines. In fact, Pure Land Buddhism and Christianity differ substantially when it comes to teaching and doctrine.[19] There is, for instance, "the idea of washing sin with the blood of Christ cru-cified," which, according to a famed master of Japanese Zen Buddhism, "will never awaken in the Buddhist heart a sacred exalted feeling as in the Chris-tian. The agony of crucifixion, death, and resurrection making up the contents of Christian faith have significance only when the background impregnating old tradition is taken into consideration, and this background is wholly wanting in Buddhists who have been reared in an atmosphere different not only historically but intellectually and emotionally. Buddhists do not wish to have the idea of self-sacrifice brought before their eyes in such a bloody imagery."[20]

There is some truth in this observation. At most Christian worship services and evangelical rallies and in some theological circles, salvation tends to be de-picted as a bloody affair, emphasizing the redemptive efficacy of Jesus' blood. "I am saved by the blood of the crucified One,"[21] is a refrain recited and sung by old-time and new Christian converts. Leaving aside such language, cruci-fixion, as a means of executing criminals in the Roman Empire, was indeed a bloody affair. There is no doubt about it. It was not merely a "symbol of cru-elty and inhumanity,"[22] but *the reality* of it.[23] The cross is all too vivid and all too realistic a demonstration of how human beings can be cruel to one another. Forms and methods may differ among societies and cultures, but the human cruelty and inhumanity the cross represents is the same at all times and in all places.

The cross is offensive to everything we human beings stand for, morally and aesthetically. It is repulsive to our sensibility and decency. The cross as religious symbolism does not apply only to the victims of Roman power many centuries ago, but to all victims of oppression and violence, political or religious, commit-ted by those in power. It stands for what is basest in human beings. It exposes the demonic forces working deep in human community. And it bears witness to story after story of human beings tortured to death, families torn apart, and societies devastated. "Buddhists do not wish to have the idea of self-sacrifice brought before their eyes in such a bloody imagery." Neither do some Christians.

The problem does not consist in Jesus' crucifixion having been a bloody affair. It *was* a bloody affair. The problem arises when crucifixion becomes an object of religious contemplation and turns into a cult object for Christian worship and spirituality. Even the blood, which was all too real for the victim of that cruel and inhuman act and all too ghastly for those who witnessed it, becomes a part of the religious symbolism that ceases to express the extreme physical pain and agony of death.

In this way, the cross, ironically, loses the power that informs its symbolism and becomes a sign that distinguishes Christianity from other religions. Is this not what the cross on the rooftop of the Christian church has become? The cross as seen in Asian societies no longer conveys that sense of human cruelty and inhumanity to Christians, not to mention Buddhists. This indicates the sad state of Christianity in Asia and in the world. Christianity has become an innocuous religion, a community of Christians seeking salvation for their souls and personal well-being at the same time.

There is no lack of stories about self-sacrifice for others' sake in any community and any religion. Most of these are bloody stories involving torture and death. There are folktales from China and Japan that remember how victims, usually unmarried young women, were thrown into the river as a sacrifice to placate the angry river god and to spare the village from floods. The religious practice of offering human beings as sacrifices to gods is as old as the history of humankind. In the evolution of religions human sacrifice was later to be replaced by animal sacrifice, which in turn was replaced by goods such as grains, food, or money. Human sacrifice gradually diminished and finally disappeared.

But the idea of self-sacrifice has persisted. Among the world religions today that continue to make its practice central to the faith are Christianity and Buddhism. For Christianity, Jesus' death on the cross is the heart of what it believes and propagates. For Buddhism it is the notion of boddhisattvas, Buddhas-to-be, who resolve not to enter the bliss of nirvana in order to save "all living creatures," that has become the heart of Pure Land Buddhism, first in China and later in Japan. As mentioned already, the parallel between Christianity and Pure Land Buddhism at the very basic level of humans pursuing the meaning of eternal and temporal life is far deeper than many of us care to believe.

What is driven home to Shinran, after his years of rigorous religious quests, is that nothing other than faith is involved in the self-sacrifice exemplified by Amida Buddha.[24] He experienced a sense of liberation and joy when he read "the account of Amida Buddha and his Pure Land," told by Sakyamuni, the founder of Buddhism, "in which all beings are the objects of Amida's unconditional Love and infinite Wisdom."[25] According to the account, Amida Buddha promises not to enter nirvana until he has fulfilled forty-eight vows. What has particularly inspired the religious imagination of Shinran and his school is the eighteenth vow, which says:

> If all beings in the ten quarters, when I have attained Buddhahood, should believe in me with all sincerity of heart, desiring to be born in my country, and should, say ten times, think of me, and if they should not be reborn there, may I not obtain enlightenment, barring only those who have committed the five deadly sins and who have abused the Good Law (*Dharma*).[26]

The vow is the Sakyamuni's mission—the mission dedicated completely to giving solace, security, and joy in the world of pain and suffering.

Imagine Shinran's excitement when he reflected deeply on this eighteenth vow of Amida Buddha. This is what he wrote in 1224 when he was fifty-one years old: "Thus, I, Shinran, the simple-hearted man with a shaven head, during the era of Kennin abandoned the practice of unessential work and found the home in the Original Vow of Amida."[27] The eighteenth vow of Amida Buddha proved to be a momentous turning point in his faith and life. He "was awakened to the oceanlike vastness of the eighteenth vow, expansive enough to embrace even the most unworthy believer. That point marked his first moment of faith, assuring him of unfathomable birth in Amida's true Pure Land."[28]

This experience occurred to Shinran when he realized that many years of hard work and arduous search were not getting him anywhere. Looking back, he is able to say:

> There are those who, in this manner, try to find their peace of mind and their way of conduct, by working most arduously, most impatiently, day and night, throughout the twelve periods of time, running after something, doing one thing or another, and belaboring themselves as if their heads were on fire. Yet, their doings, however superficially good and proper, are essentially mixed with poison. As long as their conduct remains thus mixed with poisonous matter, it will be impossible for them, however they may desire to do so, to be born in the Pure Land of the Buddha.[29]

He is one of the arduous workers he describes in this passage. In fact this is a description of himself. As he pens these words, he must be aware of the complete difference between the old world of Mount Hiei, where he spent twenty long years, and the new world into which he is about to embark.

Again we are reminded of a dramatic experience of Paul, which occurred when he was still called Saul, serving the effort of his Jewish religion to round up followers of the crucified Jesus and to snuff out the Jesus movement. In his letter to the churches of Galatia he writes how he turned from a student of Judaism into a single-minded evangelist to the Gentiles:

> You have heard, no doubt, of my earlier life in Judaism. I was violently persecuting the church of God and was trying to destroy it. I advanced

in Judaism beyond many among my people of the same age, for I was far more jealous for the traditions of my ancestors. But when God, who had set me apart before I was born and called me through God's grace, was pleased to reveal God's Son to me, so that I might proclaim him among the Gentiles ... (Gal. 1:13-16)

Paul refers to his conversion to the cause of Jesus, movingly told by Luke (Acts 9:1-9; 22:1-13). The conversion has led to his sole trust in Jesus for God's saving grace.

This is an about-face change for Paul, who was "a Jew, born in Tarsus in Cilicia, but brought up in this city [Jerusalem] at the feet of Gamaliel, educated strictly according to our ancestral law ... " (Acts 22:3). Shinran could have paraphrased Paul to describe the change that had come to him. He too was born in a Buddhist culture, was brought up on Mount Hiei, the headquarters of Buddhism, with intimate ties with the ruling family and aristocrats, sat at the feet of important priests and teachers, and was educated strictly according to the doctrine of the Tendai Buddhism. As Paul had to put all his learnings and training behind him in response to the call of Jesus to the people outside the Jewish community, Shinran too had to leave Mount Hiei behind to become a tireless "evangelist" to the masses of people, with complete trust in the mercy of the Buddha.

Shinran, armed with this newfound faith—not in his own power to save himself, but in the power of Amida Buddha to save him—had to leave the old world, like the raft in the parable.

> Be on guard not to believe in the teachings given out by the boddhisattvas and others, which are not fit [for people of latter days] to follow. They will prove to be hindrances, will cause much confusion and bewilderment and will make you lose the chance of being greatly benefited [by] a birth in the Land of Amida Buddha.[30]

A new journey of faith thus had begun for Shinran. Pure Land Buddhism was destined to become the most popular form of Buddhism in Japan, offering refuge and comfort to the men and women who trusted in the mercy of the Buddha for their life and for salvation in the Pure Land.

Dharma for Getting Across, Not for Retaining

After a detour to the beginning of Christianity and to sixteenth-century Europe, let us return to the parable of the raft. We find the traveler in the parable on the other shore, wondering whether he should "proceed taking [the raft] with him packed on his head or shoulders," since it "has been very useful" to him. This is an absurd question, monks in the parable must have said to themselves. "No, lord," they answer, the traveler should not take the raft with him. The raft that had been useful in getting him across the river would become a burden to him if he were to carry it. Besides, it is made of grass, not of precious stones or valuable metals such as silver or gold. The answer is correct, but have the monks truly understood the meaning implied in that absurd question? I am afraid they have not.

It is true that no one in their right mind would take the raft with them. But do we not do the contrary in our religious life? Our common sense tells us to discard the raft, but the sad thing is that such common sense is not followed in religious life. What should be discarded is retained to our detriment.

The raft in the parable is thus no ordinary raft. It is parabolic of what we learn and practice in religion, symbolic of what we hold as dear and important religiously. It alludes to the religious tradition we have inherited, regarded as true and absolute. It refers to the beliefs and doctrines we have learned from the religious authorities and consists of rules and regulations we are expected to follow as members of a faith community. It is what makes our religion different from other religions.

This is where the parable of the raft finally leads. More basic than the raft and utterly indispensable to the recovery of wholeness is the sense of awe in the divine presence, the sense that precedes any religious teaching and doctrine. This sense includes an awareness of one's helplessness, one's lostness.

This most primal and primordial religious sensibility in human consciousness, which has always existed unadulterated, uncontaminated, and uncorrupted, inspires Paul to make a radical change in his religious allegiance. "For I decided to know nothing among you except Jesus Christ, and him crucified" (1 Cor. 2:2). Jesus evoked in Paul that primary religious sensibility, enabling him to see beyond his own religious tradition. The risen Christ enabled him to link again with that primordial religious sensibility, suppressed by his own religious community.

For Martin Luther, the transformation is no less radical. It must be that same religious sensibility, which existed beyond his Catholicism, that prompted him to say: "At last, by the mercy of God, meditating day and night, I gave heed to the context of the words, namely, 'In it the righteousness of God is revealed, as it is written: He who through faith is righteous shall live.' There I began to understand that the righteousness of God is that by which the righteous lives by the gift of God."[31] "He who is righteous through faith shall live!" This is what Paul had said many centuries before (Rom. 1:17). A direct link between Luther and Paul is forged by that "primitive" religious sensibility.

The Believing Heart

But we Christians and theologians have ignored this basic, primal, and primordial sensibility that underlies human religious consciousness. Religions have fought one another as if their religions had made them into different human beings. Diverse sects and different schools of theological thought within the same religion also vie with one another, point fingers and condemn and excommunicate as if they had nothing in common. No amount of dialogue, no amount of effort from people of different religions to be civil, will be able to tear down the walls of separation until we all become aware once again that the "raw" religious seed is planted in us all, the seed from which all religious trees have grown in different kinds, shapes, and sizes.

Paul through his encounter with the risen Jesus, and Luther through his reading of Paul's emphasis on faith in God's saving righteousness, are touched by that basic, primal, and primordial religious sensibility. That seed of our religious aspirations connects us once again as human beings born out of God's creative love, sustained by God's Spirit in our life in the world, and inspired to continue our journey toward eternity in one another's company, helping one another, correcting one another, but moving forward together to that city of God and that Pure Land in which there is no temple (Rev. 21:22). Religions that we refuse to let go, like the raft in the Buddhist parable, have no place there. Is this an unrealistic vision?

We know that Paul and Luther shared the same religious sensibility. But what are we to make of the fact that Shinran, from a totally different religious tradition, seems to respond to that same religious sensibility and resonates with the divine saving love? Just like Paul and Luther, it was faith and a believing heart—not conformity to rules and teachings of the religious establishment—that made Shinran deeply aware of the other power—the power of the Buddha. That primal religious sensibility prompted him to strike out on a new religious path, making him a soulmate of religious pioneers in East and West who responded to God's search for humanity.

"How Much More So with a Wicked Person!"

In *The Tannisho,* consisting of sayings of Shinran compiled by an immediate disciple, there are these well-known words:

> Even a good person is reborn in the Pure Land, and how much more so with a wicked person! But people generally think that even a wicked person is reborn in the Pure Land, and how much more so with a good person![32]

These are shocking words. With them Shinran seems to stand religious faith on its head, obscuring the difference between good and evil, doing away with the line drawn to separate the sheep and the goats.

But Shinran is no libertarian, practicing freedom as a license to act without moral sensitivity. With these words he is not encouraging indulgence in worldly pleasures, saying that no matter what one does—arson, robbery, murder—all will be well in the end. He is not indulging in a game of words, teaching that a good person is wicked and a wicked person is good. Nor is he setting up a logic of his own, asserting that in order to be a good person one has to be a wicked person.

In fact, "Shinran, Honen [Shinran's teacher and mentor], and the traditional schools of Buddhism were united in their opposition to" licensed evil.[33]

What he has said may lead to misinterpretation, and Shinran is not unaware of it. But he would have nothing to do with misinterpretations of his statement. This is evident in what he wrote in a letter to a follower, reprimanding the follower for promoting a misinterpretation:

> It is deplorable that you have told people to abandon themselves to their hearts' desires and to do anything they want. One must seek to cast off the evil of this world and to cease doing wretched deeds; *this* is what it means to reject the world and to live the *nembutsu*. . . . When has it ever been said that one should act in accordance with one's mind and heart, which are evil? You, who are totally ignorant of the sutras and commentaries and ignorant of the Tathagata's words, must never instruct others in this way.[34]

Shinran is not amused. The letter shows he is very upset. This is not what he had meant by saying that even a wicked person could be reborn in the Pure Land, and he feels obliged to counter the distortion.

The situation Shinran faces recalls Paul's passionate argument in his letter to the Christians in Rome about the relationship between God's grace and human sin. This is how Paul framed the question: "But if our injustice serves to confirm the justice of God, what should we say? That God is unjust to inflict wrath on us?" (Rom. 3:5). This of course is not his own question. It is a question some had posed to subvert Paul's emphasis on dependence on God's saving grace in spite of, or even on account of, our sins.

Paul is upset. He finds himself in a similar dilemma to Shinran. Does he have to concede to the seemingly correct logic that God needs our injustice to manifest God's own justice? Does he have to admit that "human wickedness brings about the manifestation of God's uprightness"?[35] But this is not what Paul had meant. How could he encourage people to do what is unjust on the pretext that otherwise God could not show them justice? The question in Romans 3:5 caricatures Paul's stress on God's unconditional saving grace. He does not tire of saying that God's saving grace is God's gift, and not something we have earned through what we have done. Paul has to make sure people have heard his objection to their misinterpretation when he says, almost shouting: "By no means!" (Rom 3:6).

Paul is very concerned with that kind of false logic and incorrect interpretation. That must be why he comes back to the issue later in the same letter. This time he poses the misinterpretation in this way: "What then are we to say? Should we continue in sin in order that grace may abound?" (Rom. 6:1). To put it another way: "If [our] uprightness comes from faith, not deeds, why does one, even a Christian, have to worry about evil acts?"[36] This is exactly the question followers put to Shinran. How deplorable! Shinran exclaims. Paul repeats the response he had made earlier: By no means!

Neither Paul nor Shinran can allow such false conclusions to be drawn from their emphasis on faith in God's saving grace. In the case of Shinran, as with Paul, it is the consciousness of his own sinful nature and his utter inability to overcome evil that prompt him to say something that appears cryptic—even paradoxical—about the good and the wicked person. He in fact does not consider himself to be a good person, one deserving the mercy of the Buddha. It has been pointed out that the "sense of inexhaustible evil remained with Shinran to the last minute of his life."[37] He expresses this deep sense of evil in *Gutoku hitan jukkai* (Lamentation and confession of Gutoku Shinran):

> Although I have taken refuge in the true teaching
> of the Pure Land,
> The mind of truth hardly exists in me;
> Moreover, I am so false-hearted and untrue
> That there cannot be any mind of purity.
>
> Each of us shows an outward appearance
> Of being wise, good, and diligent,
> Possessing so much greed, anger, and wrong views,
> We are filled with all kinds of deceit.
>
> My evilness is truly difficult to renounce;
> The mind is like a serpent or scorpion.
> Even doing virtuous deeds is tainted with poison,
> And so is called false practice.
>
> How shameless and unrepentant a person am I
> And without a heart of truth and sincerity;
> But because the Name is transferred by Amida,
> Its virtue pervades the ten directions.[38]

One could take this for a Christian confession of sinfulness were the name Amida replaced by the name Jesus.

But why do most Christians categorically deny to Buddhism such an awareness of sin? It is partly because of our ignorance about Shinran and the sect of Pure Land Buddhism he developed. The awareness of sin expressed in Shinran's lamentation and confession is in fact much deeper and much more sincere than many Christian prayers and confessions. One can even go so far as to ask: How much deeper can one get? How much more genuine can one be? And how much more sincere can one become in one's confession of sin?

Shinran is not just identifying sinfulness as moral imperfection. Yes, our sinfulness gets expressed in our moral weakness and wrongdoings. But Shinran knows that sinfulness is part of our nature, and does not consist just of moral defects that can be corrected if we work hard enough. The sad fact is that we can never succeed in our effort. This is what drives Shinran to despair:

In all small and foolish beings, at all times, thoughts of greed and desire incessantly defile any goodness of heart; thoughts of anger and hatred
constantly consume the dharma-treasure. Even if one urgently acts and
urgently practices as though sweeping fire from one's head, all these acts
must be called "poisoned and sundry good" and "false and deceitful practice." They cannot be called "true and real action." To seek to be born in
the land of immeasurable light through such false and poisoned good is
completely wrong.[39]

Besides being a further confession of one's sinfulness, this is a candid admission of hypocrisy. It does humble us Christians, perhaps because it comes from
Shinran, who was born, lived, and died a Buddhist.

What is Shinran getting at? Why is moral perfection impossible? Why are
we always besieged by sinful thoughts and evil intentions even when we are doing something good and commendable? Such questions preoccupy Shinran. He
knows from his own experience the futility of trying to attain moral perfection,
even of ridding himself of sinful thoughts and evil intentions. He has to know
the cause so that he can, to use a Chinese expression, *dui zheng xia yao*, literally,
"give the right prescription for an illness," or "take the right remedial steps to
correct a shortcoming."

What, then, is the illness that causes sinful thoughts and evil acts? What
makes Shinran, to quote Paul, "do not do the good I want, but the evil I do
not want" (Rom. 7:19)? What is the disease that wastes his spirit and soul and
turns him into "a foolish being full of blind passions" (*bonno gusoku bonpu*)? It is
karma! *Karma* is one of the cardinal concepts in Buddhism, "that moral kernel
in each being which survives death for further rebirth or metempsychosis."[40]

There is good *karma* and there is evil *karma*. Shinran is almost exclusively
preoccupied with evil *karma*, that evil kernel in human beings that causes us not
to do good but to do evil. We cannot do anything about the situation because
evil is part of what we are. "At the root of human existence is *karmic* evil, evil
because beneath the veil of ordinary life is found insatiable greed and blind self-
centeredness, and '*karmic*' because such evil is the product of one's countless past
lives."[41] We can imagine how a sense of helplessness takes hold of Shinran when
he stares at that "*karmic* evil" at the root of his existence, and by inference, of
all human existence.

What Shinran has to grapple with is also what Christians down the centuries,
beginning with Paul, have had to grapple with—sin, and not just sin in the sense
of moral failure, but in the sense of something in our very being causing us to
think bad thoughts and to do evil things. This is what is known as "original sin"
in Christianity. "Original" in the Christian doctrine of "original sin" should not
be taken to mean that the sin that corrupts human beings originated when Adam
and Eve disobeyed God's command and ate the forbidden fruit in the Garden
of Eden (see Genesis 3). We are told that ever since human beings inherited

that "original sin," sin has not been something we acquire in the course of our lives but something we are born with.

Whether the Buddhist emphasis on *karma* as a "product of one's countless past lives" or the Christian view of original sin, the real point that these ideas try to make is that each human being is capable of both evil and good thoughts and deeds, and that we are more capable of the former than the latter. This discovery must have shocked and saddened Shinran at the same time. What is one to do? Give up in despair? Throw oneself at the mercy of the Buddha? Shinran took the latter course, just as Paul did when he said: "Who will rescue me from this body of death? Thanks be to God through Jesus Christ our Lord!" (Rom. 7:24-25).

Other Power, Not Self-Power

For Shinran it is not in Jesus but in Amida Buddha that he finds refuge from his *karmic* evil. We have already quoted him as saying that "even a good person is reborn in the Pure Land, and how much more so with a wicked person!" This is how he explains the statement:

> For a person who relies on the good that he does through his self-power (*jiriki*) fails to entrust himself wholeheartedly to Other Power (*tariki*) and therefore is not in accord with Amida's Primal Vow. But when he abandons his attachment to self-power and entrusts totally to Other Power, he will realize birth in the Pure Land.[42]

Do we not perceive behind these words a person who has come out of "the dark night of the soul" relieved, liberated, and motivated to live not for oneself but for others? This is what Shinran did for the rest of his long career, spending his life with men and women who struggled to live in adverse situations and empowering them to live in hope and to entrust themselves to the infinite compassion of Amida Buddha.

What is self-power (*jiriki*)? According to Shinran, "self-power is when one counts upon one's body, one's mind, one's power, or any of one's various good roots."[43] Much self-power is employed in Christianity as well as in Buddhism to attain salvation. But this is the wrong way, asserts Shinran, who goes on to say that "to attain the true faith you must be free from the limitations of your discriminating intellect, that the roots of the self-power's working must be overthrown."[44] This statement sounds very "evangelical," does it not? Is it not the heart of Jesus' good news in the parable of the father's love (Luke 15:11-32)[45] that we are accepted by God not because of what we are but because of God's forgiving love?

The opposite of self-power is Other Power, in capital letters. It "denotes the power of Amida's Prayer. . . . the working of Amida's compassion is free from all human agency, severed from discrimination and arguing . . . not calculated."[46] The Other Power is an unconditional power. It works for us and in us not based on who we are and what we are. It delivers us from the worries of this world and assures us entry into the bliss of the Pure Land not because of what we have achieved.

The Buddha who is this Other Power of compassion "is not very far away from them [the Other Power devotees].... they are living with him, in him, rising with him in the morning and retiring at night again with him."[47] Is this not a Pure Land version of "Immanuel"? True, this "Immanuel" is not God-with-us, but Buddha-with-us. But for an ardent soul such as Shinran, on the quest of the meaning of life and the destination of human existence, is not Buddha-with-us none other than God-with-us?

Something at the heart of this religious experience should draw a response, even from Christians. Do we not find ourselves utterly incapable of relying on our own power for doing good? This is also Shinran's self-discovery. Do we not often suppress the voice of conscience and do things contrary to what we say and believe? Shinran has been deeply troubled by this experience. Even in our religious devotion, do we not tend to be calculating, even scheming, to gain God's favor? Shinran admits that he is not above religious hypocrisy. In moments of honest soul-searching, are we not often horrified by what we are capable of in the depths of our hearts? Shinran is no exception to such self-awareness.

I do not believe such religious reflections are different for Christians or for Shinran. At that level of religious awareness we as Christians, Shinran, or people of other faiths have nowhere to hide. We are all naked before one another and before God. That self-awareness, which I believe is the awareness of our un-masked self, the self unembellished with moral niceties and religious pomp, unprotected by wealth and position, unendowed with immortality—to that self-awareness we all have to return to reclaim humanity, to seek enlightenment, and to commit ourselves together to the saving mercy of God.

We as Christians cannot but be amazed by the appearance of Shinran on the religious scene in twelfth-century Japan. It was an appalling time, when Buddhism had lost itself in legalism and was corrupted by power and wealth. External conditions were also harsh, described as "a dreadful tale of storms, earthquakes, conflagrations, plagues, starvation, and cold, when infants could be seen clinging to the breasts of their dead mothers and shivering men stole images of the Buddha for firewood and corpses remained unburied. In the city proper [Kyoto], excluding the suburbs, over forty-two thousand corpses lying in the street were counted in two months. It was a world of pollution, and famine struck not only the capital city, but also all the surrounding provinces...."[48]

It is surely providential that Shinran appeared on the scene to preach the gospel of the infinite mercy of the Buddha. If Shinran had been born in Europe in the twelfth century, he would undoubtedly have called upon people, just as Paul did before him and Luther was to do after him, to entrust themselves to the saving grace of God in Jesus. But the fact is that he was not born in Christian Europe, but in Buddhist Asia. He did not receive his training as a monk in a

Christian monastery, but in a Buddhist monastery. He became a tireless evangelist to suffering people long before the first Roman Catholic missionaries set foot in his land in the seventeenth century. Shinran taught them to put their trust not in themselves, not in the precepts of the official Buddhist church, not in the self-serving ruling power, but in the compassion of the Buddha.

We Christians have to take such historical and religious facts seriously in our appraisal of other religions. In the case of Shinran, it is obvious that he had no way of finding in Jesus that Other Power to save him and others from this suffering world. The only recourse he had was the Buddha and the latter's teaching about the Original Vow made by Amida Buddha. Is this not all that is important for Christians to know? Should this not provide cause for us to offer thanksgiving to God and make us awed by the mysterious ways in which God works within creation? Is this not all that is needed in our practice of Christian faith and theology?

Should some Christians still need evidence of God's universal presence, we could remind them of John the Evangelist's account of the life and message of Jesus:

> In the beginning was the Word, and the Word was with God, and the Word was God. He was in the beginning with God. All things came into being through him, and without him not one thing came into being. What has come into being in him was life, and the life was the light of all people. The light shines in the darkness, and the darkness did not overcome it.
>
> (John 1:1-5)

Christian theology has to go back to these words of John the Evangelist to fathom God's ways with creation. Theology has to begin at the very beginning, not midway, not at the time when Jesus was born two thousand years ago, and not at the fleeting moment of the present. Theology did not begin with Christianity, but was there at the beginning when Christianity had not even been conceived. Theology was God's theology before it became "Christian" theology. Somehow John was able to grasp this fact. That is why his theology begins at the beginning with the story of creation, and not in the recent past with the story of the nativity. Is not the story of nativity a *recent* story in view of the infinite span of time that preceded it?

When theology begins at the beginning, when we engage in theology that precedes Christian theology, then we incorporate all that has been excluded from Christian theology. In addition, what is problematic in Christian theology has to be taken up again, what gives us a headache in Christian theology needs to be diagnosed, and what is objectionable in Christian theology has to be reevaluated. Shinran offers a historical example that challenges us to gain fresh perspectives and develop new depths.

Shinran surprises us with what he says about faith in the Other Power. "As I think of the great ocean of faith," he tells us,

I find it makes no choice between the noble and the humble, between the black-robed and the white-robed. It does not distinguish between male and female, between the old and the young....[49]

With such a statement, Shinran seeks to democratize Buddhism of twelfth-century Japan, to declericalize it, and to question the tradition of strict laws against women. The struggle he initiated continues today, not in Japan alone, but in many nations.

The Believing Heart

What, then, is faith for Shinran? Let us quote a Shin "catechism" summing up its teaching on the Other Power:

Q. What is the Shin faith?

A. The easiest of all faiths. You have been in it for the last ten years and it is only that you are not conscious of it yourself.

Q. What shall I do to have the faith?

A. Nothing much but to hear.

Q. How shall I hear?

A. Just as The Other wills. When you hear a storyteller, you just hear him. All the labor is on his side. As he talks, you hear him. There is no special way of hearing. When you have heard, that is the time when *Namu-amida-butsu* has entered into your heart.

Q. If so, is just hearing enough?

A. Yes.

Q. Even then, I have fears as to my really hearing it: Did I hear or not? What shall I do with this?

A. This is not hearing but thinking. No thinking is needed here. Faith is awakened by hearing. Don't be caught here. If you reflect and begin to ask yourself whether you have faith or not, you turn your back toward Amida.[50]

"Faith is awakened by hearing." Does this not sound familiar even to Christian ears?

It is Paul, if you remember, who writes: "So faith comes from what is heard, and what is heard comes through the word of Christ" (Rom. 10:17). Hearing is of utmost importance both for Pure Land Buddhists as well as for Christians. But what do we hear? Shinran and his followers hear that it is faith not in their self-power but in the Other Power that delivers them from the evil of this world and brings them to the Pure Land of bliss. Christians hear that it is not by faith in ourselves but by the grace of God that we are restored to right relationship with God.

How do we come to have such faith? For Shinran and his followers it is through the compassion of Amida Buddha, who has turned back from the threshold of the Pure Land and returned to the world to be with suffering humanity. That is why Shinran and his followers have resorted to *nembutsu,* that is, "to think of Buddha, to keep in memory the Buddha." The aim is "to be embraced in the grace of Amida by repeatedly pronouncing his name."[51] But *nembutsu* is not merely a mental exercise or wishful thinking. It is faith in action. It is "meant to exhaust the power of a finite mind which, when it comes to this pass or *impasse,* throws itself down at the feet of something it knows not exactly what, except that the something is an infinite reality."[52]

For Christians, the heart of their faith is Jesus, the Word of God that "became flesh and dwelt among us" (John 1:14). It is

> at the name of Jesus [that]
> > every knee should bend,
> > in heaven and on earth and under the earth,
> and every tongue should confess
> > that Jesus Christ is Lord,
> > to the glory of God the Father.
> > > > > (Phil. 2:10-11)

This is a hymn that the early Christian community directed to Jesus, the Word of God, to whom God gave "the name that is above every name" (Phil. 2:9).

For past two thousand years Christians have been bending their knees to Jesus Christ their Lord and calling upon men and women to do the same. Shinran and his followers have also been calling upon the name of Amida, throwing themselves down at the feet of "something [they know] not exactly what." Thus, perhaps, ends any semblance of Pure Land Buddhism to Christianity. Thus, perhaps, resolves any similarity between the two faiths. But does it?

For Shinran and his followers, they have not left their faith vague, enigmatic, and hollow. That "something [they know] not exactly what" is "an infinite reality." Amida represents this infinite reality. Amida, insofar as he is infinite, cannot be apprehended. But as an infinite *reality,* Amida can be apprehended by faith.

In a similar way, Jesus who was born, lived, and died in Palestine two thousand years ago can be apprehended historically, but Jesus as the Word of God—as an infinite *reality* called the Word and Christ—can only be apprehended by faith. Faith, both in Pure Land Buddhism and in Christianity, is the key to unlock the mystery of the divine. It is also the code that gains us access to the reality called God, who eludes our rational cognition.

What, then, is faith? It is the heart that believes, or the believing heart (*xin xin* in Chinese, *shinjin* in Japanese). *Xin (citta* in Sanskrit) is "the heart, mind and soul. It is the seat of thought or intelligence."[53] It stands for the whole person. It *is* the whole person. This is also the way the heart is understood in the Hebrew Scriptures. It is "the innermost spring of individual life, the ultimate source of all its physical, intellectual, emotional, and volitional energies, and consequently the part of a human being through which he [or she] normally achieved contact with the divine."[54]

Faith for Shinran and for the sect of Pure Land Buddhism is the commitment of the total person of the believer to the Other Power of Amida Buddha. It is the unconditional trust in that power for one's salvation.

> [F]aith is the heart and mind without doubt; it is *shinjin*, which is true and real.... To be free of self-power, having entrusted oneself to the Other Power of the Primal Vow—this is *faith alone*.[55]

This is the "gospel" Shinran spent all his life to bring to the women and men shut out of official Buddhism and suffering under feudal rulers and warriors.

People without power and means in Shinran's day, those who lived at the mercy of those who had power over their life and death, needed this kind of faith. Faith, the heart that believes, is most vividly expressed as follows: "Sake (Japanese wine) cannot be poured into an overturned cup, but when it stands in its natural position, anybody can pour sake into it and as fully as it can hold. Therefore, have *the cup of your heart* upright ready to receive, and hear; it will surely be filled with Amida's mercy."[56]

Hold "the cup of your heart" upright, ready to receive Amida's mercy and to be filled with it! Can we not paraphrase this saying and apply it to Christian faith: Hold the cup of your heart upright, ready to receive God's saving love in Jesus and to be filled with it? Is this not how miracles of faith happen? And is it not such faith that Jesus says can move mountains?

Part Five

LOVE

No one has greater love than this,
to lay down one's life for one's friends.

—John 15:13

An Allegory

An Andalusian shepherd boy travels in search of a worldly treasure. From his home in Spain he journeys to the markets of Tangiers and across the Egyptian desert. "The wind told me that you know about love," the boy said to the sun. "If you know about love, you must know about the Soul of the World, because it's made of love."

"From where I am," the sun said, "I can see the Soul of the World. It communicates with my soul, and together we cause the plants to grow and the sheep to seek our shade. From where I am—and I am a long way from the earth—I learned how to love. I know that if I came even a little bit closer to the earth, everything there would die, and the Soul of the World would no longer exist. So we contemplate each other, and we want each other, and I give it life and warmth, and it gives me my reason for living."

"So you know about love," the boy said.

"And I know the Soul of the World, because we have talked at great length to each other during this endless trip through the universe. It tells me that its greatest problem is that, up until now, only the minerals and vegetables understand that all things are one. That there's no need for iron to be the same as copper, or copper the same as gold. Each performs its own exact function as a unique being, and everything would be a symphony of peace if the hand that wrote all this had stopped on the fifth day of creation.

"But there was a sixth day," the sun went on.

"You are wise, because you observe everything from a distance," the boy said. "But you don't know about love. If there hadn't been a sixth day, human beings would not exist; copper would always be just copper,

265

and lead just lead. It's true that everything has its destiny, but one day that destiny will be realized. So each thing has to transform itself into something better, and to acquire a new destiny, until someday, the Soul of the World becomes one thing only."

The sun thought about that, and decided to shine more brightly. The wind, which was enjoying the conversation, started to blow with greater force, so that the sun would not blind the boy.

"Well, why did you say that I don't know about love?" the sun asked the boy.

"Because it's not love to be static like the desert, nor is it love to roam the world like the wind. And it's not love to see everything from a distance, like you do. Love is the force that transforms and improves the Soul of the World. When I first reached through to it, I thought the Soul of the World was perfect. But later, I could see that it was like other aspects of creation and had its own passions and wars. It is we who nourish the Soul of the World, and the world we live in will be either better or worse, depending on whether we become better or worse. And that's where the power of love comes in. Because when we love, we always strive to become better than we are."

The boy reached through to the Soul of the World, and saw that it was a part of the Soul of God. And he saw that the Soul of God was his own soul. And that he, a boy, could perform miracles.[1]

Chapter 11

The World-Soul of Love

Life, hope, and faith. These have been stations in our theological journey. Life with all its complexity and simplicity, hope in the midst of perversity and perplexity, and faith that sustains life in hope against hope—this is the reality each of us faces, cherishes, and grapples with as we go through our pilgrimage on earth. But is there life not nurtured by love? Is hope true if not informed by love? And is faith still faith if not inspired by love?

These questions remind us of the words with which Paul ended his celebrated chapter on love in his first letter to the Christians at Corinth: "And now faith, hope, and love abide, these three; and the greatest of these is love" (1 Cor. 13:13). Paul is right. Love is the greatest of all these. It is a glorious thing; there is no question about it. But the fact is that it also creates pain, agony, and suffering. Love, in spite of its glory, is never far from tragic happenings in human life and history.

This is the paradox of love: where there is much love there is much pain; where there is little love there is little pain. The paradox seems to mean that pain and agony make love great and deep. But this is only part of the truth. It is also true, and perhaps more true, that without love agony cannot be relieved, pain healed, and tragedy redeemed. In love heaven and earth coexist. In it good and evil struggle for domination. And in love the divine purges and redeems the love that is self-serving and abusive. It is the paradox of love that we find in a story from ancient Vietnam, called "A Song of Enlightenment."

A Song of Enlightenment

"A long time ago," the story begins, "in a fight for justice a proud boy chopped off another boy's arm with his family sword. The victorious boy, believing the battle was over, gave thanks, sheathed his weapons, and went home." He got engaged to the orphan girl his grandmother had raised to be his wife. But another war broke out. He enlisted and was "gone a long time, during which he distinguished himself in many battles." He was elated and happy, totally unaware of tragic happenings at home.

> When he returned, however, he found his home in shambles. The crops had failed, the animals had run away, and the house itself was in disrepair.

267

When he opened the door, he was greeted by his fiancée, who now looked as old as the grandmother he remembered.

"What happened?" he asked in astonishment. "Why has my home been ruined? Where is my grandmother? What's happened to you?"

"It was horrible," the fiancée said, falling weeping in his arms. "After you left, the boy whose arm you cut off came back and took revenge against us. He killed your grandmother and chopped her into pieces, then he raped me, pillaged our house, and burned our farm."

The boy-turned-soldier already had his ancestral sword half-drawn in rage when he cried, "I will avenge this atrocity! Justice and virtue must prevail!"

On his way down the road, he stopped at his grandmother's grave and prayed for the strength and courage he would need to avenge her. While he was praying, his old enemy appeared. But instead of striking him from behind or calling him to combat, the enemy fell to his knees and begged the soldier to behead him for the wrong he had committed.

The soldier, believing his prayer for justice had been answered, drew his sword and prepared to strike, when a bell sounded in a nearby temple. The soldier paused as a song, borne on the wind in a chorus of ghostly voices—now his grandmother's, now the victims he and his ancestors had killed in war, now the voices of his own children yet-to-be-born—filled the air around him:

> Late afternoon—
> Hear the bell—
> The bell wakes up
> My soul—
>
> We must hurry to become
> Enlightened—
> We must kneel beneath the tree of
> Buddha—
> We look into the face of god and
> Forget the past—
>
> To forgive our brother is to forgive
> Ourselves—
> We abandon our revenge;
> Our lives have seen suffering enough.
>
> We are tired and worn out with
> Ourselves—
>
> If I take revenge, it will be the cause;
> The effect will follow me into my next life.

> Look into the mirror: see the compassion in your heart.
> Avoid all resentment and hatred for
> Humankind—

The soldier, having had his passion interrupted by the bell and his spirit awakened by the song, put away his sword and helped his enemy get up.

"Go your own way," the soldier said. "I took your arm, and that cannot be replaced; but I could have had your life, and this I have returned to you."

"Go your way in peace," the one-armed man replied. "I took your loved ones, it's true, and what's done cannot be undone; but I, too, have returned to you your life: for my brothers would have avenged me even though you had my head."

So the two men, no longer boys, parted and began new lives. To commemorate the breaking of the circle of vengeance, the temple bell now rings twice each day and reminds the people to arrest their passions long enough to think; and having thought, to hear the song of enlightenment.[1]

This is a story of vengeance, an account of human tragedy in life and in history. But this is also a story of reconciliation, of how love and compassion can heal the wounds we human beings inflict on one another. The story makes us Christians reflect deeply; it comes from a Buddhist country devastated by the war waged against it by the combined military forces of the government of Vietnam, ruled by a Roman Catholic family, and the United States of America, a nation said to be under God.

Justice and Virtue Must Prevail?

Vietnam, a socialist republic in Southeast Asia, is a nation of almost seventy million people. Like other nations in Asia, Vietnam has embarked on the road from an agricultural economy to a free-market economy. It has become a growing market and has attracted foreign investments, ended its isolation from the rest of the world, and seemed bent on following the steps of some other Asian nations that have achieved economic development. Most of these economic developments have been achieved at the cost of human development, with rampant corruption in government and in society. Still, Vietnam must have development if it is to be a competitive nation in the world. This is at once a promising and disquieting prospect, but, as for other Asians, this seems an inevitable path for Vietnam to travel in the years to come.

This fact is particularly sad for Vietnam, which has barely recovered from the colossal tragedy of the Vietnam War. We know that 58,000 American men and women were killed in action. But we also know that millions of Vietnamese—Vietcong and civilians, including women and children, Cambodians and Laotians—also lost their lives. While the war raged and devastated the land

and its people, Vietnam was an inferno of heart-breaking cries and screams from torture and death. It became a realm of terror and fear, an arena in which human beings were nothing but bodies to be counted when dead, statistics in battlefield reports. Both sides claimed to fight for the virtues of freedom and peace. The antagonists engaged in deadly combat justified the atrocities they were committing in the name of justice. But totally absent was the virtue called love; even justice checked by love was rejected as cowardice. The worst and most demonic influences in humanity were turned loose, dictating the actions of the planners of war, and the actions of those who executed the plan. Human beings ceased to be created in the image of God, but in the image of the devil—depersonalized, cold-blooded, heartless, and ferocious.

This is what happened, for instance, at My Lai in March 1968. Hundreds of unarmed civilians were herded out from their homes and slaughtered. They were stabbed to death with bayonets, killed at gunpoint, machine-gunned, and blown to bits by grenades. When the carnage was finally over, the entire village had been wiped out, leaving only a few survivors. Was this not a hell created by human beings turned devils? "When Army investigators reached the barren area in November 1969, in connection with the My Lai probe in the United States," reported a Pulitzer Prize–winning journalist, "they found mass graves at three sites, as well as a ditch full of bodies. It was estimated that between 450 and 500 people—most of them women, children and old men—had been slain and buried alive."[2]

Each child, woman, and man slain on that day in My Lai is testimony to what the world is like when love is shut out of the human heart and mind. Here is one testimony: "A woman came out of a hut with a baby in her arms and she was crying. She was crying because her little boy had been in front of their hut and . . . someone had killed the child by shooting it. When the mother came into view [she was] shot with an M16 and she fell. When she fell, she dropped the baby. . . . The infant was also killed."[3] Such scenes were repeated as if no one was in control of the universe except human beings who had turned into demonic forces intent on destroying it. The entire creation seemed shocked into silence; even God seemed to turn away, weeping, not daring to look.

A thirty-year-old peasant by the name of Nguyen Khoa had to witness an excruciating horror. He saw "a thirteen-year-old girl who was raped before being killed. GIs then attacked Khoa's wife, tearing off her clothes. Before they could rape her, however, Khoa said, their six-year-old son, riddled with bullets, fell and saturated her with blood. The GIs left her alone. . . ."[4] The story causes excruciating pain in our hearts and in our stomachs. But there is something in the story that has profound theological significance. It is this: the six-year-old son, riddled with bullets, fell and saturated his mother with his blood and saved her life.

We know how important blood is to life. Healthy blood brings good health; unhealthy blood, bad health. Good blood circulation gives us physical well-being. But blood is much more. Blood is life. When drained of blood, life expires. The Hebrew Scriptures contain a divine injunction not to eat "flesh with its life, that is, its blood" (Gen. 9:4; see also Deut. 12:23). This is a serious injunction, for "whoever eats it shall be cut off" (Lev. 17:14). Is this a stern warning against murder? Is it the implicit recognition that life is given by God and thus belongs to God, and that human beings have no right to dispose of it?

The point is that blood relates not only to our physical well-being but to our religious well-being as well. "It is," we are told in the Hebrew Scriptures, "the blood that makes atonement" (Lev. 17:11). *Atonement* is a heavily loaded theological word referring to "ways of understanding the manner in which the salvation of humanity is possible through the life, death and resurrection of Christ."[5] The Christian doctrine of atonement has its origin in the rites of sacrifice practiced in ancient Israel. The blood of the sacrificial animal was poured on the altar, its life given up to absolve human sins and to restore human relationship with God. Christianity has taken over this Hebrew rite of atonement and developed "theories of atonement." Christianity not only has made sin a necessary "prerequisite" of atonement, but has turned the doctrine into a legal transaction between God and the devil, with human beings, and particularly Christians, the sole beneficiaries.

In Christian faith and theology we have, in this way, strayed very far from what the word *atonement* meant originally and from the fundamental religious tenet it represented. It has been pointed out that "the English word 'atone' is derived from the phrase 'at one.'... Similarly, 'atonement' originally meant 'at-onement,' or 'reconciliation.' In modern usage, however,... 'to atone for' a wrong is to take some action which cancels out the ill effects it has had."[6]

It is this "modern usage" of the word *atonement* that has come to prevail in Christianity in its faith and theology of the cross. The result has been not only to misrepresent God and God's dealing with humanity but to narrow God's activity almost solely to "atonement of the sin of disobedience and salvation of individual souls."

In a very strange way—perhaps providential also?—the story of the blood of the six-year-old who saved his mother by saturating her with his blood enables us once again to grasp the word *atonement* as meaning "to be at one with" or "at-onement." The blood of the little boy that saturated his mother was his life. His life was in his blood. Fatally shot, his blood poured out from him and saturated his mother, covering her and saving her life. With his blood, he became "at one with" his mother. His life is now at one with the life of his mother. He lives as long as his mother lives. He is dead, yet alive with his mother. He is gone, yet he is present in her. Dead yet living, son and mother have become one.

Whether the boy was conscious of all this is not the question. The blood that poured out of him and saturated his mother is the testimony of that oneness of life it created. Is this not an eloquent, although tragic, testimony to the "atonement" that can take place between human beings? Does not this kind of "atonement" enable us Christians to come to grips more deeply with what has taken place between Jesus on the cross and the rest of humanity? Does it not also prompt us to look more humbly into the heart of God—the heart that bleeds for the blood human beings, such as the six-year-old Vietnamese boy, had to shed?

Wrong in Retrospect

The reflection on atonement takes us back to the Last Supper, shortly before Jesus was to be arrested, tried, and sentenced to die on the cross. It is reported that he takes the bread and breaks it, saying to those present: "Take; this is my body" (Mark 14:22; also Matt. 26:26; Luke 22:19). This is a drama both real and symbolic, for both the bread and his body will be broken. Over the wine he says: "This is my blood of the covenant, which is poured out for many" (Mark 14:24; also Matt. 26:28; Luke 22:20). This is even more real and symbolic. Wine is red; blood is also red. If his followers did not comprehend the symbolism of the broken bread, how could they fail to grasp the meaning of the red wine Jesus is pouring into their cups? Blood is life. The wine he likens to his blood is his own life. He is going to pour out his life for many—for his followers present at the supper, for tax collectors and "sinners" with whom he has kept company, for the crowd who welcomed him to Jerusalem with "Hosannas" and who later shouted for his crucifixion, even for his religious enemies who brought about his death. The world has not been the same since.

In many arenas of life and history, and particularly in war, there seems to be neither justice nor virtue. Win or lose, justice is abused and virtue is subverted. In the case of the My Lai massacre, the GIs who committed the atrocity had no justice on their side, though they might pretend that they were carrying out the order to exterminate enemy Vietcong. But how could the babies they murdered have been Vietcong? When committing the crime of murder, they also betrayed whatever virtues they learned at home, school, and in church. How could they be accountable to even the rudimentary values of human beings when they riddled a six-year-old boy with bullets?

True, there has been no lack of soul-searching in the United States in twenty years after the Vietnam War ended. This is a sign of hope, although we are not sure whether the bitter lessons thus learned will serve humanity in the future. But soul-searching we must do.

Who better to undergo soul-searching than a person heavily involved in the decision making and execution of the Vietnam War? I am referring to Robert McNamara, who served as defense secretary in the Kennedy and Johnson administrations. Because his is a candid and honest soul-searching, it makes some of us more frightful of what those in power can do to unleash the demonic power of death in the world.

We of the Kennedy and Johnson administrations who participated in the decisions on Vietnam acted according to what we thought were the principles and traditions of this nation. We made our decisions in light of these values. Yet we were wrong, terribly wrong.[7]

What are we to make of this candid and honest admission on the part of a principal policy maker?

Those who held power in the U.S. government "acted according to what [they] thought were the principles and traditions of their nation." And yet, twenty years later, one of them says: "We were wrong, terribly wrong." Does this not make one shudder to the core? Does it not prompt one to call foul on behalf of some sixty thousand Americans and millions of Vietnamese who died in the war? If the war was wrong—not only wrong, but *terribly* wrong—"in retrospect," are not the principles and traditions of the United States, according to which American GIs acted, wrong? Are they not *terribly* wrong? What are these principles and traditions? They are principles of justice and equality, traditions of peace and democracy.

What is said in retrospect amounts to an indictment of the foundation of the United States. McNamara's indictment is that in these principles and traditions there is neither justice nor virtue. This is a big indictment, because the United States is supposed to have been founded on the Christian faith. But it does not take the Vietnamese men and women who died during the Vietnam War to say that there is no justice, no virtue, in these principles and traditions. The indigenous people of the United States, their world turned upside down and their land taken away, and the African Americans with the bitter experience of slavery, would also declare that there is neither justice nor virtue in these principles and traditions, according to which "the best and the brightest"[8] in high echelons of government acted. Perhaps this is the most profound lesson anyone in the United States can learn.

If there is neither justice nor virtue, there should still be love—if not in the high places of power, then in persons and places devastated by war. The six-year-old Vietnamese boy's blood proved to be life for his mother. His blood became a living proof of love, the love that saved her and that gave her life. What is love if not a blood relationship? The mother had carried her son for nine months in her womb. For six years she nourished and protected him. Now she carries his blood in her soul and nourishes it in her memories. Her six-year-old son died tragically, but he lives in her and with her, embraced in love and affection.

This is what love is. This is the tragic sense of love. There is no true love without it. But love is not true if it does not become redeeming, if not in life then in death. But in this case death was life. The six-year-old boy died to live in his mother. The bond of love between the two turned death into life, a life no power on earth, not even M16 rifles, could destroy. Love is stronger than any power on earth, even the power of death. This is the power of love that makes Jesus victorious on the cross.

No miracle happened on the cross. God seemed powerless to intervene. Injustice and crime seemed to have triumphed. But there is the power of love with which the powers of this world have not reckoned. And history ever since the cross gives testimony of how the power of that love hidden in the hearts of humanity gives birth to life, nurtures it, and redeems it. One witness after another tells how the power of love concealed in the depths of God's creation saves life, renews it, and transforms it.

We do not know why love has to work in the midst of tragedies. But is there not a reverse side? If there were no love at work in the midst of human tragedies, what would humanity become and what would the world turn into? The cross is a tragedy, a supreme tragedy. We human beings will continue to erect crosses for ourselves as long as we live and as long as the world lasts. If this is sure, there is something else which is also sure: love will be at work to the end of the world and until the end of time. This is not empty faith. No, God cannot leave the world alone without love.

A Human Shield

Let us revisit that scene of horrors at My Lai. We are not through with it. We have not yet seen all the miraculous work of love in the midst of the hell turned loose on the helpless women, old men, children, and babies.

On that day a helicopter pilot, Chief Warrant Officer Hugh Thompson of Decatur, Georgia, was flying over My Lai. He saw how women and children were being mercilessly slaughtered, including "a bloodied but unhurt two-year-old boy miraculously crawling out of the ditch, crying," who was grabbed, thrown back into the ditch, and shot. Thompson was enraged, "almost frantic." He also "noticed a group of mostly women and children huddled together in a bunker near the drainage ditch." He landed his helicopter.

> Before climbing out of his aircraft, Thompson ordered . . . his crew that "if any of the Americans opened up on the Vietnamese, they should open up on the Americans." He walked back to the ship and called in two helicopter gun ships to rescue the civilians. While waiting for them to land, "he stood between our troops and the bunker. He was shielding the people with his body. He just wanted to get those people out of there." The helicopters landed, with Thompson still standing between the GIs and the Vietnamese, and quickly rescued nine persons—two old men, two women and five children. One of the children later died on route to the hospital.[9]

That someone—and two other soldiers who assisted Thompson—could perform such actions in a situation in which might is justice and violence is virtue is almost beyond imagination. But it did happen.

This is a story of putting one's life on the line, not to save oneself, but to save others—not to shield one's fellow soldiers from the enemies but to shield "the enemies" from one's fellow soldiers. Hugh Thompson, the American helicopter pilot, was no friend of the Vietnamese civilians. All he knew was that they were women, old men, and children and that they were totally exposed to the killing frenzy of his fellow soldiers. They were frightened victims of the GIs, who had turned into human predators. He had seen many of the civilians murdered in cold blood. He could hear their last-minute pleas, cries, and screams. He could see their faces, contorted and white with terror. He could also see their bodies strewn on the ground, full of blood but lifeless.

It seemed that nothing would prevent the same fate from overtaking these women, old men, and children "so frightened that their souls had already left them" (*hun bu fu ti*), to use a Chinese idiom, meaning that they were frightened out of their wits. Short of a miracle, their fates would be the same as the other villagers. But for them a miracle did happen. It happened in the person of Hugh Thompson, who planted himself between them and his fellow GIs to shield the Vietnamese from the bayonets, M16s, and grenades. Thompson remained in that position until they—two old men, two women and five children—were rescued and taken to safety in the two helicopter gunships he had called in for that purpose.

What motivated Thompson to put himself in harm's way? What prompted him to expose himself to an impossible position? What inspired him to take an almost suicidal action? Was it the military honor he had been trained to respect and keep? But infringement upon military honor on the battlefield and in enemy territory is a rule rather than an exception. Was it a sense of outrage that set in motion a series of actions he took to rescue those Vietnamese civilians?

The Heart of Compassion

Perhaps it was what Mencius (371–289 B.C.E.?), the most renowned Confucianist after Confucius, called *ce yin zi xin,* translated as "feeling of commiseration," in Thompson that compelled him to do what he did. According to Mencius, "the feeling of commiseration is found in all people."[10] *Commiseration* in English refers to "the feeling or expression of sorrow for another's suffering or trouble, of pity, sympathy."[11] What Mencius terms *ce yin zi xin* does encompass sorrow, pity, and sympathy caused by the suffering or trouble of others. Although it may be debatable, and it has been debated in China, as to whether all human beings are endowed with the feeling, it is generally true that most people show pity and sympathy for those in misery and pain. As for Hugh Thompson, he did show that he had plenty of such "commiseration."

But is this all that Mencius meant by *ce yin zi xin?* Is it all that prompted Hugh Thompson to do what he did? There must be something more than "the feeling of commiseration" in Mencius's *ce yin zi xin* and in what Thompson did. As far as Mencius is concerned, he seems to expand what he means by *ce yin zi xin:*

[T]he heart (*xin*) of compassion and mercy (*ce yin zi xin*) is what we call
    humanity (*ren*);
the heart (*xin*) of shame and detestation (*xiu wu*) is what we call
    righteousness (*yi*);
the heart (*xin*) of respect and reverence (*gong jing*) is what we call
    propriety (*li*);
the heart (*xin*) of right and wrong (*shi fei*) is what we call wisdom....[12]

These can be said to constitute the four basic tenets of Mencius's teaching on
human relationships in society.

The bedrock of these four tenets—compassion and mercy, shame and detestation, respect and reverence, right and wrong—is the heart (*xin*). The heart is
not just feeling. Nor is it merely sensibility. The heart does not only stand for
how we are affected by what we see and witness outside of us. It is the consciousness of what we are as human beings. It is humanity in us. It is that which
makes us what we are. The heart represents the whole of us. We as persons
are defined by our hearts. To be aware of the heart in us is to be aware of us
as human persons. To speak from the heart is to speak with all sincerity and
honesty as a human being. Human relationship is thus a heart-to-heart affair.

What then makes up the heart? In other words, what makes a person a person? Similarly, what makes a human being human? The answer relates to the
four tenets Mencius emphasizes in his discourse, and the most basic of these
four is "the heart of compassion" (*ce yin zi xin*). "The heart of compassion,"
according to Mencius, is "the heart that cannot bear to see the suffering of
others."[13] To illustrate his point, he mentions that "when people suddenly see a
child about to fall into a well, they all have a feeling of alarm and distress, not
to gain the favor of the child's parents, nor to seek the praise of their neighbors
and friends, nor because they dislike the reputation of *having been unmoved by
such a thing* [if they did not rescue the child]."[14]

This reminds us of an occasion on which Jesus encountered religious leaders
concerning the sabbath (Matt. 12:9-14; also Mark 3:1-16; Luke 6:6-11). They
were all in the synagogue on a particular sabbath. It so happened that there was
a man with a withered hand in their midst. What could be a better opportunity
to bring him to the attention of Jesus and to trap Jesus with the question on the
sabbath? "Is it lawful," they asked Jesus, "to cure on the sabbath?" (Matt. 12:10).
His answer was meant to touch their hearts rather than the letter of the law:
"Suppose one of you has only one sheep and it falls into a pit on the sabbath;
will you not lay hold of it and lift it out?"

Jesus' opponents were put on the defensive. They racked their brains to find
a reason to rebut him. But Jesus did not give them much time. He came straight
to his point: "How much more valuable is a human being than a sheep! So it is
lawful to do good on the sabbath" (Matt. 12:11-12). In another version of the
story Jesus turned the table on his adversaries, and asked them: "Is it lawful to

do good or to do harm on the sabbath, to save life or to kill?" (Mark 3:4; also Luke 6:9). His adversaries got it all wrong. When a life is at stake, the life of a sheep and, even more, the life of a human being, what is tested is not the law, however sacrosanct it may be, but your heart—you as a human being. In this Jesus got everything right.

So Mencius got it right, too. The heart of compassion (*ce yin zi xin*) is the heart moved by the sight of a child falling into the pit. It is the heart aroused to take action without any ulterior motives. If we all have that kind of heart—and Mencius teaches that we do—then the other cardinal tenets that constitute humanity can be evoked as well. He concludes:

> From such a case [of rescuing a child from the pit], we see that a person without the *heart* of compassion is not a human being; a person without the *heart* of shame and detestation is not a human being; a person without the *heart* of deference and humility (*rang*) is not a human being; a person without the *heart* of right and wrong is not a human being.[15]

This is the best of Confucian humanism. It resonates with other views of human beings developed elsewhere.

But this is more than humanism. Human being endowed with such *heart* (*xin*) can rise to the occasion when self-sacrifice is called for. Such a heart enables us to go beyond the limits of what we normally believe we can do. What else can we call it? How best do we name it? We can call it "the heart of love," the heart empowered by love, and the heart charged with love. That Mencius in ancient China could envision such love in human beings, and inculcate princes and rulers with it in the hope that there would be peace and justice in society, cannot but impress us. Although he did not use the word *love* as in the Bible and in Christianity, is this not what love is?

The Heart of Shame

What Hugh Thompson demonstrated in My Lai is what Mencius calls *ce yin zi xin* (the heart of compassion) or what we Christians call "love." His love was not soft sentiment. It was pained by the sense of shame caused by his fellow soldiers committing such unspeakable atrocities against helpless women, old men, and children. Such love was not indulgence. It was inflamed with the sense of detestation for the terrible wrong done to others. Such love was the courage not to confuse wrong with right, not to tolerate a heinous crime such as the crime committed against those defenseless Vietnamese villagers.

Love is thus not neutral. A neutral love is not love, but at most a kind of lukewarm love. One recalls what is said about the church in Laodicea in the Book of Revelation: "You are neither cold nor hot. I wish that you were either cold or hot....you are lukewarm" (Rev. 3:15-16). Lukewarm love does not have passion for life. It does not become excited by the joys of life, nor is it anguished by despair. It does not take sides. What it does is sit on the fence, watching with disinterest what is happening on both sides of the fence. Lukewarm love does not commit itself to a particular view or position. Commitment is not its virtue. Rather, it shies away from committing to a cause, runs away from people beset with trouble, and evades responsibilities relating to family, community, and society.

Mencius's *ce yin zi xin* (compassion) is not neutral love. If it were, it would not be moved by the sight of a child falling into the pit, and the person would not hasten to rescue it. Jesus' love is anything but neutral. If it were, he would not have challenged the religious leaders with the question of whether they would not rescue a sheep fallen into a ditch on the sabbath. Surely, neutral love is not the love with which Jesus dealt with poor and disinherited women and men. He committed himself to them, took their side, and identified the reign of God among them. Neutral love is not the form of compassion that prompted Hugh Thompson to place himself between the Vietnamese, stricken with the terror of death, and the GIs with their guns trained on them. If it were, he would have turned away from them, closed his eyes, and shut his ears to their desperate pleas for life. Neutral love, by being detached and indifferent, is an immoral love. And love that is immoral is not love. It is cynicism. It is a betrayal of love.

Mencius's *ce yin zi xin* is informed by a sense of shame. It is said in feudal Japan that people, particularly those of the samurai (warrior) class, would commit suicide out of the sense of shame. Even the slightest incident in which one's honor were stained or marred could cause a person to commit suicide. Mencius is not advocating such extreme practices. But he is saying that a person with no sense of shame, and, by inference, no sense of honor, is what Confucius calls *xiao ren* (a mean person) in contrast to *jun zi* (an honorable person).[16] What is the difference between the two kinds of people? "The honorable person," says Confucius, "thinks of virtue; the mean person thinks of possessions. The superior person thinks of the sanctions [of the law]; the mean person thinks of personal favors."[17]

An interesting episode illustrates how Confucius remained an honorable man in a trying situation. He and his disciples had made their way to the country of Chen. It so happens that "their provisions were exhausted, and his followers became so ill that they were unable to rise." The situation was so serious that one of his disciples, called Tse-lu, "with evident dissatisfaction . . . said: 'Has the honorable person likewise to endure in this way?' " Was this sarcasm, desperation, or anger? Perhaps all. In response,

> The Master said, "The honorable person may indeed have to endure want, but the mean person, when he is in want, gives way to unbridled license."[18]

Confucius was not to be ruffled. He used the adverse occasion to drive home to his followers the difference between an honorable person and a mean person.

One only wishes that a spirit such as the spirit demonstrated by Confucius, and not rigid teachings and rituals, had been able to shape China more deeply, its life, history, and especially its politics. As far as Mencius is concerned, he not only inherited this legacy of the Master Confucius, but expanded and promoted it in his time. An honorable person possesses a strong sense of shame and shows intense detestation for cowardice, dishonesty, and treachery, not to mention injury and murder. Such a sense of shame—shame for what his fellow GIs had done to turn themselves into savages, to create an inferno of death, and to dishonor their country—must have prompted Hugh Thompson to risk his own life to save the victims of war. Is this sense of shame not part of what we call compassion or love?

Love that has no sense of shame for the powerful oppressing the powerless is not love. Love not moved by a sense of shame for the rich exploiting the poor is not love. Love that remains indifferent to women, men, and children who suffer injustice, be it racial, sexual, political, or economic, is not love. Love not empowered by a sense of shame for crimes committed against humanity is not love. Such love has nothing to do with God. This is not God's love. God's love is the kind of love Jesus pours out for Jerusalem when he laments: "Jerusalem, Jerusalem, the city that kills the prophets and stones those who are sent to it! How often have I desired to gather your children together as a hen gathers her brood under her wings, and you were not willing!" (Matt. 23:37; also Luke 13:34). In Jesus' lament there is a deep sense of shame for the horrors committed in that "holy" city. There is also extreme sadness welling out of his heart for the city's destiny. This is love. This is Jesus' love. In it is disclosed God's love.

The Heart of Propriety

Mencius's *ce yin zi xin* is related to the heart that knows respect for others and the spirit of humility. This is what is called *li*, propriety. A person who has no *li* considers him- or herself the center of everything. One's likes and dislikes become the paramount preoccupation. One's whims dictate what one does in certain situations. There is no consideration for others for others' sake. This is what Mencius has seen in rulers and sovereigns and he, just like his mentor Confucius, has not spared effort to stress to them the importance of *li* in government, in society, and in human relationships. Above all, the heart of *li* is respect and reverence for life.

In Mencius we have a rare glimpse of an indomitable spirit similar to the prophets in ancient Israel. On one occasion he tells King Hui of Liang straight in the face:

> Your dogs and swine eat the food of people, and you do not make any restrictive arrangements. There are people dying from famine on the roads and you do not issue the stores of your granaries for them. When people die, you say, "It is not owing to me; it is owing to the year." In what does this differ from stabbing a man killing him, and then saying—"It was not

I; it was the weapon?" Let your majesty cease to lay blame on the year, and instantly from all the nation the people will come to you.[19]

Such straight talk is designed to awaken in the king the heart of *ce yin* (compassion) and the heart of *li* (respect and reverence) for his people.

It is such a heart of *li* (respect and reverence) for life that Jesus tried to awaken in the people of his time. "You have heard that it was said to those of ancient times, 'You shall not murder'; and 'whoever murders shall be liable to judgment.' But I say to you that if you are angry with a brother or sister, you will be liable to judgment" (Matt. 5:21-22). Jesus is referring to a commandment (Exod. 20:13) among the Ten Commandments, which everybody knows. He goes beyond a question of law to the heart of the matter: that respect and reverence for life and for one another is not merely for self-protection or even for a good society. The root of *ce yin*, the heart of *li*, Jesus is saying, is love rooted in God. Such love affirms that God not only allows "humans to do no damage to one another," but nothing that "gives birth to physical violence and murder."[20]

But in a very true sense, human history is a history of violence and murder. This is the case among tribes, within a nation, and in the world of nations. The Vietnam War was just one example, and what happened at My Lai was another startling testimony. But in that war and in any other war there have been exceptions. At My Lai, Hugh Thompson was one exception. Not bearing to see these Vietnamese women, old men, and children herded to death, he was able to stop the carnage long enough to get them to safety. What motivated him? Heroism? Rewards? None of these. It must have been what Mencius called the heart of *li*, "the respect and reverence" for life, that prompted him to action.

The Heart of Right and Wrong

Mencius's *ce yin zi xin*, the heart of compassion, is also the heart that stands for what is right against what is wrong. This, according to Mencius, is the heart of wisdom (*zhi*). We are often faced with dilemmas in life, having to decide what to do and what not to do, what to take and what to reject, what to choose and what to repudiate. Mencius points to the problem with a metaphor of a fish and a bear's paw. "I like fish and I also like bear's paw," he says. "If I cannot have both of them, I shall give up the fish and choose the bear's paw."[21] He then extends this metaphor and applies it to situations of life:

> I like life and I also like righteousness. If I cannot have both of them, I shall give up life and choose righteousness. I love life, but there is something I love more than life and therefore I will not do anything improper to have it. I also hate death, but there is something I hate more than death, and therefore there are occasions when I will not avoid danger.[22]

This is what is known as *she shen qu yi* (giving up one's life for righteousness), taught and practiced in China by some as the highest ideal of moral courage and conduct.

Many factors make a person decide to choose righteousness before life. One of the factors has to do with right and wrong. As Mencius sees it, it is wrong for rulers to use their power against people, to enjoy life at their expense, and to drive them to war to kill one another. On the other hand, it is right to rule with benevolence, to make food available to people in times of famine, and to strive for peace and harmony with neighboring countries, thus sparing people tragedies of war. This is "the heart" that chooses right over wrong, even danger and death instead of safety and life, the heart motivated by *ce yin zi xin,* compassion. According to Mencius, "it is not only the worthies alone who have this moral sense" of right and wrong, this heart of compassion, but "all people have it."[23]

One seems to perceive this heart of right and wrong being called into action as Hugh Thompson put himself in a dangerous situation in order to save the life of Vietnamese villagers in My Lai. For him it was wrong to kill innocent people and right to spare them. This is the heart of compassion impelled by a sense of right and wrong. Compassion without the sense of right and wrong is not compassion; it is indulgence. Compassion not inspired to choose right over against wrong is permissiveness. Compassion not prompted to take the side of right in the face of wrong is cowardice. As with compassion, so it is with love.

It is such a heart that John the Evangelist perceived in Jesus when he reported Jesus to have said: "No one has greater love than this, to lay down one's life for one's friends" (John 15:13). But Jesus goes beyond this. He is not only prepared to die for his friends and his followers, but also willing to lay down his life for his opponents and enemies, even for those who conspired to bring about his death. With that love he overcame hatred and severed the chain of animosity. And with that love he also broke the circle of vengeance.

A Temple Bell

This leads us back to "A Song of Enlightenment," with which we began this chapter. Seeing his house in ruins, a deed performed by the young man whose arm he had cut off some years ago, the young soldier set out at once to avenge the atrocity done to his family. By accident the two adversaries found themselves face to face at the grave of the soldier's grandmother. "The soldier...drew his sword and prepared to strike, when a bell sounded in a nearby temple."

Anyone who has visited a Buddhist temple, especially one on a hill in deep mountains, surrounded by trees and water, knows what a temple bell sounds like. It begins with a deep and heavy tone reverberating from the womb of nature and from the innermost part of the soul, dancing in the air, singing in the universe, and merging with milliards of sounds on the mountaintops. It then fades back into the womb of nature, filling the heart with peace with all creation as you sink into the oblivion of yourself. That sound carries you into eternity. In oblivion you hear nothing, yet you hear everything. You feel nothing, yet you feel all. You have lost yourself, but you are never so real to yourself as you become one with the sound of the bell that rises from creation and returns to it. It is a mysterious sound that pleads with you, prays with you, and quiets your fretting heart and mind. It makes its way into your distressed soul to make room for peace, with yourself and with God. The sound enables you to rise from the ruins of your old world to rebuild a new world of reconciliation, saves you from self-destruction and from destruction of others. The sound redeems your relations with others and with God, compels you to choose life rather than death—not only for yourself but for others, even for your foes. The sound carries the voice of the Buddha:

> There is no fire like the fire of lust.
> There is no grip like the grip of anger.
> There is no net like the net of delusion.
> There is no river like the river of craving.[24]

It must be this voice that the bell of the temple brought to the heart of the young soldier about to avenge his foes.

Breaking the Circle of Vengeance

Another sound arises when the soldier hears the temple bell. The sound turns into "a song, borne on the wind in a chorus of ghostly voices—now his grandmother's, now the victims he and his ancestors had killed in war, now the voices of his own children yet-to-be-born." The song bemoans human woes from ancient times to the present, and extending to the future. It is sung by victims of human atrocities from all times, who are not able to enter the joy of eternal life—a chorus of the spirits of the wrongly murdered, haunting the living.

This is not just a vision; it is living history. This is not merely a dream; it is a reality. It reminds us of a scene in the Book of Revelation that gives a rare glimpse into the hearts of early Christians faced with martyrdom.

> I saw under the altar the souls of those who had been slaughtered for the word of God and for the testimony they had given; they cried out with a loud voice, "Sovereign Lord, holy and true, how long will it be before you judge and avenge our blood on the inhabitants of the earth?" (Rev. 6:9-10)

This is an earnest cry. Yes, the blood of the innocent must be avenged. The blood cries out to God from the ground just as Abel's blood cried out after he had been murdered (Gen. 4:10).

But does God avenge our persecutors? Does God listen to our cries and punish our enemies? Is God a vengeful God? Does God ever forgive those who have done us wrong? Does God ever let them go scot-free? We often are in a vengeful mood when injustice and suffering are inflicted on us. In this we are not alone.

> O Lord, you God of vengeance,
>   you God of vengeance, shine forth!
> Rise up, O judge of the earth;
>   give to the proud what they deserve!
> O Lord, how long shall the wicked,
>   how long shall the wicked exult?
>   (Ps. 94:1-3)

This is by no means atypical of psalms in Hebrew Scripture. Do we not, even as Christians, also want our God to seek revenge against those who have caused us frustration and distress?

This may be the God of many "people of God" in the Bible and the God of many Christians, but is this God, this vengeful God, the true God? Many of us may conceive of God in this way, but one thing is certain: this is not the God of Jesus. If his God were the God of revenge, he would have cried to that God from the cross to avenge his blood, and to mete out to his tormentors and persecutors the punishment they were due. But this is not what he did on the cross. Instead, he prayed to God to forgive them.

Something in the chorus of those victims in "A Song of Enlightenment" surprises us. In that chorus of Vietnamese war dead, carried by the sound of the bell, the young soldier did not hear pleas for revenge and demands for punishment. The chorus wakes his soul, preoccupied with revenge, and urges him to break the circle of vengeance. That is a vicious circle. To avenge someone's blood one has to kill others. Then the lives of these others must be avenged. And so it goes on and on, causing more blood to flow.

The sound of the temple bell, however, breaks that circle of revenge. It makes the young soldier pause long enough to listen to these words: "Our lives have seen suffering enough." This is almost an understatement. Human history is a history of suffering that we cause ourselves, that we inflict on one another, and that spills over into our environment. Paul is right when he says that "the whole creation has been groaning in labor pains" until it can "be set free from its bondage to decay" (Rom. 8:22, 21). Who has caused the decay? Not creation itself. Not God. We now know better: it is we human beings who have caused it.

"Our lives have seen suffering enough," intones the bell. These are sensible words, words of reason. They do not come in thundering shouts that make us cover our ears. They come in a still, small voice. Here the story of Elijah, a prophet in ancient Israel, comes to mind. In the wilderness fleeing from Queen Jezebel, who was after his life (1 Kings 19:1-18), he found himself in the midst of "a great wind, so strong that it was splitting mountains and breaking rocks in pieces." It was a terrifying experience, but God "was not in the wind." Afterward came an earthquake and a fire, but God was not in them, either. These events were followed by "a sound of sheer silence." It was a soothing, assuring silence.

Embraced in the silence, secure and at rest, Elijah became aware that he was in the presence of God.

"Don't Make Vengeance Your God"

The silence Elijah discovered was a compassionate silence. The loving silence enables the turbulent mind to cease to fret and agitate. It makes the restless heart pause in serenity, once it finds itself in the vastness of the universe. It causes the soul filled with hatred for others to perceive pain and suffering in them. It is a silence that redeems ourselves and others from hostility to one another. It is a silence that tells us and others that we are not alone in the universe. It is a silence that reveals that God is love and not hatred, compassion and not revenge.

That sound of the temple bell, before fading finally into the rivers and mountains, tells the young soldier in a calm but firm voice: Abandon your revenge. The voice startles him. It exposes what is stirring in his mind and heart. It tells him to stop what he is about to do to his foe. It commands him not to take the latter's life. The first thing that comes to his mind at the sound of the bell is self-centered, if not selfish. "If I take revenge," he reasons, "it will be the cause; the effect will follow me into my next life." This is true. He has to reckon with the circle of revenge. The future generations will be caught in that circle of shedding one another's blood.

But something greater than his own self, beyond future generations, dawns on him. "Avoid," says the bell, "all resentment and hatred for humankind." Humankind is larger than the young soldier. It is far more comprehensive than his ancestors. It comprises generations of all people, and not just his own people. Humankind has been imprisoned in the circle of revenge. A crack has to be made in that circle. A breach must be made. The future not only of his own people but of all humankind depends on the little rupture he can make. The sound of the temple bell, "a sound of sheer silence," is urging him to make a tiny crack in that circle of revenge. The crack may be tiny, but it can grow into a huge crack. That circle is not invincible. Nor is it inevitable. But it cannot be broken by swords and bloodshed. It can only be broken by the power of compassion and love.

It is a soul-searching moment for the young soldier. Hate or compassion? Revenge or forgiveness? To kill or to let live? He chooses the latter. "The soldier, having had his passion interrupted by the bell and his spirit awakened by the song, put away his sword and helped his enemy get up." The circle of revenge is broken. No blood is shed. The two men embrace and go their ways, knowing that compassion and not hatred, love and not revenge, has saved them from perpetual feuds and conflicts. To deliver humankind from suffering and destruction, what is needed is not the violent power of the sword but the reconciling power of love.

Is this merely a legend impossible to locate in real human experience? The scene it depicts may be ideal but not real. The lesson it teaches may be noble but not practicable in the world of conflicts and war. Is it? But consider the story of a Vietnamese father who has gone through the fears, pains, and sufferings of the Vietnam War. In the midst of deafening explosions and agonizing cries of his friends and relatives exposed to the terror of death, he tells his daughter in a calm voice:

> Bay Ly, you were born to be a wife and mother, not a killer. That is your duty. For as long as you live, you must remember what I say. You and me—we weren't born to make enemies. Don't make vengeance your god, because such gods are satisfied only by human sacrifice.[25]

Let us not be irritated by what the father says about the duty of his daughter to be a wife and mother. Let us not import our sensitivity to sexism into the counsel of the father to his daughter. What the father tries to convey is that his daughter is not born to be a killer. His daughter, though still young in age and experience, has grown old from the relentless war. She has become experienced, even streetwise, on account of what she has had to go through. The treatment she has received not only from enemy soldiers but from her own people has made her soul and mind precocious. All she wants in her heart and mind is to avenge the blood shed on her playground and the death inflicted on her people.

From Washington, however, the war looked different:

> The one thing demonstrably going for us in Vietnam over the past year has been the large number of enemy killed-in-action resulting from the big military operations. Allowing for possible exaggeration in reports, the enemy must be taking losses . . . at the rate of more than 60,000 a year.[26]

This was 1966. The war was to continue for several more years, and the number of Vietcong killed in action was to rise dramatically. How many women, old men, children, and babies were included in this body count?

Seeing all this happening around her, how could the heart and spirit of the young daughter not be inflamed with hatred and revenge? It was this hatred and revenge that kept up the morale of the people and inspired them to fight. Meanwhile, the war planners continued to assess the war from Washington:

> The infiltration routes [to the South] would seem to be one-way trails to death for the North Vietnamese. Yet there is no sign of an impending break in enemy morale and it appears that he can more than replace his losses by infiltration from North Vietnam and recruitment in South Vietnam.[27]

That a small nation like Vietnam withstood the greatly superior enemy firepower is nothing short of a miracle. That wave after wave of young men and women went to their deaths, only to be followed by others, poorly equipped and often hungry, cannot be explained except by the sheer power of the spirit. In the end Washington planners had to concede that "this important war must be fought and won by the Vietnamese themselves. We have known this from the beginning."[28]

But such facts are not all that brought victory to Vietnam. Something else hidden in the heart and spirit of Vietnamese women and men finally brought the war to an end. How better can one express it than with the words of the father to his young daughter? "Don't make vengeance your god, because such gods are satisfied only by human sacrifice." To hear this from a father who himself has been a victim of a terrible war is truly astonishing. To listen to the words from the lips of a man in a "Buddhist" nation, under relentless attack from a "Christian" nation, cannot but make us Christians humble.

"Don't make vengeance your god," says the father. Yes, the war must be fought. Enemy attacks must be fended off. But vengeance must not be your god. How can it be a god? Vengeance is a demon, a devil. It tears apart the moral fabric of human community. It destroys what makes human beings human—their humanity. That god will not be satisfied with vengeance of an enemy. When your enemy is avenged, the enemy will, in turn, surely create chaos for you and for your community. The last enemy to achieving a lasting peace in heart, community, nation, and world is that god called vengeance. The circle of vengeance cannot be broken until that god is eliminated, and the altar erected in its honor dismantled.

Vietnam has been a Buddhist country for centuries. It was a Buddhist nation during the Vietnam War, which added another tragic dimension to that war. Presumably most of the Vietcong were Buddhists. Presumably many American soldiers, if not most of them, were Christians. The Vietnam War was an ideological, geopolitical conflict between a small Asian country and a global superpower. But in a sense it was also a religious war between a Buddhist nation and a Christian nation, a war that involved Buddhists and Christians in the brutal massacre of one another.

Partly to justify American involvement in the Vietnam War, it has been said in retrospect that America "must be for freedom, for dignity, for genuine democracy, or it is not America. *It was not America in Vietnam.*"[29] This is a lame justification at best. If America was not America in Vietnam, how could America be America at home? It was America, which betrayed its own ideals of freedom, dignity, and democracy, that got America involved in the Vietnam War. It was a misdirected effort to contain communist expansion in Asia—and Christian zeal in support—that made America lose its soul and betray its faith overseas.

Such cooperation is nothing new. It is well represented in the history of the colonial expansion of the "Christian" West to the rest of the world. Colonialism, politically motivated and religiously sanctioned, is a counterwitness to what Christianity should stand for. It is the betrayal of Jesus, of his life and mission. Western colonialism, combining political forces and religious zeal, sought to colonize the body, spirit, and soul of the colonized nations and peoples. But the Vietnam War deprived the history of colonization of moral and religious justification. What the war taught us, among other things, is that for America to be America, for a "Christian" nation to be Christian, or for Christians to be Christians, they must stand for freedom, human dignity, and genuine democracy not only at home but also abroad.

This also has to be said of a Buddhist country such as Vietnam. It has to be stressed that Vietnam is not above criticism. It does not represent a paragon of virtue as it casts itself, and is cast by its sympathizers, as a victim of the Vietnam War. We know how in Vietnam the North and the South waged a war of revenge on each other. In self-defense and armed with nationalism North Vietnam engaged in a war of revenge against invaders. But in the midst of this violence from within and without, there were still people like the elderly father who could admonish young men and women not to make revenge their god.

It is this "innate" goodness that we Christians tend to overlook in people of other faiths. Even if we take notice, we are inclined to treat it, if not with disdain, at least with condescension. In the creation story we Christians have taken over from Hebrew Scripture, did not God bless human beings after God had created them (Gen. 1:28)? And at the conclusion of the creating activities, did not God say with an unconcealed sense of joy and satisfaction: "God saw everything that God had made, and indeed, it was very good" (Gen. 1:31)? Should it then surprise us Christians that people of other religious cultures are capable of doing good out of their created nature, and not in an attempt to win God's favor?

The truth is that the advice not to make revenge one's god, coming from a Buddhist land fighting for its survival against a formidable Western nation, does make us Christians ponder deeply. The old Vietnamese father might not have been conscious of it, but his advice was deeply rooted in the Buddhist teaching of compassion for all beings, and in the Buddhist vision of a human community in which all violence would cease and peace would prevail.

Essence of Nonviolence Is Love

What triumphed in the end in Vietnam was not military prowess, either Vietnamese or American. What brought an end to the tragic war was not the victory of one determined nation over another nation. What finally brought peace to the ravaged land was the souls of the people in Vietnam awakened to the infinite mercy and compassion of the Buddha.

Folk poetry circulated among the South and North Vietnamese:

> My hand is holding a bowl of ginger and salt.
> Ginger is hot, salt is strong.
> They embrace each other:
> North and South share the same sorrow.

> We love each other;
> why have we abandoned our love?[30]

The people must have sung the poem at first in their hearts. They were afraid to be heard. But unable to keep it inside themselves, they began to hum it. Gradually it was on their lips. Before they knew it, it began to be "sung throughout the country."[31]

Ginger is hot and salt is strong. If North is ginger, South is salt. If South is ginger, North is salt. Ginger and salt together make tasty food. North and South, embracing each other, create a peaceful nation and make a happy people. But we are not embracing each other any longer, the poem says. We are not loving each other anymore. Why have we abandoned our love? The question is not asked to find answers. It is not raised to develop excuses. It is a reminder that North and South Vietnam are still bound to each other by love despite the hostilities.

It is important to note that this is a *folk* poem and not government propaganda. It expresses what is deep-seated in the hearts of people, and what has been long suppressed by the warring parties. The governments fighting for the control of the country want them to believe that North and South are "enemies who do not live under the same sky" (*bu gong dai tian*), according to a Chinese saying. But people know in their heart of hearts that they do live under the same sky, that they breathe the same air, that they live on the same ancestral land, that they eat the same rice they cultivate year after year. The folk song reminds them that nothing should cause them to abandon love for one another.

The folk song expresses the earnest desire, deeply buried in the hearts of women and men, for reconciliation between North and South. When the war was going on, when the political factions had daggers drawn against each other, when political allegiance to the powers that be was the only means for survival, even the desire for reconciliation was suspect. It was the betrayal of a political cause, regarded as a sign of weakness, and treated as nothing but capitulation to one's enemy. But for people who had to bear the brunt of political struggle for power, men and women who had fallen victim to the merciless drive for military victory, the folk song was the manifesto of their true longing.

This folk song is a lament for the love lost in the quagmire of hatred and trampled under the brutality of war—the love North and South cherished for each other for centuries. Ginger and salt may be incompatible when separate, but once they embrace each other in the making of daily food they are indispensable ingredients. Government ideologies, political struggle, and war have separated them. A moving line in the folk song tells us: "North and South share the same sorrow." The war has turned their love into sorrow. Now must be the time to turn sorrow into love again.

The folk song is short, but the stories it contains are long. It conveys its message in a quiet voice, but is bursting with tears and pain.

During our struggle, many scenes of love arose spontaneously—a monk sitting calmly before an advancing tank; women and children raising their bare hands against barbed wire; students confronting military police who looked like monsters wearing huge masks and holding bayonets; young women running through clouds of tear gas with babies in their arms; hunger strikes held silently and patiently; monks and nuns burning themselves to death to try to be heard above the raging noise of the war. And all of these efforts bore some fruit.[32]

These are all stories carried in the folk song of love. There is no end to such stories. The folk song of love has no ending. As it is sung, more and more stories will be remembered and added. It will no longer be a whispering song. It will become a mighty chorus resounding on earth and reverberating in heaven.

The scenes of terror, violence, panic, despair, protest, and horror described above are at the same time scenes of love. *A monk* sitting calmly before an advancing tank turns that scene of violence into a scene of love. *Women and children* raising their bare hands against barbed wire change that scene of despair into a scene of love. *Students* confronting military police convert the scene of violence to a scene of love. *Young women* with their babies in their arms running through clouds of tear gas make that scene of panic a scene of love. *Men and women* holding hunger strikes in silence commute the scene of protest to a scene of love. The *monks and nuns* who burned themselves to death transformed scenes of horror into scenes of love for their people and nation.

These efforts bore fruit, we are told. How strange! These people—women, men, monks and nuns, students, children, and babies—are powerless. They are unarmed. They hold no political clout. They are not decision makers. But they are awakened to the reality that they have a stake not only in their own fate but in the destiny of their nation. They know that the political decision that made them victims of the war was not their own decision. They have realized that, though unarmed with political and military power, they are armed with the power of love—the power that can stop the advancing tank, the power that can break barbed wire, the power that can overpower violence, and the power that can rouse the conscience of the nation to seek reconciliation and peace. In these scenes of love the powers that be are confronted with *love as the essence of nonviolence.*

Nonviolence is not always an alternative to violence. It can be an attitude, a posture, even a matter of necessity forced upon people without power. It can be an attitude of self-negation, a posture of self-humiliation. It can be a means necessary for survival. Such nonviolence is no virtue. It contributes to the perpetuation of violence on the part of those who possess power. It surrenders to the forces that practice injustice and oppression. And it reduces human beings to means that serves the ends of the rich and powerful. Nonviolence in this case is just another name for complicity.

But nonviolence whose essence is love is different. It does not share the passive mind-set mentioned above. Nonviolence inspired by love does not regard survival as a matter of utmost importance: that monk sitting calmly before an advancing tank risked his life to stop terror. Nonviolence motivated by love does not shrink from brutal force: those men, women, and even children behind barbed wire raised bare hands in protest against the brutal power that demanded their absolute allegiance. Nonviolence informed by love does not take the status quo for granted: it compels students to confront military police ready to subdue them with batons, bayonets, and guns. Nonviolence nurtured by love makes it impossible to remain silent before the ruling power that has turned against people: even young women carrying babies brave clouds of tear gas to be part of the demonstrations against the repressive government.

Nonviolence compelled by love becomes a redeeming power for the nation devastated by the power of hatred: it is manifested in the acts of those nuns and monks setting themselves on fire at the height of the raging war. They became torches of light in darkness, fires of hope in the midst of hopelessness, and flames of peace that brought the tragic war to an end. The war did come to an end, leavings millions of men, women, and children dead and their land in shambles. Still the war ended. The end was not brought about by nonviolence and love alone. This is true. But it is also true that without nonviolence and love the war could not have ended the way it did, leaving many other women, men, and children alive to rebuild the land and to give birth to the future.

World-Soul Made of Love

These acts of nonviolence, big or small, public or private, heroic or timid, did bear fruit. If this was the case in Vietnam during the Vietnam War, it can also be true in any country. Surely nonviolence has borne fruit throughout history, from ancient times to the present. Christians should know this, for Jesus, the soul of our being and the heart of our faith, has won the world with nonviolence nurtured, inspired, motivated, and compelled by love. It is the redeeming power of his nonviolence that from time to time throughout history turns despair into hope, hostility into peace, and death into life.

The allegory at the outset of our discourse on love is an allegory of love. In that allegory, the shepherd boy said to the sun: "If you know about love, you must also know about the Soul of the World, because it's made of love." And this was the sun's reply: "From where I am, I can see the Soul of the World. It communicates with my soul, and together we cause the plants to grow and the sheep to seek our shade. From where I am—and I am a long way from the earth—I learned how to love."

The Soul of the World is made of love. This is a revealing thought and an empowering insight. Human history is filled with stories of atrocities. Our lives are exposed to terrors we inflict on each other. But all these alone do not make up our life and our history. There is the Soul of the World made of love that does communicate with our souls. It communicates with us in the language of love. It enables us to commit acts of love in spite of ourselves. And it manifests itself in women and men compelled by love to face violence with nonviolence, to overcome hatred with love.

This Soul of the World made of love gives birth to human souls capable of love. It makes the history of humankind a history of love as well as a history of hostility. This Soul of the World made of love makes and remakes our souls to enable us to respond to each other with love. And it is in the Soul of the World made of love that we, women and men, irrespective of creed, color, gender, and class, must find ourselves in the embrace of its love. Is it perhaps deep insight into the Soul of the World made of love that enabled Paul to say: "And now faith, hope, and love abide, these three; and the greatest of these is love" (1 Cor. 13:13).

Chapter 12

The Saving Work of Love

"It was the third hour," nine o'clock in the morning our time, "when they cruci-fied [Jesus]" (Mark 15:25 [NJB]).[1] From what the writers of the Gospels tell us, the scene of this gruesome execution was anything but sad, cruel, and horrid for the crowds gathered to watch. It was a scene repeated often after Roman regime began to prescribe such punishment for lower-class non-Roman criminals and for political agitators in the third century B.C.E. It was not unlike scenes that have played out in many countries, from times past to recent times.

There were "a great number of . . . people [who] followed Jesus" on his way to Golgotha, the place of execution outside Jerusalem (Luke 23:27). "Apparently," they "were those common people who daily listened to Jesus in the temple."[2] But Luke also identified women among them, telling us they "were beating their breasts and wailing for him" (23:27). By injecting this vignette, Luke turns the festival atmosphere that accompanied such occasions into a mournful procession and shifts the crucifixion as a spectacle to a human tragedy to grieve and lament.

But were these women merely "grieving over the impending death [of Jesus] and playing the part of the mourners"?[3] Or by inserting this vivid picture was there something else Luke wanted to say? Let us remember that Jesus did not defend himself either before the supreme council of seventy-one religious mem-bers in Jerusalem or at the court of Pontius Pilate, the Roman governor. He was almost totally silent (see Mark 14:61; Matt. 26:63, 27:12). His opponents heaped one accusation after another against him, even instigated the crowds to bear false witness against him. When the crisis was mounting, his disciples denied that they had anything to do with him.

Was Luke remembering this when describing Jesus' march to death? Was he trying to let the whole world hear the women beating their breasts and wailing for Jesus? In the women's expressions of extreme anguish, the world was hearing horrendous injustice done to an innocent man and terrible violence committed against a saintly person. In their cries rising to heaven, Jesus' religious oppo-nents were hearing the distress, hurt, and alienation of the people excluded from the official religion. In the outburst of emotions, Roman rulers were hearing a protest against the miscarriage of justice inflicted on a widely popular rabbi who had not broken Roman criminal laws. Did not Pilate, the Roman governor, de-clare, "I find no basis for an accusation against this man" (Luke 23:4)? But to capitalize on the political opportunity handed to him by the Jewish authorities, Pilate broke the Roman law of justice and condemned Jesus to die on the cross.

When Jesus was finally nailed to the cross, "those who passed by derided [Jesus], shaking their heads and saying, '... save yourself, and come down from the cross!" (Mark 15:29-30; also Matt. 27:39-40). They were "people from the city, not a gathered crowd at the execution."[4] But they did not seem like innocent passersby. They had not been unaware of the furor surrounding Jesus, his entry into Jerusalem, and his controversies with the religious authorities. "Aha! You who would destroy the temple," they shouted at Jesus, "and build it in three days!" (Mark 15:29). This was a malicious taunt accompanied by sarcastic laughter. Were they part of the group that accused Jesus at the supreme religious council (Mark 14:58; also Matt. 26:61)? Were they some of those who shouted, "Crucify him! Crucify him!" at Pilate's palace (Luke 23:21; also Mark 15:13; Matt. 27:22)?

Also present at the scene of the crucifixion were the chief priests and the scribes. They had at last won their fights against Jesus, whom they had stigmatized as a blasphemer of God, opposed as a challenger to their religious authority, and feared as a political agitator against Roman rule. They lost their dignity as religious leaders when they joined the jeering crowds, "mocking him among themselves and saying, 'He saved others; he cannot save himself'" (Mark 15:31; also Matt. 27:41-42; Luke 23:35). But was it a triumph won with a clear conscience? Was it a victory gained without uneasiness and compunction?

The last accusation they hurled against Jesus as he weakened must have come back to the chief priests and the scribes as a series of questions: But why do you try to save yourselves and not others? Why do you consider yourselves to be saved while others are not saved? How can you save yourselves while others suffer in pain, distress, and misery? How can you be saved when most people struggle to bear heavy burdens of foreign domination, to cope with enormous demands of daily life, and to suffer contempt, discrimination, and intolerance under your religious establishment? Such questions set us out to explore the redemptive work of love in this last leg of our theological journey.

Love That Saves Others

The insults the passersby and the religious leaders directed at Jesus contain unintended truth. The truth is that the main purpose of religion at its best is to save others and not to save oneself. The truth is that a religious community exists not for its own sake, but for the sake of others. The truth is that women and men of true faith learn to accept others as God's children, even though others believe and practice their faith differently. To believe, in short, is not to believe in faith itself, not in religion as such, not in doctrine and creed, and not in the supremacy of one's religion over other religions.

In contrast, to believe in such things is to make faith the object of one's supreme concern. To believe in them is to regard faith or its particular expressions as a goal of religious devotion. To believe in them is to view faith that has taken form in church, in teachings, and in ecclesiastical constitutions and laws as conclusive, definitive, and final. To believe in these things as the final judgment on truth and untruth in faith and morals is to make other authorities superfluous. It is to make God superfluous.

Believing in Love

To believe is to believe in the love that can save others but that cannot save oneself. To believe is to practice the kind of love that may bring pain to the person who practices it, but that can help achieve the worthy and noble causes of others. To believe is to activate the love that stands by truth by saying no to untruth. To believe is to nurture the love not intimidated by violence or corrupted by profit or gain. To believe is to be enlivened by the love that refuses to be discouraged when it is not requited. To believe is to be sustained by the love that does not yield to cynicism when forces of evil prevail against what is good and right. To believe is to be empowered by the love that envisions hope in the midst of despair and that keeps faith when confronted with death.

Jesus lived with this kind of love. He dedicated his entire life to it and shared it with others. He sought to reform his religion and to change his society with this kind of love. As expected—and he himself anticipated it—he had to die for it. Jesus did more than believing in this kind of love. He practiced, lived, and died for it. He personified it. In this love which is Jesus we Christians come to know that God is love.

Jesus is not God. He is flesh and blood just as we are. But he reflects God as he reflects this kind of love. He shows us what God is as he lives this love and seeks to fill others with it. He is God in the world in that he is this love in the world. He is God to us as he is this love to us. As we watch him nailed to the cross for the sake of this love, we also watch God nailed to the cross. What relates Jesus to God and God to Jesus is not some abstruse trinitarian formula of Father, Son, and Spirit, but the love that has power to save others. What binds Jesus to God and God to Jesus, in spite of the infinite and qualitative difference between Jesus as a human being and God as a divine being, is not the nature of Jesus theologically defined as "human and divine," or as "more divine than human," but the love that helps others live but that cannot prevent suffering and death on its behalf.

The bond between Jesus and God does not make Jesus more divine than human and God more human than divine. It is through this bond that Jesus as a true human being and God as a true God become related in the saving work of love. In this bond between Jesus and God we human beings find ourselves—not as spectators to the crucifixion, the culmination of the saving work of love—but as participants in it.

"Were You There?"

This perhaps is the faith of which the well-known African American spiritual, "Were You There," sings and confesses from the midst of hardship, loneliness, and longing.

> Were you there when they crucified my Lord?
> Were you there when they crucified my Lord?
>
> Were you there when they nailed him to the tree?
> Were you there when they nailed him to the tree?
>
> Were you there when they pierced him in the side?
> Were you there when they pierced him in the side?
>
> Were you there when they laid him in the tomb?
> Were you there when they laid him in the tomb?
>
> (*refrain*)
> Oh! sometimes it causes me to tremble, tremble, tremble.[5]

We hear a lament in this African American spiritual. It stirs our souls and hearts. It makes us not bystanders at the cross but participants.

The lament we hear in this African American spiritual is the lament of the women who accompanied Jesus to Golgotha. It is the lament of the African Americans brought against their will from their home in Africa to be slaves in America. It is the lament of countless men and women who suffer physical and spiritual dislocation on account of political oppression, social changes, or economic hardships. The lament at Golgotha rises from the laments of human beings, echoing, resonating, and blending with them to form a powerful lament of God who created the heavens and the earth for the well-being of all creatures, including human beings.

But human beings, created to be part of God's creation, have made themselves the whole of it. And human beings, whom God "made . . . a little lower than God" (Ps. 8:5), have attempted to make themselves a little more than God. Human beings are both victims of the cross of Jesus and accomplices in turning the world into what the cross symbolizes—a world of pain, suffering, and death. "Were You There" can serve as a lament for all of human experience before and after Jesus' crucifixion.

The disciples whom Jesus chose to impart his vision were not at the crucifixion. The crowds who followed him, who had listened to him avidly, and who had recovered their human dignity were not there. Passersby were there to poke fun, to deride, and to heckle. The high priests and scribes were there to administer a coup de grâce with their taunts, making sure that Jesus was dead and that he would not cause any more trouble with his sharp tongue. Pontius Pilate, the Roman governor, was not present. Having gotten rid of a case that for him was no more than a nuisance, he washed his hands, declaring that he had nothing to do with Jesus' death, and went on with his business as a colonial ruler. When we think of these facts, do they not cause us to tremble as the spiritual intones?

Most Christians today are not there either when our Lord is crucified. We are preoccupied with the business of living, and it is a very difficult, complex, and labor-intensive business. Even many Christians who profess to be followers of Christ, who insist that there is no salvation for humanity except through him, are not there when their Lord is crucified. They are so busy trying to convert nonbelievers, to increase church membership, and to expand their influence that they have no time to be there when their Lord is crucified. They are so consumed with efforts to defend their faith against atheists and believers of other religions that they cannot afford moments of quiet at the foot of the cross. They have not time to ponder if Jesus intended his death on the cross to divide humankind into saved and unsaved, those destined for heaven and those destined for hell. Do not these thoughts cause us to tremble as the spiritual moans?

There are also many pastors and Christians busily engaged in construction work, erecting beautiful and expensive church buildings. In some countries in Asia religions prosper. Temples and shrines, ever larger and more magnificent, "mushroom like bamboo shoots after rain" (*yu hou chun xun*). How can Christianity lag behind? Even if inferior in strength as an organized body, according to a Taiwanese saying, we can never allow ourselves to be outnumbered and lose our competitive edge (*su tin bo su lang*). Pastors and members of their city congregations mobilize financial resources to build big and splendid churches, considering such building almost the only way to bear witness to Jesus and to show their faith. But by worshiping in these new and well-furnished churches, they are not there with Jesus at the crucifixion.

The love that saves others is often absent from us Christians. It has been more important for us to save ourselves than to save others. We have been more preoccupied with winning over others than with traveling with others in the search for the way, the truth, and the life. We have always been more interested in telling others to believe what we believe than in learning from them. We have taken literally what the apostle Paul once wrote to the church at Corinth: "Woe to me if I do not proclaim the gospel!" (1 Cor. 9:16). But we have not stopped to think what Paul meant by "the gospel." It has not occurred to us to ask whether by "the gospel" Paul meant the same thing Jesus did—the reign of God that belongs to the poor and the dispossessed, that gets manifested when the oppressed are set free from their oppressors, and that finds its way into those who suffer pain and affliction in body and soul. Nor do we stop to ask if the gospel we preach bears resemblance to the gospel of God's reign for which Jesus lived and died.

Love That Saves

For love to be truly love it has to be the love that can save others. This kind of love is saving love—love that saves—and the work it does is saving work—work that saves.

We use the word *saving* as an adjective and noun, avoiding the noun *salvation*. *Salvation* for most Christians has acquired the meaning of repenting for one's sin, calling upon the name of Jesus, and receiving God's gift of eternal life. The focus of salvation is this "I" who repents, this "I" who calls upon the name of Jesus, and this "I" who receives eternal life. It is always *my* salvation that is the center of religious activity. Salvation for many Christians, and for adherents of other religions, is often a self-centered undertaking.

Saving as an adjective or verb, particularly as a verb, is less loaded with religious baggage. It is not as heavily theological as *salvation* is and is used much more commonly in daily parlance. We often hear someone say "I want to save myself," meaning to spare oneself from embarrassment, blunder, or bankruptcy by luck or hard work. But in church we do not say, "I save myself from sin," because we know we cannot save ourselves. It is God who saves us. It is, to be more specific, God in Jesus that saves us. God or God in Jesus plays the active role in our experience of being saved.

But this experience of God or God in Jesus acting on us changes when it becomes the experience of "my" salvation. Salvation becomes something that has become secure in my possession, something that I own, and even something that I have but others, those outside Christianity in particular, do not have. Since others do not have it, they must either strive for it or be prepared to be excluded from it. In thinking this way I forget that I have not saved myself, but that God or God in Jesus has saved me.

We have also refrained from using the familiar word *redemption*. But how can one avoid the word when dealing with religion? Just as with *salvation*, there is no religion that does not make *redemption* its central concern. Is not redemption always the central theme in religious ritual, teaching, and artistic representation? What is religion if not a religion of redemption? To mention religion is to mention redemption. To teach religion is to teach redemption. To practice religion is to practice redemption. The sole business of religion has to be redemption. Whether devotional practice, offering of tithes, or ordination, all theological roads lead directly or indirectly to redemption.

What is redemption? What does the word mean? The word *redemption* comes from the Latin word *redimere*, to buy back. In the ordinary use it means buying back something or "recovering possession or ownership by payment of a price or service."[6] As this dictionary meaning shows, redemption is not free. It comes with payment. It has to be achieved by performing a mandatory service. Originally, redemption was a "secular" concept practiced in all societies. But it "became of great theological importance in the Old Testament...and to a lesser degree in the New Testament" and came to acquire a "central position in the vocabulary of modern Christian theology, where the terms [*redeem, redeemer, redemption*] have a currency quite disproportionate to the relative infrequency of their appearance in the New Testament."[7]

The point made here is important. The blood Jesus shed on the cross, in Christianity, is the sacrificial blood that cleanses and absolves our sins. The death he died on the cross is the price or ransom paid by God to the devil to free us from evil's clutch. The term *redemption* in "secular" use relates to a business transaction between concerned parties. This "secular" meaning has been converted to religious use, making what takes place between God and humankind an exchange or bargain God made with Satan. But did a business transaction take place at Jesus' crucifixion? Did Jesus himself undergo the pangs of death on the cross while considering himself a price paid by God to free humanity from sin? It is of course difficult to surmise what was going through his mind as he was nailed to the cross to face his imminent death. But it can be said that as someone who practiced the reign of God, proclaimed it, and used it to empower the powerless, the poor, and the dispossessed, Jesus would not have thought of himself as playing a part in a business deal such as a redemption or ransom. He would not have regarded the God he called "Abba" as one who might use him as payment, as ransom money, in order to satisfy the conditions required for the forgiveness of sins allegedly committed by human beings against God.

No, love that saves has nothing to do with redemption as a price to be paid or as a ransom to be made. Hearing spectators and opponents saying that he could not save himself, Jesus must have responded in his heart: "So be it!" Without knowing it, they uttered the truth that Jesus had come to free others from social humiliation, to liberate them from religious alienation, and to deliver them from self-pity and resignation. Without realizing it, they articulated the meaning of his life and mission: to lift up the downtrodden, to comfort the broken-hearted, to kindle hope for those in despair, and to make the presence of the loving God real in their lives.

This is all that he lived for, all that mattered to him. If this is what saving others means, Jesus could respond with an Amen. Instead of hurting him, these words confirmed and even blessed what he had done. But then another thought must have come to his mind. He had freed others from social humiliation, but he had been condemned to a humiliating form of death. He liberated others from religious discrimination, but he was subjected to undignified punishment. He delivered others from self-pity and resignation, but was he not tormented in death by self-pity and resignation?

Who are we to say that such thoughts never crossed Jesus' mind when he was suffering on the cross? Could it be that Jesus was tempted to agree with what the passersby said? Is this not a very human thing to do? We often yield to the thought that we are repaid with ingratitude, even with betrayal, by those whom we have helped. "You cannot save yourself!" This was a cruel taunt thrown at Jesus. It could have broken the dignity he had maintained. It could have prompted him to cry "injustice!" at the top of his voice. It could have aroused him to shout complaints to God whose bidding he believed he was doing.

Suffering unto Love

But Jesus, according to what we know, did not do such things. He was in fact incapable of such thoughts. The cruel taunts confirmed why he had come into the world. He did not come to the world to save himself, but to save others. He did not engage in the ministry of God's reign to establish his prestige and to gain power over others, but to enable others to be part of it. He did not plot with other revolutionaries to overthrow Roman rule and to install himself as messiah-king. He enabled women and men to have the strength of the spirit to stand on their feet in the world of human suffering.

The world has never ceased to be a world of suffering. This is a fact and does not require great wisdom or rigorous asceticism to realize. But growing used to the fact is another matter. We do not get used to natural disasters that bring loss of property, injury, and even death. We do not grow accustomed to the anguish and pain diseases inflict. And we cannot accept the death of our loved ones with equanimity and anticipate our own death without anxiety or fear. What gives us strength to go on living and hoping is the faith that God will carry us along in God's continuing effort to bring a new creation into being to replace the old creation.

But there is suffering we human beings inflict on one another, suffering that reveals the darkest part of human nature and that even makes God shudder. I am referring to horrendous crimes we human beings have committed against one another since the beginning of history, including the Holocaust. The cross on which Jesus suffered and died is both the reality and symbol of such human suffering.

The cross stands for suffering, but also for saving power. The question is how this cross, which in itself has no saving power, has come to possess it? Why has this cross, itself nothing but a horror, become the source of faith and hope for Christians and non-Christians? Suffering—this is what the cross represents— has nothing to commend itself to anyone. Simply to suffer has no religious merit. Suffering per se is not salvific—that is, "tending to save, providing or causing salvation."[8] We try to avoid and free ourselves from suffering.

But what transforms the cross into a source of inspiration? What makes it the supreme evidence of God's presence with Jesus and with men and women who suffer imprisonment, torture, and death? What is the power that changes it from a demonstration of human cruelty into testimony to the God who so loved the world? The answer is: LOVE. It is not the suffering that Jesus endured on the cross that saves, but the love he manifested through it. It is not the pain he suffered on the cross that saves, but the love emanated from it. Nor is it the death he died on it that saves, but the love that was not overcome by it.

Suffering cannot save, but love can. Suffering does not save, but love does. Suffering by itself and for itself is meaningless, but *suffering unto love* provides meaning. The cross is Jesus suffering unto love. His cross is suffering that turns into the manifestation of love. His cross evokes compassion as well as passion (agony, distress, rage). His cross becomes the power of love that gives birth to life. Because the cross is Jesus suffering unto love, a new life has already begun on the cross. Suffering unto love is suffering unto life. It is suffering unto hope. And it is suffering unto faith.

This is what the cross of Jesus is. It can speak to many crosses in the world—crosses on which many women and men suffer and die. It can help break the silence of the crosses they have to carry to their graves. It appeals to the world and pleas with it to end the hideous practice of nailing people to the cross. It attests to the world that its mission is to transform the suffering of those crosses into the crosses of suffering unto love, suffering that has the power of love to give birth to new life and to new human community.

Let us see how the cross of Jesus as the cross of suffering unto love can share the pain and despair of other crosses and enable them to turn suffering into the creative force of love. A poem called "You Are the Crucifix of Korea" will help us begin. It was written and read by a Korean woman poet in 1990 at the forty-fifth anniversary of the end of the Pacific War, in memory of Korean women forced to become "comfort women" for Japanese soldiers in Southeast Asia:

> Who can wash all of your bloodstained body?
> Who can stitch together your torn heart
> and bring it to its lasting place?
>
> You were crushed underfoot sooner than the fatherland.
> You were forgotten sooner than the liberation,
> You who are the flowers of history's tears.
>
> Who can dull your revenge-filled heart
> to sleep, in its last resting place?
> You! You are the victim, fallen, as war plunder,
> as public toilets. You are like a pakkokt.
>
> You, pain-filled crucifix of earth,
> You blossom anew like flowers trampled under weed,
> You challenge us, who are burdened with shame and resentment.
> You touch the fatherland who betrayed you, filled with anger.
>
> We want to give you a secure shelter,
> come back and rest, when you
> are no longer a long-haired sixteen-year-old virgin.

> Today we want to construct a memorial for you
> so that no more women will fall victim to colonial brutality.
> You are innocent. You are our mother.
>
> Now wrap up your wings.
> No longer waver from side to side.
>
> You who are the crucifix of Korea
> Repose in comfort,
> You who are the flowers of Korea's tears.[9]

The heart of the poet must have been filled with deep sorrow and anguish when she was writing these verses. She must have been unable to control her tears.

As she read it at the anniversary service, the audience moaned and sobbed with her, crying and wailing for their sisters forced to serve Japanese troops as sex slaves during the war. Most of the women died; those who survived to tell of the inhumanity and atrocities inflicted on them have been physically, psychologically, and spiritually maimed for the rest of their lives. This is one of the darkest chapters in the history of humankind. It is further evidence of how human beings, left to their own devices, can turn themselves loose against defenseless human beings, ravaging, plundering, raping, and disposing of them as if they were trash.

There were as many as three hundred thousand "comfort women."[10] Most of them were young girls in their teens and early twenties, some as young as thirteen. Police and military agents abducted them on their way from school, enticed them with the promise of a job, or forced them to follow with threats of imprisonment or death.

These women were virtually "sex slaves," treated as nothing more than sexual outlets for Japanese soldiers. Most of them came from Korea, but others came from Taiwan, China, the Philippines, and Indonesia. The stories of their inhuman treatment exploded when three former Korean "comfort women" submitted their demands for government apologies and compensation to a Tokyo District Court in December 1991. Their stories embarrassed the Japanese government and shocked the Japanese public and people of Southeast Asia. The stories exposed war crimes of the first degree and darkened the already dark history of Japan's Pacific War.

Scars of Suffering

How can one read these stories without deep sorrow? Who can hear them and not experience being in the pit of terror? "In 1934 when I was 14 years old," recalls a Korean woman, "I was taken as 'comfort woman' for the Japanese army." In the years that followed, she was raped, tortured, and mutilated. "When I lost consciousness, they threw me into the garbage dump."[11] Chong Jin-Nim, the Korean poet, is right. "Who can," she asks, "wash all of your bloodstained body?" Most of these "comfort women" died with bloodstained bodies in army barracks, in the streets, or on the battlefields with no one to wash their bodies. Was not Jesus' body, pierced on the cross by Roman soldiers, also stained with blood? Did not blood drip from his head torn by the crown of thorns?

The women who survived their horrible traumas washed their bloodstained bodies. But they were not able to wash away the scars. "Though many years have passed since then," says the woman quoted earlier, "physical and mental scars still remain. No matter how the Japanese Government may pay compensation, they can never wipe out the deep-rooted grudges and scars left in my heart and on my body."[12] After Jesus had died, he was taken down the cross, wrapped in a linen cloth, and prepared for burial. But the scars on his body could not be erased by the linen cloth.

Do these stories not make us recall the suffering of that unknown "servant," lamented and eulogized by a prophet among the Jewish exiles in Babylon in the middle of the sixth century B.C.E.?

> He was wounded for our transgressions,
>   crushed for our iniquities. (Isa. 53:5)

We do not know in what circumstances "the servant" was wounded and crushed. But we do know the transgressions and iniquities that led to his suffering. These were the transgressions committed by those in power against the powerless, the iniquities perpetrated by the rich against the poor—transgressions and iniquities the prophets such as Isaiah, from the eighth century onward, exposed and castigated. That "suffering servant" could have well been the men and women wounded and crushed by the rich and powerful during the centuries that preceded the downfall of Judah in 586 B.C.E.

There is one thing the "suffering servant," the "suffering Jesus," and the "suffering comfort women" have in common: scars of suffering on their bodies. No lament, apology, or compensation could wash them away. If no power on earth is able to wash the bloodstained bodies of "comfort women" and to remove the scars from their bodies, perhaps the love generated from Jesus' suffering would be able to do it. Even Jesus' suffering alone could not do it. But suffering unto love, made real by Jesus—practiced even on the cross when he said, "Father, forgive them; for they do not know what they are doing" (Luke 23:34)—can do it. That love is not forced upon a person, nor does it make a person drag out an ignominious existence. The love born out of and tested by suffering cannot be easily defeated by malice, give in to despair, or give up in resignation.

In telling their stories publicly and demanding justice from society, the survivors of the war crimes make sure that young women of future generations will not have to suffer the same fate. They may not know it, but in this way they are practicing "suffering unto love" on their own behalf and on behalf of their sisters who died painful and humiliating deaths in faraway lands. One of the writers who interviewed former "comfort women" concluded: "We neither need violence nor domination in our world. And no one has the right to treat others as tools, absolutely not, not even for what is believed to be a great cause. *I have, during this past year, learned so much about human dignity and love.*"[13]

Broken Hearts

The poem read in memory of former "comfort women" raises another question: "Who can stitch together [a] torn heart" of women crushed underfoot? Another Korean woman poet writes:

> To recollect the dreadful past
> The pitiful bygone nightmare
> Giving pain
> To the women of the world.[14]

The crimes against female humanity were committed by Japanese soldiers, but they should make all men shameful. These crimes testify to the sin of men in a world they dominate—sins of treating women as less than human and of using them as means to satisfy their carnal desires.

Males have prostituted God's gift of sexuality. Sexual love is an essential part of God's creation of humankind. The story of creation in the second chapter of Genesis shows deep insight when it says that a man and a woman "become one flesh," and that they "were both naked and were not ashamed" (Gen. 2:24-25). The union of a man and a woman in one flesh is a bodily union, a sexual union. At the same time, it is a union of a female spirit and a male spirit, a union of spirits and souls, a spiritual union, a soul union. And as a sexual and spiritual union it is a union blessed and sanctified by God.

This means that a sexual union between a man and a woman should be a spiritual union. It also means that a spiritual union between a woman and a man is realized in their sexual union. One should, then, speak of a sexual-spiritual or spiritual-sexual union between a woman and a man. It should be an ecstatic union, a union in which the man and the woman lose themselves in each other, become immersed in each other, become oblivious of the self as a separate individual, and together achieve the depth of a vision of God who is "love divine, all loves excelling."[15] This is what a sexual union must mean. Unfortunately, because of traditions shaped and dominated by men, this most sacred of all human unions has too often been desecrated, abused, and exploited by men to the detriment of both sexes. The abuse and exploitation of the female sex have become so common that, even when men seek to reclaim the sexual union as sacred, such overtures can be met with suspicion and rejection. That the Christian church has always treated sex as something beneath faith, even as something that betrays it, has contributed to the false view of sexual union as a hindrance to one's spiritual growth and well-being. The church's teaching on human sexuality, as an issue to be suppressed or to be spoken of in derogatory terms, has fostered a hypocritical attitude toward sexuality among its members.

The sexual union practiced as a spiritual union should, in fact, be beautiful and beatific. It must be for this reason that Genesis, after saying that man and woman would become one flesh, adds that they "were both naked, and were not ashamed." This is a healthy view of human sexuality. Sexuality practiced as a gift from God strengthens mutual relationship, deepens mutual acceptance, and enhances mutual well-being. It also makes us realize that other creatures with which we share God's creation are also born, live, and give birth to new lives on the strength of sexual relationships. The biblical story is right. When sexuality is respected as a divine gift and sexual union is practiced as a spiritual and physical union, there is nothing to be ashamed of. On the contrary, sexuality is to be treated with reverence and celebrated with both joy and awe, knowing that it reflects the union of God with humanity and the union of humanity with God.

But what happened to "comfort women" at the hands of Japanese soldiers during the Pacific War was shameful—not only shameful, but blasphemous. By treating women as they did, the soldiers blasphemed God's creation. When they excluded the spiritual from the sexual-spiritual union, they not only degraded women but themselves, and sank to the lowest level of inhumanity. It was their own humanity that they abused, and not the humanity of the women they abused carnally. It was their own humanity that they denied, not the humanity of the women they crushed under their boots. They committed crimes against humanity and sinned against God. The same should of course be said of all instances of rape—sexual acts that violate the humanity and will of others.

It never occurred to the Japanese soldiers, who committed the crime and sin, that they were breaking the hearts of the women subjected to their sexual abuse and torture. These women's hearts were so broken that the poem dedicated to their memory had to ask a painful question: "Who can stitch together your torn heart?" No one can stitch the heart of the "comfort women." It was broken into a thousand small pieces. Who could put them together again? The heart was removed and thrown away to make a body without a heart, a corpse without life. No one could stitch the heart into their body and make them human beings again.

On December 9, 1992, a privately organized hearing was held in Japan. After a former "comfort woman" from North Korea finished her testimony, another former "comfort woman" from South Korea rushed to the podium and embraced her. The other Korean women at the meeting quickly surrounded the two, embracing one another, bursting into tears, crying with their faces toward heaven in an expression of extreme sorrow and anguish, saying: "What a dreadful thing Japan did to you! How could one die in this way unrequited!" The hearing ended with a lament:

> The body broken as a young girl still trembles with pain,
> The heart torn as a young girl still hurts terribly. . . . [16]

Indeed, who could mend the body so cruelly mutilated? Who could stitch together the heart so mercilessly torn?

Jesus was also humiliated, and his body was broken. At his trial at the council of religious leaders, "some began to spit on him...and to strike him" (Mark 14:65; also Matt. 26:67-68; Luke 22:63). After Pilate the Roman governor sentenced him to death, the Roman soldiers "struck his head with a reed, spat upon him" (Mark 15:19; also Matt. 27:30; John 19:3). On the cross one of the soldiers "pierced his side with a spear, and at once blood and water came out" (John 19:34). If his body was thus cruelly attacked and broken, his heart too was so mercilessly torn that just before he died he burst into a loud cry: "My God, my God, why have you forsaken me?" (Mark 15:34; also Matt. 27:46).

The cry was so loud that "bystanders heard it" (Mark 15:35; also Matt. 27:47). It was a heart-wrenching cry. Abandoned by opponents, crowds, and disciples, and forsaken by God, Jesus let out a cry that must have drawn many hearts to him, especially the hearts of those women who followed him faithfully, and who accompanied him to Golgotha to be with him during his last hours. In his cry we seem to hear the cries of those "comfort women" who died with their bodies broken and hearts torn. In his cry we perceive the cries of those women who were with him, and the cries of those women who surrounded and embraced the former "comfort women."

But Jesus' suffering did not end in that heart-breaking cry. His death did not occur with that cry echoing in the air and lingering in the universe. According to Luke's account, Jesus said: "Father, into your hands I commend my spirit" (Luke 23:46). He said it "crying with a loud voice." This cry must have been as loud as the previous cry of forsakenness. It was a cry saying that his struggle with death was over. It was an invocation that his suffering should create new hearts and a new world. And it was a prayer to God to receive his suffering, to turn his suffering into suffering that loves, heals, and restores.

Is it not such suffering, love, and suffering unto love that we hear in the testimonies of the "comfort women"? A Filipino woman had to witness her father tortured to death by Japanese soldiers as well as the deaths of her two-year-old brother and seven-month-old sister. She herself was severely wounded and left for dead. She bled so much that her clothes were soaked with blood and stuck to her body. She concluded her testimony saying:

> Nothing good, literally nothing, could come out of war. Having to choose between war and peace, we must choose peace. We must love children and nurture them. And we must teach our children to love each other and help each other. *Where there is love, there is peace.* And when there is peace, there will be no war.[17]

For this Filipino woman suffering is not the last word, but love is. After her extreme suffering she still finds love possible. But her testimony goes even further.

The suffering she has gone through strengthens her faith in love, and calls us to love one another, even the people of the nation that plunged her into suffering.

Is this not suffering unto love, not unlike the suffering of Jesus, who died with love in his heart and on his lips? It is suffering unto love and not suffering itself that has the power to create peace in the world. It must be this suffering unto love that consoles the hearts and souls of the young women who died with their bodies broken and their hearts torn. And it is love born out of the excruciating birthpangs of suffering that could stitch their hearts.

Another Korean woman poet composed verses dedicated to the "comfort women," living or dead:

> Young as a rosebud
> your life
> has not even begun to blossom
> You are so young
> so sweet
> still so innocent
> that you could not have just been
> upon your mother's warm embrace
> drinking in from her tender
> breasts.[18]

The poem refers to the former "comfort women" in their youth, when they did not suspect that their world of love and peace would be turned upside down.

How could men subject those innocent lives to their bestial desires and insane carnal tyranny? Tens of thousands of Japanese soldiers inflicted abuse on virgin girls who, as the poet states, had not long ago "been drinking from [their mothers'] tender breasts." These soldiers, if they survived the war, returned to their country to become ordinary citizens, raised families, and had daughters of their own. How could they have told their families, and especially young daughters, what they had done? This utterly defies comprehension. But human nature often defies comprehension.

But in contrast to lowly human nature, some can rise to a moral height and show a noble side to humanity.

> O but arise now
> our ancient motherland flower
> stand high in our midst
> to sing a new song—
> yours
> ours
> for the peace, hope, justice,
> and love of the world.[19]

This is a summons to all the "comfort women" who died in confusion, shame, and pain. Their mutilated lifeless bodies could not respond, but one hopes and prays that their spirits, though broken and torn, can.

Jesus did rise from the realm of death. He was "laid...in a tomb that had been hewn out of the rock" with "a stone against the door of the tomb" (Mark 15:46; also Matt. 27:60; Luke 23:53). The tomb was sealed. But as it turned out, the spirit of Jesus was not sealed. It rolled away the stone placed against the tomb (see Luke 24:2; also John 20:1) and rose to sing a new song through millions of men and women who, like Jesus, had suffered and died. The new song these spirits sing is a song of peace, hope, and justice. Above all, it is a new song of suffering unto love, the love that grows out of suffering to give peace, hope, and justice to the world.

"Crucifix of Earth"

The cross of Jesus became the saving work of love. The cross cannot save others, but as suffering turned into love it can. The cross as the denial of enemies cannot save, but as an affirmation of them it can. The cross as a rejection of those who have committed sins and crimes against others and against God cannot save, but the cross that forgives can. The cross as condemnation of the world cannot save. What is left in the world to be saved when all has been condemned? But the cross that faces the world with suffering unto love can save it.

The cross of Jesus is this kind of cross. This is why men and women in suffering have, over the centuries, found themselves at the foot of the cross, receiving the courage to live, the faith to hope, and the vision for the future. This is the clue to why the cross has the power to give strength to those who "walk through a valley of deepest darkness" (Ps. 23:4 [REB]). That is also why it is a symbol, a supreme symbol, not of despair but hope, not of defeat but victory, not of death but life. Why is the cross of Jesus a secret? Because the saving love it embodies is of God. Why is it a clue? Because the saving power that emanates from it comes from God. And why is it a symbol? Because the saving reality it symbolizes is the reality of none other than God. The cross of Jesus testifies that God in Jesus and Jesus in God is this saving love, this saving power, this saving reality. It also testifies that since it is a saving power, love, and reality, it embraces the crosses men and women have to bear and re-creates them as crosses of saving power, love, and reality.

Is this why Chong Jin-Nim addresses the "comfort women" as "You, pain-filled crucifix of earth"? This "crucifix of earth" bears a striking resemblance to the cross of Jesus; crosses in opulent churches do not. It is a pain-filled cross just like the cross of Jesus, unlike the crosses that glitter in well-decorated church buildings that are pain-free. It holds in itself the agonies and afflictions no language can convey.

But this "pain-filled crucifix of earth" also has other aspects to remind us of the cross of Jesus.

> You blossom anew like flowers trampled under weed....
> You are innocent. You are our mother....
> You who are the crucifix of Korea...
> You who are the flowers of Korea's tears.

Is not the crucifix of Korea—and of other Asian nations—also the crucifix of Jesus, the crucifix of God who made the heavens and the earth, and the crucifix of God who created human beings? Since Jesus embraces this pain-filled crucifix just as God embraces it, it is not going to rot away in the ground and be forgotten. It will blossom anew, claiming its right to be the mother of the future generations of women and men. It will become part of God's new creation.

To be a mother is to nourish the seed of a new life in the womb, and to give birth to it in the fulfillment of time. Is not the cross of Jesus such a mother to generations of men and women? It has nurtured many lives in its womb, made them grow, and given them birth. From the crucifix of suffering humanity we learn what the cross of Jesus means as the cross of suffering unto love. At the same time we also learn how the cross of Jesus transforms the crucifix of human beings, who suffer pain and death, into the mother that gives life and hope to the world.

Life-Force Called Love

We have come full circle, have we not? We began our journey with a life-and-death matter. We know that if there is life, there is also death. We know that the shadow of death always hangs over life. We know that the process of dying is part of the process of living. We all die—all sentient beings, all living creatures, all things in creation. Even the universe itself, which lives billions and billions of years, will one day die to give way to new universes. But is it not also true that the process of living is part of the process of dying? All creatures live to die, but they also die to live, living in the generations to come, living in God's creation, and living, finally, in God who is life itself.

Could this be what Jesus was saying when he was told that Lazarus, whom he loved, had fallen fatally ill (John 11:3)? Jesus replied: "This illness does not lead to death" (11:4). Was John setting the stage for Jesus to raise Lazarus from death? However one may understand the story, "the ultimate issue of this sickness would not be death. Rather it would be for God's glory,"[20] the glory of God being the source of life and not death.

This is faith. And this faith gives rise to hope. Holding this faith and hope Jesus carried on his ministry, knowing full well what was in store for him: death on the cross. If the ultimate issue of Lazarus's illness for Jesus is not death, the ultimate issue of the cross is not death either; it is life. This is a difficult faith, not only for us Christians, but for Jesus himself. This is an impossible faith, not only for human beings at large, but for Jesus. What makes this faith possible is not blind faith, not courageous faith, not single-minded faith. It is the faith that God is love, that God cannot be other than love, that for God to be God, God must be love. In a life and ministry filled with pain and suffering, followed by the shadow of death, the deepening experience of God as love strengthened Jesus' awareness that the ultimate issue of the cross is not death. The awareness grew into the assurance, not just hope, of a new life through death on the cross.

Life as an Ultimate Issue

What, then, is this love? Of what does it consist? Love is life-force, a force that gives birth to life, a force that sustains it, gives meaning to it, and re-creates it. As such, love is a life-making force. Does not life begin with the union of love between a woman and a man? Making life is a biological act. This is what takes place in the world of nature. Human life-making is also a part of the natural world, but if it is only biological and physical, it is a union of impulses, and not of love. And when it takes place with force and violence, it is rape and not a union of love.

In the story of the woman caught in adultery, John does not tell us whether it was a case of rape or mutual consent. But by exposing and condemning her in the name of the law, the people who had brought her to Jesus were violating her as a human being and as a woman. What they exhibited was not life-making force, but life-destroying force. It may be that this was how Jesus felt. "Neither do I condemn you," Jesus said to her. "Go your way, and from now on do not sin again" (John 8:11). That was a turning point in her life, for Jesus' love as a life-making force enabled her to start her life all over again.

Love is a life-affirming force. Love is love because it affirms others, even though others are different in how they live and what they believe. It does not try to make others just as we are. Others are others precisely because they are different from us. Is not the reverse also true? We are others to them because we are different from them. If there are no others, there is no us; and if there is no us, there are no others. Life is possible when it is based on affirmation of others by us and affirmation of us by others. It is this love as affirmation of others that Jesus practiced when he associated himself with social and religious outcasts. "Yours is the reign of God," he told them (Luke 6:20-23; also Matt. 5:3-12). He also practiced this love when he affirmed the faith of a Roman centurion: "In no one in Israel have I found such faith" (Matt. 8:10).

Love is a life-saving force. Love, if it is life-making and life-affirming, can save a lot of things. It can save broken relationships—relationships between parents and children, between married people, between sisters and brothers, between friends. Is it not too unrealistic to talk about love in our society in which power and greed prevail? Is it not too idealistic to mention the word *love* in the world of conflicts? But is it not precisely for this reason that love as a life-saving force is most needed? Love as a life-saving force is not a sentimental love, not the love that patches things up, that saves face, that keeps the semblance of peace. This is a costly love. Something has to go: power, greed, privileges, cherished ideas and practices. Love is not saving if the person practicing it does not get hurt. It is not healing if it does not make the person exercising it suffer. It is not liberating if it does not demand us to give up what is dear to us, even life itself. Did not Jesus say, "Those who seek to preserve their life will lose it; and those who lose their life will gain it" (Luke 17:33)?[21] And his love as life-saving force cost his own life, but gained many lives.

Love is also a life-renewing force. Our life is not a self-growing, self-preserving, and self-perpetuating entity. This is true both physically and spiritually. Left to itself, a life will become weak, shrivel, and die. It has to be fed, nurtured, trained, and cared for, again both physically and spiritually. But there is a biological clock that we cannot turn back, the clock that reminds us of the finitude of our life. Is there something we can do about that clock? Yes, there is. It is the life-renewing force called love. We do not have to wait until our biological time runs out to get that love activated. The end of biological time would be too late even for love. The fact is that physically, in terms of billions of cells that make up our body, we die each moment, each day. We do not have to wait until our last day and the last moment on the earth to die. We die each day of our life.

But love as the life-renewing force can renew us also each day of our life. It does so by motivating us to extend a helping hand to those in pain and suffering, inspiring us to strive for justice, enabling us to pursue what is true and right. And it gives us the power to believe in the love that renews our lives and the lives of others. It is this love as life-renewing force to which Jesus must be referring when he says, "No one puts new wine into old wineskins" (Mark 2:22; also Matt. 9:17; Luke 5:37). Love is this new wine. Some of the physical cells in our body die each day, but when love grows and works inside us, the spirit in us, the self in us, the humanity in us, gets renewed little by little until we are transformed into "a new creation" (2 Cor. 5:17), to use Paul's expression. On that day and at that moment we are born again from the womb of death. This is a great mystery of love. And as we strive to practice love as a life-renewing force and experience, in joy as well as sorrow, both in frustration and encouragement, in despair on the one hand and hope on the other, we may come to grips with it as a mystery of life, not only here but also hereafter.

God as love is this kind of life-force. Is this not the reason why God is said to have "created the heavens and the earth" when "the earth was a formless void and darkness covered the face of the deep" (Gen. 1:1-2)? If it were not for God as the life-force as mentioned above, how could one account for the fact that the cross of Jesus has become the faith and hope for millions of women and men? And if God were not this life-making, life-affirming, life-saving, and life-renewing force of life, how can one explain why hundreds of thousands of people in history have gone to their deaths for the sake of what they believe to be true, good, and noble? Even in Jesus' case, could he have gone to die on the cross if he had not believed in God who is love?

"There Is No Fear in Love"

"There is no fear in love," we read in the First Letter of John. In the light of love we have discussed so far, we can only agree with the saying. Love that creates fear is not love. It is something other than love. It is fear disguised in the form of love. It is not a life-force, a force that gives birth to life, but a fear-force, a force that gives rise to fear, that spreads fear and pollutes the world with fear. It is not a life-creating force, but a force that intimidates life, frightens it, and alienates it. It is not a life-saving force, but a force that judges, punishes, condemns, and destroys.

If God is love as the life-force, it is wrong to portray this God as the God of wrath, the God of judgment, the God of punishment, and the God who condemns. Is this not the way God has been portrayed in religions, even in Christianity? God is often portrayed in this way in sermons, in apocalyptic literature, and in popular religious literature. God who shows love to believers and bestows blessing on them after raging against infidels and inflicting punishment and death on unbelievers is an anticlimactic God, not God at the beginning who created the heavens and the earth in love, but God who comes at the end of the world to collect those who survived the horrors of destruction.

This is not the God portrayed by Jesus. For Jesus, God, from beginning to end and beyond the end, from start to finish and beyond the finish, is the God of the life-giving and life-saving love. Is this not why Jesus told the parable of the loving father (Luke 15:11-24)? "This son of mine was dead and is alive," says the father upon his son's return. "He was lost and is found!" (Luke 15:24). There is no word about the father's anger toward his son, only words alluding to the anxious wait for his son's return. Jesus also tells a story of a shepherd who, after having found the lost sheep, invited his neighbors to come and celebrate the happy occasion with him. "Rejoice with me," he said, "for I have found my sheep that was lost" (Luke 15:6). Again there are no complaints on the part of the shepherd about the hardship he had to go through in his search for the lost sheep. There is only joy and happiness. How could there be fear in this kind of love?

If love that has no fear takes away from us fear for God, it should also remove from us fear of death. One of the reasons that attracts people to religion is fear of death.

Human beings are born, live, and must die. What then happens after death? Grief-stricken parents at the side of the deceased child they loved, sons and daughters weeping at the death of their parent, bitter separation caused by a friend's death, by the death of the beloved spouse, or by the death of the person with whom one was deeply in love—all this creates unbearable loneliness for the bereaved. The deceased is gone forever, raising for the survivors the question of where death has taken them, and casting doubts about eternal life and about reunion with them. Since the ancient times philosophers and thinkers have wrestled with the question of death, speculated about it and meditated on it. Religious teachers, too, have prayed for revelation from above to be enlightened. As for most people, they have lived and died with one kind of view on life and death or another.[22]

The questions posed are perennial and seem destined to remain perennial. Death is inevitable, but there seems no answer to the questions it raises.

Where has death taken our beloved ones? Is the separation caused by death absolute? Is the hope of reunion with them mere wishful thinking? These were also the questions of Jesus' disciples. With his death becoming more certain and inevitable with each passing day, Jesus seemed to become more and more preoccupied with such questions. It is John who captures Jesus in this meditative and prayerful situation in what is known as Jesus' farewell discourses (John 13:1—17:26). At one point Jesus, according to John, tells his disciples: "Little children, I am with you only a little longer. You will look for me; and as I said to the Jews [the Jewish leaders who opposed him] so now I say to you, 'Where I am going, you cannot come'" (John 13:33).[23]

These words leave both his opponents and disciples puzzled and mystified. They completely misunderstand him. This is how his opponents responded: "Is he going to kill himself? Is that what he means by saying, 'Where I am going, you cannot come'?" (John 8:22). As for his disciples, Peter spoke up on their behalf: "Lord, where are you going? . . . Why can I not follow you now? I will lay down my life for you" (John 13:36-37). Peter's response was followed by Jesus' prediction that Peter would deny him three times before the cock crowed. But the point John the Evangelist is making is that neither Jesus' opponents nor his own disciples understood him. Jesus and his conversation partners were talking about two different things, one referring to the heaven and the others to the earth, as the Taiwanese would say.

For Jesus, he was focused on the inevitable prospect of his departure from this world. He could speak about it only in a vague language, in metaphors of coming and going, of being with his disciples only a little longer, of their not being able to find him. These are allusions to his death. As allusions, what Jesus said does not make it clear whether he himself had sure knowledge of what was going to happen to him after death.

This seems to lead us to the conclusion that Jesus was not any wiser than philosophers, thinkers, and religious teachers who have said much about death only to realize that they could only say little. Death and what happens after death, if not matters of speculation, have to be matters of faith. Christian preachers today, instead of painting fanciful pictures of what life after death is like, should stress that the ultimate matter of life after death is a matter of faith, and not a matter of achieving desires and ambitions not fulfilled in this world.

But Jesus, according to John the Evangelist, did not in fact leave the question of death totally in the dark. After saying to his disciples that they could not go where he was going, he went on to give them "a new commandment of love": "Just as I have loved you, you also should love one another. By this everyone will know that you are my disciples, if you have love for one another" (John 13:34-35). From the talk on death to the commandment on love—this seems to be a big jump in discourse. It is not. What happens is a change of orientation and direction.

To face death one must practice love. Love in this case is not something optional, something with which one engages in one's spare time. If one does not deal with death as an option or in one's spare time, one cannot treat love in a halfhearted way. Since love possesses the key to the questions posed by death, we have to engage ourselves with it in all seriousness. This is what love as a commandment means. In reminding us of this compulsory nature of love, Jesus is not turning love into a law, making it a legal case. Just the contrary. Love as a commandment requires us to continue practicing it so that it becomes second nature to us and part of us, so that it takes hold of us and takes form in us.

If this love works in us, motivates us in our relationships with others, and empowers us in our daily encounter with death, then we do not have to fear death. Wherever there is no love, there is fear of death; but wherever there is love, there is no fear of death. This is because there is no fear in love. Whenever love is absent, then fear of death becomes real; but whenever love is present, then fear of death loses its power. Faith is the practice of living and dying in love in which there is no fear.

The life lived in such love is a liberated life. It is a life lived for others and for God. And the death died in such love is a death leading to a new life with God and with those who have gone to be with God. Death is not the end of life, but the beginning of life, a new life, an abundant life. We do not know what it is like, but we can be sure it is a life to be lived in love without fear. It is a life with God and in God. Can we say more than this about life after death? No. This is perhaps all we can say about it. Do we need to say more about it? No. This is all we need to say about it. Life in love that has no fear is to be born each day in God who is LOVE. And death in love that has no fear is to be born once for all eternity in the LOVE that is God.

Resurrection of Love

This takes us back to the moving post-Easter scene depicted by John at the end of his Gospel. To the distraught disciples who had returned to their old fishing trade by the Sea of Tiberias, the risen Lord appeared in his full presence. There was a miraculous catch of fish, a sacramental event reminding them of how they had been called to follow him three years earlier. On the shore were bread and the fish prepared on a charcoal fire. Jesus invited them to have breakfast with him. This was a sacramental meal, a meal that made the disciples remember the Last Supper they had with Jesus and the many meals they and Jesus had with women, men, and children on the fringes of their society and religious community. John has created a scene that brings to a distinct relief what Jesus means to him, to the disciples, and to the rest of the world.

The conversation that ensued between Jesus and Peter is a conversation on love. Jesus asks Peter: "Do you love me?" The question is repeated three times, and Peter responds yes three times. This exchange has usually been taken to mean that "Peter [is] completely restored to his position of leadership. Three times he had denied his Lord. Now he has three times affirmed his love for him, and three times he has been commissioned to care for the flock."[24] This might have been part of what John had in mind when he crafted this story with so much sensitivity and affection. But is this all he was trying to say?

What is the real theme of the story: Jesus' naming of love or Peter's restoration to leadership? It must be the former. Who is the main character of the story: Jesus or Peter? It must be Jesus. Standing before Peter and the other disciples is the Jesus who loved them, and who loved the people that followed him. He loved them so much that he was not afraid to offend the political and religious authorities. He loved to the extent that he was willing to defend their rights and dignity as human beings. He loved them in such a way that he was for them the presence of God who so loved the world. It is this love the risen Lord must be driving home to the disciples. It is this love that he is trying to resurrect in their hearts. It is the love that has no fear, the love that is not afraid of opposition, hostility, and even death.

Then there is this "me" in the question Jesus asked Peter, with the other disciples listening to him in quiet and rapt attention: "Do you love *me?*" (John 21:15, 16, 17). Who is this "me"? This "me," first of all, is Jesus himself. Do you love me with the love that has no fear, the love that enables you to stand with me no matter what happens? This "me" is the community of men, women, and children with whom Jesus used to associate himself, people exploited by the rich and the powerful. Do you love them with the love that has no fear, the love that does not allow you to leave them in the lurch? This "me" is the world God so loved. Do you also love this world, John seems to have Jesus asking them, so that the world would know that God so loved it?

If we recall how John began his Gospel by saying, "In the beginning was the Word, and the Word was with God, and the Word was God" (1:1), we may assume that this "me" also relates to God's creation. It is not just "me" as an individual person, "me" as human community, and "me" as the world. This "me" is all this, but more than this. This "me" is the cosmic "me," the "me" that makes all things come into being, loving them, affirming them, saving them, and renewing them. This "me" is God, who was in the beginning and always is from now to the end, the end which in reality is a new beginning.

However one may understand what the resurrection means, it means, above everything else, the resurrection of this love as the life-force in the individual "me," in the "me" as human community, as the world, as creation, and as God. If this is what the resurrection of Jesus means, then resurrection did not take place only after Jesus' death on the cross. It took place when Jesus healed the sick, comforted the sorrowful, lifted up the downtrodden, strengthened the weary, and gave courage to those in despair. And if this is what resurrection signifies, it did not take place only within the Christian community but also in other communities. And if this is what the resurrection of Jesus symbolizes, should it seem strange if it takes place in all parts of God's creation at all times?

Whenever there is resurrection of love, there is resurrection of life. Jesus comes to resurrect love in the world so that there will be life in the world, the life that is saved and renewed by love, the life that does not die in spite of death, and the life that is fulfilled in God who so loved the world yesterday, so loves it today, and will never stop loving it tomorrow. To have faith is to have this kind of love. To hope is to be inspired by love. And to live is to learn to practice love in our lives. Life, Hope, and Faith are companions of our journey in LOVE—love that has no fear, love that makes us aware of God in us and with us, love that enables us to identify that God in others, the God who is behind us and before us, the God who is also behind others and before others. For Christians it is Jesus who deepens that faith and hope in that God of love, that "one God...who is above all and through all and in all" (Eph. 4:6).

Notes

Part One: Invitation

1. *De unit. eccl.* 6; quoted in J. N. D. Kelly, *Early Christian Doctrines,* rev. ed. (New York: Harper & Row, 1978), 206.

2. See Kelly, *Early Christian Doctrines,* 206.

3. Hans Küng, *Christianity and the World Religions: Paths of Dialogue with Islam, Hinduism, and Buddhism,* trans. Peter Heinegg (Garden City, N.Y.: Doubleday, 1986), xiii.

4. Even the figure of 309.1 million computed in the 1992 *Encyclopaedia Britannica Book of the Year,* quoted in "Religions of the World Gather in Chicago," *San Francisco Chronicle,* August 27, 1993, p. A4, seems too low. The article was written on the occasion of the international gathering in Chicago, August 1993, to mark the one hundredth anniversary of the Parliament of the World's Religions.

5. See the cover story, "The Generation That Forgot God: The Baby Boom Goes Back to Church, and Church Will Never Be the Same Again," *Time,* April 5, 1993, 46–47.

6. See ibid., 46.

7. Ibid., 47.

Chapter 1: We Piped for You and You Would Not Dance

1. Francis Wright Beare, *The Gospel according to Matthew* (San Francisco: Harper & Row, 1981), 262.

2. See *Webster's New World Dictionary,* 2d ed. (New York: World Publishing Company, 1970).

3. See D. T. Suzuki, *Essays in Zen Buddhism,* 1st ser. (London: Rider, 1970), 376.

4. She Cheng Yen, *Chin Su Ch'eng Yu, "Morning Meditations"* (Taipei: Ch'u Chi Wen Hua Press, 1992), 216. Translation from the Chinese by C. S. Song.

5. See Suzuki, *Essays in Zen Buddhism,* 2d ser. (London: Rider, 1970), 41–42. The story is taken from *Kao Shen Chuan* (Biographies of high monks), 24, comprising the periods extending from the Liang (502–57), T'ang (618–907), and Sung (960–1279) dynasties.

6. Suzuki, *Essays in Zen Buddhism,* 2d ser., 45–46.

7. Ibid., 48.

8. John Macquarrie, the British theologian, uses the term in the latter sense in *God-Talk: An Examination of the Language and Logic of Theology* (London: SCM Press, 1967). Theology, he tells us, "is a form of discourse professing to speak about God" (11).

9. See Lao Tzu, *Tao Te Ching,* trans. D. C. Liu (New York: Penguin Books, 1963), 117.

10. Confucius, *The Analects* 2.22. See *The Chinese Classics,* trans. James Legge (Hong Kong: Hong Kong University Press, 1960), 1:153.

317

Chapter 2: Birds of the Air and Lilies of the Field

1. NRSV translations have been slightly altered throughout for gender inclusiveness.

2. For my treatment of this subject see *Jesus and the Reign of God* (Minneapolis: Fortress, 1993).

3. Jaroslav Pelikan, *Jesus through the Centuries: His Place in the History of Culture* (New Haven: Yale University Press, 1985), 47.

4. Ibid., 56.

5. See footnote on Matt. 18:24 in *The New Oxford Annotated Bible* (NRSV), ed. Bruce M. Metzger and Roland E. Murphy (New York: Oxford University Press, 1991).

6. See footnote on Matt. 18:28 in ibid.

7. Quotations are taken from *The Prayers and Meditations of Saint Anselm with Proslogion,* trans. Benedicta Ward (Middlesex, England: Penguin Books, 1975), 244.

Chapter 3: Come and See

1. D. T. Suzuki, *Essays in Zen Buddhism,* 1st ser. (London: Rider, 1970), 237.

2. It is interesting to note that the author of the Fourth Gospel has Philip, who had joined Jesus as a disciple, say to Nathanael when the latter questioned Jesus' credentials, "Come and see" (John 1:46).

3. Quoted from the paper, "Protestant Christianity in China Facing the Challenges of Modernization," presented by Chen Zemin, vice president of Nanjing Theological Seminary, at the "International Consultation on Christian Culture and Modernization," Beijing, October 10–14, 1994.

4. Ibid.

5. I use the phrase "the kingdom of God," here following the translation in the NRSV. But it is better rendered as "the reign of God," or "the rule of God." I have used the rendering "reign of God" in some places. See my book *Jesus and the Reign of God* (Minneapolis: Fortress, 1993).

6. In my book *Jesus in the Power of the Spirit* (Minneapolis: Fortress, 1994), I tried to address the issues raised here.

7. The reader is referred, for instance, to Jaroslav Pelikan, *Jesus through the Centuries: His Place in the History of Culture* (New Haven: Yale University Press, 1985).

8. See *Webster's New World Dictionary,* 2d ed. (New York: World Publishing Company, 1970).

9. Ibid.

10. The Ami tribe is one of some eleven aboriginal tribes in Taiwan with a total population of about 150,000.

11. According to the exchange rate, current at this writing (1997), of one U.S. dollar per 26 yen, 400,000 yen is approximately U.S. $15,000, and 300,000 yen about $11,500.

12. The story, which I abridged, paraphrased, and translated from the Chinese, is found in *Po Hi-bang* (Repairing fishing nets), published by the Fishermen Service Center, the Presbyterian Church in Taiwan, 1991, 44–45.

Part Two: Life

1. The date of the Buddha's birth has been a matter of conjecture by scholars. Here I follow the dating by Hajime Nakamura. See his *Genshi Bukkyo, sono Shiso to Seikatsu* (Primitive Buddhism: Its thoughts and ways of life) (Tokyo: NHK Books, 1970), 35.

2. See *The Buddhist Tradition, in India, China, and Japan,* ed. William Theodore de Bary (New York: Vintage Books, 1972), 60–64.

Chapter 4: Death Is Not the Wages of Sin

1. The idea that the human being is formed from dust "is also commonplace outside the OT. The Gilgamesh Epic (1:34) tells how Aruru created Enkidu from clay. Egyptian monuments portray the god Khnum making man out of clay. The classic myths tell of Prometheus creating the first man from soil and water. It is evident then that Genesis is here taking up a very ancient tradition of the creation of man and is giving these old ideas its own distinctive flavor.... Other peoples too regarded man as constituted of clay plus a divine element. The Babylonians spoke of man as a mixture of clay and the blood of a god. The Egyptians held that men had souls like the gods. Similarly, Prometheus made the human body from clay and gave it life with divine sparks" (Gender-exclusive language has been retained; see Gordon J. Wenham, *Genesis 1–15*, Word Biblical Commentary 1 [Waco, Tex.: Word Books, 1987], 59–60).

2. *Yi qi mian dui sheng si* (Facing life and death together) (Taipei: Yuan Shen Publishing House, 1994), 38–39. Chinese translation by Chen-Mei Lin of the Japanese original entitled, *Byoyin de sinu to yu ko to* (Dying at the hospital), by Yamazaki Shozo. The English excerpt here is translated from the Chinese by C. S. Song.

3. The discovery of twenty thousand-year-old paintings of animals in a Paleolithic cave near Avignon in southern France is said to have "reopened some of the oldest and least settled of questions: When, how and above all why did Homo sapiens start making art?" It is suggested that the oral spray painting used to create these cave paintings "may have had a spiritual dimension: 'Spitting is a way of projecting yourself into the wall, becoming one with the horse you are painting. Thus the action melds with the myth. Perhaps the shamans did this as a way of passing into the world beyond.'" See "Behold the Stone Age," *Time*, February 13, 1995, 52–62.

4. Brian L. Weiss, for example, head of the psychiatry department at Sinai Medical Center, in *Many Lives, Many Masters* (New York: Simon & Schuster, 1988) made public his exploration of reincarnation based on the psychiatric treatment he carried out on one of his patients.

5. Walter Brueggemann, *Genesis,* Interpretation (Atlanta: John Knox Press, 1982), 45. This is a departure from the biblical and theological expositions focused on the tree of the knowledge of good and evil and on the human desire to "be like God, knowing good and evil [i.e., everything]" (Gen. 3:5).

6. Wenham, *Genesis 1–15*, 67.

7. The story of Abraham offering Isaac his only son as a sacrifice to God in Genesis 22 indicates that child sacrifice was also practiced in ancient Israel at one time.

8. J. G. Frazer, *The Belief in Immortality* (London, 1913), 74–75. Quoted in Mircea Eliade in *From Primitives to Zen: A Thematic Sourcebook of the History of Religions* (New York: Collins/Fount Paperbacks, 1967), 140.

9. Wenham, *Genesis 1–15*, 73.

10. Pope John Paul II, for example, says in the encyclical *Evangelium vitae:* "Death came into the world as a result of the devil's envy (cf. Genesis 3:1, 4-5) and the sin of our first parents (Genesis 2:17, 3:17-19)." See "The Gospel of Life: The Encyclical Letter on Abortion, Euthanasia, and the Death Penalty," in *Today's World* (New York: Times Books/Random House, 1995), 13.

11. Anselm, *Cur Deus Homo.*

12. Ibid.

13. See Lau Su-Kuang, *Zhong guo zhe xue shi* (A history of Chinese philosophy), rev. ed., 3 vols. (Taipei: San Min Publishing House, 1984), 1:256.

14. See *A Source Book in Chinese Philosophy,* translated and compiled by Wing-Tsit

Chan (Princeton, N.J.: Princeton University Press, 1963), 209; from *Chuang Tzu*, "Chi lo" (Bliss), 2.

15. *Chuang Tzu*, chap. 6, *"Da zong shi"* (The great teacher): "Si sheng, min ye, qi you ye dan zhi chang, tian ye, ren zhi you suo bu de yu, jie wu zhi qing ye." For the English translation see *The Sayings of Chuang Tzu*, trans. James R. Ware (Taipei: Confucius Publishing, 1970), 68. The phrase, "beyond the interference of human being," however, is the rendering by Wing-Tsit Chan in *A Source Book in Chinese Philosophy*, 193.

16. See Fu Wei Xun, *Si wang zhi zun yen yu sheng min zhi zun yen* (Dignity of death and dignity of life) (Taipei: Zheng Zhong Press, 1993), 166.

17. *Zhu xin we zhang* in Hinayana Buddhism. This is one of the three signs or proofs of a Hinayana sutra called nonpermanence. The other two signs are nonpersonality (or nonself), and nirvana.

18. *The Sutra of the Heart of Prajina* (*bo re xin jing*) is composed of some 260 Chinese characters representing the essence of the six hundred volumes of the Heart Sutra (*xin jing*). This famous quotation in Chinese is as follows: *Se bu yi kong, kong bu yi se. Se zhi shi kong, kong zhi shi se.*

19. See Nakamura Hajime, *Gen shi bukkyo, so no si so to se kai* (Primitive Buddhism: Its thoughts and world) (Tokyo: NHK Bukkus, 1970), 97–99.

20. *The Compact Edition of the Oxford English Dictionary* (London: Oxford University Press, 1971), 1:968.

21. *Webster's New World Dictionary*, 2d ed. (New York: World Publishing Company, 1970).

22. *Sayings of Chuang Tzu*, chap. 5, *"De chong fu"* (Evidences of complete excellence), 58.

23. This is a paraphrase of Lau Su-Kuang's interpretation in his *zhong guo zhe xue shi*, 1:262.

24. Ibid., 1:263.

25. Ibid., 1:260.

26. *The Chuang Tzu*, *"De chong fu."* See *Sayings of Chuang Tzu*, chap. 5, 52.

27. Fu Wei Xun, *Si wang zhi zun yen yu sheng min zhi zun yen*, 167.

28. See Joseph A. Fitzmyer, S.J., *The Gospel according to Luke, I–IX*, Anchor Bible 28 (New York: Doubleday, 1981), 658.

29. *Webster's New World Dictionary*, 1086.

30. See Hugh Anderson, *The Gospel according to Mark* (London: Marshall, Morgan & Scott, 1976), 152.

31. *The Analects* 3.12. See Chan, *A Source Book in Chinese Philosophy*, 25.

32. This verse should directly follow v. 7a, for "the discussion of a dubious journey to Judea without any mention of the Lazarus theme in verses 7-10 [is] interpolated in order to emphasize the risk of a return to Judea" (see Ernst Haenchen, *A Commentary on the Gospel of John 7–21*, trans. Robert W. Funk [Minneapolis: Fortress Press, 1984], 59).

33. See ibid., 57.

34. Ibid., 56.

Chapter 5: In the World There Is Suffering

1. See Heinrich Dumoulin, *Zen Buddhism: A History*, vol. 1: *India and China* (New York: Macmillan, 1988), 171.

2. The story is from *Chan jue* (Zen awakening), ed. Chiu Han-jue (Taipei: Yau Wen Books, 1990), 181; translation from the Chinese by C. S. Song.

3. For some gruesome Buddhist stories written from this perspective see, for example, Elizabeth Wilson, "The Female Body as a Source of Horror and Insight in Post-Ashokan Indian Buddhism," in *Religious Reflections on the Human Body*, ed. Jane Marie Law (Bloomington: Indiana University Press, 1995), 76–99.

4. Cf. Chiu Han-jue, *Chan jue*, 183f.

5. *San Francisco Chronicle*, April 14, 1995, A1 and A4.

6. Ibid.

7. François Barton, "Health in a City Environment," *World Health* (The magazine of the World Health Organization), May–June 1994, 24.

8. Ibid.

9. Ibid.

10. Dominique Lapierre, *The City of Joy*, trans. Kathryn Spink (New York: Warner Books, 1985), 37.

11. Ibid., 31.

12. "Revenge of the Killer Microbes," *Time*, September 12, 1994, 62.

13. Ibid.

14. Ibid.

15. Samir Ben Yahmed, "Population Growth and Disasters," *World Health*, May–June 1994, 26.

16. Albert Camus, *The Plague*, trans. Stuart Gilbert (New York: Penguin Books, 1960), 78.

17. Ibid., 80.

18. Ibid., 82. No attempt is made to replace sexist language in order to preserve the way the author has the priest deliver his sermon.

19. Ibid., 84.

20. Claus Westermann, *Genesis 1–11*, trans. John J. Scullion, S.J. (Minneapolis: Augsburg Publishing House, 1984), 256f.

21. Lila Abu-Lughod, *Writing Women's World: Bedouin Stories* (Berkeley: University of California Press, 1993), 132.

22. Ibid.

23. Ibid., 90.

24. There is a parallel story in Gen. 12:10-20.

25. Judy Cannato, in *Womenpsalms*, compiled by Julia Ahlers, Rosemary Broughton, and Carl Koch (Winona, Minn.: Saint Mary's Press, 1992), 111–12.

26. The Hebrew phrase translated as "in toil" (NRSV) and "by labor" (REB) is *he'itsabon* (בעצבון), literally "in pain."

27. One recalls a well-known book by S. N. Kramer, *History Begins at Suma*, to which Mircea Eliade referred in his *A History of Religious Ideas*, vol. 1: *From the Stone Age to the Eleusinian Mysteries*, trans. Willard R. Trask (Chicago: University of Chicago Press, 1978), 56.

28. Nyein Chan, in *Voices from the Jungle: Burmese Youth in Transition* (Tokyo: Center for Christian Response to Asian Issues, 1989), 66.

29. Ibid.

30. Eugene Borowitz, *The Mask Jews Wear* (New York: Simon & Schuster, 1973), 99. Quoted in Michael Peterson et al., *Reason and Religious Belief: An Introduction to the Philosophy of Religion* (New York: Oxford University Press, 1991), 92.

31. Fyodor Dostoyevsky, *The Brothers Karamazov*, trans. David Magarshack (New York: Penguin Books, 1958), 285.

32. The source from which this quotation was taken is lost and cannot be identified.

33. Hajime Nakamura, "Basic Teachings of Buddhism," in Heinrich Dumoulin, ed., *Buddhism in the Modern World* (New York: Macmillan, 1976), 5.

34. Rita M. Gross, *Buddhism after Patriarchy: A Feminist History, Analysis, and Reconstruction of Buddhism* (Albany: State University of New York Press, 1993), 150.

35. See *The Wisdom of Buddhism*, ed. Christmas Humphreys (London: Curzon Press, 1979), 57.

36. See Marvin H. Pope, *Job*, Anchor Bible 15 (New York: Doubleday, 1965), 13.

37. "No passage could be structurally closer than this to Job 3. It could even be said that Job 3 and Jeremiah 20:14-18 are two of the most structurally parallel passages in the Bible." This does not mean that there is a direct dependence of one on the other, but "more likely, we are dealing with a particular genre (in this case a lament genre) that both Jeremiah and the poet of Job draw on for their own particular purposes" (Bruce Zuckerman, *Job the Silent: A Study in Historical Counterpoint* [New York: Oxford University Press, 1991], 124).

38. C. S. Mann, *Mark*, Anchor Bible 27 (New York: Doubleday, 1986), 277.

39. Hugh Anderson, *The Gospel according to Mark* (London: Marshall, Morgan & Scott, 1976), 148.

40. Joseph A. Fitzmyer, S.J., *The Gospel according to Luke, I–IX*, Anchor Bible 28 (New York: Doubleday, 1981), 738.

41. From the *Mahayana-abhisamaya Sutra*, quoted in D. T. Suzuki in *Outlines of Mahayana Buddhism* (New York: Schocken Books, 1963), 45.

42. Mann, *Mark*, 278.

43. Claus Westermann, *Isaiah 40–66: A Commentary* (Philadelphia: Westminster Press, 1969), 262, 263.

44. For the whole story see John 9:1-41.

45. Raymond E. Brown, *The Gospel according to John 13–21*, Anchor Bible 29a (New York: Doubleday, 1970), 737.

Part Three: Hope

1. Song from Zaire (author unknown), quoted in Bernadette Mbuy-Beya, "African Spirituality: A Cry for Life," in *Spirituality of the Third World*, ed. K. C. Abraham and Bernadette Mbuy-Beya (Maryknoll, N.Y.: Orbis Books, 1994), 74–75.

Chapter 6: Elusive Hope

1. *Serving One Another*, report of the "Consultation on the Mission and Ministry to Filipino Migrant Workers in Hong Kong," April 28 to May 1, 1991, Kowloon, Hong Kong (Hong Kong: Christian Conference of Asia/Urban Rural Mission, 1991), 67–68.

2. Ibid., 70.

3. See Feliciano V. Carino, "Towards an Ecumenical Mission and Ministry to Filipino Migrant Workers in Hong Kong," in ibid., 40.

4. Maria Teresa I. Diokno, "Asian Realities and the Migrant Worker," in ibid., 45.

5. Ibid., 45.

6. Ibid., 46.

7. "The ASEAN Declaration" (Bangkok, 1967). See *ASEAN Reader*, compiled by Francisco A. Magno, *Asian Issues* (Hong Kong: Christian Conference of Asia/International Affairs) 2 (January 1990): 12.

8. Ibid., 15.

9. Ronald Reagan won the U.S. presidential election in 1980, in part, by asking voters if they were better off economically than in 1976, when Jimmy Carter, Reagan's opponent, was elected.

10. Diokno, "Asian Realities and the Migrant Worker," in *Serving One Another*, 46.

11. Ibid., 47.

12. Ibid.

13. Ben Barioso, "Philippines: The National Situation," in *Serving One Another*, 54.

14. Elisso Tellez, Jr., "An Overview of Filipino Migrant Workers in Hong Kong," in *Serving One Another*, 80.

15. Diokno, "Asian Realities and the Migrant Worker," in *Serving One Another*, 48.

16. In 1985 there were nine million migrant workers in the United States, four million in South America, 1.5 million in West Africa, 300,000 in South Africa, six million in the Middle East, and 200,000 in Oceania. See Andre Jacques, *The Stranger within Your Gates* (Geneva: World Council of Churches, 1986), appendix 3: "World Migrant Workers Map, Estimated Numbers."

17. *Migrant Women Speak* (Geneva: World Council of Churches, 1978), 103.

18. Ibid., 106.

19. This statement, however, contradicts the account later in the same chapter, when Moses asks to see the glory of God: "You cannot see my face," God tells Moses, "for no one shall see me and live. . . . See there is a place by me where you shall stand on the rock; and while my glory passes by I will put you in a cleft of the rock, and I will cover you with my hand until I have passed by; then I will take away my hand, and you shall see my back; but my face shall not be seen" (33:20-23). The contradiction could be due to these two stories having originated from different traditions. Theologically, the second story is much more profound.

20. For the story of the golden calf see Exodus 32.

21. Also Matt. 14:13-21; Luke 9:10b-17. Another version of the story is found in Mark 8:1-21 and Matt. 15:32-39.

22. Claus Westermann, *The Promises to the Fathers: Studies on the Patriarchal Narratives*, trans. David E. Green (Philadelphia: Fortress Press, 1980), 130.

23. Ibid.

24. Ibid.

25. Ibid., 156. Gerhard von Rad is also of the view that God's covenant with the patriarchs and with Israel at Sinai comes from the Yahwist. See particularly his *Old Testament Theology*, trans. D. M. G. Stalker, vol. 1 (New York: Harper & Row, 1962), pt. 2.B.

26. B. Davie Napier, *The Book of Exodus*, Layman's Bible Commentary 3 (Richmond: John Knox Press, 1963), 14.

27. "Testimony of Nolly Pereda," in *Serving One Another*, 72.

28. As an English proverb puts it, "a leopard never changes its spots."

29. Exod. 7:14; 8:1; 8:16; 8:20; 9:1; 9:8; 9:13; 10:1; 10:21.

Chapter 7: Ethics of Hope

1. *Roget's 21st-Century Thesaurus*, ed. The Princeton Language Institute (New York: Bantam Doubleday Dell, 1993), 378.

2. M. Kannan, "Testimony to an Unshakable Belief," in *Witnessing Together amidst Asian Plurality*, preparatory materials for the Asian Mission Conference, Seoul, South Korea, April 25–May 2, 1994 (Hong Kong: Christian Conference of Asia, 1994), 18–19.

3. *The New Encyclopaedia Britannica* (Chicago: Encyclopaedia Britannica, 1987), 3:601, col. 1.

4. Ibid.

5. Ibid.

6. Kannan, "Testimony to an Unshakable Belief," 18–19.

7. *New Encyclopaedia Britannica,* 224.

8. *A Source Book in Indian Philosophy,* ed. Sarvepalli Radhakrishnan and Charles A. Moore (Princeton, N.J.: Princeton University Press, 1957), xvii. There are "four Vedas (Rig Veda, Yajur Veda, Sama Veda, and Atharva Veda), each of which has four parts, known as Mantras, Brahmanas, Aranyakas, and Upanishads. The Mantras (hymns), especially the later ones in the Rig Veda, constitute the actual beginning of Indian philosophy" (xviii).

9. Ibid., 23–24.

10. Ibid., 29–30.

11. Mircea Eliade, *A History of Religious Ideas,* vol. 1: *From the Stone Age to the Eleusinian Mystics,* trans. Willard R. Trask (Chicago: University of Chicago Press, 1978), 198.

12. Karen Armstrong, *A History of God: The 4,000-Year Quest of Judaism, Christianity, and Islam* (New York: Ballantine Books, 1994), xvii.

13. See Mircea Eliade, *From Primitives to Zen: A Thematic Sourcebook of the History of Religions* (London: William Collins Sons/Fount Paperbacks, 1977), 268–69. The *rugo* "is the fence surrounding the homestead and, by metonymy, the homestead itself" (269).

14. Ibid., 268.

15. Ibid., 273.

16. I. C. Sharma, *Ethical Philosophies of India,* edited and revised by Stanley M. Daugert (Lincoln, Neb.: Johnson, 1965), 73.

17. See William K. Frankena and John T. Granrose, eds., *Introductory Readings in Ethics* (Englewood Cliffs, N.J.: Prentice-Hall, 1974), 1.

18. Robert L. Stivers et al., *Christian Ethics: A Case-Method Approach* (Maryknoll, N.Y.: Orbis Books, 1989), 4.

19. Ibid., 4–5.

Part Four: Faith

1. "A Peasant Catechism from Peru," in *Confessing our Faith around the World,* Faith and Order Paper 126 (Geneva: World Council of Churches, 1985), 93.

Chapter 8: Faith in the World of Divided Loyalties

1. The clause emphasized is listed in an NRSV footnote as an alternative reading to "so that you will be a blessing."

2. Jean Zaru, "May God's Peace, Mercy, and Blessings Be Unto You," in *Speaking of Faith,* ed. Diana L. Eck and Devaki Jain (London: Women's Press, 1986), 51, 53.

3. See "Notes on Contributors" in Eck and Jain, *Speaking of Faith,* 285.

4. Leviticus 19:18 does not contain the second part of Jesus' citation of the verse in Matthew 5:43, namely, "... hate your enemy." Jesus was probably reacting to "the strictest Pharisees (school of Shammai)," who "added to this command what they thought it implied: Hate your enemy (Matt. 5:43)." See *The NIV Study Bible,* note to Leviticus 19:18.

5. The statistics and related information are taken from *Pa le su chi na, gen-zai to shyo-lai* (Palestine: Present and future), ed. Pa le su chi na nin-gen ken-kyu-kai

(Symposium on problems of Palestinians and Jews) (Tokyo: San Ichi Books, 1985), 51–52.

6. See ibid., 52.

7. Nora Kort, "God Hears the Cry of My People," in *Faith and the Intifada,* ed. Naim S. Ateek, Marc H. Ellis, and Rosemary Radford Ruether (Maryknoll, N.Y.: Orbis Books, 1992), 129.

8. Munir Fasheh, "Reclaiming Our Identity and Redefining Ourselves," in Ateek, Ellis, and Radford Ruether, *Faith and the Intifada,* 67.

9. Don Wagner, "Holy Land Christians and Survival," in Ateek, Ellis, and Radford Ruether, *Faith and the Intifada,* 47.

10. Samia Khoury, "Foreword," in Ateek, Ellis, and Radford Ruether, *Faith and the Intifada,* vii.

11. Ibid.

12. Fasheh, "Reclaiming Our Identity and Redefining Ourselves," 66.

13. Elias Chacour, "A Palestinian Christian Challenge to the West," in Ateek, Ellis, and Radford Ruether, *Faith and the Intifada,* 86.

14. Kort, "God Hears the Cry of My People," 125.

15. Fasheh, "Reclaiming Our Identity and Redefining Ourselves," 67.

16. Ibid.; emphasis added.

17. Nadia Abboushi, "The Intifada and the Palestinian Churches," in Ateek, Ellis, and Radford Ruether, *Faith and the Intifada,* 60.

18. Fasheh, "Reclaiming Our Identity and Redefining Ourselves," 66.

19. Jean Zaru, "The Intifada, Nonviolence, and the Bible," in Ateek, Ellis, and Radford Ruether, *Faith and the Intifada,* 126.

20. Chacour, "A Palestinian Christian Challenge to the West," 88–89.

21. *Time,* November 13, 1995, 71.

22. Ibid., 61.

23. Zaru, "May God's Peace, Mercy, and Blessings Be Unto You," 53.

Chapter 9: Our Faith and God's Grace

1. A Social Worker in Hong Kong, "Perceiving God Anew," in *Your Will Be Done: Reflective Writings, Prayers, and Hymns Related to the Discerning of God's Will for Our Lives* (Hong Kong: Christian Conference of Asia/Youth, 1984), 19.

2. Hwang Pi Yun, "Political Participation of the Christian Churches in Hong Kong—Looking Back and Looking Forward," in *From East Europe to Hong Kong: The Communist Regime and the Church* (Hong Kong: Hong Kong Christian Patriotic Democratic Movement, 1990), 98–99; translated into English from the Chinese by C. S. Song.

3. See *The Interpreter's Dictionary of the Bible* (Nashville: Abingdon Press, 1962).

4. The parallel in Matthew's Gospel (5:3-11) is known as the Sermon on the Mount. "Happy" is what the Greek word *makarios,* used by both evangelists to introduce each blessing, means literally.

5. Padma Hensman, *In God's Image* (Asian Women's Resource Center for Cultures and Theology, Seoul, South Korea) 14 (Winter 1995): 41.

6. Malini Deuananda, "Creed," *In God's Image* 14 (Winter 1995): 49.

7. Karen Armstrong, *A History of God: The 4,000-Year Quest of Judaism, Christianity, and Islam* (New York: Ballantine Books, 1993), xix.

8. See Kwok Nai Wang, *Hong Kong 1997: A Christian Perspective* (Hong Kong: Christian Conference on Asia/Urban Rural Mission, 1991), 64.

9. Ibid., 51.

10. These lines from Rabindranath Tagore are quoted in the Indian Preparatory Group, "An Indian Search for a Spirituality of Liberation," Conference on Asian Spirituality, Seoul, South Korea, July 3–8, 1989. See *Asian Christian Spirituality: Reclaiming Traditions,* ed. Virginia Fabella, Peter K. H. Lee, and David Kwang-sun Suh (Maryknoll, N.Y.: Orbis Books, 1992), 82.

11. *The Great Learning* 2. See James Legge, *The Chinese Classics* (Hong Kong: Hong Kong University Press, 1960), 1:361. This well-known dictum reads in Chinese, *gou ri xin, ri ri xin, you ri xin.*

12. *The Great Learning* 1.4. See Legge, *The Chinese Classics,* 1.357–58.

13. See Legge's commentary in *The Chinese Classics,* 1:358.

14. The so-called story of the Fall.

15. Lao-Tzu, *Tao-te ching,* a new translation based on the recently discovered Ma-Wang-tui texts, translated with an introduction and commentary by Robert G. Hendricks (New York: Ballantine Books, 1989), 71.

16. See Wing-Tsit Chan, *A Source Book in Chinese Philosophy* (Princeton, N.J.: Princeton University Press, 1963), 149.

17. Ibid.

18. See "The River of Humanity," *Image: Christ and Art in Asia,* no. 65 (December 1995): 2.

19. Ibid.

20. Ibid.

21. Ibid.

Chapter 10: The Heart That Believes

1. This parable is taken from *The Wisdom of Buddhism,* ed. Christmas Humphreys (London: Curzon, 1979), 85–86.

2. Ibid., 81.

3. From *A Buddhist Bible,* ed. Dwight Goddard (Boston: Beacon Press, 1970), 84.

4. "Bhikhu" means Buddhist monk. The verses, from *Thera-gatha* 620–31, are quoted in Richard H. Drummond, *Gautama the Buddha: An Essay in Religious Understanding* (Grand Rapids, Mich.: Eerdmans, 1974), 57.

5. From Kukai's so-called *Testament,* written by another hand. Quoted in Moriyama, ed., *Kobo Daishi Den (Life of Kobo Daishi),* 85. See *The Buddhist Tradition in India, China, and Japan,* ed. William Theodore de Bary (New York: Vintage Books, 1972), 288, and n. 2 on the same page.

6. See de Bary, *The Buddhist Tradition,* 304.

7. Ibid., 308. "Nine kinds of medicines" refers to "the first nine teachings or stages of religious consciousness" Kukai developed in *The Ten Stages of Religious Consciousness,* "a systematic evaluation of the principal schools of Buddhist teaching, as well as of Confucianism, Taoism and Brahmanism" (see de Bary, *The Buddhist Tradition,* 304, 308 n. 14). "The Diamond Palace" refers to "esoteric Buddhism," brought back from China by Kukai and Saicho. It strives to get at the reality hidden by appearances and involves changing oneself through strenuous effort, thus obtaining the key to the secret storehouse of truths (see Matsunaga Yukei, *Mitkyo: Esoteric Buddhism* [Tokyo: Iwanami Shoten, 1991], 65–69).

8. From de Bary, *The Buddhist Tradition,* 279.

9. Ibid., 279–80.

10. *Jodo* means "Pure Land" and *shin* means "true." The official name of the Shin sect reputed to be founded by Shinran is Jodo Shin (the Pure Land True Buddhism), not just Shin. See Daisetz Suzuki, *Collected Writings on Shin Buddhism* (Kyoto: Shinshu Otaniha, 1973), 51.

11. Hee Sung Keel, *Understanding Shinran: A Dialogical Approach* (Fremont, Calif.: Asian Humanities Press, 1995), 35.

12. From Shinran, *The Kyogyoshinsho: The Collection of Passages Expounding the True Teaching, Living, Faith, and Realizing of the Pure Land*, quoted in James C. Dobbins, *Jodo Shinshu: Shin Buddhism in Medieval Japan* (Bloomington: Indiana University Press, 1989), 24. "The Principal Vow" or "the Primal Vow" refers to "the working of Amida Buddha (dharma-body as compassionate means) issuing forth as the profound desire, wish, or prayer from the deepest source of life itself, to free all beings from the weight of karmic evil in the ocean of birth-and-death" (see "Glossary," in *Letters of Shinran*, trans. Mattosho [Kyoto: Hongwanji International Center, 1978], 79).

13. Shinran, *Kyogyoshinsho*, quoted in Keel, *Understanding Shinran*, 35.

14. Ibid.

15. *Gutoku* in Japanese. Shinran often refers to himself in such a self-deprecating way. "Literally, *gu* is 'ignorant' and *toku* 'bald-headed.' 'Ignorant' implies a humble acknowledgment of one's unenlightened state (*avidya*). *Toku*, in general usage, referred to one who was cast out from society because of criminal acts or heterodoxy, after [which] such men had their hair shaved off" (see "Glossary," in Shinran, *Kyogyoshinsho*, 211–12 n. 26).

16. Shinran, *Kyogyoshinsho*, 140. "Ran" is the second character of his name Shin-Ran.

17. Martin Luther, "Preface to the Complete Edition of Latin Writings," in *Martin Luther: Selections from His Writings*, ed. John Dillenberger (New York: Anchor Books, 1961), 11.

18. Takeo Ashizu, "Shinran als 'japanischer Luther,' über das Nembutsu," in *Luther und Shinran—Eckhart und Zen*, ed. Martin Kraatz (Cologne: E. J. Brill, 1989), 1.

19. Daisetz Suzuki lists a number of differences between the teachings of Pure Land Buddhism and Christianity in *Collected Writings on Shin Buddhism*, 57–69.

20. Ibid., 59.

21. Quoted in ibid.

22. Ibid.

23. See, for example, "The Cross Is Human Violence," in C. S. Song, *Jesus, the Crucified People* (Minneapolis: Fortress, 1996), 98–99.

24. Amida Buddha is "generally rendered as the Buddha of Infinite Light (*amitabha*) and Eternal Life (*amitayus*). 'Infinite Light' means the light of transcendental wisdom, while 'Eternal Life' connotes unconditional love—two essential and inseparable aspects of all Buddhahood" (see "Glossary," in Shinran, *Kyogyoshinsho*, 203).

25. Ibid.

26. See Suzuki, *Collected Writings on Shin Buddhism*, 6–7. "Five deadly sins," according to the early tradition, are "(1) killing one's mother, (2) killing one's father, (3) killing an arahat, (4) causing blood to flow from the body of a Buddha, (5) disrupting the harmony of the assembly of monks" (see "Glossary," in *Notes on "Essentials of Faith Alone*,*"* a translation of Shinran's *Yuishinsho-mon'i*, ed. Yoshifumi Ueda [Kyoto: Hongwanji International Center, 1979], 88).

27. Shinran, *Passages Collected to Show the Truth of the Pure Land Doctrine*, quoted in Kakunyo Shonin (1270–1351), *The Life of Shinran Shonin*. See Suzuki, *Collected Writings on Shin Buddhism*, 172. "Shonin" means sage.

28. Dobbins, *Jodo Shinshu*, 29.

29. Shinran, *Kyogyoshinsho*, 93.

30. Ibid., 95.

31. Luther, "Preface to Latin Writings," 11.

32. Shinran, *The Tannisho: Tract of Developing the Heterodoxies*, trans. Tosui Imadate, in Suzuki, *Collected Writings on Shin Buddhism*, 208–9.

33. Dobbins, *Jodo Shinshu*, 48.

34. *Letters of Shinran*, ed. Yoshifumi Ueda, trans. Mattosho (Kyoto: Hongwanji International Center, 1978), 52–53. The term *nembutsu* has several meanings in the history of Buddhism, based on the various connotations of *nen* (meditating, thinking, pronouncing, and so forth): meditating on the special features of the Buddha image, holding onto the thought of the Buddha, and pronouncing the name of a Buddha (see "Glossary," 77). "Tathagata" is "a synonym of Buddha, frequently used by Shinran to refer to Amida Buddha" (see "Glossary," in Ueda, *Notes on "Essentials of Faith Alone,"* 105).

35. Joseph A. Fitzmyer, S.J., *Romans*, Anchor Bible 33 (New York: Doubleday, 1993), 329.

36. Ibid., 432.

37. Keel, *Understanding Shinran*, 46.

38. *Shozomatsu Wasan: Shinran's Hymns on the Last Age* (Kyoto: Ryukoku University Translation Center, 1980), 94–97. Translation is altered and quoted in Keel, *Understanding Shinran*, 46.

39. Quoted in Keel, *Understanding Shinran*, 48.

40. William Edward Soothill and Lewis Hodous, compilers, *A Dictionary of Chinese Buddhist Terms* (Delhi: Motilal Banarsidass, 1977) 403.

41. See "Glossary," in Ueda, *Letters of Shinran*, 76.

42. Shinran, *The Tannisho*, trans. Dennis Hirota (Kyoto: Ryukoku University Translation Center, 1982). Quoted in Keel, *Understanding Shinran*, 31. Gender-exclusive language has been retained for clarity.

43. See "Glossary," in Shinran, *Kyogyoshinsho*, 243 n. 119.

44. Ibid.

45. It is also known as the parable of the prodigal son.

46. Cf. "Glossary," in Shinran, *Kyogyoshinsho*, 243–44 n. 120.

47. Suzuki, *Collected Writings on Shin Buddhism*, 54.

48. George Samson, *A History of Japan to 1334* (Stanford, Calif.: Stanford University Press, 1958), 286. Quoted in Keel, *Understanding Shinran*, 18–19.

49. Shinran, *Kyogyoshinsho*, 118.

50. See Suzuki, *Collected Writings on Shin Buddhism*, 100–101. *Namu-amida-butsu* "is the Japanese reading of the original Sanskrit phrase *namo amitabhabuddhaya*, meaning 'Adoration of the Buddha of Infinite Light.' But with the followers of the Pure Land teaching the phrase is far more than mere adoration...for by this they express their absolute faith in Amida who makes it possible for them to be born in the Land of Purity and Bliss..." (see "Glossary," in Shinran, *Kyogyoshinsho*, 229–30 n. 80).

51. See "Glossary," in Shinran, *Kyogyoshinsho*, 220 n. 79.

52. Ibid.

53. *Dictionary of Chinese Buddhist Terms*, 149.

54. *The Interpreter's Dictionary of the Bible* (Nashville: Abingdon Press, 1962).

55. Ueda, *Notes on "Essentials of Faith Alone,"* 29.

56. Emphasis added. Suzuki, *Collected Writings on Shin Buddhism*, 109.

Part Five: Love

1. Paul lo Coelho, *The Alchemist* (San Francisco: HarperSanFrancisco, 1993), 156–60.

Chapter 11: The World-Soul of Love

1. "A Song of Enlightenment," in Le Ly Hayslip, *When Heaven and Earth Changed Places: A Vietnamese Woman's Journey from War to Peace* (New York: Penguin Books, 1990), 363–65.

2. Marvin E. Gettleman et al., eds., *Vietnam and America* (New York: Grove Press, 1995), 424.

3. Ibid., 416–17.

4. Ibid., 424.

5. Alister E. McGrath, ed., *The Blackwell Encyclopedia of Modern Christian Thought* (Oxford: Blackwell Publishers, 1993), 20.

6. "Atonement," *The Interpreter's Dictionary of the Bible* (Nashville: Abingdon Press, 1962), 1.309.

7. Robert McNamara, *In Retrospect: The Tragedy and Lessons of Vietnam* (New York: Vintage Books, 1996), xx.

8. Ibid., xix.

9. Gettleman et al., *Vietnam and America,* 420.

10. *The Book of Mencius* 6.1.6. See Wing-Tsit Chan, *A Source Book in Chinese Philosophy* (Princeton, N.J.: Princeton University Press, 1963), 54.

11. *The World Dictionary* (Chicago: World Book, 1984), 1:417.

12. *The Book of Mencius* 6.1.6. See Chan, *A Source Book in Chinese Philosophy,* 54. The Chinese word *xin* (heart) in the translation quoted is rendered "feeling." But I retain its literal and original meaning of "heart." The reason will become clear in our discourse and exposition.

13. *The Book of Mencius* 2.1.6. The word *xin* (heart) is rendered "mind" by most translators (see, for example, Chan, *A Source Book in Chinese Philosophy,* 65, and James Legge, *The Works of Mencius,* vol. 2 of *The Chinese Classics* [Hong Kong: Hong Kong Chinese University Press, 1960], 201). *Xin* (heart) in Chinese usage certainly refers to the thinking capacity (mind) of a person, but it is the thinking *subject* or *person* to which it primarily refers.

14. *The Book of Mencius* 2.1.6. For the translation of this passage I have combined Chan's rendering (*A Source in Chinese Philosophy,* 65) and that of James Legge (*The Works of Mencius,* 202) to bring out more effectively the meaning of the Chinese text.

15. *The Book of Mencius* 2.1.6. The English translation is from Chan, *A Source Book in Chinese Philosophy,* 65, with *compliance* replaced by the word *humility.* The Chinese word for humility is *rang,* as in *li rang,* meaning "to make way humbly or modestly." Hence, "humility" rather than "compliance" or "complaisance" (Legge's rendering in *The Works of Mencius,* 202) seems more to the point Mencius is making.

16. *Jun zi* is always translated as "a superior person," *xiao ren* almost always as "an inferior person." James Legge uses "a superior person" for *jun zi* but sometimes renders *xiao ren* as a "mean" person (see *The Chinese Classics,* vol. 1). I have followed here his rendering of *xiao ren* as "a mean person," but have translated *jun zi* as "an honorable person" instead of "a superior person." I think "an honorable person" is not only a better contrast to "a mean person," but is more faithful to what Confucius and Mencius meant.

17. *The Analects* 4.11. See Chan, *A Source Book in Chinese Philosophy,* 27.

18. *The Analects* 15.1. See Legge, *The Chinese Classics,* 1:294.

19. *The Works of Mencius* 1.1.3.5. See Legge, *The Chinese Classics*, 2:132.

20. Douglas R. A. Hare, *Matthew* (Louisville: Westminster John Knox, 1993), 51.

21. *The Book of Mencius* 6.1.10. See Chan, *A Source Book in Chinese Philosophy*, 57. A "bear's paw" and bear palm "have been a delicacy in China from the earliest times" (Legge, *The Chinese Classics*, 2:411).

22. *The Book of Mencius* 6.1.10. See Chan, *A Source Book in Chinese Philosophy*, 57.

23. *The Book of Mencius* 4.1.10. See Chan, *A Source Book in Chinese Philosophy*, 57.

24. From Tykheo Thich Minh Chan, *Some Teachings of Lord Buddha on Peace, Harmony, and Human Dignity* (Ho Chi Minh City: The Dharma Executive Council, 1984), 17.

25. Hayslip, *When Heaven and Earth Changed Places*, 200.

26. McNamara, *In Retrospect*, 262.

27. Ibid., 263.

28. Ibid.

29. Loren Baritz, *Backfire: A History of How American Culture Led Us into Vietnam and Made Us Fight the Way We Did* (New York: William Morrow, 1985), 42. Quoted in Gettleman et al., *Vietnam and America*, 519. Emphasis added.

30. The poem is quoted in Thich Nhat Hanh, *Love in Action: Writings on Nonviolent Social Change* (Berkeley: Parallax Press, 1993), 42.

31. Ibid.

32. Ibid., 40.

Chapter 12: The Saving Work of Love

1. In John's Gospel it was "about the sixth hour" (19:14), that is, about noon.

2. Fred B. Craddock, *Luke,* Interpretation (Louisville: John Knox Press, 1990), 271.

3. John Nolland, *Luke 18:35—24:53,* Word Biblical Commentary (Dallas: Word Books, 1993), 1139.

4. C. S. Mann, *Mark,* Anchor Bible 27 (New York: Doubleday, 1986), 647.

5. *The United Methodist Hymnal* (Nashville: United Methodist Publishing House, 1989), no. 288.

6. *Collins English Dictionary,* 3d ed. (Glasgow: HarperCollins, 1991), 1298.

7. *The Interpreter's Dictionary of the Bible* (Nashville: Abingdon Press, 1962), 4.21.

8. *The World Book Dictionary* (Chicago: World Book, 1984), 1839.

9. The poem, by Chong Jin-Nim, is found in *In God's Image* (Asian Women's Resource Center for Culture and Theology, Seoul, South Korea) 15 (Summer 1996): 35–36. "Pakkokt" is a plant that blooms in the night; it withers as soon as the sun appears.

10. See Meiko Yamada, *Yianfu tachi no Taiheiyo Senso* (Comfort women's Pacific War: Women's secret war stories) (Tokyo: Koninsha, 1995), 9.

11. See Jong Ok-Sun's testimony, "Former 'Comfort Woman' for the Japanese Army," *In God's Image* 15 (Summer 1996): 22–23.

12. Ibid., 23.

13. Emphasis added. Ishikawa Itsuko, *"Jiugun Yianfu" ni sareta Siojotachi* (Young girls forced to become comfort women) (Tokyo: Iwanami Publishing House, 1993), 210. Translation from the Japanese by C. S. Song.

14. Lee Ok-Nyo, "Pay It Back Now," *In God's Image* 15 (Summer 1996): 68.

15. Charles Wesley, "Love Divine, All Loves Excelling," in *The United Methodist Hymnal,* no. 384.

16. See Ishikawa Itsuko, *"Jiugun Yianfu" ni sareta Siojotachi,* 158–59. Translation from the Japanese by C. S. Song.

17. Ibid., 173. Translation from the Japanese by C. S. Song.

18. Kwak Song-Hee, *In God's Image* 15 (Summer 1996): 95.

19. Ibid.

20. Leon Morris, *The Gospel according to John* (Grand Rapids, Mich.: Eerdmans, 1998), 478.

21. Also Matt. 10:39. The quotation here combines the renderings of the NRSV and the NEB.

22. Sakabe Yoshio, "Sei to Si no Kobo" (Hope concerning life and death), in *Seimei no Imi* (Meaning of life), ed. Takenaka Masao and Satohara Kenichi (Kyoto: Sibunkaku Press, 1992), 180. Translation from the Japanese by C. S. Song.

23. That John has Jesus repeat what he said to his opponents on other occasions (see John 7:33-34 and 8:21) indicates that he wants to show that the question of death was very much on Jesus' mind.

24. Morris, *The Gospel according to John*, 772.

Index

Abraham, 148–49, 192–93
African American slavery, 142–43
Alienation, 126–27
Amen, practice of, 16–18
Ami tribe, 70, 71, 318 n.10
Amida Buddha, 246, 247, 251–53,
    259–60, 261, 263, 264, 327 n.24
Ancestor veneration, 100, 236
Anselm of Canterbury, 91–92
Anxiety, 32–37, 127
Art, origins of, 319 n.3
Arteaga, Nikita, 105–6
Asceticism, 20
Asia
    Christianity in, 54–57, 227, 229–30
    economics in, 138–41
    migrant workers in, 135–38
    stories/myths in, 67–68, 71–73
    See also specific countries
Association of Southeast Asian Nations
    (ASEAN), 138–39
Atom bombs, 2
Atonement
    defined, 271–72
    theology of, 91–92

Baptism, 15
Bartimaeus, 243
Betrayal stories, 70–72
Bible
    Beatitudes, 222
    Exodus, 143–47, 156–59
    Genesis, 36, 52, 79, 83, 86, 102, 109,
        111–12, 148–49
    Isaiah, 48, 127, 220–21
    James, 29
    Jeremiah, 124–25, 322 n.37
    Job, 123–24, 171, 322 n.37
    John, 30, 50–51, 261, 265
    Luke, 38, 48, 97–98, 189, 292

Mark, 131, 184
Proverbs, 174
Psalms, 179, 283
Revelation, 277, 282
Samuel, 46
See also Scriptures, Hebrew
Birth/childbirth, 96, 112–17. *See also*
    Creation stories
Blood, 270–72, 273, 298
Boddhisattvas, 251
Buddha, 18, 77–78, 84, 109, 282, 318
    n.1. *See also* Amida Buddha
Buddhism
    ascetic story, 104–5
    on death, 93–94, 96
    detachment in, 20
    on grace of God, 241–42
    Pure Land, 246, 250, 253, 255, 257,
        263–64
    on reality, 126, 237
    sects, 244, 247
    on self-sacrifice, 250–51
    Shin, 247, 262
    statistics, 3
    on suffering, 122–23
    on women, 262
    Zen, 18–23, 51, 92, 250

Camus, Albert, 110–11
Catholicism, in Philippines, 141
Center, defined, 64
Charity, 182
Cheng of Ch'in, King, 133
Childbirth. *See* Birth/childbirth
China
    Christianity in, 54–55, 224
    on death, 93
    historical events, 133
    male heirs in, 235–36

Chong Jin-Min, 300–301, 307, 330 n.9
Chosen people, 53
Christ. *See* Jesus Christ
Christendom, 14–15
Christianity
  change in, 1–7, 9
  expansion, 3–4
  on God-talk, 25–26
  and Judaism, 143
  statistics, 2–3
  as theology of history, 148
Church
  change in, 5
  church-centered faith, 61
  and non-Christians, 53–57
  relationship of Christians to, 1
  and salvation, 60–61
  theology as serving, 13–14
"Circle, The." *See* Marketplaces
Clay, human beings from, 319 n.1
Come and see invitation, 51–52, 69
Compassion, heart of, 275–77
Community, theology of, 37–41
Confucius, 100–101, 275–79
Conversation, theological, 68–69
Coolies, 165–66
Creation stories, 36–37, 65–66, 67, 79,
  86–90, 169–71, 303
Crucifixion, 250–51, 273, 292–93,
  295–96, 298–300, 307–8. *See also*
  Death
Cyprian, 1

Death
  Buddhism on, 93–94, 96
  doctors' stories, 80–81
  fear of, 311–12
  of firstborn, 153–61
  God's responsibility, 83, 85–90
  Jesus and, 81–82, 92, 97–103, 128,
  250–51, 292–93, 295–96, 298–
  300, 307, 312–13
  as wages of sin, 90–92, 98, 102
Despair, 127

Disease
  Nikita Arteaga's story, 105–6
  and poverty, 107–9
Dostoyevsky, Fyodor, 120–22

Ecclesiology, 38, 47
Economics
  in Asia, 138–41
  military vs. consumer, 167
  Philippine statistics, 140
  world statistics, 167
Egypt
  death of firstborn in, 153–61
  Israeli slave labor in, 152–53
Elijah, 283–84
Enemies, loving, 196–99
Enlightenment, 20, 22
Ethics
  of hope, 182–87
  and theology, 175
Evangelism, 45
Exodus, 53

Faith
  Chinese character for, 29
  church-centered, 60–62
  defined, 206, 263–64
  effect of stories on, 66
  as freedom, 221–26
  in future generations, 235–37
  and God's grace, 215, 220–21, 237,
  241–42
  and hearing, 262
  Jesus-oriented vs. Christ-centered,
  61–65
  and justice/injustice, 217–21, 256
  keeping, 239–40
  and loving enemies, 200–7
  and loyalty, 212–14, 215
  as practice of amen, 18
  as spiritual renewal, 231–35
Firstborn, death of, 153–61
Fly now and pay later scheme, 141–42
Forgiveness, 196
Freedom, faith as, 221–26

Gautama the Buddha. *See* Buddha
Gilgamesh epic, 319 n.1
God
  and death, 83, 85–90
  dichotomy of, 172
  and injustice, 218–19
  grace of, and faith, 215, 220–21, 237,
    241–42
  likeness of, 121
  as love, 29–30
  mercy of, 242
  perceived anew, 215–17, 224, 227–28
  preoccupation with, 31–32
  relation with world, 53–57
  truth-claims for, 226–27
  will, theology of, 44–49
  See also Kingdom of God; Theology
God-talk. *See under* Theology
Good Samaritan. *See* Samaritan parable
Great Learning, The, 233–34

Handmaid of the church. *See* Theology
Hannah story, 115
Happiness, 222
Hearing. *See* Listening/hearing
Herod, King, 160
Hinduism, history, 169
History, 133–34
  of Christian Israel, 52–53
  theology of, 148
Holocaust, 2, 120, 122
Hong Kong, Christianity in, 229
Hope
  as contemporaneous, 191
  defined, 163–64
  empty, 185
  ethics of, 182–87
  history of, 134
  incense sticks of, 186
  meaning of, 70
  and promise, 136–37
  purpose of, 135
  quality of, 167–68
  as self-transforming, 182
  theological questions, 162–63
  and uncertainty, 191–92

Hsin, 29–30
Hui-K'o, 20–21
Hui-neng, 22–23
Human beings
  African poem, 131–32
  creation of, 79, 82, 319 n.1
  God-in-us, 82–83
  as historical, 133–34
Human-talk. *See under* Theology
Humanity, faith in, 237–39

"I Am a Child of Burma," 118–19, 120
Imana, prayer to, 177
Incense sticks of hope, 186
Indonesia, creation story, 88–90
Injustice. *See* Justice/injustice
Isaiah, 17–18
Israel
  Christian history of, 52–53
  importance of, 192
  use in slave labor, 142, 152–53, 159

Jairus's daughter story, 99–101, 103
Japan
  Buddhism in, 244, 247
  comfort women for soldiers, 301–7
Jesus Christ
  accusations against, 292–93
  birth, 116, 159–60
  come and see invitation, 51–52, 69
  and death, 81–82, 92, 97–103,
    128, 250–51, 292–93, 295–96,
    298–300, 307, 312–13
  divinity of, 294
  on enemies, 196–99
  on forgiveness, 196
  as healer, 126, 128
  on human nature, 172
  Jesus-oriented vs. Christ-centered
    faith, 61–65
  as Lamb of God, 50
  listening by, 74
  on love, 17, 294
  at marketplaces, 11–13
  as Other Power, 261

Jesus Christ (*continued*)
    on prayer, 28
    on prosperity, 138
    as reformer, 16
    on suffering, 125, 128–29
    as teacher, 32
    on theology of God's reign, 41–44
    on theology of God's will, 44–49
    on theology of human community,
        37–41
    on theology of life, 32–37
    who is Christ questions, 194–95
John the Baptizer, 15, 50–52
Judaism
    ancient, 181
    Christianity and, 143
See also Scriptures, Hebrew
Julius Caesar, 133
Justice/injustice, and faith, 217–21, 256

Kannan, 164–66, 168–69, 176, 180,
        185
Karma, 258–59
Khnum, 319 n.1
Khoa, Nguyen, 270
Kingdom of God, 41–44, 59–60, 75,
        131, 318 n.5
Kukai, 244–46
    The Precious Key to the Secret Treasury,
        244
Küng, Hans, 2, 3
Kuo An
    on enlightenment, 20
    "Ten Cow-Herding Pictures," 18–20

Language
    as communal, 27
    religious, 28
    See also Speaking in tongues
Lao Tzu, 28, 92, 238–39
    Chuang Tzu, 92–93, 94–96
    Tao-te Ching, 237–38
Lapierre, Dominique, 107
Lazarus stories, 98–99, 102–3, 182–83,
        308
Legion story, 125–26

Life
    love as life-force, 309–11
    theology of, 32–37
Listening/hearing, 74, 262
Love
    believing in, 294
    God is love, 29–30
    heart of, 277
    as life-force, 309–11
    neighborly, 16–17
    nonviolence as, 287–91
    and pain, 267
    that saves, 296–99
    and suffering, 267, 299–300, 302
    weakening bond of, 196–97
Loyalty
    concept of, 212–13
    to country, 209–12
    divided, 193, 212–13, 215
    and faith, 209, 212–14, 215
    to Jesus, 193–200
    to people in need, 200–9
Luther, Martin, 249, 254–55

"Magnificat of the Midwife, The,"
        116
Makashi, Yoko, 240
Mao Zedong, 133
Marketplaces
    culture/theology in, 10, 11–12
    Jesus at, 11–13
    in Tainan, Taiwan, 9–10
McNamara, Robert, 272–73
Men
    male heirs in China, 235–36
    and sexuality, 303–4
Mencius, 275–81
Mercy, God's, 242
Migrant workers, 155
    Asian, 135–38, 141–42
    in Switzerland, 142
Monasticism, 20, 21
Mondo, 51
Money, power of, 15
Moses, 144–47, 150–51, 153–55,
        157–58, 323 n.19

Nain story, 97–98, 103
Nonviolence, 287–91

Orientation, defined, 64
Original sin, 258–59

Pai-chang, 104
Pain. *See* Suffering
Palestinian Christians, 193–209
Paul the Apostle, 57–60, 250
    conversion of, 252–54
    on death, 91, 96
    on good and evil, 248–49, 257
    on gospel, 59, 296
    on injustice, 256
    on love, 267
    religious sensibility of, 255
    on salvation, 59–60
    as Saul, 58, 252
    on speaking in tongues, 29
Peruvian Magnificat, 189
Peter the Apostle, 57–59, 314
Philippines
    Catholicism in, 141
    economic statistics, 140
Pilate, 292–93, 305
Ping fan, 224
Population statistics, 106–7
Poverty, 106–9, 184
Power, self vs. Other, 259–62
Prayer, 28
Prometheus myth, 319
Promise, theology of, 148–49
Propriety, heart of, 279–80
Pure Land Buddhism. *See under*
    Buddhism

Quilim, Mediatrix Jane, 135–36, 141,
    142, 155

Raft parable, 241–42, 253–54
Reality, 126
Reconciliation, and solidarity, 211
Redemption, 297–98
Reign of God. *See* Kingdom of God
Religious reform, 16

Repentance, 59, 60
Resurrection, 57, 250, 314–15
Roman Catholic Church. *See*
    Catholicism
Rule of God. *See* Kingdom of God

Saicho, 244, 246
Sakyamuni, 251–52
Salvation, 53–55, 60–61, 227–29,
    297–99
Samaritan parable, 38–41
Scriptures, Hebrew, 56, 85, 92, 123, 143,
    174, 264, 271
Self-sacrifice, 250–51
Sexual union, 303–4
Shame, heart of, 277–79
She Cheng Yen, 20
Shen-hsiu, 22–23
Shinran, 247–50, 251–53, 255–64
Sin, and death, 91–92, 98, 102
Slavery, 142–43
Sleep, and death, 101–2
Solidarity, and reconciliation, 211–12
Solomon, King, 162
"Song of Enlightenment, A," 267–69,
    281, 283, 284
Speaking in tongues, 29
Spiritual renewal, faith as, 231–35
Success stories, 72
Suffering
    Buddhism on, 122–23
    and innocence, 121
    Jesus on, 125, 128–29
    and love, 267, 299–300, 302
    meaning of, 70
    and religious authority, 146
    vulnerability to, 109
Sumero-Akkadian prayer, 178, 180
Sunita, 242–43
Syncretistic religion, 208–9

Taiwan
    betrayal story, 70–73
    Tainan, marketplace, 9–11
Tannisho, The, 255

Ten thousand talents parable, 43–44
Taoism, 92
Ten Commandments, 280
Testimony, 26
Theology
  basis of, 45
  conversation in, 68–69
  defined, 23–25
  in everyday life, 12–13
  of God's reign, 41–44
  of God's will, 44–49
  as God-talk, 23–26, 36
  of history, 148
  of hope, 162–63
  of human community, 37–41
  as human-talk, 27–30
  of life, 32–37
  as practice of amen, 16–18
  of promise, 148–49
  root of word, 23
  as serving church, 13–16
  theocentrism, 62
Thompson, Hugh, 274–75, 277, 281

Toil, 117–18, 120
Truth, search for, 21

Vedas, 169, 173–74
Vengeance
  breaking circle of, 282–84
  story, 267–69, 281, 283, 284
Vietnam, 267, 269–70, 285–87, 290
  My Lai horrors, 274–75, 270

"Were You There?" (spiritual), 295–97
Wisdom, heart of, 280–81
Women
  and Buddhism, 262
  as comfort women, 301–7
  and faith, 222–25
World Christian Encyclopedia, 2
World Health Organization (WHO),
  106–7

Zacchaeus story, 175
Zaru, Jean, 193–94, 195, 199, 210–11
Zen Buddhism. *See* Buddhism